W9-AHJ-819

Teaching Recent Global History

Teaching Recent Global History explores innovative ways to teach world history, beginning with the early 20th century. The authors' unique approach unites historians, social studies teachers, and educational curriculum specialists to offer historically rich, pedagogically innovative, and academically rigorous lessons that help students connect with and deeply understand key events and trends in recent global history.

Highlighting the best scholarship for each major continent, the text explores the ways that this scholarship can be adapted by teachers in the classroom in order to engage and inspire students. Each of the seven main chapters highlights a particularly important event or theme, which is then complemented by a detailed discussion of a particular methodological approach.

Key features include:

- An overarching narrative that helps readers address historical arguments;
- Relevant primary documents or artifacts, plus a discussion of a particular historical method well-suited to teaching about them;
- Lesson plans suitable for both middle and secondary level classrooms;
- Document-based questions and short bibliographies for further research on the topic.

This invaluable book is ideal for any aspiring or current teacher who wants to think critically about how to teach world history and make historical discussions come alive for students.

Diana B. Turk is an associate professor and the Director of Social Studies Education at New York University.

Laura J. Dull is an associate professor and the Coordinator of the Graduate Secondary Social Studies Program at SUNY New Paltz.

Robert Cohen is a professor of social studies education and history at New York University.

Michael R. Stoll is an instructor of education at William Jewell College in Liberty, Missouri.

Transforming Teaching

Series Editor: James Fraser, NYU Steinhardt School of Education

Assessment for Equity and Inclusion
Embracing All Our Children
edited by A. Lin Goodwin

Real Learning, Real Work
School-to-Work As High School Reform
Adria Steinberg

Unauthorized Methods
Strategies for Critical Teaching
edited by Joe L. Kincheloe and Shirley R. Steinberg

Teaching African American Literature
Theory and Practice
edited by Maryemma Graham, Sharon Pineault-Burke, and Marianna White Davis

Reinventing the Middle School
edited by Thomas S. Dickinson

Where's the Wonder in Elementary Math?
Encouraging Mathematical Reasoning in the Classroom
Judith McVarish

Teaching Authentic Language Arts in a Test-Driven Era
Arthur T. Costigan

Teaching US History
Dialogues among Social Studies Teachers and Historians
edited by Diana Turk, Rachel Mattson, Terrie Epstein, and Robert Cohen

Teaching Recent Global History
Dialogues Among Historians, Social Studies Teachers, and Students
Diana B. Turk, Laura J. Dull, Robert Cohen, and Michael R. Stoll

Teaching Recent Global History

Dialogues Among Historians,
Social Studies Teachers, and Students

DIANA B. TURK, LAURA J. DULL, ROBERT COHEN,
AND MICHAEL R. STOLL

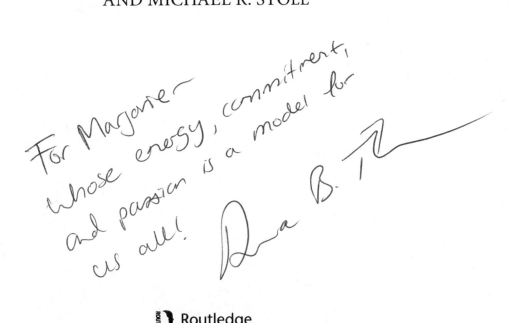

For Margarer —
whose energy, commitment,
and passion is a model for
us all!

Dina B. T

Routledge
Taylor & Francis Group

NEW YORK AND LONDON

First published 2014
by Routledge
711 Third Avenue, New York, NY 10017

and by Routledge
2 Park Square, Milton Park, Abingdon, Oxon, OX14 4RN

Routledge is an imprint of the Taylor & Francis Group, an informa business

© 2014 Taylor & Francis

The right of Diana B. Turk, Laura J. Dull, Robert Cohen, and Michael R. Stoll to
be identified as authors of this work has been asserted by them in accordance with
sections 77 and 78 of the Copyright, Designs and Patents Act 1988.

All rights reserved. No part of this book may be reprinted or reproduced or utilized
in any form or by any electronic, mechanical, or other means, now known or
hereafter invented, including photocopying and recording, or in any information
storage or retrieval system, without permission in writing from the publishers.

Trademark Notice: Product or corporate names may be trademarks or registered
trademarks, and are used only for identification and explanation without intent to
infringe.

Library of Congress Cataloging-in-Publication Data
Teaching recent global history : dialogues among historians, social studies teachers
    and students / Diana B. Turk, Laura J. Dull, Robert Cohen, Michael R. Stoll.
      pages cm
    Includes bibliographical references and index.
  1. History—Study and teaching.   2. History, Modern—20th century.   I. Turk,
Diana B., editor of compilation.
    D16.2.T43 2014
    907—dc23
    2013029791

ISBN: 978-0-415-89707-5 (hbk)
ISBN: 978-0-415-89708-2 (pbk)
ISBN: 978-0-203-80411-7 (ebk)

Typeset in Minion Pro
by Apex CoVantage, LLC

Printed and bound in the United States of America by Publishers Graphics,
LLC on sustainably sourced paper.

Contents

Series Editor Introduction

It is a pleasure to introduce *Teaching Recent Global History* to Routledge's Transforming Teaching series and to its readers. As Robert Cohen notes in his introduction, the "subtitle—*Dialogues Among Historians, Social Studies Teachers, and Students*—suggests one of the central goals in our work is to connect working history teachers, and their students, with historical scholarship and to dialogue with historians." This is exactly the goal of the Transforming Teaching series, and *Teaching Recent Global History* does a masterful job of achieving that goal.

This volume is much more than a sum of its parts, although its parts—thoughtful and engaging dialogues about the recent history and ways to teach the recent history of Africa, Asia, Latin America, the Middle East, and the former Soviet Union as well as key international issues from war crimes to the place of the United States in the world and world history—are very impressive. At the same time, the authors provide the teacher of global history or world history with a way of approaching the enterprise that is much more than a collection of different regions and topics. No student will emerge from any of the lessons offered here with the old stereotypes of the rest of the world, or of the study of history, intact. The history of the 20th century as it emerges in this volume is a fascinating story of people in many different places taking actions to change their lives; actions that will make sense to and encourage the activism of today's students. Global history, as projected in *Teaching Recent Global History*, is a study of the connections between parts of the world and between topics. It is especially fitting in this context that the last chapter focuses on the place of the United States in world history. Too often students are taught two quite separate courses, one on the history of the United States and one on the history of the world—which means every part of the globe *except* the United States. Such an approach fosters an odd sort of American exceptionalism—"the rules of the world don't apply to us." It also leads students to misunderstand the rest of the world. The 20th century history of Korea, or Cuba, or the former Soviet Union simply cannot be understood except with reference to those countries' long-standing interactions with the United States, and the history of the United States is distorted if it is not told as a relationship to others.

Many of us bemoan the fact that too many of today's high school and college students have little interest in studying history and that too many of today's young—and not-so-young—people lack much historical knowledge or the ability to place current developments in historical context. In our increasingly interdependent world, such a lack of interest and knowledge can be a dangerous thing. The best response, of course, is excellent history teaching. And *Teaching Recent Global History* is a very valuable resource to teachers committed to excellence in their teaching.

This book is full of information, first rate interviews with a number of leading historians, but also very specific examples of how that information can be used in today's classrooms to transform the teaching that is taking place: to engage students in the study of history and to move the history classroom from a place where knowledge is simply transmitted to a place where students become historians, do their own historical research—becoming "historical detectives," as the teachers of the unit on Africa say—draw their own conclusions, and make history their own. For teachers concerned with the Common Core, as every teacher must be, there is also a detailed graph aligning the material in the chapters with the Common Core Standards.

In these examples, as teachers drew on the research included in the interviews in this book, high school students were able to look at history afresh, understanding the agency of people in Asia or Latin America or other parts of the globe in new ways: ways that they found interesting, indeed fascinating, rather than boring, the usual complaint. In the hands of these teachers, the past that was to be studied was no longer dead but a living and vital reality. This volume is a tool of great value to the world history teacher who uses it that will, indeed, transform other classrooms as it transformed those described here and spark the curiosity of a new generation of citizens. Read on. It will be a rewarding experience.

James W. Fraser
New York University

Acknowledgments

The authors wish to thank the following people for their support and assistance during the long process of bringing this volume to fruition: Stacie Brensilver Berman, our wonderful doctoral assistant in the Department of Teaching and Learning at NYU-Steinhardt, whose organization and attention to detail helped keep this project coordinated and streamlined; the teachers who participated in the roundtable discussion we held about teaching global history and who helped us frame our ideas for what form this book would take (not all of whom ended up contributing to chapters due to moves and changed teaching assignments); the eight historians and scholars whose expertise helped shape the arguments for each chapter: Fred Cooper, Greg Grandin, Charles Hanley, Stephen Kotkin, Zachary Lockman, Mary (Molly) Nolan, Moss Roberts, and Marilyn Young; Alejandro Velasco for providing us with documents on Nixon's visit to Caracas and Jen Lewis and Angela Carreno from the Center for Latin American and Caribbean Studies (CLACS) at New York University for assisting with background documents and guidance for the Latin America chapter; the many middle and secondary level classroom teachers who collaborated with us on writing lessons and units for this volume, not all of which curricula ended up being featured in our chapters or included in our discussion; the numerous principals who saw the value in this project and granted us access to their schools' classrooms; and finally, the parents and students who granted us permission to observe and talk with students, evaluate the work completed for our teaching units, consider the implications of their learning, and otherwise step back and take stock of how students had experienced the teaching and learning that took place in our teaching units.

We also thank Catherine Bernard and Madeleine Hamlin of Routledge, for their support, expertise, and patience in understanding that a project like this, involving teams of historians, education faculty, and teachers, invariably will encounter obstacles to meeting deadlines that don't happen in smaller, less disparate projects. Our series editor Jim Fraser proved, as he did on our Teaching U.S. History project, a reliable cheerleader and sage counselor; his support particularly during the challenging times of the project made all the difference in reminding us that excellence and innovation, not completion, were the goals here.

The authors also wish to thank the following individuals, without whose expertise, guidance, editorial support, and/or moral encouragement, it would have been difficult to bring this project to fruition: Dolores Byrnes (who also indexed the book), Matt Meisner, Maia Merin, Emma Price, Dejan Ristić, and Karen Thomson. In the final stages of the project, Gail Newton and Sue Cope of Taylor and Francis provided crucial editing and proofreading of the document. In addition, we would like to thank Lena Singh and Juliana Thrall for their administrative support throughout this project. Finally, Robby Cohen would like to thank his former classmates at UC Berkeley's International House and the historians of Africa, Europe, Asia, the Middle East, and Latin America with whom he studied at Berkeley and SUNY Buffalo for sparking his interest in global history and NYU's historians for sustaining that interest.

Introduction

Robert Cohen

In his brilliant essay "The World We have Lost," the late Tony Judt, America's most distinguished historian of post-World War II Europe, expressed regret that in the early 21st century we live in "an age of forgetting," in which we have great difficulty "making sense of the turbulent century that has just ended" and "in learning from it." Rather than expressing an interest in the complexities of the global history of the 20th century, our ahistorical society seems, in Judt's words, to act as if that history "*has nothing of interest to teach us.* ... With too much confidence and too little reflection we put the twentieth century behind us and," after the fall of communism in 1989–1991, "strode boldly into its successor swaddled in self-serving half-truths: the triumph of the West, the end of History, the unipolar American moment, the ineluctable march of globalization and the free market" (Judt, 2006, 2008).

Judt's jeremiad has a special resonance for high school history teachers, who find their field so consistently undervalued and neglected by school officials and Washington. Just recently, in fact, the members of New York State's Board of Regents showed how little concerned they were with serious study of the past. Amidst an educational era in which standardized tests in math and literacy have been proliferating at an unprecedented rate, the Regents seriously entertained moving to eliminate the *only* statewide exam in global history as a cost-cutting measure (Decker, 2012). The U.S. Congress has been even less history friendly, voting in 2011 to de-fund the federal government's only national professional development program for history teachers—the Teaching American History program (Brinkerhoff, 2011). This lack of support for history teaching and learning attests that, just as Judt claimed with regard to historical knowledge, we do indeed live in "an age of forgetting." Global history teachers thus have good reason to feel as though they are often sailing against gale force winds as they labor to engage their students in deep, meaningful, and critical study of the past.

In some ways the challenge of teaching 20th century global history in the schools is more daunting even than Judt's words relay. High school teachers are, after all, engaged in teaching the one part of the population with the least experience and firsthand knowledge of the 20th century. A 15- or 16-year-old high school sophomore today would have been born close to the turn of the 21st century and so came to political and historical consciousness after the 20th century was over. Given the historical amnesia of their parents and other elders, as Judt suggested, teenagers are in even worse shape, since they never knew enough about that century to have forgotten it. It is little wonder, then, that many teachers find their students enter high school with enormous gaps in their knowledge of recent global history and geography, often viewing major regions of the world such as the Middle East through stereotypes, popular misconceptions, and prejudices (Rundquist, 2011).

You might think that such major learning deficits would fill global history teachers with horror or leave them demoralized. But on the contrary, we found in the focus groups we held at the start of the school–university history partnership that led to the writing of this book that the teachers participating viewed their entering students' ignorance of 20th century global history as evidence of just how important their own work as teachers really was. In fact, part of the excitement they felt in teaching recent global history was the opportunity to push their students to question stereotyped views of the world and start judging the world beyond America's shores on the basis of historical evidence rather than via xenophobic rhetoric popularized by demagogic politicians and shock jocks.

Although eager to dispel their students' misconceptions and help them expand their intellectual horizons, the teachers who were part of this book project recognized how large the task is of introducing the entire 20th century's history—its roots before that century and legacies into our own—for the *whole globe*, to teens with little background in global history. And of equal importance, the teachers candidly acknowledged that in taking on such global history teaching, they had to come to grips with the limits of their own teacher training and history education. Even teachers who had been history majors in top colleges often admitted that they lacked sufficient global background because as they advanced through college, they became more specialized in their historical studies, perhaps focusing on one area of the world, while doing little global history work after their freshmen survey courses. So, for example, one could graduate from a history program knowing a great deal about modern Europe or the United States, but with very little course work in African, Asian, Latin American or Middle Eastern history. For the newly minted global history teacher, this often meant that they were teaching about parts of the world that they had not studied in any sustained way, and so they had to school themselves just before, or even as, they were teaching their students this history.

How, then, can teachers manage to lead intellectually stimulating classes in 20th century global history when their own knowledge of some regions of the world tends to be limited? The answer is in part conceptual and in part organizational and logistical. Global history as a field does not approach the world of the 20th or 21st centuries via detailed micro-studies of separate, disconnected, or fully autonomous countries or regions. Rather, this field of study works, as history itself does, dynamically, with parts of the world *in interaction with each other*. Trade, culture, technology, ideology, revolution, war—all these topics involve interaction, cooperation, and conflict that transcend the nation state, and draw us into studying the world internationally, continentally, and globally. This does not mean, of course, that the local, the national, or the regional do not matter since global trends take their specific forms at more local levels. But the focus on global trends and global history themes means that one can teach a very meaningful high school unit on comparative 20th century revolutions without delving into the kind of detailed national history one would need to have mastered in order to conduct, say, an intensive doctoral seminar on the

Bolshevik Revolution. And then there are the organizational and logistical imperatives of high school teaching. Global history is, after all, the mother of all high school survey courses, in which teachers in two short years (or less, depending on the state) must race through a tremendous amount of history, from the ancients to today. "From Plato to NATO" was the way it used to be phased, but even that phrase is too narrow to cover the non-western and post-Cold War portions of world history. And so even if high school teachers had the knowledge to do so, they simply lack the time to explore a single nation's 20th century history in the kind of depth possible in an advanced seminar.

What all this adds up to is that in organizing global history teaching, it is necessary to be selective and to prioritize the aspects of national and regional histories that are part of important international trends that have shaped the global experience in and since the 20th century. This means thinking thematically about global history (Tignor, Adelman, & Kotkin, 2011). This is why the chapters in *Teaching Recent Global History* are centered around pivotal historical themes, issues, problems, and developments that have shaped and re-shaped the world in the 20th century—including colonialism and decolonization, social democracy and reform, revolution, war, terrorism, war crimes, religious practice and conflict, consumer culture and the competition between communism and capitalism, and finally globalization and the role of superpower(s) in dominating international relations.

Even while being thematic and focused on the larger global forces and trends, global history teachers realize that the building blocks for such macro-history is the development of deeper understanding of each region of the world. Unless one really understands the major regions and nations, it is difficult to make meaningful comparisons—and the danger of uninformed ventures in comparative history is that they can end up descending into something akin to comparing two unknowns. This is a key reason why all of the teachers who collaborated in developing lessons and units for this book proved so eager to work with the area specialists. Teachers who had never before had the chance to take advanced college courses with an historian of Africa or Latin America, the Soviet Union and Eastern Europe, the Middle East or Asia took great delight in enhancing their understanding of these areas under the guidance of experts who have conducted research on, and published extensively in, each area. In the interest of promoting greater mastery of the history of the major regions of the world, the chapters in this book explore recent global history's grand themes in intentionally diverse settings. Toward this end, in the scholarly interviews and teaching units described in this book, we: spotlight the toppling of European colonialism and independence in Africa; study revolution by assessing its meaning and costs in the Chinese Cultural Revolution; gauge the struggle in Latin America for social democratic reform, along with its foes from the Cold War era U.S.; probe religious loyalties and conflict in the Middle East; portray consumer culture and its ramifications in the uneven economic competition between the Soviet Union and the capitalist West; offer a comparative history of war crimes that features the recently uncovered story of how U.S. forces at No Gun Ri in the Korean War perpetrated a My-Lai style massacre, a forgotten chapter in a forgotten war; and explore debates over American power in the post-Cold War years as the world shifted from a bipolar to unipolar world.

As this book's subtitle—*Dialogues Among Historians, Social Studies Teachers, and Students*—suggests, one of the central goals in our work is to connect working history teachers, and their students, with historical scholarship and to dialogue with historians. We have done this via the most accessible form available, interviews, which are focused on key themes in global history as well as on biographical figures and primary sources that seemed to be most useful for teaching recent global history. In other words, the interviews were done with teachers in mind, spotlighting the most teachable issues, questions, and sources.[1] Those interviewed were without exception experts in transnational history, having written about whole regions and comparative history as well as national studies, authors who are accustomed to thinking about history at the macro- as well as the micro-level. They offer important insights into how teachers might acquaint their students with how people in other parts of the world experienced the 20th century and interacted with each other and with the United States.

We were especially pleased that this dialogue yielded historical insights that teachers could and did use to shatter their students' misunderstandings about 20th and even 21st century global history. For example, teachers working on our chapter on religion mentioned that their students, like many Americans, often reflect the erroneous tendency to equate Islam with terrorism and autocracy. The teachers found evidence in Middle East historian Zachary Lockman's interview to counter such misconceptions, including his point that the most populous Muslim nation in the world, Indonesia, is a democracy. And for the teachers whose students knew little about the fall of the Soviet Union other than the popular notion that the Cold War was "won" by U.S. military might, Sovietologist Stephen Kotkin offered powerful evidence that economic not military factors ended the Soviet era. Students who thought of the My Lai Massacre as an aberration in U.S. military history would be startled to find that more than a decade earlier, U.S. military forces committed a similar atrocity in the Korean War, massacring hundreds of civilians at No Gun Ri—a tragedy discussed in the interviews of historian Marilyn Young and AP reporter Charles Hanley, whose work breaking the story won him and his investigative team a Pulitzer Prize. And then there is Marilyn Young's startling conclusion that the United States, which prides itself on its international peace-making efforts, has been at war so often from the mid-20th century to the present that war, rather than peace, is now the American norm.

Teachers and teacher educators involved in this book, too, were surprised by some of the insights offered in the interviews, as with Moss Roberts' finding of a strong international aspect of the Cultural Revolution, or Frederick Cooper's challenge to the notion that tribalism pervaded modern African history. Mary Nolan complicated our understandings of Nazi Germany's war criminality by explaining that it extended far beyond the SS and even involved the *Wehrmacht* (the regular German army) in massive atrocities. Another groundbreaking conclusion came from Greg Grandin, who found that it was not Western Europe or the U.S. but Mexico that led the way in enshrining social democracy in its constitution, written back in 1917.

Empowered by the insights, data, and primary sources from these interviews, our teacher co-authors, together with university-based social studies faculty, worked to meld them into thought-provoking history lessons, activities, and units for middle and high school global history classes. Then these lessons and units were field tested in diverse classroom settings. Our use of the term "diverse" here is neither casual nor merely rhetorical. Our teaching was done in truly diverse settings ranging from inner city to suburban, from high performing to struggling. And this was intentional. We set out to test our view that cutting edge global history scholarship from university-based historians can be used effectively with middle and high school students of all ability levels and in a wide range of educational settings so long as teachers adapt them appropriately for use in their classrooms. We are happy to report that the field testing of these lessons proved us right. One need not be an Advanced Placement student to benefit from the best historical scholarship. In fact, some of our most successful teaching occurred in high-need school settings, as will be made clear in the chapters that follow. Note, too, that the project was open to any interested teacher—there were no special criteria for selecting those who collaborated with us. We found that when committed teachers worked together and with social studies faculty on lessons—grounded in stimulating scholarship from our historian interviews—they generated thought-provoking historical sources, questions, and arguments that engaged broad student interest and involvement in every type of school. This makes perfect sense, because historical teaching that challenges common stereotypes and assumptions, that surprises, and that offers dramatically new ways of looking at the world can stimulate student interest, and such interest can motivate student learning regardless of reading levels or previous performance on any kind of standardized test.

The chapters that follow are designed to walk readers through the collaborative process that our teachers (most of whom became chapter co-authors) experienced as they worked with education school faculty and historians on new approaches to the teaching of recent global history. Each chapter begins with an historian interview, which our teachers read and discussed at the start of this teaching collaborative. Then the chapters describe the teachers and the school environments in which they work and explore the planning processes that began with historical content discussions and involved gleaning from the historian interviews the most teachable themes, questions, and sources. Next we describe the teachers considering how to convert these new ideas and materials into exciting lessons and units. Taking as our starting point that history "begins with—and often ends with—questions, problems, puzzles, curiosities, and mysteries" (Bain, 2005, p. 181), all the units are built around "essential questions" aimed at helping students achieve certain "enduring understandings" about the topic and region under study (Wiggins & McTighe, 2005).

The teaching narrative proceeds from planning to implementation, and we see how the lessons fare in the classroom via vivid descriptions of what worked and did not work to promote effective historical teaching and learning in these diverse middle and secondary school settings. Teacher reflections and student work are then integrated into assessments of the units. Chapter Resources include outlines of the units and lessons linked to Common Core Standards, worksheets, sample student work, and other relevant teaching materials. The teaching narratives aim to be three dimensional and candid, not just for the sake of accuracy, but also to provide teachers reading this book enough specific information to give them the confidence and background they need to adapt these lesson ideas and learning activities for their own global history classes.

Through every phase of this teaching work—from the initial brainstorming right up through the final assessments of the lessons—what continually impressed us was that the collaboration between the teachers was every bit as stimulating as their interaction with the historians on this project. Most teachers remarked on how rare it was for them to have the opportunity for extended dialogue with their colleagues about their teaching work and how they can improve it and link it to some of the most illuminating scholarship of global historians. One of the central conclusions from this book project is that teachers can do some of their most innovative instructional work when they find the time and make the effort to run their teaching ideas by their fellow educators and jointly assess their lessons—candidly confronting their weaknesses as well as their strengths. In other words, when teachers have the opportunity to build a community of practice, great things can happen in their classrooms.

As the chapters in *Teaching Recent Global History* attest, those great things centered on active student learning, sparked by creative pedagogy that placed students in conversation with the key global history themes, questions, and controversies that our global historians had articulated with such eloquence in their interviews. The teachers got students out of their seats for process drama, role plays as investigative journalists, mock UN hearings, construction of video narratives, historical debates, and gallery-style exhibits. The students created and then critiqued revolutionary poster art, wrote political correspondence, constructed surveys on religion, and deconstructed documentary and feature film clips. What made these learning activities so exhilarating was that they were not merely lively and fun but were also intellectually rigorous and rewarding: they pushed students to think critically and independently about the world the 20th century made and its legacies. These activities empowered students to sail against the winds of historical ignorance that Tony Judt warned against, and ensured that our students will be among those resisting the tendency for ours to be an "age of forgetting" 20th century history.

The one thing our teaching groups did not get to do during the involved process of planning and teaching these units was to step back and consider how all of the historical scholarship that went into this book's seven chapters cumulatively fit together and relate to one another. And since global history is all about how the parts of our world interact with one another, it is worth reflecting—both here and by readers as they make their way through this book—on what conclusions this global history lead us to when viewed as a whole. What is most striking in this regard is the tug of war between national/regional experience and global power. In probing colonial and neo-colonial relationships, at times the historical imperialism borders on dictating a kind of historiographical imperialism: when writing about, say, Africa, the western powers are so intrusive that we find ourselves repeatedly discussing Africa primarily in terms of its relationship to the West. Similarly, with the Cold War, Latin America is so coupled with the history of U.S. intervention that it can almost seem like the 51st state. In other words, when we use a global history frame and speak of world systems, the powers at the top tend to fill so much space in historical narratives that at times there is a danger that our students may *only* envision those other regions as having a history when they are in relationships to hegemonic powers. One does not, for example, have to buy into the notion that the 20th century was "the American century" to notice the U.S. footprint all over Latin American, Asian, European, and Middle Eastern history. The irony, of course, is that as a school topic, U.S. history is usually separated out from global history and taught in an entirely different grade level, almost as if it were not a part of the globe. Yet with regard to the 20th century, the U.S., first as a rising then as a hegemonic global power, cannot seem to help but hog the global history spotlight.

To their credit, however, the historians interviewed in this book—especially those who study Asia and Africa—pushed back on this western-centered history. Their words remind us that the experience on these continents, including their most appropriate chronological frames, do not conform to the themes that some of the greatest western historians have sought to impose on 20th century global history. For example, in his classic global history *The Age of Extremes,* the eminent British Marxist historian E. J. Hobsbawm (1996) argues for—as the book's subtitle, *A History of the World, 1914–1991,* indicates—a "short 20th century," whose start (the outbreak of World War I) and end (the collapse of the Soviet Union) are framed by events that originated in Europe. As such, this is not a formulation that, for example, our African historian Frederick Cooper or China scholar Moss Roberts find persuasive or even useful. In fact, Cooper expressed great skepticism over whether any 20th century chronological frame is useful for understanding the African experience since the colonial–decolonization story's critical earlier chapters occurred well before the 1900s and its breaking point in the 20th century came well before the Soviet collapse.

Similarly, the 12 epigrams Hobsbawm (1996) uses to open his influential global history, ostensibly providing a "bird's eye view" of the 20th century, also suffer from Eurocentrism. Most of those epigrams are deeply pessimistic about the 20th century, seeing it as a sad story of bloody war and genocide. These include René Dumont terming the 20th "only a century of massacres and wars," and William Golding concluding that it was "the most violent century in human history." Such reflections eloquently convey the historical sensibility of these dozen prominent and justifiably war-weary Europeans, but not Latin Americans or Africans who had nothing to do with initiating the 20th century's tragic world wars. And even the "age of forgetting" that Tony

Judt evoked so powerfully in his reflections on the 20th century is a western construct aimed at speaking to and for an American and European readership. These are useful reminders that as we struggle against an "age of forgetting" in America, we ought to try not to assume that our own tendencies toward historical amnesia constitute a global phenomenon. In places like the Middle East, for instance, it is remembrance of historic enmities, not amnesia, that seems the greatest affliction. Thus as we work to make the teaching of global history manageable via thematic chapters and time frames, we need to keep in mind that sometimes cramming the history of our complex world into a small and tidy set of categories can distort as much as it illuminates. If we want a bird's eye view of 20th century global history, those birds should not be confined to Western Europe but should be migrating across the globe—as do the chapters of this book.

Our hope is that history teachers will find *Teaching Recent Global History* useful on several levels. The first is as individual educators. The lesson, unit, and activity planning and teaching narratives offer teachers ideas they can adapt for use in their own history classes. And the historian interviews afford teachers the opportunity to connect with cutting edge historical scholarship globally, and so to experience the excitement of looking anew at important events and regions of the world in and since the 20th century. But we also hope that the book works on a second level that transcends solo teachers, and that it serves as a model for building teachers' communities of practice. Whatever merits this book has were made possible by just such community building among teachers and the creation of dialogues between teachers and historians, breaking down the walls that often separate schools and universities. If our under-resourced public school history classes are to become effective in challenging and toppling this "age of forgetting," those of us who value knowledge of the past need to work together. By working collaboratively, we can enhance our historical knowledge and pedagogical skills so that our students will come to see history as an essential way of understanding the problems of our own century and their roots in, as Judt put it, the 20th century "world we have lost."

Note

1   Note that while the teachers worked with entire interviews, those provided here have been edited as we selected the most relevant content for each chapter.

Works Cited

Bain, R. (2005). "They thought the world was flat?" Applying the principles of *how people learn* in teaching high school history. In J. Branson and S. Donovan (Eds.) *How students learn history, mathematics and science in the classroom* (pp. 179–214). Washington, D.C.: The National Academies Press.

Brinkerhoff, N. (2011, May 15). House Republicans move to eliminate grants for teaching American history. Allgov.com. Retrieved from www.allgov.com/news/where-is-the-money-going/house-republicans-move-to-eliminate-grants-for-teaching-american-history?news = 842664

Decker, G. (2012, Sept. 10). Instead of eliminating global studies exam, state could revamp it. *Gotham-Schools*. Retrieved from http://gothamschools.org/2012/09/10

Hobsbawm, E. J. (1996). *The age of extremes: A history of the world, 1914–1991*. New York: Vintage.

Judt, T. (2006). *Postwar: A history of Europe since 1945*. New York: Penguin.

Judt, T. (2008). *Reappraisals: Reflections on the forgotten twentieth century*. New York: Penguin.

Rundquist, J. (2011, July 19). Most students lack proficiency in geography, results show. *Newark Star Ledger*. Retrieved from www.nj.com/news/index.ssf/2011/07/most_us_students_lack_proficie.html

Tignor, R., Adelman, S., Aron, S., & Kotkin, S. (2011). *Worlds together, worlds apart: A history of the world*. New York: Norton.

Wiggins, G., & McTighe, J. (2005). *Understanding by design*. Upper Saddle River, NJ: Pearson Education Inc.

One
Africa

Up from Colonialism: Change and Continuity in Africa

By Laura J. Dull, with Michelle Lewis-Mondesir
and Alejandro Sosa

Framing the Questions: An Interview with Frederick Cooper,
conducted by Robert Cohen

Frederick Cooper is a professor in the Department of History at New York University. He earned his Ph.D. from Yale University. His books include: *Plantation Slavery on the East Coast of Africa* (1977); *From Slaves to Squatters: Plantation Labor and Agriculture in Zanzibar and Coastal Kenya, 1890–1925* (1980), for which he won the Melville Herskovits Prize of the African Studies Association in 1981; *On the African Waterfront: Urban Disorder and the Transformation of Work in Colonial Mombasa* (1987); *Confronting Historical Paradigms: Peasants, Labor, and the Capitalist World System in Africa and Latin America* (1993); *Decolonization and African Society: The Labor Question in French and British Africa* (1996); *Beyond Slavery: Explorations of Race, Labor, and Citizenship in Postemancipation Societies* (with Rebecca Scott and Thomas Holt) (2000); *Africa Since 1940: The Past of the Present* (2002); *Colonialism in Question: Theory, Knowledge, History* (2005); and *Empires in World History, Power and the Politics of Difference* (with Jane Burbank) (2010), a recipient of the World History Association Prize for 2011. Cooper is the recipient of several grants and fellowships and has lectured at universities worldwide.

Robert Cohen: *What are the biggest American misconceptions about Africa?*

Frederick Cooper: The biggest misconception is Africa as primitive. Sometimes I think that every time a reporter from a major newspaper … gets assigned to cover Africa, he thinks he is re-living Joseph Conrad's [famed novel] *The Heart of Darkness*. So you're constantly getting this evocation of cultural peculiarity. So the starting point for what most Americans know about Africa is that it's strange, it's impoverished, it's got images of wild nature, the jungle … And that leads one to think of explanations of why Africa has certain problems and what the nature of the issues are in a circular fashion. Africa is the way it is because it's Africa.

I think the way you do start to break this down is to say, "Okay, this is a part of history, [and] like every place else it has its particularities." And that you try to ask good questions which aren't all necessarily that different from the questions you'd ask about any society, be it in North or South America, Europe or Asia. My own approach is to say, "We are dealing with human societies that all have common problems—how to get food, how to develop relationships across generations, between the sexes, and here are ways in which these things are dealt with in different contexts." What you might call an anthropological approach. One other way of dealing with these kinds of things is to emphasize variety, to say, "Okay, you do have instances of famine, say Somalia today." You could deal with that and say that you don't want to let Somalia stand in for Africa as a whole because Africa is a continent of great variety and complexity that has confronted the problems of being human on the earth in a variety of ways. And sometimes produced horrific results and sometimes produced ways in which people can manage.

RC: *In terms of the 20th century in Africa, what central historical themes would you advise teachers to focus upon?*

FC: Well, I think one of the most important things to get at really starts earlier than the 20th century—and the 20th century is best framed in terms of it—and that is the connection between Africa and the world. I don't want students to think that Africa was an isolated continent living in a time warp forever and a day, and then in the 20th century you're dealing with colonialism and then efforts to end colonialism and become free, independent nations. So you'd want to go back a little and try to say that Africa was never isolated either from connections within the continent or from connections overseas. The Indian Ocean had connections abroad; the east coast, for example, had connections to India, to Arabia, and even to China that go back 2,000 years. The Sahara was something to cross not an impermeable barrier.

And what that means is that when you get to 20th century history you're not dealing with, "Here's this tribe here, there's that tribe there, which has always led its self-contained existence." The very nature of society and culture has been shaped interactively by people who are in contact or in motion. We can see this quite vividly in cases of African groups that are Islamic—obviously they were in contact with people in North Africa or the Persian Gulf, or Egypt, or Arabia. But we know that with a little more probing, you see this is true even of most of sub-Saharan Africa. So the notion of Africa as a conglomeration of distinct cultures is very artificial. The complexity that an individual sees in the way that person is culturally located, there is enormous variety, but it's not separation of each from each other. So I think that base line is very important—and not to see the 20th century as starting from a kind of anthropological zero.

The colonizations of the late 19th century, which happened very rapidly, were certainly a big event, but it wasn't as if this was the first time that Africans had contacted outsiders. And certainly not the first time that you have forms of cultural symbiosis, hybridity, interaction, and change. So one starts the 20th century, then, with a view of something new happening in societies that are already involved in historical processes, that are connected to each other, [and] to other parts of the world.

Well, let's try to trace what they are: in some ways the colonial period cut into connections. It created new barriers as well as creating new connections [such as] linguistic barriers between Francophone Africa and Anglophone Africa and Portuguese Lusophone Africa. These are creations of the late 19th, early 20th century, and they have become quite important sets of distinctions. It's actually hard to get conversations between people even in neighboring countries who were under French or British colonial rule.

If you look at a railroad map of Africa, [the] railroad enhances connections at one level. But if you look at the map, all the railroad lines outside of southern Africa run from the interior to the coast. They're drainage networks. They're not web-like networks. So your physical image of the kind of connectivity that colonial rule produces is a very specific one. And in that sense the incentives created by this type of connectivity are for more relationships to the inside–outside rather than among African economies, [and those economies are] orienting themselves toward European economies and not toward each other. And that's a huge problem in the 21st century, the lack of, [and] the costs of, connections within Africa and the encouragement that that gives to particular sorts of connections that are often quite insidious, like the arms trade.

So one trend over the 20th century we might call externalization, that economic activities enhance political perceptions that were oriented toward privileging the outside over the inside. And that's [related to] the concept that I use a lot in my book, *Africa Since 1940* [2002], the "gatekeeper state," which is important [in understanding modern Africa]. I think externalization goes back, at least in West Africa, to the days of the slave trade before colonialism. Colonial rule very much externalizes the process [of privileging the outside]. Once you start to have that [externalization], then the key question about what shapes the possibilities of an African country today has to do with the interface between the inside and the outside. Hence the incentives toward gatekeeping by elites that are trying to enhance their own power—[externalization] focuses your attention at this one point of connectivity, which it can't do in situations where you have a whole variety of more web-like connections among people.

[This] is not something that's easy to overcome. But if one wants to try to understand why things are the way they are—this is one important element of an explanation, of the way in which certain elites have a lot [to] gain from the narrowness of the connections to the outside world … the possibility of controlling them. And why African leaders, knowing quite well that their econo-mies are relatively small, would have had difficulties in establishing anything comparable to the European common market. If you are a ruler of a country you have something to be gained by being at the gate between the inside and the outside, everything passes through you. You collect the toll of everything that goes through. Is it in your interest to have tighter connections with other people who are in the same boat as you? Not necessarily. The people, the citizens of the country would benefit from it; the elite, not necessarily.

[T]he extremes of gatekeeping are found in the oil producing states. Maybe the extreme of the extreme is Angola, where you have a narrow elite that's based in Luanda, the capital city, that basically collects revenue from Chevron, Total—the French oil company—and a couple of others. And they spend it on their own luxury living, and they spend it on military goods. They fought a nasty civil war, but now that that's over, the gatekeeping phenomenon is not over. Here you have the extremes of gatekeeping because most of the production of the product occurs with very little labor … What matters most is you get a few Texans in to dig the wells, and then you sit and turn the spigot and collect a lot of money in rent for it. So there you have an elite that has very little relationship with its own people. They can get rich. And there is absolutely no reason why it should do anything else.

Gabon is another example. A country with a huge oil revenue and a population of only a couple of million, a *tiny* population. Everybody could be rich in Gabon, but only a few hundred people, maybe a thousand people, are. And there is no particular reason why the ruling elite should do things differently. What matters for them is their relationship with the outside. So you now have this scandal that is going on in France, with accusations that the leaders of Gabon financed political campaigns in France—a sort of reverse neo-colonialism. Why is it even imaginable that something like that could happen? Because what matters here is the relationship of the elite, particularly the family of [the late president of Gabon] Omar Bongo and now his son Ali Bongo [president of Gabon since his father's death in 2009] to oil companies. And the control of that connection. The Bongo clan doesn't need its own people ... What matters here is the relationship between a governing group and the leading actors of the outside world.

RC: *Do you see this pattern is one that was established under colonialism and has just been perpetuated or is this new in any way?*

FC: I think that externalization happened—you see its roots—even earlier [than the era of colonialism]. But, contrary to the image that we sometimes have of the colonial state as being this totalizing institution, [this image] doesn't work very well for most of Africa, with relatively dispersed populations and very few white officials or white military people after the initial conquest, or even during the initial conquest. So you're dealing with colonial regimes that did not impose a grille of power over the place but rather concentrated power in a few places ... by concentrating force, they could punish people who were causing trouble. And colonial wars could be extremely brutal. But they didn't routinize administration, and they didn't routinize economic structures over large expanses. They did it where there was something very lucrative, say the copper mines of northern Rhodesia. But what they didn't do is spread out authority in a uniform way. [They would] make their deals with local kings, local chiefs. They did all sorts of things to have a very low cost structure of authority, which will allow extraction of things that are relatively easy to extract.

In some cases, however, [colonizers] need actually fairly complex kinds of structures of order to get anything at all. And in some cases they're presented these by African communities that organize production themselves. The best case of this is the production of cocoa in what is now Ghana, formerly the British colony of Gold Coast. There, unbeknownst to the colonial government, people started in the late 19th century to plant cocoa bushes. They plant this product, having gotten the initial shoots from Swiss missionaries. And this takes off and allows African cultivators to obtain a moderate degree of prosperity, and then the colonial government can start to fill its coffers by taking exports—for a product for which they were not responsible. For the colonial government, the interest is in the export of it. For Africans, a lot of Africans are involved in the production of it ... It is partially family labor but most often it's actually beyond the family, but people have figured out ways of getting workers, either as wage laborers or more likely as tenants. Sometimes people who will be promised that in the long term they will get help to become cocoa farmers themselves. So it softens the class relations within the cocoa producing areas. But from the point of the colonial government, they get a good thing without having to be too deeply involved in how it is produced—they're not going to ask very many questions. So colonial gatekeeping can work in that way, which isn't particularly terrible for the Africans involved. Some people did fairly well off this.

In other cases [like Rhodesia and South Africa], you're dealing with all these settlements of white farmers. Those are usually extremely oppressive, and only work because Africans in the surrounding areas are denied opportunities to produce things that the market can use themselves ... Rhodesia would be a fine example of that. South Africa is even more concentrated because they have gold and other kinds of things. It's true of central Kenya as well, where ... up until 1947 or 1948 or so, Africans in central Kenya, the highlands, were denied the right to plant coffee. Coffee was the most lucrative crop. Only white people could plant coffee. When that ends ... you start to see some Africans doing the same thing as white people, in getting poor laborers to work for them, and some of them can do relatively well for themselves—but it's the same structure.

But you get variation on these themes in which you have relatively autonomous African communities that produce but then have a narrow range of things for marketing. But because many Africans are involved it means that those people have to be taken seriously. And governments have to be very careful about leaning too heavily on them or they might kill off the very thing that's giving them resources. And colonial governments sometimes figure this out, but sometimes they killed the goose that is laying the golden egg.

And independent African governments afterwards faced some of those same questions. And some of them, including Kwame Nkrumah's Ghana, were more restrictive on cocoa producers than the British colonial government had been. And they actually damaged considerably the cocoa economy. So gatekeeping triumphs over increasing production. But Nkrumah was worried not just that somebody else would be rich; he was worried that people who were rich would use their resources to organize against the government. That wasn't foolish. There was a real possibility that could happen.

RC: *What chronological frame might you use for Africa?*

FC: Well, think about processes. I find it useful to think of moments of uncertainty when things look as if they could have gone in a different direction. There's no doubt about the importance of colonization. But then one has to be careful about it because it doesn't change everything. Like the history of externalization, which we've been discussing, goes back way before it, and certainly in certain parts of Africa that were affected by the slave trade. And it might have taken [some remotely situated] people 20 years before they learned they were colonized. But nonetheless [it's a big deal] in terms of certain kinds of structures like the building of railways, the collections of taxes, the imposition of different languages. So we want to see it in terms of the broader picture, and that the rhythms of change may not coincide with that, but it's important nonetheless.

The point which I see as one of these moments of uncertainty and possibility is right after World War II where the two biggest European powers, France and Britain, realize that they can't play [the usual colonial] game anymore. They have to take more seriously the possibility of increasing the productivity of Africa but also making their rule more legitimate. And these two begin to be in direct contradiction to each other. You wanted to exploit more but look as if you're exploiting less. Or maybe actually make it more in the interests of Africans to be involved in the imperial economy, to convince them by something other than naked force that they have an interest in it. Well, this sets up all sorts of possibilities, of which a kind of developmental imperialism is one. But if you look at the period after World War II what you're seeing here is a set of possibilities that are on the table. There's not only one pathway. So to look at this period in terms of multiple possibilities rather than a neat change from A to B.

RC: *Could you elaborate on how this late history of colonialism looks when you hold these competing imperial powers side by side?*

FC: In France there is a very strong notion of citizenship both for itself and in terms of how it relates to its overseas territories. Up until 1946, there was a sharp distinction between people who were citizens and people who were subjects, even though both were French nationals. And so an African in Cotonou was a French national but not a French citizen. After [World War II], the most important claim being made from that generation of African politicians is for French citizenship. And France thinks that the only way it's going to make a long-term viability out of its African colonies is to accept that and say, "Well, everybody will be a citizen, and we'll see what that means." And so you have some people trying to make the meaning of that as narrow as it could be and others trying to make it as expansive as it could be. There's a lot of politics around citizenship.

In the British case, the reigning concept is the individual nature of each territory—Gold Coast, Nigeria, Kenya, etc. And in a way the model is Commonwealth … they could say to Nigeria "Well eventually you'll be like Canada." Well, is eventually going to be 5 years? 15 years? Or 115 years? That they don't say. In fact, the speed was much more rapid than the British in 1945 would have thought it was going to be. So it's only in retrospect that the decolonization of British Africa looks like it was following a plan that was written in London. But the model there is territorial. So what the British would have liked to do after the war was to see Africans start with a focus on local government, then territorial, set autonomy, and then perhaps independence in the context of the Commonwealth. In fact the post-war generation of African politicians doesn't want anything to do with local politics. What they're focusing on is how to take a colonial regime that's been a gatekeeping state and gain control of that. So the focus becomes territorial.

What it doesn't become is imperial. So whereas you have French Africans from October 1945 sitting in Paris in parliament—not *many* of them but nonetheless every territory is represented—you don't have African politicians sitting in parliament in London. Even though they're a minority, the French African politicians in Paris think they can gain access to resources that are imperial France as a whole, and to quite a significant extent they do. The game of politics in British Africa is about the territory and what one can gain there … So you have a very strong notion of citizenship in France, you have a very weak one in British Africa, although under the Nationalities Act of 1948 everybody in the Commonwealth had a kind of second order of British citizenship. A Canadian can show up in England and has a right to be let in. That was actually true of Jamaicans and Guineans for a time. It was taken away from them but not really until Thatcher.

The Portuguese government after World War II was a dictatorship. So the notion of extending political rights to Portuguese Africa was a question that was never posed because people in European Portugal had no political rights either. But what Portugal did is a part of what Britain and France were [doing], which is economic development. But economic development in Portuguese Africa turns out to be "let's bring whites from Portugal and put them in certain key sectors of the economy," playing roles that Africans were playing in British and French Africa. So the politics of development are quite different in those cases.

In British and French Africa the governments lose control over the timing. You end up with independence, which the French hadn't thought was what the people needed or wanted. The British think it will take decades or even longer. By 1960 it's clear what's happening there. But of the options of making citizenship meaningful, making the Commonwealth meaningful, the option that people end up with is one that wasn't the most desirable for anybody, which is the autonomous nation state, the independent nation state.

Portuguese Africa didn't end up that way. But with everybody around Angola, Mozambique, and Guinea Bissau becoming independent by the 1960s you end up with guerilla movements having a base in neighboring countries. You end up with the normality of colonial rule being severely compromised. You end up with the fact that it's very difficult to do colonialism in one colony. And by the early 1970s the costs of fighting these wars for the Portuguese Army are so severe that the Portuguese Army then rebels against their own government, overthrows the fascist state in Portugal, and Portugal is actually liberated from its African colonies. So that's another trajectory.

[T]he government of South Africa in 1945–1946 is considering reforms in its structure, which [are] parallel to what is being done in some parts of British Africa, particularly in regard to labor. After the 1948 elections, won by the Nationalist Party, they do exactly the reverse, making South Africa more racially segregated, rolling back some of the trends toward urbanization of African populations, forcing Africans to remain in local farms, in many cases forcing them to shuttle back and forth between temporary jobs in mines and the city and impoverished rural homelands … [A]partheid wasn't really a whole new invention but it becomes more severe after 1948 with the enforcement of the pass laws, the enforcement of segregation, the forcing of people to keep their seat in these impoverished rural homelands, the pretense that Africans are really tribal people and not citizens of South Africa. And that dynamic remains despite all that opposition from African political activists.

RC: *Why did it take so much longer in South Africa for the old regime to fall?*

FC: You're dealing with a population that is 15% non-African rather than 2 or 3%. It has much more resources to maintain white domination. Also that white population has really become Africanized. It's not as if they have a home to go back to. Whereas in Africa where you don't have [European] settlement, in Nigeria, Ghana, for example, the only white people who live there are either businessmen or government officials, neither of whom have set down roots in the country. In South Africa the largest part of the white population there have started calling themselves Afrikaners, which means Africans … So they're going to fight to keep what they have for a long time—until the contradiction of pretending to be part of the civilized world and running a white-dominated government that the rest of the world repudiated became more than they could bear. And the violence that they need to impose to keep the system becomes more than they themselves can tolerate.

RC: *I am struck by the theme of disappointment about decolonization [in your book] since it so reminds me of a similar feeling in Charles Payne's* I've Got the Light of Freedom *[2007] on the black freedom movement in Mississippi. In both cases you have social movements that battled for democratic rights in the face of horrendous violence. Then when the social movements win and secure democratic rights, there is the expectation of great social change and leaders connected to the people. But then the elected leaders get cut off from the social movements that helped carry them to power and begin acting in ways that benefit the leaders rather than the formerly oppressed people … It's not as if nothing has changed, yet there is this striking sense of disappointment.*

FC: Lots of Africans would articulate that theme. I was in Dakar in the summer of 2010, which was the 50th anniversary of Senegal's independence … So I was on a panel with two Senegalese scholars, both with very strong international connections … And all three of us on the panel dealt very summarily with the issue of celebration of the 50th anniversary, "Let's focus on what possibilities opened up. And how were these shut down? And try to see that the narrative of triumph is inadequate." But that doesn't mean that you want to say, "Everything was great until 1960 when we were struggling and then everything was bad after we won the struggle." So how do you re-narrate this story? And particularly when the audience got into it and people of different generations, there you see some people really wanted the heroic narrative. Some were demonizing the France narrative. And others were trying to say, "There really were possibilities that were developing here and what we want to see is how far one could go with them. And it didn't all turn bad in 1960 after independence. There were things that got pushed in very positive directions."

But maybe the date of 1960 is not the most important date in fact. And the "rise and fall" narrative needs to be read along with one which sees that maybe the 1945 to the 1970s narrative [is one] in which the question was "how wide was the opening going to be?" And it was never [fully opened] but it opened up to a degree and then gets compressed particularly in the economic crisis of the 1970s. And governments feared that they could no longer deliver what they had promised. African governments were saying, "We're Africans. We can deal with the needs of our citizens in a way that outsiders are never going to do." But then what happens when they don't? And governments started to become very defensive. And over time they both tried to deliver and to suppress alternatives. Then when they can't deliver all they do is suppress alternatives. And that is a phenomenon more of the 1970s and 1980s than it is of the 1960s.

Part of the way I would re-tell this is to say that independent governments had raised expectations in the period when they were politically mobilized. And when the world economy did reasonably well, as it did during the 1960s, they can actually deliver on some of these things. You have a degree of social progress in many African countries, especially those that avoid bad things like civil war, like in the former Belgian Congo. Then the world depression of the 1970s is a really important part of the story … after that [economic crisis] weakens states they both become more repressive—because they can't deliver things they're supposed to—and they become more dependent on outside sources.

And then what the IMF [International Monetary Fund] and other outsiders impose in the 1980s is absolutely catastrophic—the so-called structural adjustments, which essentially say that governments have to cut back on social services. And that means that the governments are cutting back on the one thing they can actually promise citizens. It can only be disastrous because it undermines the long-term capacity of African societies to do anything.

So here's a way in which the question isn't one of, "Well, African governments triumph and then they blow the whole thing." [Rather,] African governments come in to power. There are certain things they can do and certain things they cannot do given the economic situation, given their own political vulnerability. You have a wide variety of outcomes in the 1960s and early 1970s. And then in the 1970s you start to see most places having real crises—and most governments finding their incapacity to do anything increases. And the political crisis takes on a new dimension by the 1980s.

RC: *Also there is the issue that even after you're independent politically that's not the case economically, as with the IMF …*

FC: Yes, the structures are there. But the IMF imposed the "structural adjustment" in the 1980s. You still have to ask the question of why African governments didn't make themselves more autonomous so they weren't so vulnerable to the selfish and destructive policies of the IMF in the 1980s. So you are faced with having to see just what were the possibilities and limitations of governments run by elites that are intent on controlling the relatively limited range of resources that they have. That's the fundamental question about that period in the 1960s and 1970s.

RC: *I wonder what you think the prospects are of Africa following the example set by Europe in the common market?*

FC: The interesting thing is Pan-Africanism seemed very much a viable political tendency in 1945. And the Manchester meeting of 1945 turned out to be the end rather than the beginning. Nkrumah tries to revive it. But the closest he comes [is] the All Africa Peoples' Congress of 1958, by then it is already clear that this is a meeting in which key actors are going to be states not peoples. The game has changed between 1945 and 1958. So it becomes quite difficult for African rulers who are very concerned about the fragility of their power within their states to say, "Well, I'm going to give up a bit of sovereignty in order to work with other countries."

And if you look at what the European Union does, it is a surrender of sovereignty [in which] quite a few economic decisions will be made outside of the national boundaries—and including now both currency, with the Euro, and border control with [the] Schengen [agreement]. Those are huge issues in regard to any concept of sovereignty. Are African rulers who are, if my argument is sound, very concerned with gatekeeping, going to think in those terms? It is very hard for people to do that. And because the world is so unequal and the degree of inequality between most of Africa and Europe is greater than between the poorest European countries (Greece and Portugal) and the richest (Germany).

If you want to say from the point of view of poor countries, do their leaders want to have relationships with other equally poor countries? Or do they want a relationship with the rich counties? The temptation is to say, "Well let's have the vertical relationship between ourselves—poor—and somebody else who is rich" rather than horizontal relationships with other countries that are equally poor. If you could have a West African economic union, an East African economic union, a Southern African economic union, that could be really positive thing for the little guy—but not necessarily for the rulers.

RC: *There seems to be an irony to all this, in that nationalism was needed as an instrument of liberation from colonialism but then nationalism becomes itself an obstacle to progress.*

FC: That's what Leopold Senghor argued in the 1940s and 1950s … He used the image of Balkanization. But for him the phrase Balkanization signified the break-up of empires into non-viable units, which would be at each others' throats, which would be internally unstable. In retrospect Senghor was right, including his own role in Senegal. He was playing some of the same games as everyone else was playing. He was in the same trap as everyone else. The difference being that he was very clear about recognizing it before the trap was sprung. But he couldn't prevent it from springing.

Works Cited

Cooper, F. (2002). *Africa since 1940: The past of the present.* New York, NY: Cambridge University Press.
Payne, C. (2007). *I've got the light of freedom: The organizing tradition and the Mississippi Freedom Struggle.* Los Angeles: University of California Press.

Essay: Up from Colonialism: Change and Continuity in Africa

By Laura J. Dull, with Michelle Lewis-Mondesir and Alejandro Sosa

A recent video by four African college students cleverly mocks excessively violent portrayals of Africans in films as they seek to "Stop the Pity" and promote positive images of the continent (*Huffington Post*, 2012). While such efforts provide a welcome balance to patronizing campaigns of other aid-seekers (for example, Invisible Children's Joseph Kony video), it is true that many Africans remain poor and oppressed by bad governance. Some historians argue that colonizers' arbitrary borders and exploitation account for ongoing problems. Certainly, many European decisions proved disastrous—think of King Leopold's pillaging of Congo and British actions during the Mau Mau Revolt in Kenya. However, often missing from the story are the actions of Africans who took advantage of colonization or, as leaders, perpetuated misery once they gained power. Inspired by historian Frederick Cooper's interview and book (*Africa Since 1940: The Past of the Present,* 2002), the teaching unit for this chapter aimed to acknowledge Africans as historical agents and not just victims, by asking: who is to blame for the lack of development and democracy in Africa? What could be done to improve life for all Africans? We hoped that students' views on these questions would be challenged by the lessons we developed.

We started by showing students jubilant moments from independence days and the end of apartheid—Ghanaians dancing in the streets; lines of first-time black voters in South Africa that streamed across the landscape; a highlife song celebrating freedom in Ghana; and speeches by leaders like Jomo Kenyatta. Next, we turned to contemporary statistics about life in these countries, asking: what has happened since independence? Did the dreams of independence come true? The results show a mixed picture: some countries like Ghana and South Africa are stable, while others, like the Democratic Republic of Congo (DRC) and Kenya, still face economic and political troubles. We then chose two pivotal events from April 1994: South Africa's first democratic elections and Rwanda's genocide, to get students to think about how social change happens and how historians use sources to reconstruct the past. Next, students learned about different "suspects" who have committed "democracide" (Mazrui, 2002); that is, European colonizers, African military leaders, and others who have impeded the development of democracy in Africa. At the end, the students had to choose one suspect and make a case as to why that group was responsible for problems in contemporary Africa at a mock United Nations (UN) hearing.

There were many powerful learning moments during these lessons, just as there were ways in which we fell short of our objectives. A major roadblock of course was time—a week or so is not enough to cover the vast and complex history of multiple African countries. But in dealing with the questions, the students developed theories about how power works and learned about the diverse actors who have created modern Africa. In addition, they confronted the difficulties of finding causes for significant events, itself a form of historical thinking. As one student who studied the unit with us asked in regard to the question of blame, "Is there a real answer to that question?"

African Gatekeepers

Africa scholar Frederick Cooper argued in the interview on which this chapter is based that many Americans misunderstand the degree to which Africa has been linked with the rest of the world, viewing the continent as "primitive" and disconnected from international currents of trade and cultural diffusion. One of the students in our project described Africa as a "land of mystery, uncivilized lands, turmoil, wars … a land of pureness touched by the hands of death." These views are understandable given the media's focus on wild animals, violence, and village life or urban slums that seem untouched by the modern world. In fact, many well-meaning people, Africans and non-Africans alike, focus on the bad news in order to keep foreign aid flowing, garner support for charity, or justify despotic rule (Chabal & Daloz, 1999; see also Mentzer, 2012). But Africans are neither "pure" nor "uncivilized" and have always been connected to the outside world. These relationships have often taken place within the context of what Cooper calls "the gatekeeper state." This form of governance means that certain groups or leaders maintain tight control over resources that bring wealth, blocking the ambitions of other elites and impoverishing the rest of the population. As Cooper explains,

> If you are a ruler of a country you have something to be gained by being at the gate between the inside and the outside … You collect the tolls of everything that goes through. Is it in your interest to have tighter connections with the other people who are in the same boat as you? Not necessarily.

Since rulers look outside to form connections, other groups within the country turn to corruption or violence to pass through the gate.

Cooper noted that gatekeeper states are characterized by "externalization," which orients economic relationships towards the exterior. This preference has literally sculpted the landscape. Maps of railroad systems show that they are "drainage networks" rather than "web-like networks"—linked from the interior to the coast, not to neighboring towns and countries. This helps explain why African nations continue to struggle with development and democracy, as in Gabon:

> A country with a huge oil revenue and a population of only a couple of million, a tiny population. Everybody could be rich in Gabon, but only a few hundred people, maybe a thousand people, are. And there is no particular reason why the ruling elite should do things differently. What matters for them is their relationship with the outside.

Outsiders include large private businesses or multinational corporations, "supercitizens" (Rothkopf, 2012) with more wealth and power than most countries.

Gatekeeping also explains the failure of nations to embrace pan-Africanism and form economic unions that might have done more to benefit ordinary citizens. In the post-colonial era, alliances such as the European Union would have required a "surrender of sovereignty" over certain economic decisions, a submission that African rulers, whose hold on power was already fragile, were generally unwilling to make. Moreover, other newly independent African countries did not make attractive partners, as Cooper explains: "If you want to say from the point of view of poor countries, do their leaders want to have relationships with other equally poor countries? Or do they want a relationship with the rich countries?" The answer, of course, is the latter.

According to Robert Cohen, the scholar who conducted our interview with Frederick Cooper, "there is this striking sense of disappointment" in looking back on the independence movements in Africa and the black freedom movement in the U.S. This observation inspired our group to start our unit with independence and then seek to understand what happened since that time. Our essential questions were drawn from the historian's conversation about what led to political crises in post-colonial African countries. Cooper argued that while the global economy was relatively healthy, African governments were able to fulfill some of their promises to citizens, to build infrastructure or support local farmers. However, world depression during the 1970s caused African states to become weaker, more repressive, and more dependent on outsiders. This led to what Cooper called "absolutely catastrophic" structural adjustments imposed by the International Monetary Fund (IMF) and others in the 1980s, economic policies that led to cutbacks in governmental programs vital to social and political stability. Cooper considered the role of Africans in creating this situation:

> You still have to ask the question of why African governments didn't make themselves more autonomous so they weren't so vulnerable to the selfish and destructive policies of the IMF in the 1980s. So you are faced with having to see just what were the

possibilities and limitations of governments run by elites that are intent on controlling the relatively limited range of resources that they have.

Similar questions arise when students confront difficult history such as genocide or the African slave trade: why do people allow bad things to happen? Why didn't people just "fight back"? One of our students pushed back against victim narratives: "If the Africans knew they were getting control, and they knew they had access to all these resources, why did they let it [present-day exploitation] happen?"

With these questions in mind, one of our goals in our unit on Africa in the 20th century was to teach about the diverse actors who have contributed to historical and social change in Africa. We drew from Cooper's insistence that, "Africa is a continent of great variety and complexity that has confronted the problems of being human on the earth in a variety of ways. And sometimes produced horrific results and sometimes produced ways in which people can manage." For example, European imperialism and rule were not homogeneous across the colonies, as Cooper emphasized when comparing forms of citizenship promoted by different colonial rulers. These conditions combined with unique local histories and geographies to shape present-day life. Cooper's book (2002) starts by addressing contrasting events in Rwanda and South Africa during the same month. In April, 1994, Rwanda began its terrible genocide. Several weeks later, black South Africans voted for the first time as the apartheid system finally crumbled. These examples should not be used to show "Africa's two possible fates—either dissolving into 'tribal' or 'ethnic' violence or uniting under a liberal democratic system." Rather, Cooper underscores the complicated histories that led to these outcomes, outcomes that were not "inevitable" due to Africans' inability to develop their own forms of government or to overcome their "ancient" rivalries (2002, p. 2). Likewise, our teaching group wanted students to view Africans as capable of misrule and benevolence, generosity and greed, creativity and destruction as any other human.

Teaching Africa in New York City

Our group consisted of two New York City public high school teachers, Michelle and Alejandro, and a teacher educator, Laura. Both Michelle and Alejandro taught at themed schools that grew out of the drive to create smaller learning communities. At the time, Michelle was teaching at the Academy for Environmental Leadership in Brooklyn, a "college-preparatory" school "committed to ensuring that every student is held to the highest standards, has consistent opportunities for intellectual engagement, and becomes knowledgeable about, and active leaders in, the preservation of the earth and its peoples" (Academy for Environmental Leadership, n.d.). The school opened in 2006. At the time of this project, there were 359 students, 75% of whom were Hispanic and 23% of whom were black. 93% of the students qualified for free or reduced lunch. There was a 74% graduation rate, and about 50% of students plan to continue on to college (New York State Education Department, 2010–2011a, 2010–2011b). Michelle chose to conduct the lessons in her tenth grade honors class of 22 students.

Alejandro teaches at World Journalism Preparatory School, also opened in 2006. Reflecting the immigrant population of its Queens neighborhood, 51% of the students at World Journalism Prep are white, 21% Hispanic, 19% Asian, and 8% black, with 45% of students qualifying for free or reduced lunches. Almost 90% of the students graduate, and 83% of those students go on to college (Inside Schools, 2012; New York State Education Department, 2010–2011c). The school, guided by the motto "Everyone has a story," is equipped with a film studio, and students publish a school paper, *The Blazer*. Alejandro conducted the lessons in his two regular-level tenth grade global history classes. Neither of the two schools has significant barriers such as testing for admission (World Journalism Preparatory School, n.d.).

Laura teaches in the Secondary Education Department at the State University of New York in New Paltz. She taught social studies in New York City public schools for seven years. One of the schools served recent Chinese immigrants as well as students who had struggled in regular comprehensive school environments. She then taught humanities in a block schedule at another alternative school. Laura was also a Teachers for Africa volunteer in Ghana, and wrote her dissertation and a book, *Disciplined Development: Teachers and Reform in Ghana* (Dull, 2006) based on her research there.

In designing our unit, we considered how to make the concept of the "gatekeeper state" comprehensible to youth. For Cooper, this idea proved vital to understanding political and economic problems that Africans continue to face. Since there have been different players who have controlled or sought access to the "gate," we agreed that the question of who is to blame for Africa's problems would be a good hook. Through this question, we sought to show that there were many different people—African and non-African—who have contributed to ongoing oppression and poverty. This question fits the qualifications for a good essential question: it was brief, compelling, and did not have a single or simple answer. In addition, the question was linked to enduring issues, such as why are societies unequal, how should wealth be distributed, how might democracy be established in diverse cultural and post-colonial contexts, and so on (Wiggins & McTighe, 2005; Zmuda & Tomaino, 2001). We also asked what could be done to improve the lives of all Africans. This question invited students to reflect on historical change and to understand that Africans are not doomed to failure.

In the spirit of "backwards planning" (Wiggins & McTighe, 2005), we developed a final project that we hoped would engage the students deeply in the essential questions. Based on a previous experience, Michelle suggested we hold a UN hearing. Early ideas included having students take on the role of different stakeholders in a country and making a speech about who was responsible for the problems in their country. In the end, students in both schools chose from a list of possible perpetrators and made a case for that group in front of their classmates. The list was inspired by an essay, "Who killed democracy in Africa?" by Kenyan professor Ali Mazrui (2002). Mazrui uses powerful imagery to describe various "murderers": "The magician who came in from the North" (European colonizers), "The soldier who came in from the barracks" (militaries that carried out *coups d'état*), "The spy who came in from the cold" (U.S. and Soviet Cold Warriors), and "The cultural half-caste who came in from Western schools and did not adequately respect African ancestors" (pro-Western African leaders).

After crafting our essential questions and final project, we confronted a dilemma familiar to global history teachers: how does one teach about a region with over 50 countries? Looming over the unit, of course, were the New York State Regents exams and curricula that shape not only what is taught in the classroom, but also the prior knowledge students would bring to the lessons. Therefore, the decision over what to teach was in some ways already determined, because preparing students to take (and pass) the state exam was a real concern for our two teachers: South Africa and Rwanda are the only African countries regularly mentioned on state tests, and sometimes Kwame Nkrumah and Nelson Mandela are cited as noted leaders. We agreed that Rwanda and South Africa would be included in the unit and were happy that Cooper highlighted these countries in his book. We chose Ghana, South Africa, and Kenya to illustrate moments of freedom in our first lesson that featured "stations" with films, music, photos, and speeches. In the second lesson, students embarked on a WebQuest (see Dodge, 2007) to learn about the different degrees of development and freedom in the DRC, Ghana, Kenya, Rwanda, and South Africa. The third lesson drew from the strategy of "history as mystery" (Gerwin & Zevin, 2010), where we asked students to select a hypothesis about what caused historic change in South Africa or Rwanda in 1994, and then study a series of clues to decide which hypothesis was best supported by the evidence. The fourth lesson involved learning about the "murderers" of African democracy and making "Wanted" posters of a suspect. The unit culminated with the UN hearing (Chapter Resources I). Both teachers taught introductory lessons to provide a historical outline of contemporary Africa, and both made modifications to the lessons based on their particular circumstances.

Illustrative Classroom Moments

We accumulated a great deal of material to assess student learning and reactions to our unit: worksheets, posters, blog postings, and other student work, observation notes and videos, and teacher and student surveys. In the following sections, we describe learning experiences from each lesson to illuminate what happened when students interacted with the material. We consider the ways in which students did, and did not, achieve the unit's enduring understandings, offering suggestions on how we would enrich or modify the lessons in the future.

Michelle's Class: What Did Independence Look and Feel Like?

In the introductory lesson, students visited several stations to become immersed in the images and words of Africans imagining their futures as free people: students viewed newsreels of independence in Ghana and Kenya and photos of South African voters; listened to a Ghanaian song celebrating freedom; and read excerpts from the speeches of Kwame Nkrumah, Jomo Kenyatta, and Nelson Mandela, each of which captured the joy of freedom ("At long last the battle is ended! And thus, Ghana, your beloved country is free forever!"), but also warned that, as Mandela declared, "The task at hand will not be easy" (Chapter Resources II). We wanted students to understand that at the time of their independence from colonial powers and oppressive regimes, sub-Saharan African leaders and their people envisioned a prosperous, democratic, and peaceful future. Besides marking an important transition from colonization to independence, this lesson set the stage for thinking about the extent to which the promises of self-government have and have not come true.

Laura was present when Michelle conducted this lesson. Michelle started by asking students to anticipate the lesson: what did the students think was going to happen now that Africans got their independence and what changes did African people expect? After introducing the stations, we circulated among groups to help students interpret the texts and provide additional historical context. Worksheet responses and a "word web" constructed the following day indicated good understandings of what freedom felt like. The students used words like "ecstatic," "extremely happy," and "excited to vote for the first time" to describe the celebratory spirit, while they explained future aspirations as "a sense of self-esteem and confidence in the future," "they felt equal," and "imagined a country to be one [in] which they could live and work with dignity." Students also noted that all three leaders warned citizens that they had to "work hard" to achieve their dreams. One student remembered the concept of pan-Africanism from a previous lesson, pointing out Nkrumah's famed declaration that, "Our independence is meaningless unless it is linked up with the total liberation of Africa." Michelle's students would return to this idea when they pondered the reasons for Africa's ongoing problems.

Alejandro's Class: What Has Happened since Independence?

To find out how life has changed since independence, students embarked on a WebQuest to examine economic and political indicators that show the position of African countries relative to others in the continent and in the world. Freedom House (2012) tracks "freedom" in terms of human rights and democratic governance, giving a ranking of free, partly free, and not free to every country. Color-coded world maps give viewers a sense of what regions and countries enjoy the most freedoms, and country pages include news accounts about rights violations or progress toward equality. Groups of students used laptop computers to research the freedom of an assigned country. Five countries were selected to represent the conditions of freedom in Africa: about 40% of countries are free (Ghana and South Africa), another 40% are not (Rwanda and Democratic Republic of Congo), and 20% are partially free (Kenya).

Students then looked at a development map to learn the degrees of economic prosperity across countries and to think about the link between development and freedom (UNDP, 2011). Next, students examined statistics such as life expectancy and education indices for their individual countries. Finally, students analyzed charts that illustrate development trends since 1980, comparing their country with world averages and the rest of sub-Saharan Africa. A summative assessment asked students to imagine they were a citizen of their assigned country and to write a "letter to the editor" discussing: have our dreams of independence come true? What problems still remain? Through this work, we hoped students would understand that while the majority of African people do not have political and social freedom, and most African nations dwell in the lowest ranks of development, there is also hope and stability, as reflected in Ghana's "free and fair" elections and South Africa's gracious hosting of the 2010 World Cup Soccer Games.

In Alejandro's classes, student letters captured the tone and emotion of typical letters to editors, suggesting the influence of the school's focus on journalism. The strongest letters incorporated statistics and other information gathered during the WebQuest to demonstrate an understanding of change since independence. For example, reports noting that "discrimination against women and the LGBT (lesbian, gay, bisexual, and transgender) community remain serious problems" (Freedom House, 2011, 2012) troubled these two student writers, whose words are reprinted here, including their own spelling and grammatical choices:

Dear NY Times,
There are 10,943 people in Rwanda living in terrible conditions. They once dreamed of prosperity, a democratic country, to stop poverty and reshape the economy. However, today they face the problems of lack of adherence to the role of law, infringements on the freedoms of expression and association, widespread corruption and discrimination against women and the LGBT community. The life expectancy in Rwanda is only a staggering 55 years, the education index is at 0.407 and their human development index rank is only 166. This are extremely low numbers for a country hoping to prosper and if they continue at this rate there will be no hope for them. Although the human development index rank is only 166 [out of 187 countries], it is still better than what it was since 1980, however this means nothing because compared to the United States, Rwanda is in need of a lot of economic help.

Dear local news paper
There is about 25 million people living in Ghana and quality of life is slowly improving as time passes … We are granted freedom of press, so we are free to express ourselves. Places like Rwanda and Ethiopia don't have this privilege. But personally, I still don't think my dream of independence came true. I dreamed of everyone being treated equally however my country condemns homosexuals. People who are being suspected of gay or lesbian would be punished severely. I really don't like this way my country is treating people just because of different interest. Some areas that still need

some improvement are better drinking water, sex education, and more farms. I saw our citizens going hungry from crop failure, lack of healthy water, and high percentage of girls dropping out of school. I hope that these issues will meet a solution one day. Ghana is a country with both positive and negative. As a citizen here, I wish to cooperate to strengthen our government and citizen's power.

For homework, Alejandro asked his students to reflect in a blog on whether life in Africa had improved since independence. Most students argued that there was both improvement and ongoing problems, demonstrating opinions of Africa as more than simply a continent of failure. Responses fell under four general categories: "Yes," "No," "Improved, but," and "Not improved, but ..." Out of 40 respondents from the two classes, 10 students argued that no, life had not improved and Africans continue to face problems such as "dictatorships," "civil wars," and "poverty." Five students argued that yes, life in Africa had improved. But the majority of the students argued both sides (21 said there was mostly improvement, while 4 argued that problems outweighed the positives). Several students drew upon specific cases, as in this response: "Africa has improved since certain areas gained independence but conflict still does exist on some other regions of Africa such as Congo and Rwanda ... Places like South Africa and Ghana really have been improving since independence." For many, the fact that outsiders were no longer ruling explained why life was better: "Yes, I think they have improved since gaining back their independence because they're free from British control ... and can gain a more stable government." The idea that Europeans were to blame for many of the problems in Africa would arise again at the UN hearing.

A post-unit survey asked students what lessons they liked the most, the least, and during which lesson they learned the most. Out of 23 respondents, 6 students liked and 6 disliked the WebQuest, whereas 7 students preferred the posters and 7 others chose the hearings. The Web-Quest activity was cited by the highest number of students (8) as leading to learning. Perhaps students felt they learned a lot because they had gathered facts by looking at maps and graphs, as in a regular social studies activity. But some students struggled with the work, because they were "not good at reading maps" or it was "boring and confusing." When teaching this lesson in the future, teachers might conduct the lesson as a whole-class activity to help students interpret the visual materials and make comparisons across time and space. Photos and other illustrations would also underscore the abstract data in this lesson: what does life actually look like in these countries? In addition, teachers might choose other indicators for evaluating African life. For example, the kingdom of Bhutan has developed the Gross National Happiness Index (Centre for Bhutan Studies, 2012) as an alternative to other measures for quality of life. Economists Amartya Sen (1999) and Martha Nussbaum (2000) argue for examining citizens' "capabilities" to pursue activities that raise their quality of life as a better way of determining people's freedom.

Alejandro's Class: What Caused Dramatic Change in Rwanda and South Africa?

Our next lesson asked students to become "historical detectives." First they chose from one of three hypotheses about the causes of Rwandan genocide or the downfall of apartheid. The following were the choices for South Africa:

1. Boycotts by foreigners led the racist South African government to stop oppressing blacks.
2. Black South Africans drove white people out of the country and took power.
3. Protests inside and outside the country put pressure on the government to end apartheid.

The following were the choices for Rwanda:

1. The Hutus and Tutsis were fighting because of ancient tribal rivalries.
2. Hutu leaders manipulated citizens to kill Tutsis, who had been favored by German and Belgian colonizers, so that Hutus could retain power.
3. Africans are prone to violence and have a lot of civil wars.

Then students looked at a series of "clues"—for South Africa, newspaper accounts and clips about the international sports boycott and Soweto riots (ACTSA, 2010; BBC News, 2006a, 2006b; BBC Radio 4, 2010) and a quote from Frederick Cooper (2002, 152–153)—each providing different answers to the questions. For Rwanda, students read a *New York Times* article that described the situation in Rwanda as related to a "centuries-old feud" (1994), while a clip from the documentary *Do Scars Ever Fade?* explained that Belgian colonizers created the ethnic categories that fuelled bloodshed. Based on these clues, students could affirm their initial hypothesis, choose another one, or create a new one. The goal was for students to learn that historical change has multiple causes and can be driven by great leaders as well as ordinary people. We also strove to reinforce the idea that historians consult multiple sources in order to make an argument about what happened in the past.

This lesson got little mention on the survey (2 out of 23 liked it the most, 1 learned the most from it, and 3 liked it least) and when Michelle began the unit, we did not have a chance to use the activity. But Alejandro noted that of all the lessons, this one most engaged students in "historical thinking" (Holt, 1990; Kobrin, 1996; VanSledright, 2004). Though many of Alejandro's students had sufficient background knowledge to pick the most valid hypothesis from the beginning, we encouraged students to reconsider their perspectives after reading each clue. We were pleased that many groups carefully drew from each clue to support the hypothesis they chose. Teachers interested in teaching this lesson need to underscore how the activity is related to the work of historians, and how ordinary citizens, such as the murderers in Rwanda or the protesters of South Africa's apartheid, contributed to dramatic historical change.

Michelle's Class: Who Killed Democracy in Africa?

In wrapping up the WebQuest with her class, Michelle introduced the "gatekeeper state": "Now for the why [African countries still struggle with democracy and development], let's talk about this concept of gatekeeping. What is a gatekeeper?" The students defined the gatekeeper as the person who "guards," "protects," and "watches the gate." Their responses to, "How do you get past him?" showed creative understandings of how power works: "killing them," "bribe them," "permission," "compromise," "sneak," "manipulate," "drugs, tranquilize," and "seduce him." At the end, Michelle compared the gatekeeper to an "Invisible person holding Africa back from development, the voices of many are not being heard, and the privileged are benefiting on the backs of many … Many continued governing like the colonizers … Are they any different from the colonizers?" Several students answered "No," to which Michelle replied, "I don't know, we will see."

Michelle then introduced the characters that Ali Mazrui blames for killing democracy in a slide show that included: "soldiers" (e.g., Flight Lieutenant J. J. Rawlings who later presided over the transition to democracy in Ghana); "Cold Warriors" (an image of Ronald Reagan shaking hands with Mobutu Sese Seko of Zaire [now DRC]); "African Leaders" (Daniel Arap Moi of Kenya who stole large amounts from the country's treasury); and "magicians" or colonizers (a cartoon image of different European characters pulling on the borders of Africa). Groups of students created a wanted poster of one murderer and prepared a defense of their choice at the hearing to be held the next day. Students struggled with pinpointing only one suspect, asking "But who is to blame?" and "Is there a real answer to that question?" They then pulled out atlases and textbooks to help them sketch Africans and maps.

One goal of the lesson was for students to understand that while colonizers have played a role in Africa's exploitation, African leaders and elites also have contributed to instability and poverty. In fact, this group of students was inclined to blame Africans: four of the posters were of African leaders, one was of African soldiers, and "wanted" on another poster was "Africa's inability to be united." One group recognized the interconnection of suspects by blaming both Europeans and soldiers: the former for "supporting African soldiers" (as in providing arms and aid) and the latter for "overthrowing leaders!" and "creating chaos!" (as happened in Congo during the early 1960s). Gatekeeping was invoked when students listed "charges" against African leaders: "promised to aid his people, only leads for his own benefit, killed democracy in Africa"; "wanted for the abuse of their power to increase their money … control all of the country's resources, and ignoring all of the Africans, and causing corruption"; and "the African leaders have been increasing power, by taking away rights and controlling everything. As a community we have to put a stop to these leaders before it gets more violent and becomes a trigger situation." The African disunity group rebuked Africans for "being originally divided; when Europeans divided them, their conflict grew … didn't help themselves when they got their independence," and "continue to be manipulated." Their reasoning echoed that of historian John Thornton (1998), who argues that larger states were better able to protect their people from enslavement than smaller ones. Their views also relate back to Cooper's question as to why Africans were so vulnerable.

In post-unit surveys, most students reported that making the posters was "fun" and "creative." Their posters included humorous touches such as, "if seen please contact the police station" and a warning to approach suspects "with extreme caution." But the posters were also particularly powerful because they expressed viewpoints different from what Laura had seen in her college-level class on African history. Michelle's students refused to see Africans as mere victims, and in fact were disappointed and angry that Africans had allowed events to happen. As one student explained, "after all, they sold people out before"—in reference to the slave trade.

Same Questions, Different Answers: The UN Hearings

In our culminating lesson, students acted as "expert witnesses" at a mock UN hearing. For this activity, we asked students to answer the essential questions in a speech about who is to blame for poverty and lack of democracy and what should be done to make a better future for Africa. We instructed students to incorporate materials from each lesson to make their arguments. For example, one of Alejandro's students started the speech with independence:

> In the early 1900s all Africans shared a dream. A dream of independence. We thought independence would mean unity, freedom and equality but instead we have watched as tension and rivalries have crumbled our governments. The problems started with the Westerners, those magical magicians that cast a spell of fascination on the African people and started what I believe to be the beginning of the turmoil in Africa.

In addition to practicing their skills in oral presentation and argumentation, we wanted students to understand that there are many historical and contemporary reasons for Africa's poverty and lack of democracy, including the endurance of gatekeeper states. Interestingly, answers to the question of blame differed in each school.

Almost half (17 of 39) of Alejandro's students blamed Westerners for Africa's problems in the post-hearing Blog #3, "Who is to blame?" For example, one student wrote, "They [Europeans] ignored

African traditions and culture as a result leaving multiple countries with borders that encompassed rival groups which were several civil wars waiting to happen." These responses were consistent with those expressed in Blog #1 about the challenges Africans faced upon independence—"sabotage" and "neo-colonialism" by other countries that sought control of "resources" continued to hold back African growth. The remaining responses to Blog #3 went to half-castes (5), soldiers (5), and "governments" (6), with two students blaming two suspects. Four students argued that everyone was at fault. One stated, "You just cannot blame one single event or person on the current situation in Africa. Rather, let it be on a series of events." Another argued, "I don't think that the situation in Africa was affected by one but by many different events and people."

While students tended to pick one suspect as mainly responsible, the hearing exposed students to multiple actors and reasons for contemporary Africa's condition. For example, the students quoted below implicitly invoked gatekeeping as one of the "roots" of the problems:

> Today we gather to beg to differ [about] who is to blame for the circumstances of today's Africa. We are here to happily dispense all of the blame to the Magicians from the North. Although many of you here today [think] corruption today in Africa only has to do with the African people. And yes to some aspects that is true; however, have you ever stopped to ask yourself about the truth? About the roots of the equation? Think way back to the beginning. When the Magicians from the North went in and conquered everything, preying on Africa's disadvantage in technical weapons … The sad part is that after the Magicians left, Africa still had no chance to redeem themselves. When the Magicians planted themselves into Africa, they made sure that they designed their governments so that it was hard to flourish when they left. They made it so that Africa depended on them. And when they left, instead of the former kings and queens working together to regain Africa's once wealthy and strong state[s], they fought against each other for power and control.

Along similar lines, one student argued that, "if they [Europeans] would have set up a functioning democratic government that probably would have conflicted with their plans of taking Africa's resources," and another explained how colonial borderlines left enemies to compete for power, drawing on Sudan's dissolution into two states as a recent example. One group claimed that "each [suspect] contributed in their own way," as when Westerners supported dictators like Mobutu Sese Seko.

Alejandro's students had read a part of Mazrui's article (2002), and its lyrical tone was captured in their speeches, as when two students stated that Europeans "mesmerized Africans with these little flecks of civilization [schools, hospitals] … but unfortunately they [Africans] followed them [Europeans] down a path of destruction." This same pair took a realist approach to politics: for Africans to earn respect in the world and protect themselves, they needed to build strong armies. Note we had not taught the students about political realism (see Mearsheimer, 2005 for a good explanation of this theory). For her solution, another student recalled Mazrui's condemnation of half-castes for disregarding their traditions to recommend a return to Africa's indigenous democratic institutions, noting, "Look at our ancestors, they survived, why can't we?"

In contrast to Alejandro's students, Michelle's students argued that Africans were mostly at fault for contemporary problems. In a pre-unit survey, 7 students blamed "governments" or Africans, 2 blamed Europeans, and 9 said they did not have enough knowledge to answer the question. In the post-unit survey, all the students answered the question. About three-quarters blamed Africans (11 chose leaders, 4 chose "governments," soldiers, or "African people"), while 5 selected Europeans and 2 chose both Africans and Europeans. In their notes evaluating the presentations, many (9) students were particularly convinced by 2 students who argued that Africans need to overcome disunity and help themselves:

> But are the Europeans to blame? Why were there divisions in Africa that have the power to cause people of the same continent to despise each other if they were disturbed in the first place? Africa was never united. If they were, the divide and conquer technique wouldn't have worked. As a result of this, Africans fought causing them to embrace Europeans' ideas and ignore one another's. Once they got their independence, they knew they needed to work hard, but even with independence their lack of unity made them weak. Statistics show that in Kenya … human development has stayed the same since 1980. Nobody can make changes for Africa but themselves. They now determine how successful or unsuccessful they are. They can no longer blame their failure on someone else's poor leadership … They should also welcome trade with other countries but not let their culture be taken over by that of the Europeans. Nobody can help Africans if they can't help themselves.

Similar perspectives appeared in comments on worksheets and post-unit surveys that Africans "should not put their fate in other people's hands," but rather "unite together to help themselves." This argument is related to Michael Barratt Brown's call (1996) for grassroots initiatives in Africa to replace the failed development policies of the World Bank and other donors and lenders.

In blaming African leaders or Europeans, students linked political power to control over valuable resources, describing problems that characterize the gatekeeper state: "We believe this is the Europeans' fault because they abused their power and took everything they could from Africa. They stole many of the natural resources that could have been used for trade to increase their [Africa's] economy." While some African leaders were good, most of them were not:

> The people responsible for Africa's underdevelopment and lack of democracy [are] the African leaders. Some African leaders had abused their powers, try to control the country's natural resources, they had ignored the African citizens and caused corruption in Africa's economy. However, not all African leaders are to blame for Africa's problems. For example, Nelson Mandela who was the first democratically elected president of South Africa.

Similarly, bad leaders were described in surveys as "selfish," "greedy," "abusive" of their power, wanting to "control resources," and only seeking to "be rich."

While Alejandro's students were split on the question of whether Africans or Europeans were at fault, Michelle's students were more inclined to blame Africans. Students' prior knowledge and lessons could have shaped their responses. In Laura's view, though, the self-help argument was persuasive because the students understood, as poor and minority youth, that they have to work harder to prove themselves. Laura observed similar attitudes among Ghanaian educators: acutely aware of outsiders' negative portrayals of Africans, teachers promoted "discipline" and "hard work" to overcome bad stereotypes and achieve the development that eluded them (Dull, 2006).

Concluding Thoughts

Students at both schools were hungry for immersion in African history. One student asked her teacher, "Are we going to learn about Haile Selassie [of Ethiopia]?" and another asked Laura, "What was Africa like during slave times?" Students simply do not get sufficient exposure to African history to overcome certain conceptions: even after completing the unit, some students continued to view "Africa" as one country or tended to assign a unified history to all Africans. Nevertheless, what was noteworthy is that students invoked different theories about power—including theories we had not taught—as they made their arguments at the UN hearing. While some of their ideas were insufficiently based in history, the students understood the ill-effects of colonial boundaries, the disadvantages small states face unless they join larger entities or form alliances with more powerful states, and how monopolistic access to resources can lead to abuses of power. All of these ideas are related to the theories Cooper raised in his interview and book and to those put forth by other scholars of Africa. Moreover, as they used Mazrui's language to talk about soldiers and magicians, the students acknowledged the multiple players in African history.

As we step back and reflect on this unit and on the questions that framed it, it is clear that the questions orienting this unit could provide a frame for the study of world history in general: how do we explain inequalities that continue to shape life across the globe? What can people do to make their lives better? These questions underscore the fact that all humans struggle with questions of equity and distribution of resources, not just Africans. A unit built around these questions would help students to provide stronger explanations for ongoing poverty. Global financial institutions like the IMF, the World Bank, and others' pro-business economic policies tend to harm ordinary citizens. For example, agricultural subsidies of G8 countries, combined with reduced support for agriculture by "downsized" governments, stifle the opportunities for farmers in developing countries to compete in the world market (Kwa, 2008; Oxfam International, 2009). In South Africa, proponents of neo-liberalism "outmaneuvered" South Africa's ANC party leaders during negotiations over new political and economic institutions, making it impossible to implement the plans of their egalitarian Freedom Charter (Klein, 2011). Other potential "murderers" of democracy are capitalists, the powerful private and corporate institutions that wield more power than most nations in the world, like Shell Oil in Nigeria (Rothkopf, 2012; see also African Greed, 2011).

At the same time, students should learn about populist movements that drive change and indigenous cultures and institutions that could provide alternative ways of solving social problems. One group in Michelle's class hinted at the ability of people to demand change, declaring that to make life better, "Now as citizens, they [Africans] shall come together as a whole and fight not in violence but public speeches and protest." Before embarking on a study of individual countries or regions, then, we suggest that students learn about the multiple players and factors that create—and work against—hegemonies within and across societies. Such lessons would strengthen students' ability to engage with questions of power and agency and to envision ways to build a better future for Africans and others.

Works Cited

Academy for Environmental Leadership. (n.d.). *Welcome page.* Retrieved from http://aelnyc.com

ACTSA (Action for Southern Africa). (2010, February 25). International sports boycott against apartheid. Retrieved from www.actsa.org/newsroom/2010/02/the-international-sports-boycott-against-apartheid

African Greed. (2011, June). African greed—exposing corruption in Africa [Web log comment]. Retrieved from http://africangreed.blogspot.com

BBC News. (2006a, June 15). Audio slideshow: Soweto remembered. *BBC News.* Retrieved from http://news.bbc.co.uk/today/hi/today/newsid_8536000/8536131.stm

BBC News. (2006b, June 6). S. Africa marking Soweto uprising. *BBC News.* Retrieved from http://news.bbc.co.uk/2/hi/africa/5085450.stm

BBC Radio 4. (2010, February 25). Sporting blacklist revisited. *BBC News.* Podcast retrieved from http://news.bbc.co.uk/today/hi/today/newsid_8536000/8536131.stm

Brown, M. B. (1996). *Africa's choices after thirty years of the World Bank.* Boulder, CO: Westview Press.

Centre for Bhutan Studies. (2012). *Gross national happiness.* Retrieved from www.grossnationalhappiness. com

Chabal, P., & Daloz, J. (1999). *Africa works: Disorder as political instrument.* Oxford, UK: James Currey.

Cooper, F. (2002). *Africa since 1940: The past of the present.* New York, NY: Cambridge University Press.

Dodge, B. (2007). *WebQuest.org.* Retrieved from http://webquest.org/index.php

Dull, L. J. (2006). *Disciplined development: Teachers and reform in Ghana.* Lanham, MD: Lexington Books.

Freedom House. (2011, August 8). LGBT population in Ghana under threat. Retrieved from www. freedomhouse.org/article/lgbt-population-ghana-under-threat

Freedom House. (2012). *Sub-Saharan Africa.* Retrieved from www.freedomhouse.org/regions/sub-saharan-africa

Gerwin, D., & Zevin, J. (2010). *Teaching US history as mystery.* New York, NY: Routledge.

Holt, T. (1990). *Thinking historically.* New York, NY: College Entrance Examination Board.

Huffington Post. (2012, April 30). Mama Hope, African nonprofit, addresses African stereotypes with "Stop the Pity" campaign. *Huffington Post.* Retrieved from www.huffingtonpost.com/2012/04/30/kony-2012-mama-hope_n_1464139.html

Inside Schools (2012). *World Journalism Preparatory.* Retrieved from http://insideschools.org/high/browse/school/1369

Klein, N. (2011, February 13). Democracy born in chains: South Africa's constricted freedom. In *The shock doctrine: The rise of disaster capitalism* (Chapter 10). Retrieved from www.naomiklein.org/articles/2011/02/democracy-born-chains

Kobrin, D. (1996). *Beyond the textbook: Teaching history using documents and primary sources.* Portsmouth, NH: Heinemann.

Kwa, A. (2008, May 12). Food crisis symptom of dubious liberalization. *Inter Press Service* (IPS). Retrieved from www.ipsnews.net/2008/05/development-food-crisis-symptom-of-dubious-liberalisation

Mazrui, A. (2002). Who killed democracy in Africa? Clues of the past, concerns of the future. *DPMN Bulletin, IX*(1), 15–22. Retrieved from www.dpmf.org/publications.php

Mearsheimer, J. J. (2005). Hans Morganthau and the Iraq War: Realism versus Neo-conservatism. *openDemocracy. net.* Retrieved from www.opendemocracy.net/democracy-americanpower/morgenthau_2522.jsp

Mentzer, A. (2012, March 13). Kony 2012: Fake advocacy? *Huffington Post.* Retrieved from www. huffingtonpost.com/the-state-press/kony-2012_b_1339081.html

New York State Education Department. (2010–2011a). *New York State report card, accountability and overview report.* Retrieved from https://reportcards.nysed.gov/files/2010–11/AOR-2011–333200011403.pdf

New York State Education Department. (2010–2011b). *New York State report card, comprehensive information report.* Retrieved from https://reportcards.nysed.gov/files/2010–11/CIR-2011–333200011403.pdf

New York State Education Department. (2010–2011c). *New York State report card, accountability and overview report.* Retrieved from https://reportcards.nysed.gov/files/2010–11/AOR-2011–342500011285.pdf

New York Times. (1994, April 16). Tribes battle for Rwanda; New massacres reported. *New York Times.* Retrieved from www.nytimes.com/1994/04/16/world/tribes-battle-for-rwandan-capital-new-massacres-reported.html?src=pm

Nussbaum, M. (2000). *Women and human development.* New York, NY: Cambridge University Press.

Oxfam International. (2009, April 17). G8 summit: Poor farmers are the answer to global food crisis. *Oxfam International* Press Release. Retrieved from www.oxfam.org/en/pressroom/pressrelease/2009–04–17/g8-agriculture-summit-poor-farmers-are-answer-global-food-crisis

Rothkopf, D. (2012). *Power, Inc.: The epic rivalry between big business and governments—and the reckoning that lies ahead.* New York, NY: Farrar, Straus and Giroux.

Sen, A. (1999). *Development as freedom.* Oxford, UK: Oxford University Press.

Thornton, J. (1998). *Africa and Africans in the making of the Atlantic world, 1400–1650.* New York, NY: Cambridge University Press.

United Nations Development Program (UNDP). (2011). *International human development indicators.* Retrieved from http://hdr.undp.org/en/data/map

VanSledright, B. (2004). What does it mean to think historically and how do you teach it? *Social Education, 68*(3) 230–233.

Wiggins, G., & McTighe, J. (2005). *Understanding by design.* Upper Saddle River, NJ: Pearson Education Inc.

World Journalism Preparatory School. (n.d.). *Homepage.* Retrieved from www.wjps.org/home.aspx

Zmuda, A., & Tomaino, M. (2001). *The competent classroom: Aligning high school curriculum, standards, and assessment.* New York, NY: Teachers College Press.

CHAPTER RESOURCES

I. Unit Plan: Modern Africa

Common Core Standards

CCSS.ELA-Literacy.RH.9–10.7 Integrate quantitative or technical analysis (e.g., charts, research data) with qualitative analysis in print or digital text.

CCSS.ELA-Literacy.RH.9–10.8 Assess the extent to which the reasoning and evidence in a text support the author's claims.

CCSS.ELA-Literacy.RH.9–10.9 Compare and contrast treatments of the same topic in several primary and secondary sources.

Essential Questions

- Who is to blame for poverty and lack of democracy in Africa?
- Where does Africa's future lie?

Enduring Understandings

Students will understand that:

- At the time of their independence from colonial powers or oppressive regimes, sub-Saharan African independence leaders and their people envisioned a prosperous, democratic, and peaceful future.
- While some countries (like Ghana and South Africa) have achieved stability and democracy, there are still many countries (like Congo and Rwanda) that struggle with poverty and poor governance.
- There are many historical and contemporary reasons for Africa's poverty and lack of democracy, including the endurance of "gatekeeper" states, a form of governance present in colonial and independent times.
- Gatekeeper states seek to maintain exclusive access to political and economic power. This can cause instability as social groups seek to bribe officials for entry to the gate, or tear it down through revolution.
- There is often a link between development and democracy: the more economically wealthy a country is, the more likely there is to be freedom in that country.
- While colonizers and western corporations played a role in causing Rwandan genocide, oppressive systems such as apartheid in South Africa, and economic exploitation of resources such as oil and diamonds, African leaders and elites have also contributed to instability and poverty.

Culminating Assessment

Mock UN hearing on who is to blame for Africa's problems and what can be done to build a better future.

Selected Learning Activities

Lesson 1:* How did Africans envision their future at the dawn of independence?

- **Activity:** Students will visit stations with images, speeches, and videos of independence and freedom celebrations to learn about hopes and goals at the time.

Lesson 2: What has happened in Africa since independence?

- **Activity:** Students will gather evidence in a WebQuest to consider the fates of several countries in Africa since independence. While some like Ghana and South Africa are functioning as a democracy, others, like Congo and Rwanda, struggle with civil war, poverty, and poor leadership.

Lesson 3: What caused dramatic historical change in Rwanda and South Africa?

- **Activity:** Students will act as detectives to solve historical mysteries about the causes of Rwandan genocide and the fall of apartheid in South Africa.

Lesson 4: Who killed democracy in Africa?

- **Activity:** Students will create "Wanted for Democracide" posters of the "Murderers" of African democracy.

Lesson 5: Who is to blame for poverty and lack of democracy in Africa? Where does the future of Africa lie?

- **Activity:** Final Assessment is a UN hearing on who is to blame for Africa's problems and what can be done to build a better future. For an example of how to approach their speech, students could read "What can be done about Africa" [www.economist.com/node/630684].

---

*Independence Stations Lesson, WebQuest, and History as Mystery Lessons (Lessons 1–3) are available at: http://faculty.newpaltz.edu/lauradull/index.php/modern-africa-lessons

II. Lesson Plan: Visions of Independence

Aim: How did Africans envision their future at the dawn of independence?

Objectives: Students will understand that: At the time of their independence from colonial powers or oppressive regimes, African independence leaders and their people envisioned a prosperous, democratic, and peaceful future.

Do Now: Show class a map of Africa: Have students find Ghana, Kenya, and South Africa. Today we will look at the independence and freedom movements in these countries to find out: How did Africans respond to independence? How did they envision their future?

Activity: Explain that students will visit three stations to gather evidence to answer two questions. On a worksheet, describe images and jot down words or phrases that: 1) Express Africans' feelings about independence and freedom; 2) Show what they imagined for their country and Africa now that they were free from colonial rule or oppression.

1) Ghana

a) Videoclip of Independence, March 6, 1957: Ghana was the first sub-Saharan country to receive its independence, in 1957, from Britain. What images do you see? What feelings do they convey?

www.youtube.com/watch?v=yxukN7hKpeE&feature=results_video&playnext=1&list=PL59DDD9C2E6D23161

b) Audioclip of Ghana freedom song (scroll down this blog)

http://foreignpolicyblogs.com/2010/06/21/50-years-of-african-independence-the-music-of-west-africa

c) Excerpt from Kwame Nkrumah's Independence Day Speech: What are the visions of Africa that Nkrumah describes?

http://panafricanquotes.wordpress.com/speeches/independence-speech-kwame-nkrumah-march-6-1957-accra-ghana

> From now on, today, we must change our attitudes and our minds. We must realize that from now on we are no longer a colonial but free and independent people.

> But also, as I pointed out, that also entails hard work. That new Africa is ready to fight his own battles and show that after all the black man is capable of managing his own affairs … It is the only way we can show the world that we are ready for our own battles …

> We have won the battle and again rededicate ourselves … OUR INDEPENDENCE IS MEANINGLESS UNLESS IT IS LINKED UP WITH THE TOTAL LIBERATION OF AFRICA …

2) South Africa

South Africa did not undergo the same process of colonization that other sub-Saharan African countries experienced. Europeans migrated there in the 17th century and began taking political power. Blacks saw their rights further eroded in 1948 with the implementation of a system of apartheid, "separateness." In 1994, apartheid was finished and Nelson Mandela was elected as its first black president.

a) Black South Africans vote, April 27, 1994. Select 2–3 images from Google image search.

Voting lines:

http://ryanhassebrook.files.wordpress.com/2008/10/south-africa1.jpg

Man votes for first time:

www.britannica.com/bps/media-view/90400/1/0/0

b) Videoclip of Inauguration, May 9, 1994, 43 seconds:

www.youtube.com/watch?v = S2FE0yeyxag

c) Excerpt from Nelson Mandela's Inauguration Speech at Cape Town:

www.blackpast.org/?q=1994-nelson-mandela-s-inaugural-address-president-south-africa-0

On May 9, 1994, Nelson Mandela was inaugurated as the first democratically elected President of South Africa. This is an excerpt from his inauguration address given at Cape Town, South Africa.

> Today we are entering a new era for our country and its people. Today we celebrate not the victory of a party, but a victory for all the people of South Africa …
>
> We have fought for a democratic constitution since the 1880s. Ours has been a quest for a constitution freely adopted by the people of South Africa, reflecting their wishes and their aspirations. The struggle for democracy has never been a matter pursued by one race, class, religious community or gender among South Africans … The task at hand will not be easy. But you have mandated us to change South Africa from a country in which the majority lived with little hope, to one in which they can live and work with dignity, with a sense of self-esteem and confidence in the future.

3) Kenya

a) Videoclip of Jomo Kenyatta, including Independence Day, play up to 2:17 (his death).

www.youtube.com/watch?v=MaeUMjGTuuA&feature=related

b) Jomo Kenyatta, Independence Day message to the people, December 12, 1963:

> Many people may think that, now there is *Uhuru* [Swahili word for freedom, independence], now I can see the sun of Freedom shining, richness will pour down like manna from Heaven. I tell you there will be nothing from Heaven. We must all work hard, with our hands, to save ourselves from poverty, ignorance, and disease.

Closure: Have students share their answers to the questions. Ask: What has happened since those days? Have independence dreams come true? (While there is some stability and freedom, as in Ghana and South Africa, many countries still struggle with underdevelopment, poverty, and lack of democracy.)

Homework: Who is to blame for the poverty and lack of democracy that still affects many Africans? Why? What would help Africans to achieve a better life? We will spend the next few days thinking about these questions.

Two
Asia

On Revolution and Rights: China's Cultural Revolution

By Laura J. Dull, with Bernadette Condesso and
Dawn Vandervloed

Framing the Questions: An Interview with Moss Roberts, conducted by Robert Cohen

Moss Roberts is a professor of Chinese at New York University. He received his Ph.D. from Columbia University. His publications include *Three Kingdoms: China's Epic Drama* (abridged translation with introduction and postface) (1976); *Critique of Soviet Economics* (translation of Mao Zedong's Reading Notes) (1977); *Chinese Fairy Tales and Fantasies* (edited and translated) (1979); *Three Kingdoms* (complete annotated translation with textual notes and critical essay) (1992, 2004); *Historical Overview of the Nanjing Massacre* (Chinese only) (1995); "Contra Ideocracy" in *Bulletin of Concerned Asian Scholars* (1997); "Bad Karma in Asia" in *Bulletin of Concerned Asian Scholars* (2000); and Laozi, *Dao De Jing: The Book of the Way* (annotated translation with textual notes and critical introduction) (2001, 2004), in addition to various articles, reviews, and essays in English and Chinese. He was the recipient of the Golden Dozen Teaching Award (1996) and received the National Endowment for the Arts Translation Fellowship (1983–1984) and the National Endowment for the Humanities Fellowship (1985–1986).

Robert Cohen: *What are the most wrong-headed assumptions Americans tend to make when they discuss China—Asia—and its history?*

Moss Roberts: The basic problem is not to realize that China is an equal. Equality is the heart and soul of the American value system, and yet we have enormous difficulty in looking at China as an equal. I don't mean this for ordinary people … But at the level of leadership discourse there is a problem, of "taking the high ground" and "instructing" the Chinese in how they can improve themselves in a variety of areas. Washington stands as if on some superior moral high ground issuing rhetorical declarations about what China *must* do. This word "must" … comes up *all* the time in editorials, in leadership discourse, with political commentators, in the media. You often see the phrase, "They 'must' be more transparent." What military is transparent? Military secrets can't be disclosed; it's treason. Besides that, no state behaves like that … Maybe they should, but they don't. So to demand that of the Chinese, publicly—and as is often the case, the accuser is no less culpable, and in some cases perhaps even more culpable, of the accusations leveled at others.

[W]e [the U.S.] do many of the things that we accuse the Chinese of. The Chinese have maintained positions on finance that the U.S. Treasury would like relaxed. But our own financial conduct has been widely criticized as well, and by the Chinese. For example, the Chinese hold a large piece of U.S. debt, as they do in the area of about a trillion dollars, so any decrease in the value of the dollar, or a relative increase in their dollar, the Yuan—we keep telling them, "Raise the value of your Yuan." But that would make their total dollar holdings worth less.

RC: *What do you see as the key themes in Asia's history since 1900?*

MR: I think the dominant pattern is the interaction of war and revolution: back and forth, war and revolution. Maybe also, connecting to another historic theme in Chinese history, is an alternation between the unified and the divided. It is the pattern of division, and then again finding some kind of unified order, and then that order, after a hundred, or two or three hundred, years breaking apart, and the regions set up separate governments, and someone else comes along after a while and re-unifies them. India has no historical pattern of unification. Sometimes they pretend that it does: they use the word *barat*, an "ancient Indian unity." But it's a *very* subdivided area, with so many languages and separate cultures; it doesn't really think of itself as "India" until the British period.

RC: *Some people talk about Mao in [China's] tradition of emperors, and there's this whole tendency to see continuity between ancient and modern Chinese history. But doesn't that negate what could be seen as unique about what's gone on with Sun Yat-sen, and then Mao? To see the idea of social-ism and communism as being some combination or hybrid of Eastern and Western influence?*

MR: Raising this issue of Sun Yat-sen is exactly the right point. Because, first of all, Sun Yat-sen is rather Westernized as a figure and somewhat different from Mao, who was much more rooted in the countryside of China and never left China until he went to Russia in 1950. But Sun Yat-sen was looking at the French Revolution, looking at the American Revolution—one of his earliest ideas of having China become a republic came from being in Hawaii where he saw a republican movement and wanted to transfer that to China. He wrote about the five-part Constitution, which is actually in effect in Taiwan.

So, I think the modern aspects, the enlightenment aspects, the republican aspects—the question of the republic—is enormous for China. And it is heightened by the fact that they were in opposition to Japan, which is an emperor-ruled country, at least theoretically … And they've been in constant conflict with Japan, really, from the mid-1870s. Although the first war doesn't occur until 1894, this idea of an emperor-centered country which is attacking them just made them all the more receptive to ideas of Western government and organization. And Sun Yat-sen was Christian. That was an element that did not survive as strongly as the idea of republicanism, but both Chinas are called republics. Taiwan is called "the Republic of China" and China is called "The People's Republic of China." Japan is called: "Japan." Nothing. No reference to the government reform now.

Sun Yat-sen's first goal was to get the Manchus out of China … And that is another persisting theme. There is a partial revolution in 1911. He realizes that the Manchus are not overthrown. The

Manchu emperor abdicates [in 1911] to Yuan Shih-kai. Who was Yuan Shih-kai? He was a kind of warlord, strong-man general who had been the governor-general in Korea.

And Sun Yat-sen realized that his group did not have the power to go into the capital, to go into Beijing, and to set up a government. So he calls himself the "Provisional President," and he let Yuan Shih-kai have the power. Yuan Shih-kai just dismissed the whole parliament very soon after that and ruled as a strong-man. There was a sort of short war after that. Sun Yat-sen's forces were defeated. And through the figure of Yuan Shih-kai, much of the nature of the Manchu rule was continued. Yuan Shih-kai himself tried to make himself emperor, in 1916, just before he died. In the summer of 1916, he thought he could make himself emperor, and then there was one other brief episode where one of the leading figures was trying to make himself the emperor of China again. So there were these little, sporadic moments where the emperor would try to become an emperor.

But then the Japanese invaded Manchuria in 1931, and the following year they put up Aisin-Gioro Puyi, from the Manchu royal house, as the emperor of Manchuria. So there you have the restoration of the imperial figure, complete, and in power until 1945. I mean, theoretically he was just a puppet of the Japanese. So the idea of the struggle between the republic and the emperor does not end with the last dynasty; it goes on through 1945. Then it becomes the struggle against the Manchus. And it then becomes wrapped up in the struggle against the Japanese.

Sun Yat-sen was an admirer of Henry George. He thought that capitalism would lead to socialism in China. He said at one point,

> Why are they wasting all that money on World War I? It's a stupid thing. Why don't they just take all the money they're spending on fighting and invest it in China? And then we'll get rich, and that'll make them rich, too.

He was very much like Deng Xiaoping, a developmentalist: whatever works. If capitalism is going to make the economy grow, good. Socialism? He also was very conscious of the need to protect people who are defenseless economically. So socialism was always part of his vision. [He wrote] a very unusual pamphlet, "The Vital Problem," in 1917. It was really a denunciation of [World War I] and a refusal to condemn the Germans. Which certainly puts him [on the side of] a plague on both your houses.

Sun Yat-sen, in his first years would definitely be classified as a terrorist … He was trying to lure members of the Manchurian imperial army over to his side. He was involved in weapons deals. He was always trying to organize some kind of military action. And he thought that China would never break free of the stranglehold of the treaty system and the treaty powers. There were many different foreign interests there in China. And he thought to break free of that you needed an army. He admired the Red Army. That's one of the main reasons that he brought in Russian advisors in the early 1920s. Even in 1918 he was in some kind of correspondence with the Russians and saluting their achievements. He wanted their military aid—and he got it. That's how Chiang Kai-shek goes to Russia for his training, and the Russians give them a lot of money, and advice, and arms … Sun Yat-sen doesn't get the kind of excitement that Mao does, but he is looked upon as the Founding Father. He is the George Washington figure for Taiwan and for the Mainland.

RC: *Can you explain why you selected Mao Zedong, Ho Chi Minh, and Gandhi to center one of your courses around?*

MR: Gandhi is the most sympathetic figure. I mean, we all love Gandhi, and he was "reincarnated" as Martin Luther King. We [in Greenwich Village, New York City] have a revealing statue of him right on the southwest corner of Union Square Park: he's in the *khadi* (that is the simple, self-woven cloth, which was so important to him, as a personal sacrifice, as a personal dedication) and he's holding a cane—a walking stick—and his knees are enlarged. [H]e's walking all over the place, from village to village to village and trying to find out what their problems are, and using his training as an attorney in England. And then he went to South Africa where he spent over 20 years fighting for the rights of the Indian community. He was in conflict with the Dutch; he was in conflict with the English. And he already had a [reputation] for that when he went back to India. [T]he legal training is really important because it gave him contact with an idealized value system that Britain had. He knew perfectly well that their practice was constantly in violation of their ideals and there was very little of the ideals that got into the practice. But still, he would "hold their feet to the fire"; he would hold them to those values, he also was a little bit of Abraham, a little bit of Moses. He was a mass leader with a phenomenal touch about how to organize and what kinds of issues to organize around. But he was *steadfastly* non-violent.

So this whole streak of militarism with Sun Yat-sen, Mao Zedong, Chiang Kai-shek, and today in China: this whole connection of revolution and war yields militarism, right? *Not* in India. In India, Gandhi is fighting against militarism. He refuses any kind of violent action and he calls off nationwide demonstrations because of a violent incident in one village. His own followers were furious at him. But he said, "I'm not going to let my men do this kind of thing. I don't care if everybody says I'm wrong; I think I'm right." So you hear this kind of moral, personal, political, different aspects, which you don't hear in Mao. Mao is a strategic thinker, globally.

[Gandhi was] working through the institutions, trying to get reforms through—you can have a kind of legality, even if it's artificial, even if it's marked by fraud and deception—but if you have a single authority, like the secretary of state for India in London and the raj, the British civil service—what they call their "steel case"—[Indians are] asking for more participation in the British civil service. They're asking for more participation in different legislative bodies. And Gandhi always stuck to what's called "dominion independence," rather than complete independence. You would very rarely see Gandhi or the Indian National Congress talking about the American Revolution … they want to remain within the Empire but have control of their own affairs. [W]hen India got independence in 1947 even after this horrendous split with Pakistan, both nations entered the Commonwealth. Pakistan first joined the British Commonwealth, and Jawaharlal Nehru was left with no choice. And they both entered the Commonwealth on the grounds of having no allegiance to the British sovereign. That was the condition. And probably you could argue that World War II brought all these changes about: the transformation of China, the transformation of India.

That's why I say, "war and revolution; war and revolution": don't separate them. Because all of these movements are accelerated and intensified, like a forcing house. You know, where plants have to grow twice as fast as they're supposed to? War is a forcing house. Who knows what would have happened without the war between Britain and Germany? Even World War I against Germany yielded promises to the Indians: "You're going to have more self-government; we're going to do more for you; we'll give your local capitalists better access to our markets." All kinds of promises were made, and reneged upon.

RC: *Why do you think Mao was so different from Gandhi on these issues? Was it because he didn't have a Western connection?*

MR: Yes. You can call it imperialist anarchy. So there's no raj in China. And there is constant fighting [with] the Japanese, the Russians, British, Americans. The French have holdings in southern China, which are an extension of their colony in Vietnam, so they're pushing into southern

China; the Japanese are pushing beyond their Korean colony into Manchuria. Everyone is at each other's throats. So with no over-arching legal system … And so no possibility of having some kind of governmental control that can both suppress, but also negotiate; that can punish, but reward as in India. In China, it's just a pandemonium there.

RC: *I think you were comparing Mao to Napoleon. Why was Mao so effective as a leader?*

MR: Now the first and most obvious thing is he knew how to pick other leaders. He could spot the talent of negotiators like Zhou en Lai—and tacticians like Lin Biao. But I think he had an uncanny sense of timing of what he could rely on … knowing who your friends and your enemies are. And at what point he realized that he had to break away from the Russians. Remember, Sun Yat-sen brings in the Russians and fuses the Nationalist Party and Communist Party into a single organization for military purposes to mount an expedition to the North, to take the capital, to throw out the warlords, and to push back against the Japanese. [T]his expedition is partially successful; it ends in 1928, and Chiang Kai-shek has a semi-precarious control over the entire country, or most of the country. But the Japanese are terrified of Chinese nationalism. And they immediately begin to plan to strike back at China.

[I]n 1927, Chiang Kai-shek decides to break with the Communists. He wants to be an international player. And he realizes that the Japanese are going to be very hard to handle, and he thinks he can't [be an international player] tied to the Communists … And probably he had plenty of encouragement from the British and from the Americans; they were not happy about the connection with the Communists and the connection with Russia. So getting rid of [the] Bolsheviks, getting rid of the Russian connection, getting rid of the Chinese Communists, becomes a key element in his strategy—in the course of the Northern expedition. So right there, you have war, revolution, counter-revolution, foreign invasion, civil war. It's just a kaleidoscopic set of moving factors, and they're all moving at different tempo.

So Mao's reaction to that was that the revolution would never be an urban phenomenon … And Mao is the one against many of the people in the Communist Party [and the] one who pushed the idea that "We have to develop organizations in the countryside." Peasant unions … and attack landlords [because] if you're going to build an army out of the peasantry, you have to change the terms of landholding. A lot of Chiang Kai-shek's officers came from land-holding families. They were the cream of the crop. And they didn't like the idea of having a Communist put pressure on the landlords—or even evict them. Mao saw that strategic vector [to re-distribute land], I think, just about before anyone. [S]o many [other] people were tied into the dogmas and the prestige of the Russian Revolution … it's true that while the Russians made some noises about developing the peasantry, they didn't know much about that, and that wasn't the pattern of their own revolution.

[The] Nationalists decided to make war against the Communist areas. The Communists had set up in one of the southeastern provinces (Jiangxi) a small "soviet." And they had a fairly aggressive land re-distribution program, and Chiang Kai-shek decided that he would clean out the "Communist bandits," as he called them, and then deal with Japan. So that was his strategic line of thinking from 1927 to 1937.

The Long March comes in the middle of that period; that's just a *huge* defeat for the Communists. Finally the nationalists had succeeded in evicting them from their strongholds, just by overwhelming military force, and the Communists had to vacate their little soviet [in 1934]. But they did something very clever. In 1931, they declared war on Japan. Right after Japan invaded Manchuria. It was meaningless in military terms, but it had a huge symbolic significance … Meanwhile, Chiang Kai-shek is saying, "We can't fight the Japanese."

And after a period of 10 years the Communists force through a second united front, in 1937. And the Japanese attack in force [at] the Marco Polo Bridge Incident in July 1937, bringing the war southward into China proper. They've consolidated their position in Manchuria, set up "Manchu-Guo," their little kingdom, a little piece of Mongolia, and now they want to move into China proper. And their strategic thinking was very much influenced by Britain in the sense that they realized that Britain, as an island and naval power, was so overwhelmingly dependent on India (or India and Egypt, technically) for their global power. And they now wanted the same thing. They wanted a raj in China. And they weren't going to get it.

RC: *How would you compare Ho Chi Minh to these other figures?*

MR: Ho also had ideals, French ideals, and there were times in his career when he thought the French could be made to walk their talk, to live up to the idea of making the Indo-Chinese people on [their] level—he [went to] Versailles [to submit] a petition. This was the [Paris] Peace Conference of the first half of 1919 [at which the Treaty of Versailles was signed after World War I]. He was trying to call their attention, but the reaction was, "Get away." They didn't want anything to do with him.

[With Vietnam's Declaration of Independence in 1945], Ho looks to France [and] like Sun Yat-sen, he looks to the U.S., citing the Declaration of Independence. He was hoping that the Americans would remain anti-Japanese. Roosevelt made a lot of promises. The Vietnamese gave a lot of assistance to the American military. They helped rescue downed flyers and they were spotters for Japanese forces. The Japanese had come into Vietnam and pushed out the French … There's a wonderful British film called "Uncle Sam, Uncle Ho" [Bradley, 1995] with a lot of interviews with the OSS (Office of Strategic Services) agents [who were in Vietnam], the predecessor to the Central Intelligence Agency (CIA). They felt betrayed by Truman, they felt that they owed Ho Chi Minh something. And the Americans just let the French come back in—they helped the French come back in. So again: betrayed ideals [as in India].

But again, it's World War II that puts an end to [colonization]; it's not the Vietnamese. There were local rebellions, communist rebellions (a big one in 1930) … The Chinese revolution benefited from the conflict among the powers. Lenin said, "Our revolution would have died if they hadn't been at each other's throats," whereas in India you had a much better organized rule, because it's unitary, and the same with France [in Vietnam]. But all of these structures, all these different forms of colonialism, are destroyed in the war—the Japanese power, the British power. Roosevelt would say to Churchill, "You know, you really have to let the Indians have their freedom and stop hanging onto your colony. That day is over." And those are the kind of promises that the Vietnamese heard and expected to be fulfilled. And Churchill … was furious: "The sun will not set on the British Empire. I will not be in office [presiding over the fall of the British Empire]."

And Churchill didn't want Roosevelt to bring China up as a power. Roosevelt elevated China, in the person of Chiang Kai-shek, as one of the Four Powers. And that's how they got into the UN. Churchill was not happy with that. He thought that would give people in Hong Kong and India ideas, and then they would want independence.

RC: *Do you think there was logic to the idea of Mao being compared to an emperor?*

MR: Ho always stayed thin. Gandhi was thin. Mao was fat … Gandhi ate pineapple, maybe a piece of bread. And he practiced marital abstinence. Ho may have had girlfriends, but he was called "Uncle Ho." He wouldn't go into the palace; he always lived in a more modest dwelling … The "emperor thing" comes back in [China in] a rather unpalatable form. But Ho and Ghandi were self-denying people, and much more appealing.

I don't like the word "emperor," but Mao became an icon in the revolution. This has a lot to do with detaching the Chinese Revolution from the world Communist movement, and the struggles with Russia over this as the 1950s come to an end. So the apotheosis of Mao was, "I was the Rising Sun," all these images of him, people wearing badges, and this cult of personality, cult of leadership. All these things are quite unhealthy and lead to people [viewing it as] a religious thing.

And it's also, maybe, a defense mechanism to China's isolation. Because all of this is happening in the late 1950s and early 1960s. Between the Dalai Lama's leaving Tibet, and Nehru giving him an area, Dharamsala, to [establish] an exiled community and the Indian War, the Sino-Indian War of late 1962, China is really being pushed into a corner. Everyone is against them. In the late 1950s, they lose India, which was so friendly to them … also Russia had been very friendly to them; now they're hostile to them. The Americans, always hostile to them, were delighted to see former friends turning against them. Then there's Taiwan, the incidents in Laos and the catalytic factor is the Vietnam War. And that war was all about China. The war in Vietnam was fought to prevent China from spreading its form of communism. And China's really isolated. The only friend it has—and this is a friendship of convenience, but it is a friend—is Pakistan.

So out of that isolation and out of the defensiveness, you get the circling of the wagons around a leader: "Mao steered us through the Revolution; he's steered us through the war; he's steered us through the Cold War. He is infallible. He has negotiated and maneuvered, through Scylla and Charybdis. He has gone back and forth—he commutes—through the whirlpool!" It's like Washington in that rowboat, that iconic figure of survival. And, "He's figured out so many things, how can he be wrong?" And of course, he's going to be wrong. The worst thing that can happen to anyone is accolades. And he got accolades. So many accolades that, I think, it damaged his judgment.

Even the Cultural Revolution has a certain logic to it, because it has everything to do with the Vietnam War [and also] the Great Leap Forward, which caused famine. It's hard to say how much, but it really was a catastrophic failure in certain respects … the Cultural Revolution also had a military aspect which nobody talks about. These phenomena are normally treated as purely Chinese, as things that emerge out of the irrationality of revolution, the irrationality of Mao's mind, or of communism or the Communist Party—but they are never seen in the framework of a regional conflict that includes Laos, Vietnam, Thailand, Japan, or a global conflict with the U.S., with Europe.

If you look at some of these really extreme moments in Chinese history, moments of hyper-stress, like the Great Leap Forward or the Cultural Revolution: would these things have happened had China not been so under the gun? How much can you attribute to purely internal factors? And how much can you leave off the table? These so-called external factors really aren't that external—they are interactive with internal factors. Just as we [in the U.S.] interned Japanese citizens in California because we were at war with Japan … [I]f you're looking at India, you've going to have to look at Britain. If you're looking at Vietnam, you're going to have to look at France. If you're looking at China, you've got to look at Russia and Japan and Korea and America.

RC: *How would you define the Chinese and Asian 20th century, and when does the 21st century begin?*

MR: Actually the 20th century was followed by the 19th century. This is a cycle, the imperial cycle. We're going back in time. I remember Clinton talking about the bridge to the 21st century. And

I'm thinking, "Maybe not." Chronology is just artifice. It has no content, it has no significance: it's just numbers … So these timelines—there are many timelines.

The Chinese will date modern history from 1839. That's when the Opium War starts. The treaties begin in 1842. And then they keep piling on, with more and more treaties. And then the Japanese want in on that. Nobody expects Japan to beat China [in 1895]. China is huge. Japan is tiny, Japan is untested, just scrambling about. All of a sudden … Goliath is down, David is triumphant. And that's why the British made a deal with them in 1902. And that's why Japan is thrilled: "We're a 'made' country!" That leads to the Russo-Japanese War. The Russo-Japanese War is crucial to [historian E. J.] Hobsbawm's [1996] timeline because it means that Russia gets slapped down so hard in Asia that they're going to re-orient their foreign policy toward the West. They're going to start worrying a lot more about the Turkish Straits, which connect the Black Sea to the Mediterranean.

After the Japanese beat them in 1905, the czar says, "We've had it in Asia, we can't maintain the Trans-Siberian; it goes so slowly, it's one track; it takes a month: we've got to worry about the West." Germany is making a huge bid for the Muslim world. They're building a Baghdad–Berlin railway; they've got another railway they're building right along the edge of where Palestine and Israel is now. They're going to contest Britain for world power. This is the build-up to World War I.

So once the Russians re-orient this policy, the British make a deal with them. Russia and Britain had been at odds over India for a hundred years. They'd never, never had any kind of understanding. All of a sudden, in 1907, two years after they get beaten by the Japanese, the Russians are making a deal … What does that mean? It means Germany is surrounded. Now, you have the configuration of national military force that makes World War I a "logical" thing to do. And that's how World War I starts: with Russia mobilizing, the minute Russia mobilizes, Germany declares war on Russia. So that's why Hobsbawm's timeline strikes me as artificial, and the Asian, and Indian, and Muslim parts of the context have to be gently shepherded into the frame so you get a more complete picture.

I don't agree with any timeline. First of all, World War I never ends. World War I gives you the Russian Revolution. It gives you the Chinese Revolution. Because the German holdings were given to Japan. That's what ignites the May Fourth Movement, which leads to the formation of the Communist Party. It gives you German fascism: the punitive [settlement of the war]. It gives you Italian fascism, gives you Japanese militarism. What a legacy.

I would make World War II go in Asia from the Japanese invasion of Manchuria in September 1931, to the end of the Vietnam War. I don't think World War II ever ended in Asia … That's why I say it's "war and revolution, war and revolution." The reason the war continues is the Chinese Revolution, and the refusal of the Americans to live with it. The Americans had a choice. They could have said, "Make a deal with the Chinese. You've got problems with the Russians … You could use them against the Russians. Mao always had conflicts with the Russians anyway."

There's a huge amount of scholarship trying to prove that the Chinese would not form any kind of relationship with the Americans. But the Chinese condition was intolerable, which was why we couldn't support Taiwan. Why not make a deal? Where is it written that you had to do this? Or why not recognize the new government? The British said, "Recognize the new government. We will." The Indians said, "You really should recognize the new government, we will." The Americans were in their "No" mode. They were in vindictive mode. When the state is in vindictive mode there's going to be hell to pay.

It was racism. It was pique: pure, infantile pique. They [Americans] were angry that [Chiang Kai-shek] had lost. What were we fighting Japan over? Why did we go into World War II? How did World War II start? It was over China. The strategic objectives of Washington in World War II were to get control over Japan—which was completely out of control—and to have a dominant position in China. That's why I mentioned to you that [President] Roosevelt wanted to bring China up, because Japan was out of the picture. They didn't want to deal with Japan anymore. And most of the American leadership couldn't stand the Japanese. They were very happy to build up China as "their" country in Asia. That was the idea, and [with] Chiang Kai-shek, they would have a treaty; it would be a new world order.

RC: *And they "lost" that, and they were angry about it.*

MR: [S]omething like the Anglo-Japanese alliance of 1902 was in the mind of Roosevelt: we will bring on an American-Chinese relationship. Japan is prostrate. And they just didn't ask the owners of the country, "Is this okay with you?" or, "How can we do this to make it okay with you?" So when the War ends, what does the U.S. do? They're flying Marines into cities, to hold them for Chiang Kai-shek. They're using Japanese troops that have surrendered—remember, they'd raced to disarm the surrendering troops. They used Japanese troops after that war in China. Do a thing like that? It's really not smart in many ways. And then aiding Chiang Kai-shek in the civil war during 1945–1949, the period they called "the War of Liberation." The previous war was a war of resistance against Japan. Now the name changes: it's a war of liberation to get Chiang Kai-shek overthrown and to get the Americans out of there. Think about that. People like to talk about how many people died because of Mao's policy. They never ask how many people died because we [the U.S.] prolonged the civil war there. A lot of people died. Prolonging the civil war for four years did a huge amount of damage. A huge loss of life. This has a lot to do with the harshness of Communist rule. They had to rebuild a country that's been devastated by war, for basically, for a hundred years. On and off, but mostly on, particularly in that last segment, from the Japanese invasion of 1931.

That's why the Vietnam War was "marketed" to the American people as a war to stop China … It makes no sense, to fight Vietnam: it's this little, pipsqueak country—which, it turned out, knew how to fight. They [Americans] forgot that the Vietnamese heritage is completely military—they defeated the Mongols. They defeated the Chinese … They're tiny, they're very gentle, and they speak French—but they're very tough, particularly if you try to invade them.

The war in Korea was [General Douglas] MacArthur's vision. MacArthur was always opposed to the European orientation of Washington. That's what made him a maverick, and that's why Truman sacked him. And that's why he was pushing the war: to get it to go into China and reverse the revolution. Truman didn't want to do that. And later, after that, the Americans did not want Chiang Kai-shek to attack, either. They were cautious about tackling the Chinese—there's a lot of them and they'd been through a lot. Any country that's been through war has a cohort of a very well-trained military.

I think the initial construction of Washington's ideology was [that China was] a subdivision of Russia. So it was seen as—in the Communist world—all subject to Russian authority. So [they were] so European focused that you couldn't even recognize the separateness, the distinctiveness, of what was going on in China. The Americans completely misread the Revolution; they never saw that tsunami coming, and I mean it was a tsunami. The mobilization of the countryside just swept through—it's an astonishing victory, how could that happen? The population was so aroused and the only leadership they were getting was from the Communists.

Are the Chinese going to behave like a State? Are they going to behave like a great power? Yes, they are. Are they going to be a rival? ... Now, that's not something that's going to be decided only by them ... Our behavior will have a lot to do with where they see themselves. Will they see themselves as a competitor, as they do now? Or will that advance to rival, or, further, to adversary or enemy? That means war. So right now I would say the first two, competitor and rival. I don't think we're at the level of adversary. But the interdependence is overwhelming.

RC: *I also want to get to the ending of this period ... with the end of the Vietnam War.*

MR: Now we've gone full circle, China has reconstructed itself through revolution, rebuilt a nation, essentially defeated the Americans in the Korean War, essentially defeated the Americans by backing the North Vietnamese in the Vietnam War, [they've] held off all these wars of aggression ... So clearly the Vietnam War had taught Washington the lesson that Truman was trying to teach MacArthur, don't fight a land war in Asia.

So, the Vietnam War ends, Nixon has already gone to China ... and recognition comes in '79. The dust is settling, the Chinese, for better or worse, are ruled by the Communist Party, and they are going to hold onto power ... They are not going to give up power, certainly not at the behest of the Americans although they may have to for internal reasons. I think people around that area are kind of relieved that there hasn't been another major war in the area since 1975.

Are they [the Chinese] always going to behave like gentlemen? I don't think so. How big a problem is this? I don't think its unsolvable now; I think it's probably better if the Americans stay out of it. [Polish American statesman Zbigniew] Brzezinski's argument is that China should be a regional power, not a global power, and this should be encouraged by the Americans to that extent. He probably doesn't like the Africa stuff [Chinese investment], but within that general sphere of the Philippines, the South China Sea, the little islands, the atolls, and even Japan, Korea, Eastern Russia, the Americans should stay out of the picture.

Works Cited

Bradley, R. (Producer). (1995). *Uncle Sam and Uncle Ho* [motion picture]. BBC/Arts and Entertainment Networks co-production.

Hobsbawm, E. J. (1996). *The age of extremes: The short twentieth century, 1914–1991*. New York: Vintage.

Essay: On Revolution and Rights: China's Cultural Revolution

By Laura J. Dull, with Bernadette Condesso and Dawn Vandervloed

During the Chinese Cultural Revolution that started in 1965, Mao Zedong engineered a massive social campaign to tear down class barriers. To stir up the population, propagandists made banners and posters proclaiming the party's new values, and citizens held struggle meetings to denounce colleagues, friends, and relatives who allegedly clung to the "Four Olds"—customs, culture, ideas, and habits associated with capitalist and foreign values. In the quest for social equality, party members confiscated property and possessions of the wealthy and sent urban youth and others to be "re-educated" in rural areas. Particularly striking was the power of young people, who eagerly joined the effort to enforce the "Four News" throughout the population. In the chaos and tragedy that the Cultural Revolution aroused, there are estimates that between 15 and 45 million people died (death estimates are a source of controversy in this area), killed by the military, but also by disease, famine, and suicide. The Cultural Revolution ended with Mao's death in 1976 and the appointment of Mao's rival, Deng Xiaoping, as the country's paramount leader. Slogans like "to get rich is glorious" replaced public criticism of "black" classes such as landlords, as the government shifted to a "socialist market economy."

It might be tempting for citizens in the U.S. to view the Cultural Revolution as a frightening challenge to capitalist and liberal values of social mobility, individual liberty, and freedom of thought. Often, people comfort themselves that such events were the result of people being "brainwashed" or frightened into submission by a charismatic leader, or as an event isolated in time and space, thus rare or unlikely to happen in America. These perspectives fail to account for the many reasons people are attracted to revolutions, including the sincere belief that society will be made better with the implementation of certain ideals. Moreover, as China scholar Moss Roberts explained, revolutions take place in an international context that can influence leaders' decisions and actions, as well as larger transformations in a society. For students and citizens alike, the history of the Cultural Revolution raises important questions about massive social movements: How and why do revolutions happen? To whom do they appeal? Do ordinary people have the power to change things? Grappling with the multiple and fascinating insights that emerged in an interview conducted with China scholar Moss Roberts, we developed a unit that would incorporate his perspective on these and other questions related to the history of modern Asia. Study of the history of this region strikes us as particularly important, given contemporary political discourse and ongoing mystifications of "the Orient."

War and Revolution

Moss Roberts' interview covers a wide swath of recent Asian history, thus offering many fruitful possibilities for teaching. For Roberts, an important theme in the modern era is war and revolution, which drove rapid social and economic changes in the region:

> War and revolution; war and revolution: don't separate them. Because all of these movements [in China and India] are accelerated and intensified [by World War II], like a forcing house … where plants have to grow twice as fast as they're supposed to[.] War is a forcing house.

In addition to helping people understand modern Chinese history, the theme of war and revolution underscores how internal events are deeply connected with external politics. Working against the "tendency [of historians and others] to minimize the external factors," Roberts explained,

> if you're looking at India, you're going to have to look at Britain. If you're looking at Vietnam, you're going to have to look at France. If you're looking at China, you've got to look at Russia and Japan and Korea and America.

For example, unlike in India, which had been united under a common civil service, "imperialist anarchy" reigned in China at the end of World War II. The Japanese, French, Russians, British, and Americans all had interests or holdings there, and so the country was wide open for "pandemonium," in Roberts' view, as different factions struggled to take power.

In fact, according to Roberts, it would be impossible to understand the dynamism of China during the 20th century without an understanding of global currents of thoughts and ideas. In seeking to "break free of the stranglehold of the treaty system and the treaty powers," Sun Yat-sen sought to build an army. His admiration for Russia's Red Army led him to seek military assistance. As Roberts noted, "That's how Chiang Kai-shek goes to Russia for his training. And the Russians give them a lot of money, and advice, and arms." Sun Yat-sen also pondered China's economic future by looking to other models:

> He [Sun Yat-sen] was very much … a developmentalist: whatever works. If capitalism is going to make the economy grow, good. Socialism? He also was very conscious of the need to protect people who are defenseless economically. So socialism was always part of his vision.

This negotiation between socialism and capitalism arose again as Mao and Deng grappled over the future of the country.

In arguing that he does not "agree with any timeline," Roberts alluded to the difficulty of establishing a clear beginning or end point for events in Asian history. He claimed,

> I don't think World War II ever ended in Asia. I think it just continued … That's why I say it's war and revolution … The reason the war continues is the CR, and the refusal of the Americans to live with it.

America's attempts to defeat Mao protracted the agony in China:

> People like to talk about how many people died because of Mao's policy [Great Leap Forward]. They never ask how many people died because we prolonged the civil war there. A lot of people died. Prolonging the civil war for four years did a huge amount of damage.

Roberts also described the Cultural Revolution as "maybe, a defense mechanism to China's isolation." In the late 1950s and early 1960s, India and Russia began to turn against their ally China, to the delight of the Americans. The war in Vietnam was another "catalytic factor" in isolating China, as it was "fought to prevent China from spreading its form of communism." Out of this isolation and defensiveness, according to Roberts,

> you get the circling of the wagons around a leader: "Mao steered us through the Revolution; he's steered us through the war, he's steered us through the Cold War. He's infallible … how can he be wrong?" And of course, he's going to be wrong. The worst thing that can happen to anyone is accolades … it damaged his judgment.

The isolation facilitated Mao's ascension as an "icon" in the revolution:

> So the apotheosis of Mao, you know, "I was the Rising Sun," and all these images of him, people wearing badges, and this cult of personality, cult of leadership. All these things are quite unhealthy and … it becomes a religious thing, and people want to appropriate a symbol, so they fight over the symbol.

At the same time, noted Roberts, Mao was concerned about abuses of power, which helps explain his appeal to many Chinese:

> He [Mao] believed in the State … he wanted to build a certain kind of state, and he had anarchic impulses too. He was kind of hostile to the Party, bureaucracy, people settled into their own niche and getting tiny … He would always say, just give them a tiny, tiny piece of power and they treat people so badly. He did have that humane instinct about abuse of power and the little guy.

Complementing his deep insights into the psychological aspects of Mao's leadership, Roberts' perspective on the entanglement of external and internal factors further reveals the limits of mere nation-based history. Instead, he foregrounds the multiple and complex factors that drive historical change:

> [W]ould these things [the Great Leap Forward or the Cultural Revolution] have happened had China not been so under the gun? How much can you attribute to purely internal factors? And how much can you leave off the table? These so-called external factors, which really aren't that external. They really are interactive with internal factors. Just as we [the U.S.] interned Japanese citizens in California because we were at war with Japan. There's an example of an external factor that's interacting with an internal factor and causing us to alter many of our standard legal practices.

Overall, the interview with Roberts provided our group with many tantalizing threads for analysis, as well as rich background knowledge about modern Asia and China that helps sketch out key contexts for the Cultural Revolution. Roberts also challenged the way educators and others often simplify the past, by ignoring external factors, for example, to make it understandable (McNeil, 1999). But how might we make sense of his arguments to help middle and secondary level students develop a clearer understanding of the history of China in the 20th century?

A Unit on Modern China

Picking up on some of Roberts' major themes, we invited students to become immersed in the texts and images of the Mao and Deng eras in order to grapple with these essential questions:

- How and why do revolutions happen?
- To whom do they appeal?
- Is a "single story" dangerous?
- Do young people have any power to change things?

Our unit was taught in two very different settings in upstate New York: a small private school and a large suburban/rural public school. In both places, students recognized that a "single story" was imposed in China during the Cultural Revolution and gained a sense of how that story pervaded daily life by taking on the roles of Chinese youth. Students also identified the shift in economic ideologies through a comparison of the symbols, images, and text used by Mao and Deng and the creation of their own propaganda posters. At the end, students could name the Party's policy shifts, how they were being presented to people, and what drove these changes.

Our group consisted of two high school social studies teachers and a social studies teacher educator. Dawn Vandervloed teaches global history at Washingtonville High School, a public school with approximately 1,550 students located in a village in Orange County, New York. In 1812, the New York Common Schools Law prompted the process of consolidation of the many schools in the area into one district, and in 1933, the community built a single K-12 school that is now the middle school. The high school currently serves an economically diverse population, with 21% of the students eligible for free or reduced lunch. According to No Child Left Behind standards, the school does a good job of educating youth, having achieved "Adequate Yearly Progress" in 2010–2011. Washingtonville has a 95% graduation rate for its population of 15% Hispanic, 7% black, 1% Asian, and 76% white students (New York State Education Department, 2010–2011). High school classes are 90 minutes, and students in Dawn's class sit at desks arranged in a "U" shape. Dawn taught this unit to all three of her tenth grade global studies classes.

Bernadette Condesso teaches social studies and is a guidance counselor at Poughkeepsie Day School (PDS), a private school founded in 1934. Set within 35 wooded acres, the school features two buildings, including a former mansion, which house classrooms and additional space for 300 students from pre-K to grade 12. Nineteen percent of students receive financial assistance, and 25% are students of color. Teachers at PDS are not required to follow state curricula, so teaching is non-traditional. As the school website declares, "Learning [at PDS] is joyful, creative, innovative, and fun!" (2012). Bernadette's classroom resembled a college seminar: students sit around a large conference table to facilitate discussion. Like Dawn, Bernadette teaches 90-minute classes; she taught this unit in one of her classes.

Since 2002, Laura Dull has taught prospective teachers and coordinated the Secondary Social Studies program at the State University of New York (SUNY) in New Paltz. Both Dawn and Bernadette are former students. Laura taught social studies for seven years in two alternative public schools in New York City. She worked on the Lower East Side in a school for Chinese immigrants and for American students who had failed to thrive in regular school environments. She was also a teacher of humanities at a school that required students to create portfolios to demonstrate competence in all their subjects.

In our initial planning meeting, the two teachers and one education professor struggled to select from the many themes that arose in Roberts' interview. The idea of comparing three leaders (Mao Zedong, Ho Chi Minh, and Mohandas Ghandi) as Roberts and a colleague were doing in a college course seemed appealing, and Roberts provided us with some references to help formulate this project. However, since much of the interview centered on China and Mao, and the teachers had already gathered some compelling resources from this era, we ultimately chose to build our unit around Mao's leadership. In talking about the goals, supporters, and causes of the Cultural Revolution, we felt that students would be especially interested in the incredible mobilization of millions of youth as drivers of social change. As a culminating question to the unit, we wanted to ask students' views on the role of youth: do young people have any power to change things? While the Chinese case displays the extraordinary capacity of young people to embrace and impose new social norms, it also raises the question of whether or not students were willing soldiers in this cause: was this simply a matter of "thought reform" or brainwashing of impressionable youth, as psychologist Robert Jay Lifton (1961) contended? Was it "an authentic expression of student protest against authority," as leftist scholars argue (see Milner, 2002)? Or, as Graham Milner (2002) contended, was the Cultural Revolution a "cynical misuse of the idealism of an entire generation in China," because "youth were largely being manipulated for the purposes of intra-bureaucratic faction fighting within the party-state hierarchy" (para. 14)? These were questions we wanted students to evaluate and, ultimately, to answer for themselves.

The striking stories, films, and propaganda of this era are powerful ways of presenting Chinese history through multiple media: there are many excellent first-hand accounts of the period (Chang, 2003; Cheng, 2010; Jiang, 1997; Ma, 1996), and evocative posters, films, and official statements and quotes are easily found online (see also Landsberger, Min, & Duo, 2011). These sources helped students hear, see, and feel how and why this revolution happened, what goals were being promoted, and the symbols and ideas used to attract people to the revolution. We started the unit with a clip from a technology, entertainment, design (TED) talk, the "Danger of a Single Story," by Nigerian novelist Chimamanda Adichie (2009). As schoolchildren, she and her peers read textbooks written for British schoolchildren, learning a limited narrative that did not include their nation's literature and history. Adichie's speech provided students with the language to talk about, and think about the effects of, the constricted messages we receive from various institutions around us, including families, schools, government, and news media. With this talk in mind, students then viewed a clip from a documentary film (Williams & Dietz, 1994)[1] in order to hunt for clues of the "story" Mao was telling and the symbols, such as Mao's *Little Red Book*, used to promote the story.

The next day, students engaged in a role-playing experience based on scenes from Ji-Li Jiang's book about her childhood during the Cultural Revolution, *Red Scarf Girl* (1997).[2] Through this kinesthetic activity (Gardner, 2011), we wanted students to think about who was attracted to the revolution, how it shaped everyday life, and why people were willing to denounce their neighbors, teachers, and even parents. The teachers chose moments that reflected the destruction of old ways—including people's memories and histories—and illustrated how a climate of fear was produced. For example, some Red Guards harass a boy wearing tight pants and pointy shoes that "are detrimental to the revolution," punishing him by cutting up his pants and shoes. In another scene, Jiang's parents furtively burn photos of travels and clothing that reveal a comfortable lifestyle. These brief and provocative excerpts, we believed, would create excellent, engrossing drama for students—and they did, as we explain below.

In the next lesson, teachers gave students posters and slogans to examine and categorize. Based on their knowledge of the Cultural Revolution, students had to decide whether texts would most likely come from Mao or Deng's times and what policy shifts they signaled. Students then had to explain to their classmates why they made their choices. For example, Maoist propaganda had more militaristic imagery, while Deng's celebration of scholarship reflected a de-emphasis of class struggle.[3] In the last lesson, students created posters that reflected the imagery and concepts promoted by one of the two leaders, Mao or Deng. Classmates were required to identify the period to which the poster corresponded. They used sticky notes to comment on their classmates' work. As a culmination to the unit, we asked students to respond in writing to the essential questions noted at the beginning of this section.

Language and Youth in Revolution: Teaching the China Unit

Laura was able to observe many of the lessons taught in the two schools. The teachers also gathered worksheets, surveys, and other materials created by the students to assess their learning and understandings from the unit. Below we present our descriptions and evaluations of the lessons in the order in which they were presented. Note that these lessons were conducted in 90-minute blocks, so teachers with regular schedules will need two periods to cover them. Also, after Bernadette taught the unit, we made some modifications for teaching the lessons in Dawn's classes. For example, we put more emphasis on the question of youth power in the final reflections for Dawn's classes, as students seemed particularly attracted to that theme.

Is a Single Story "Dangerous"? Why did Mao Include Youth in His Campaign?

Before embarking on a study of the Cultural Revolution, both Dawn and Bernadette gave mini-lectures setting the context and covering these topics: Mao's rise to power, the Great Leap Forward and its problems, the alleged decline in "revolutionary spirit" that led to disagreement among Communist Party members, and external governments' hostility toward China. In the 1960s, Mao decided to re-energize the population by rooting out foreign and capitalist elements in the society, putting his rivals on alert and distracting citizens from China's economic and other troubles. His plan required the mobilization of vast numbers of people, especially youth, and he brilliantly used images and slogans to spread his message. Chimamanda Adichie (2009) would call this message a "single story," and warns in her talk that this is "dangerous" because other perspectives are absent or repressed. This repression leads to stereotyping, fear, and conflict. In our first lesson, we showed a clip from Adichie's speech and another film segment about the Cultural Revolution (Williams & Dietz, 1994) to initiate discussions about why the Cultural Revolution happened, how it was presented to people and for what purposes, and what symbols and practices were used to change minds and incite action.

In both classes, the films sparked thoughtful reflection by the students on the attractions of propaganda and revolution. Dawn's students turned the conversation to their experiences with "single stories" about their ethnicities. After identifying Adichie's argument as "you hear so much of something it's hard to know what's true" and "without any prior knowledge, you have to believe it," which leads to "stereotyping," several students offered firsthand experience with the "dangers" of a single story. An Asian student noted that, "People keep asking me if I eat dogs or cats," and a student from Jamaica said that she feels people think the "mindset of Jamaicans is: you love Bob Marley, smoke weed—but I was born into a middle class family with the American Dream!" Several students blamed "the media": "People get the idea of Africans being poor; it's not every ten minutes a middle class kid eats a piece of bread, you hear every ten minutes a kid dies."

After viewing the film excerpt on the Cultural Revolution (Williams & Dietz, 1994), which included footage of public criticism and humiliation of authorities, a re-casting of plays and other arts into revolutionary stories, and massive marches of exuberant youth, Bernadette's students engaged in a conversation about how purveyors of a single story must constantly work to quell other stories. One student explained that leaders "needed a certain amount of fear" in order to control the population and get rid of the Four Olds. Books were often burned because "they have different stories." After students also noted that statues were torn down, schools were closed, and an anti-intellectual feeling was cultivated, Bernadette asked, "Why?" Students explained that since educated people "could challenge the story," Mao encouraged "chaos" so that people would want change and "turn to him for an easy solution."

While the single story theme was popular with students, they also evoked some of Roberts' own insights about the Cultural Revolution. Students in both schools drew upon psychological explanations as to why Mao targeted youth. Bernadette's students argued that young people would have "total loyalty" to Mao, it was "easier to manipulate what they believe," and they were "more susceptible to propaganda." Dawn's students argued that young people were "uncorrupted," "easily brainwashed," "naïve," and "don't know the effects of their actions." But earlier, Dawn's students came up with different reasons when the teacher framed the question as: "Would my father be interested in revolution?" After the students answered, "No," Dawn asked if the students would be interested, to which they enthusiastically declared, "Yes!" Students argued that because they "like change" and "were young" with "nothing to lose," they could easily adjust to new situations and thus would be more likely to join a revolution. The students would be asked to grapple again with this tension between agency and coercion when they assessed the role of youth in the Cultural Revolution.

How did Language Lead to Action? What Role did Youth Play in the Revolution?

For our next activity, we borrowed from the ideas of "process drama" (see Mattson, 2008) to bring sections of Jiang's memoir (1997) to life. The teachers gave groups of students a portion of the text to read and turn into a scene. The scenes included: Jiang's parents burning old photos (pp. 122–125); Red Guards confronting a youth wearing "inappropriate" pants and shoes (pp. 30–33); people destroying shop signs, such as "Great Prosperity," that "still stank of old culture" (p. 21); criticism of Jiang for calling a student "Pauper" (which had been her usual nickname) (pp. 64–66); and authorities pressuring Jiang to denounce her father as "an enemy of the people" (p. 226). After each presentation, teachers helped students debrief the performance, asking students to describe what had happened, who had the power in the scene and who was being targeted, and what symbols and language the actors were using to enforce the revolutionary spirit.

Students at PDS were clearly comfortable with public performance and came to class prepared. While some of them read from a script, others improvised their scenes. Most of the groups used simple props, like store signs and a Mao hat, and one group modernized their scene, with the youth defending his tight pants by saying, "But I got these from H & M!" As often happens with drama, students laughed, applauded, and generally enjoyed watching their classmates' performances. In addition, the scenes evoked good understandings and connections among the students. For example, students returned to the theme of the destruction of the past after the photo-burning scene, with one student explaining why Mao so feared the past: he "would have wanted to suppress any good memories … of the past because that would have meant that some things had worked prior to the revolution." Students also linked the skit about tight pants back to internal power struggles in the government. During the post-performance discussion, one of the play's actors read from the book, noting that the youth's defense of his pants was that he "had bought them in a government store." This, the student said, indicated that the government itself was insufficiently revolutionary and needed to be reformed. In talking about the symbolic meanings of clothing, another student brought up the anti-bourgeois *sans-culottes* movement during the French Revolution. The PDS students' assessment of the activity revealed much about their consciousness of alternative pedagogies: the performances helped "you remember it [history] more" and through acting, there was "more of an emotional aspect to it [the story]."

The students in the class Laura observed at Dawn's school exhibited more hesitation about performing the scenes. Many of the students came to class unprepared, and Laura and Dawn had to circulate among the groups to help students write up the scenes and create props. Still, out of 32 respondents to a post-unit survey, the majority of the students (22) liked the activity, with 9 disliking it and 1 both liking and disliking the scenes. Like Bernadette's students, Dawn's students felt it helped them to "visualize" what was happening in the book and "showed how the girl was treated." One student described the scenes as a "memory hook." Many of the students felt they were "funny" and "cute and fun to do." Those who disliked the activity were afraid of public performance—one described it as "embarrassing" and another said, "I don't really like getting up in front of the class." Dawn felt that part of the problem was that students simply did not know how to go about preparing the scenes. In addition, as proponents of drama in the classroom argue (Prendiville & Toye, 2007), students need to feel comfortable with their peers and with public speaking. Drama warm-up activities and the integration of role playing from the start of the year can help reduce students' reservations about performing.

Even with the student reticence, the performances in Dawn's class were often clever and engaging, and as in Bernadette's class, led to laughter and joy at the novelty of seeing classmates act. The teacher also saw new sides to her students: one young woman who seemed disengaged during the group's preparation did an excellent job of capturing the tone and attitude of her character. To ensure that all students paid attention and participated in debriefing the skits, Dawn assigned specific groups to take responsibility for answering the questions. Worksheets and discussion illustrated in-depth understanding of how the revolution affected people's everyday lives, and how youth joined in the effort to eliminate the Four Olds. Students noted that it was a "stressful and nervous" environment as people, particularly the "rich" and "upper class," were afraid of "being humiliated." The revolution was attractive to peasants and other "people from 'good' classes" who "got special treatment" and "gained power" as the upper classes "lost power." Students acknowledged the primacy of class in determining status by noting that "it doesn't matter about poor grades or anything because power is changing." Dawn also asked students, "Where else in history do we see this?" Students mentioned the Russian and French Revolutions as other periods of class struggle.

These lessons illuminate the tension as well as the exhilaration that can result from using drama in the classroom. While some students found performance challenging, and the teachers themselves were concerned about incorporating drama, the scenes sent students visually and physically into a unique moment in the past when poor people wielded power over the rich. By viewing or taking on the roles of characters from Jiang's memoir, students were able to see and hear multiple perspectives on the essential questions of why the revolution happened, and to whom it appealed.

What Economic, Political, and Social Shifts did Changes in Mao and Deng's Language Represent?

In order to transition from Mao to Deng and help prepare students to make their own posters, the teachers created folders with several posters and slogans from each time period. Rather than just telling students the changes they reflected, we wanted students to figure out the similarities and differences on their own by comparing the symbols and language that were used in each set of materials. We asked pairs of students to examine the materials and categorize them as from either Mao or Deng's times. Then, we asked them to defend their choices and explain what had changed. The following discussion focuses on Dawn's class.

What was striking about this activity was students' immediate interest in the arresting visual materials and the strips of paper with slogans. It appeared that this exercise was both approachable and challenging: that is, the texts were just difficult enough to intrigue the students, but not so complicated as to overwhelm them (Willingham, 2009). After the groups finished looking at the materials, Dawn held up the poster or had students read the slogan and then asked them to explain what period the items were from and what stories they told. For example, one poster showed a smiling Mao as a sun shining down on marching citizens. Another Mao-era image showed angry workers using their implements—shovels, guns, red-stained paintbrushes—to harass a wealthy business person.

The primary source documents helped illustrate how Deng softened the class struggle and militarism of the Cultural Revolution. Dawn held up another poster of smiling citizens wearing the uniforms representing different professions (a doctor, a miner, a sailor) and asked, "Why is this one Deng?" A student pointed out, "Mao did not want them to learn," but in Deng's time, it was okay for people "to do what they want." In addition, unlike the communist uniforms in Mao's posters, Deng's people wore what the students called "modernized" clothing. In discussing similarities and differences, one student noted that "both are looking to the future with the kids" and "both want to reform China." However, Mao seemed to want to "scare the people" while "Deng calms everyone down" and encourages citizens to "study more." As another student put it, "Mao wanted landlords and intellectuals to be bullied and not treated equally; now [with Deng], mental workers should be respected." In the end, students recognized that "Mao and Deng both wanted the success of China, [but] in different forms." This lesson led students into the next part of China's history: why did Deng move away from radical class struggle? What had changed, inside and outside of China?

How did Chinese Leaders Communicate Their Ideas?

In our last lesson, we asked students to take on the role of propagandists for either Mao or Deng and create a poster that expressed that leader's social visions. By creating their own propaganda, students had to think about how to create a powerful and appealing message in a limited space, as well as to display their understandings of the similarities and differences between the two periods.

In Bernadette's classroom, we displayed the posters on the wall, and students put up sticky notes with positive and critical feedback about their classmates' work. The posters, most of which were about the Cultural Revolution, captured the tone and messages of the era, but their starker and simpler imagery reflected a more modernist influence than the highly detailed, realist propaganda of Mao and Deng. For example, one poster included the graphic repetition of a word that combined Mao with obey—"MaObey" (Chapter Resources II)—with the first three letters in red and the second part in black against a white background, evoking the conformity and fear of the Cultural Revolutionary times. Bernadette's students conducted some research to add creative touches: for example, a poster of a frowning face and a smiling face used Chinese characters as eyes. In the frowning face, the eyes read in old characters, "Four Olds," while the smiling eyes read "Four News" in new characters. Another poster was adorned with the phrase "Revolution is not a dinner party," taken from Mao's *Little Red Book*. The student explained the phrase as meaning that there were "going to be some hard times but it's [Cultural Revolution] something for everybody." Another student drew a picture of Mao pouring new ideas into the world, while putting old ideas, along with parents, teachers, and books, into a jail cell. The artists stated that the messages was, "I [Mao] will give you the world, but [I am] taking these things out so as to give you a different world." They also included an image of the Red Guards, all looking exactly the same, in keeping with the idea that this was a collective effort and people should not try to distinguish themselves from others. Another poster from the Deng era featured the phrase "In with the New, Out with the Old," over a background that included words associated with old ideas on the top half and others associated with new ones on the bottom half.

Only one of Dawn's classes had time to make the posters. Their posters, created on colored paper, had more text and less imagery than those of Bernadette's students, who had done them for homework, while Dawn's were done in class. Many of the posters focused on the transition from Four Olds to Four News. For example, one listed the positive changes that the Four News brought for women, such as "women did not have to bind their feet" and "women were treated equally." Another wrote the Four Olds as featuring "Education" and "Bourgeois" while the Four News emphasized "No education," "Agriculture," and "Students work with peasants." One poster of the Deng era included slogans such as "It doesn't matter if a cat is black or white as long as it catches mice." Symbols of strength (barbells), agriculture (wheat), education (book), and industry (factory) were drawn to express Deng's values. A poster on the Cultural Revolution used the modern image of a circle with a slash over something that is prohibited: landlords, rich peasants, counter-revolutionaries, criminals, and rightists were listed in a circle with a slash across them. This symbol was surrounded by slogans such as "beating down Jesus following" and "beating down the bad elements." Another poster was done in the style of Da Zi-Bo, the banners used to publicly criticize "bad class" individuals (of elite or middle class origins)—and seemed to mix both new and old critiques of the "teacher" who "yells too much," gives "too much homework," and has "capitalist ideals."

The students in both schools did not have the time to replicate the highly detailed, colorful propaganda of professional Chinese artists. Rather, their work either captured the atmosphere of the times (as in the "MaObey" poster emphasizing strict obedience) or reflected the general messages that people received (as in the Da Zi-Bo banner or the poster with Deng slogans). In other words, through their drawings, students learned how revolution happens by illustrating the different visions of society invoked during the Cultural Revolution and Deng's era, and how this felt for people in the past.

Reflections on Learning: Do Young People, Like You, Have Any Power to Change Things?

In Bernadette's class, students ended the unit by responding in writing and in a discussion to the questions: how and by whom was the Revolution presented to people? Were Mao's methods effective? Many of the students spoke about Mao's skillful mobilization of young people. One student alluded to the generational conflict that Mao unleashed: "He [Mao] gained his following through the children who saw him as a revolutionary leader who gave them power and control over their elders. For the children especially, the revolution was exciting and grand." The same student sought to explain Mao's success, mentioning a strategy that appears to be universal: "The crux of his power lies in being able to present complex problems in society with simple, easy solutions." During discussion, she evoked a powerful metaphor to explain how revolutionary ideas were spread, describing the Red Guards as a "human microphone" broadcasting the "simple ideas from the *Red Book*" out to the population. In their written reflections, several students mentioned the brainwashing or susceptibility of children:

> This [the Revolution] was done through Mao and his Red Guards who used violence as a way to get people to conform and education as a way to target the most impressionable people of the population ... the youth. Mao started with the youth ... because he said that a movement took great devotion and what better people to choose than those who could be easily brainwashed and who would be willing to give everything (including their life) for the cause ... Mao didn't want any ideas but his own to infiltrate the minds of these blind followers ... [and] Mao's *Red Book* and speeches were the source of the arguments, and his views were incredibly inspirational to the susceptible teenagers and children.

According to this last student, Mao's methods were "all highly effective" because they convinced "the working class of an inevitable reform and [were] scaring the upper class into submission."

Several students drew from the film and book to understand Mao's appeal, as in this response:

> One of the striking things I got from the movie … was when it said that Mao believed that if he could take China's most beloved opera and give it new meaning, that he could change anything and essentially infiltrate their culture's history and make it seem bad, pictures, clothing, shops, even parents that were representative of the "old way" were condemned.

One student gave a fascinating analysis of the ultimate failure of the Cultural Revolution, arguing that it could not be sustained because "all they were doing was destroying the old ways," not doing anything to push the country forward. At the end of the discussion, Laura asked the students to think of other reasons, besides propaganda and impressionable youth, for people's enthusiasm for the Cultural Revolution. In addition to Mao's charisma, students noted that fear motivated people: people "followed along" and turned on neighbors before neighbors could denounce them.

For final reflections in Dawn's class, we decided to focus on the theme of youth power that Bernadette's students were so drawn to. Students read an excerpt from Jiang's epilogue that begins with "Many friends have asked me why, after all I went through, I did not hate Chairman Mao and the Cultural Revolution in those years. The answer is simple. We were all brainwashed" (1997, p. 265). After reading the text, students were asked to write their answers to the questions: were young people just being brainwashed by Mao or did they genuinely have the power to make changes? Why is a single story dangerous? Perhaps influenced by the reading, the majority of the students (30) argued that indeed people were brainwashed. Sample responses include: youth only learned "good things of Mao" so they "didn't know any better" and they were "basically only spies for Mao." But 7 students were not so sure and acknowledged both the limits and potential of youth power: "They were brainwashed considering Mao controlled everything they learned but if they didn't go along with Mao's teachings they could've overthrown them [the government]" and youth "had power to make changes but only the changes Mao allowed." Another stated, "ideas put into the youth's minds were generated by Mao, but the young people PROVED [capitals in the original] in their actions that they're capable." In fact, what makes youth powerful is perhaps their idealism and energy, which can be turned to good or bad: "no matter what the young people believed, they could still make changes." Students cited several dangers of a single story, including discrimination and stereotyping, manipulation and control over thought, and the fact that a small group or leader could take control. This last response was taken from the epilogue in which Jiang argues, "Without a sound legal system, a small group or even a single person can take control of an entire country" (pp. 265–266). One student's answer echoed part of Milner's thesis (2002): "Their leader had taken advantage of their trust and loyalty to manipulate the entire country of China."

Concluding Thoughts

Students were enthusiastic about the multiple texts and exercises that they encountered during this unit. As one of Bernadette's students put it, "I liked the mixture of art, theater, cinema, and text. I think that by choosing these [materials] the ideas of the Cultural Revolution were really made clear to all." Through these media, students were able to reflect on enduring questions about the power of a single story: how it was told, how it was spread, to whom it appealed, and how it ended with the new leader and his introduction of a different direction for the country. As often happens when lessons "go live," students' contributions and interpretations took us down paths we teachers had not anticipated. Their reactions suggested interesting ways to extend certain questions. For example, given the general conclusion that "impressionable" youth were manipulated by Mao, a next step for teachers might be to challenge this idea by looking at youth movements elsewhere, such as those of the 1920s and 1930s in the U.S. (see Cohen, 2010) or anti-apartheid demonstrations in Soweto in 1976. How were these cases similar to and different from the Cultural Revolution? Were young people's motivations in America or South Africa really so different from those of the Chinese? What was at stake for people who did not "just follow along" and accept leaders' decisions? More broadly, educators must strive to ensure that we do not make the "single story" approach our own approach in the classroom—that is, we must remember to consider multiple interpretations of events, just as historians do.

Another possible teaching direction, in keeping with Moss Roberts' emphasis, would be to consider the global context that shaped Deng's actions. Deng, who had been educated in France and the Soviet Union, presided over the famed meeting with President Nixon that signaled the end of the two nations' hostilities. What personal beliefs and external influences contributed to Deng's disagreement with Mao during the Cultural Revolution (Deng was purged twice during the Cultural Revolution) and his ability to reform China once he took power? What had changed internationally in the shift from Mao to Deng that enabled Deng to cultivate warmer relations with other nations?

Mao and Deng both recognized the power of the arts in persuading people to take the country in new directions. Familiar theater productions were re-cast to promote a revolutionary spirit, and Chinese artists created vibrant posters to present the aspirations and visions of leaders. To honor the importance of the arts in education, we asked students to imagine life in China by acting in scenes, examining and illustrating propaganda posters, and viewing and discussing films. These activities were often unsettling or difficult for students, but they also gave rise to pleasure, humor, thoughtfulness, and pride over their achievements. Most of all, they gave rise to deep—and accurate—insights about how historical actors may have felt about their experiences during this era.

Notes

1   The section on the Cultural Revolution begins at 1:02. We stopped the film after about 20 minutes.
2   While writing this chapter, we learned of a curriculum guide called *Teaching Red Scarf Girl*. For teachers interested in devoting more time to the book, the resource is available from Facing History and Ourselves at: www.facinghistory.org/resources/publications/teaching-red-scarf-girl.
3   Moss Roberts gave further insight into the two leaders' differences after reading this chapter: "Mao was essentially a military leader … He mobilized youth … in preparation for dealing with an expansion of the Vietnam war, preparing them politically to serve as soldiers (Red Guards). These measures (combined with Vietnamese resistance and international condemnation) ultimately persuaded Washington to cut a deal with the Chinese and reduce their role in Vietnam ('Vietnamization,' 1972–3). Once this happens, once Kissinger and Nixon have been to China, there's no longer a need for mass youth mobilizing and a transition to civic order and civil society gets underway."

Works Cited

Adichie, C. (2009, July). The danger of a single story. *TED Talk*. Retrieved from www.ted.com/talks/chimamanda_adichie_the_danger_of_a_single_story.html

Chang, J. (2003). *Wild swans: Three daughters of China*. New York, NY: Touchstone.

Cheng, N. (2010). *Life and death in Shanghai*. New York, NY: Grove Press.

Cohen, R. (2010). An interview with Robert Cohen. In D. Turk, R. Mattson, T. Epstein, & R. Cohen (Eds.), *Teaching U.S. history: Dialogues among social studies teachers and historians* (pp. 109–116). New York, NY: Routledge.

Gardner, H. (2011). *Frames of mind: The theory of multiple intelligences.* New York, NY: Basic Books.

Jiang, Ji-Li. (1997). *Red scarf girl: A memoir of the Cultural Revolution.* New York, NY: HarperTrophy.

Landsberger, S. R., Min, A., & Duo D. (2011). *Chinese propaganda posters.* Cologne, Germany: Taschen.

Lifton, R. J. (1961). *Thought reform and the psychology of totalism: A study of "brainwashing" in China.* New York, NY: Norton.

Ma, Bo. (1996). *Blood red sunset: A memoir of the Chinese Cultural Revolution.* New York: Penguin Books.

Mattson, R. (2008). Theater of the assessed: Drama-based pedagogies in the history classroom. *Radical History Review, 102:* 99–110.

McNeil, L. M. (1999). *Contradictions of control: School structure and school knowledge.* New York: Routledge.

Milner, G. (2002). China: Youth and the Cultural Revolution. *Links: International Journal of Socialist Renewal.* Retrieved from http://links.org.au/node/1326

New York State Education Department. (2010–2011). *New York State report card: Accountability and overview report.* Retrieved from https://reportcards.nysed.gov/files/2010–11/AOR-2011–440102060003.pdf

Poughkeepsie Day School. (2012). *Home page.* Retrieved from www.poughkeepsieday.org

Prendiville, F., & Toye, N. (2007). *Speaking and listening through drama, 7–12.* London: Sage Publications.

Williams, S., & Dietz, K. (1994). *China: A century of revolution, Part 2, The Mao years 1949–1976.* United States: Zeitgeist Films. Retrieved from www.youtube.com/watch?v = 0m7YoNlkWzM

Willingham, D.T. (2009). Why don't students like school? *American Educator,* Spring. Retrieved from www.aft.org/pdfs/americaneducator/spring2009/Willingham(2).pdf

CHAPTER RESOURCES

I. Unit Plan: Modern China

Common Core Standards

CCSS.ELA-Literacy.RH.9-10.2 Determine the central ideas or information of a primary or secondary source; provide an accurate summary of how key events or ideas develop over the course of the text.

CCSS.ELA-Literacy.RH.9-10.6 Compare the point of view of two or more authors for how they treat the same or similar topics, including which details they include and emphasize in their respective accounts.

CCSS.ELA-Literacy.WHST.9-10.10 Write routinely over extended time frames (time for reflection and revision) and shorter time frames (a single sitting or a day or two) for a range of discipline-specific tasks, purposes, and audiences.

Essential Questions

- How and why do revolutions happen?
- To whom do they appeal?
- Is a "single story" dangerous?
- Do young people have any power to change things?

Enduring Understandings

Students will understand that:

- While some revolutions begin among ordinary people, the Cultural Revolution was initiated by Chairman Mao.
- Revolutions have multiple causes, including internal power struggles, relations, support, or ideological influences from other countries, and social and economic conditions that harm certain groups.
- Government leaders use propaganda, education, rallies and marches, and other forms of persuasion to convince people of the value of their policies.

- People join revolutions for many reasons, including attraction to certain ideals, desire to gain benefits from participation, fear or pressure to conform, or manipulation by leaders and others.
- Mao's Cultural Revolution emphasized class struggle, while Deng Xiaoping moved the country toward a blend of socialism and a market system.

Culminating Assessment

Create posters that reflect the imagery and concepts promoted by either Mao or Deng. Classmates should identify the period to which the poster corresponds and use sticky notes to comment on their classmates' work in a Gallery Walk activity. Students then respond in writing to one of the essential questions.

Selected Learning Activities

Lesson 1: Is a single story "dangerous"? Why did the Cultural Revolution happen? Why did Mao include youth in his campaign for reform?

- **Activities:** View and discuss Adichie and Cultural Revolutions clip.

Lesson 2: How does language inform, influence, or lead to action? What role did youth play in the Cultural Revolution? How was the revolution presented to people, by whom, and for what purpose?

- **Activities:** "Re-creating the Revolution" through re-enactment of scenes from Red Scarf Girl (1997). Suggested scenes:

   1. "Shops still stank of old culture" (pp. 21–25).
   2. "Tight pants and pointed shoes" (pp. 30–33).
   3. "*Yang-san* [umbrella] is fourolds" (pp. 33–37).
   4. Election of Red Successors (pp. 56–59).
   5. "Reflect on your class origin" (pp. 64–66 or pp. 67–70).
   6. "Burning family pictures" (pp. 122–125).
   7. "Name change" (pp. 211–215).
   8. "Break with family" (pp. 224–227).

Lesson 3: How did leaders in modern China communicate their ideas? How was the language used by Mao and Deng Xiaoping similar and different? What economic, political, and social shifts, if any, did the changes in their language represent? Did their campaigns really change China, and, if so, how?

- **Activities:** Distribute speeches, statements, and posters from the Mao and Deng eras without any identifying information (dates, authors). Ask students to categorize the texts: when do they think they were written? Who wrote them? What stories are these speeches/images telling? Write down words/symbols that illustrate the messages.

Lesson 4: What were the symbols and symbolic practices used by China's leaders? Were they effective? Why is a single story dangerous? To whom did the single stories of Mao and Deng appeal?

- **Activities:** Museum installation of student-made propaganda posters. Have students identify the era which each represents and discuss why. Alternative plan: assign students a "red" or "black" card. Black symbolizes the landlords, rich peasants, counter-revolutionaries, and rightists that Mao was opposed to, while red symbolizes the revolutionary cadres, revolutionary martyrs, revolutionary soldiers, workers, poor and lower middle class peasants. Ask them to list on one side of a sheet of paper those posters that would have struck fear in them, and those that they would have supported. Have them list the symbols or words that appeal or cause fear. Debrief with students.

II. Student Work: Propaganda Poster

Figure 2.1   "MaObey" poster, by Natasha Vega

Three
Latin America

Struggling for Social Democracy: Latin American Visions and Cold War U.S. Resistance

By Diana B. Turk, Laura J. Dull, and Michael R. Stoll, with Brittany Rawson

Framing the Questions: An Interview with Greg Grandin, conducted by Robert Cohen

Greg Grandin is a professor in the Department of History at New York University. He received his Ph.D. from Yale University in 1999. His publications include *Blood of Guatemala: A History of Race and Nation* (2000), for which he received the Latin American Studies Association's Bryce Wood Award; *The Last Colonial Massacre: Latin America During the Cold War* (2004); *Empire's Workshop: Latin America, the United States, and the Rise of the New Empire* (2005); and the critically lauded *Fordlandia: The Rise and Fall of Henry Ford's Forgotten Jungle City* (2009), which was a finalist for the Pulitzer Prize in History, as well as for the National Book Award and the National Book Critics Circle Award. His edited volumes include *A Century of Revolution: Insurgent and Counterinsurgent Violence During Latin America's Long War* (with Gilbert Joseph) (2010) and "The Imperial Presidency: The Legacy of Reagan's Central American Policy" in *Confronting the New Conservatism: The Rise of the Right in America* (Michael Thompson, editor) (2007). He has also published in the *New York Times, Harper's, London Review of Books, The Nation, Boston Review, Los Angeles Times,* and *American Historical Review.* He served as a consultant to the UN truth commission on Guatemala and is the recipient of a number of honors and awards, including the John Simon Guggenheim Memorial Fellowship in 2004.

Robert Cohen: *What do you think are the most common mistakes, misconceptions, or wrongheaded assumptions that North Americans make when they think about Latin America and the Caribbean?*

Greg Grandin: There are two really big ones. One has to do with violence. People look at Latin America and they think, "This place has chronic violence"—and there has been—but I think that they conflate war with internal repression. In terms of the first category, war, Latin America has been a remarkably peaceful continent. At least since the early 1930s, [with] the Chaco War between Bolivia and Paraguay, there hasn't been a major, inter-state war between countries. There've been a few skirmishes here and there, which were consequential, but nothing compared to the violence of Europe. Europe, just in terms of the sheer numbers killed, has been a much more violent continent than Latin America. All of the violence has been internally directed, at social movements. While I think Latin America does have that reputation, I think it's also important to distinguish between the two.

The second has to do with Latin America's contribution to social democracy. Everybody knows Latin America as a place of revolutionaries: from Augusto Sandino in the 1930s to Emiliano Zapata to Che Guevara, it's a region that throws up these kinds of militant revolutionaries, insurgents, Latin American guerillas. There's a conflation of these groups. Mostly unknown is Latin America's contribution to both social democracy and liberal multilateralism. Just in terms of social democracy, Mexico's 1917 constitution was the first fully conceived social democratic charter in the world. It pre-dated India; it pre-dated the European charters. And what I mean by social democracy is protection or guarantees, not just of individual rights—the right to free speech, the right to religion—but social rights to education, to health care, to social security, and the right to unionize.

RC: *That sounds like something that came much later in the U.S., with Franklin Roosevelt's second bill of rights near the end of World War II.*

GG: Yes, right. This was 1917 in Mexico's case. Almost all of the social rights that made it into the UN Declaration on Human Rights come from Latin America. The first international human rights charter is the Organization of American States (OAS) Declaration on the Rights of Man [1948], which attempts to balance these individual rights with welfare, and education, and gender equality.

RC: *So using the Declaration [and] the constitution of Mexico are primary sources that teachers might want to start off with?*

GG: Yes, certainly. Those social rights migrated into every Latin American constitution. It would be unthinkable having a constitution in Latin America that didn't guarantee social rights. Whether it is actually delivered upon and protected—whether the guarantee is actually fulfilled—is another question, but there's just a common-sense notion. I think this is related in a very complicated way, but Latin American jurists at the end of the 19th and beginning of the 20th centuries made significant contributions to what we think of as liberal multilateralism. Basically the very notion of a confederation of nations [like the League of Nations and the UN] that see their interests as aligned and see that the purpose of international diplomacy is cooperation and not real power rivalry, is a Latin American contribution. It was invented by Latin America, which was born into confederation after independence from Spain, in which they affirmed a number of principles: *uto posseditis* ("as you possess"), which becomes the foundation of the liberal international order, tentatively with the League of Nations and then fully with the United Nations.

RC: *You have discussed the way Latin America has a continuing New Deal-like tradition, and the recent shift left there in the last decade or so, while America since the Reagan era has been going off on a politics of hyper-individualism. Latin America continues to model a more egalitarian alternative.*

GG: Yes, and I think that's deep in Latin American political culture. There [are] a lot of intellectual sources of it. There's a Catholic humanism, a kind of French rights tradition, an ongoing power of these collective experiences, whether it be the peasantry or the working class. What I like to say is that for the last 20 or 30 years, social scientists have organized their approach to Latin America around one question: how do you explain the fragility of democracy in Latin America? But I think you have to explain the endurance or persistence [of social democratic ideals and movements]. That's the real historical question: in the face of all of this violence and all this repression against democrats of all stripes, why does that social democratic ideal not dissipate? It continues. And the persistence of that ideal, and of democracy understood not just as individual rights but some kind of social justice.

RC: *What do you think that is? Why do you think it's proved so enduring?*

GG: I think there are a number of different reasons for it. Part of it has to do with the political and religious culture of the region, the Catholic Church, and the revitalization of a certain kind of Thomism and the notion of natural rights and human rights that comes out of the [Spanish] conquest. There's a kind of dialectic in Latin America where the very nature of the [colonial] genocide was just so overwhelming, it provoked and sparked debates over the nature of individual rights and natural law that become the foundation of the human rights movement. I think that there's a certain kind of influence of the French rights tradition that emphasizes more positive rights and the role of the state in creating and cultivating a virtuous society. And, the ongoing power of the peasant class, the peasantry, and the working class—these sources of collective experience allow for a certain kind of solidarity.

Then, also, the big question, the elephant in the room, so to speak, is the United States. You could almost think of the U.S.–Latin American relations over the last 200 years as a kind of imminent critique in which the U.S. and Latin America are fighting to define a shared set of nominally common values—democracy, republicanism, liberalism—but in very distinct ways. The U.S. is this kind of liberal, universalizing empire (for lack of a better word). Yet, often times [there has been] a gap between their actions and their ideals. Latin American nationalists defined themselves in between that gap, or identified that gap, and it allowed them to identify [themselves]. So the more individualistic the U.S. became, the more affirming of some kind of social democracy Latin Americans became.

RC: *I was going to ask you about the key themes in Latin America since 1900. That seems like one of them: this idea of Latin America as being this source of a socially democratic ideal. I wonder, why do you think it is that that's been sort of obscured in U.S. culture? Whether you think about Castro, there's almost such a condescending view, "it's our backyard." I wonder, whether it's a legacy of this Protestant disdain, or condescension toward Catholics …*

GG: I think there's that. There's "the Black legend," in which Anglo-Protestants, even before they arrived in the Americas in the 17th century, defined themselves vis-à-vis Spain, and all that was wrong with Spain. Spain [was seen] as Catholic, superstitious, lethargic, corrupt, brutal, and militaristic, while Anglo-Protestants saw themselves as dynamic, commercial, modern, and forward-looking. Obviously there's a lot of influence there. There are ways in which Cold War social scientists saw it in a very particular way, as almost refracted through the politics of the Cold War. There's a way in which all of those things I've talked about as potential sources of social democracy have also been sources of turmoil. Take the [Latin American]

Right's drive for some kind of restored, organic social unity—intellectual historians in the U.S. tended to see that as a source of authoritarianism and militarism. The Catholic Church has obviously been involved, not just on the progressive side of social movements, but also the reactionary side. A lot of modernization theory and Cold War social science was elaborated vis-à-vis thinking about Latin American populism and the constant mobilization of these social movements and the chronic chaos and conflict that emerged from that. And there are some ways in which Latin America is just taken for granted. It's almost so comfortable that you don't see it.

RC: *I want to ask you a question about chronology. Talk about [historian] E.J. Hobsbawm: He has this concept of a short 20th century that's framed as starting with World War I and then ends with the fall of the Soviet Union. It's very centered on the Long Cold War and based on Europe. I'm wondering if you see that as a frame that is applicable to Latin American history. And how do you think of the 20th and 21st centuries? Do you see those two periods as being different? Do you think that idea of a short 20th century works for Latin America?*

GG: I think it works to some degree. What I tried to do in *A Century of Revolution* is to look at a short 20th century. But I wouldn't start it with the Russian Revolution; I would start with the Mexican Revolution, and then run through the Central American conflicts of the 1980s. I see that as a coherent epoch in which in Latin America by 1910, after close to a century of independence, there was a general sense among modernizing elites that they had to overcome the legacy of colonialism. And what was the legacy of Spanish colonialism? A dependent economy based on one or two or three no-value-added exports of raw materials. A kind of rural clientele-ism that still allowed these pockets of private power to exist, particularly embodied in the landed oligarchy, outside of state control. An exclusionary nationalism that in the 19th century tended to be kind of positivist liberalism. The period of Diaz in Mexico is an example of this. And there was in general widespread consensus by the early 20th century, that that had to be transcended. I would say the Mexican Revolution was the first sustained effort to do that. Every country had different moments and different attempts to overcome that legacy. The Mexican Revolution in the 1910s, populism in the southern cone in Brazil and Argentina and Chile in the 1930s and the 1940s, a much more focused import-substitution program and nationalism in Guatemala and Bolivia in the 1950s, a much more radical New Left that was informed by a much sharper critique of dependency theory in the 1960s and 1970s, and then the crisis in Central America in the 1980s. In each country, all of the countries' experiences of trying to transcend or to overcome that legacy of colonialism were distinct, but they were sequential and so they built off each other. The Cuban Revolution comes out of the experience of these failed nationalist projects in the 1950s and populism in the 1940s.

Then, the next periodization [from the 1980s to 1999] would be this attempt by the U.S. to impose neo-liberalism, the Washington consensus, and not just to open up Latin American countries' economies to U.S. finance and U.S. corporations and do away with that import-substitution model, but also to get Latin American countries to move away from populist direct democracy and adopt more representational forms of democracy, much more like we would think of in the United States. I think that that failed, and that it failed mostly because of the failure of neo-liberalism to deliver the goods. In the heyday of state developmentalism, the cumulative growth between 1960 and 1980 in Latin America was at something like 89% of the GDP in terms of per capita income. It wasn't as impressive as South Korea or Taiwan but it was pretty good. It was enough to create a middle class. Between 1980 and 2000 the per capita growth, using the same statistics, was 7%. It was this enormous failure. Added to this was the fact that financial neo-liberalism creates a much more volatile environment in which these rolling financial crises can destroy accumulated wealth—whether it be in Mexico, Argentina, or Brazil—in the blink of an eye. So what you begin to see around the 1990s, basically with the election of Hugo Chavez in 1998, is the emergence of a new developmentalist class, of new modern, local, national elites, who were trying to get some grip on their economies, and I think that accounts for the return of the Left.

RC: *How would you define neo-liberalism for the teachers, in terms of what was going on in the 1990s?*

GG: Neo-liberalism is a term that everyone else in the world knows, except the United States. The way that I like to talk about it is "Reaganism on steroids"—that Reagan represented this attempt by the New Right in the U.S. to respond to the multiple crises of the 1970s, particularly the economic crisis of New Deal Keynesianism, by basically de-industrialization, banking everything on finance capital. Substituting debt for high wages, breaking unions, and then managing to keep consumerism going through an extension of debt and credit rather than high wages, and the rollback of the state in order to jumpstart a lethargic economy. What you saw in Latin America was that times 10. Latin American countries came out of the Cold War—and even before the end of the Cold War—deeply indebted. And that debt was a kind of leverage that the IMF [International Monetary Fund] used in order to enforce what in Latin America was called "structural adjustment," which was basically an opening up of their economies. In the 1970s you saw a lot of countries engage in quite a bit of nationalization, as a way of creating and nurturing national industrialization. What you saw in the 1980s was a complete rollback of that. In exchange for restructuring loans, the IMF insisted that countries privatize their national industries, remove subsidies, remove tariffs, weaken labor protection, and roll back state services, and then open up their currencies to bond trading houses in the United States. So it really was like Reaganism times 10 in Latin America. It was a complete disaster. Its success was basically predicated on creating an urban consumer class that anchors the whole project. Except in a few very key places—Mexico City, Sao Paulo, Santiago, Chile—that didn't happen. What it did was basically disrupt the local agricultural markets and push people into the cities, or in the case of Mexico, migrants north. It just created this very volatile political situation.

RC: *Why do you think that in the last few decades America has been shifting to the Right while Latin America has been shifting to the Left?*

GG: Well, I just think it is what we've talked about: the failure of neo-liberalism and the emergence of a new political class. In some countries, that class, like Venezuela and Bolivia and Ecuador, emerges out of the complete collapse of the old order that was very much tied to this neo-liberal model. In countries like Brazil, where there wasn't a complete collapse, you saw the consolidation of a social democratic Left that offered both a better, more equitable distribution of resources to the poor and a way of advancing the interests of a national elite, which didn't find its interests being advanced under the neo-liberal model. So you see that at least—and it's all, obviously, relative—but part of what passes for the Left in Latin America means breaking out of the United States as being the only game in town; instead, promoting a diversification of sources of capital, of sources of credit, markets, promoting integration among Latin American countries.

That all falls under the rubric of the Left in Latin America. In the U.S., I think, it's a much more complicated answer of why there's been a move to the Right.

RC: *If you were to take a biographical approach to 20th century Latin America, who do you think would be good for teachers to focus upon?*

GG: Well, I mean I have a few idiosyncratic ones, but I guess the most useful in the early 20th century would be somebody like Augusto Sandino in Nicaragua. He, in some ways, was this home-grown, organic insurgent in Nicaragua who forced the U.S. Marines to withdraw, and forced the U.S. to rethink its militarism. He wasn't the only one, but certainly [pointed out] the disaster of these sequential occupations in Nicaragua, Dominican Republic, Haiti, and other places in Central America and the Caribbean. [Y]ou could think of it as the equivalent of the Middle East today: a place where sequential military interventions didn't pacify the region, but instead led to certain radiuses of radicalization throughout Latin America. That forced the New Deal to rethink how the U.S. could best project its power, in terms of the "good neighbor" policy … I think José Martíne, in Cuba, is somebody who very much charted out the distinctions between the U.S. and Latin America, in terms of race, in terms of democracy. Later on, in the 20th century, people like Salvador Allende in Chile: trying to steer a middle ground between the Soviet Union and the United States and believing you can draw on Chile's deep democratic traditions to advance a kind of democratic socialism would be also an interesting person.

RC: *And are there any writers, or cultural figures you think that would be really important for teachers?*

GG: Rigoberta Menchú was a Nobel Peace Prize winner for her biography, *I, Rigoberta Menchú,* which was published in the early 1980s. Menchú was born a poor, indigenous Mayan woman in the highlands of Guatemala. And her family got caught up in the violence of the civil war. They were peasant activists; they were involved in liberation theology organizations. Her family got really, really active, and then they were all killed by the military except for her; she went into exile. She gave a series of interviews that became *I, Rigoberta Menchú,* which, all of a sudden, took off. It developed a life of its own. It was both a memoir of what was going on in Guatemala but then got caught up … as a kind of emblematic book of multiculturalism. In the late 1990s she was singled out by an anthropologist [David Stoll] who, after a 10-year investigation into her life story, found that some of the things in her book weren't quite true, and that led to a widespread discrediting of her work. And [people on] the Right, like David Horowitz, seized on it—while there are a lot of different ways of thinking about it, there's nothing in that book that are out-and-out fabrications. You know, in some ways she stretched the truth, she combines certain experiences, she telegraphed certain experiences. But it came under much greater scrutiny than other books—you know, Henry Kissinger wrote a book that won a Nobel Peace Prize, and I'm sure nobody has subjected his memoirs to such a fine-toothed examination. I think there's something about the reaction to her, her book that says something about the way violence in the Third World is understood. What the anthropologist who went after her tried to do was not so much to discredit her but to discredit the larger narrative that she was putting forth, that the violence was an inevitable outgrowth of social exploitation. And his argument was that the violence was instead a reaction to Menchú and others' romanticism of a Cuban revolutionary-inspired Left. And I think there's a way in which that trope maps onto different ways of discrediting social movements.

RC: *Because your books on Latin American history raise such key themes that teachers can focus on, I'd like to discuss these. For example, in* Empire's Workshop, *what are some of the main arguments that you make? What do you think are some of the key themes of the 20th century—and 21st century too—in Latin America that we should be thinking about?*

GG: The thing about Latin American history is the U.S. actions in Latin America have just been so egregious—supporting the coups, interventions, and assassinations, in which the consequences were so overwhelmingly disastrous. One example is the U.S. support of a coup in Guatemala in 1954 against reformist social democrats kicks off more than three decades of intense political violence that leads to genocide with 200,000 dead. It's so overwhelmingly outrageous and morally bankrupt that there's a way in which Latin America dumbs down thought. Because it doesn't force you to think about the actual importance of Latin America in terms of politics, in terms of culture, in terms of ideas, to the United States. So what I tried to do in *Empire's Workshop* was [to] think about Latin America's contribution to U.S. domestic politics. Part of the idea for it came out in the run-up to the war in Iraq, developed during the invasion of Iraq, when we had a teach-in here at NYU [New York University]. I gave a five-minute talk on why so many members of the George Bush administration seemed to be old Iran-Contra hands: Elliot Abrams, John Negraponte, Otto Reich. There was this whole slew of Iran-Contra luminaries. And from that short little talk I began to work out a larger argument about the role of Latin America in the formation of the U.S.'s governing political coalitions. And so the argument of *Empire's Workshop* is that the two great governing political coalitions of the 20th century—the New Deal and the New Right—largely worked out their ideas and strategies and developed and deepened the relations and alliances between their constituencies in Latin America. It was the New Deal that through the Good Neighbor policy basically developed the idea of liberal multilateralism, and early on I talked about Latin America's contribution to that idea. The big, bedrock, fundamental principle of liberal multilateralism is recognition of the absolute sovereignty of individual nations, and the creation of these elite confederations of nations, whether it be the League of Nations or the United Nations. Both of those largely came out of Latin America. The U.S. had long resisted that, until it really had no other option because of the Great Depression.

When that [New Deal] coalition reaches its exhaustion and falls apart in the 1970s, the New Right turns again to Latin America. And this explains why so many of the politicians and officials of the Bush administration had come out of Iran-Contra. Under Reagan, Central America largely becomes the crucible that brings together the New Right. And this is why Iran-Contra is not just a conspiracy and is not just a crime—although it was those two things. It was also a coming-out, the framework that brought together the two main constituencies of the New Right: the intellectual neo-conservatives who gave this new militarism its intellectual and legal justification, and the Religious Right, which gives the new militarism its grassroots force and power and energy. It was Central America that deepened this alliance between the neo-cons and the Religious Right. It was Central America that also brought together other minor players within the new coalition: radicalized Vietnam vets, but radicalized to the Right, people like Oliver North, as well as other kinds of militarists and soldier of fortune mercenaries. It was liberation theology, the major intellectual organizing force of the Central American revolutionaries, that became the first political religion that unites the New Right in terms of figuring out how to roll it back. It was also in Central America that the Republican Party doesn't just rehabilitate militarism and project it into the Third World; it re-moralizes that militarism. So that's what I mean by the title, *Empire's Workshop*: there's a way in which Latin America becomes key in the formation of the ideas, the tactics, and the constituencies of governing coalitions [in the U.S.].

RC: *Let's talk a bit about what you were writing about in* The Last Colonial Massacre.

GG: Well, *The Last Colonial Massacre* was a book that came out of research that I was doing when I worked with the Guatemala truth commission. Basically I was an historical advisor. And I wanted to write a book that looked at the relationship of the overthrow in 1954 to the unfolding of the war and to the violence that comes. And how the experience of the land reform in the communities of Guatemala, how they experienced 1954 and then the violence of the 1960s, 1970s, and 1980s. But increasingly, I focused on this one area that had a massacre in 1978, the Panzós massacre, [which] in many ways [was] a turning point in the war. And the massacre itself corresponded to all the forms of violence: it was carried out by the local elites, over a local grievance. The massacres of the 1980s were much more centrally directed by a nationalized counter-insurgent military. And what I found was almost a hidden history of the Communist Party in this one region that stretched back to the 1920s. So *The Last Colonial Massacre* is a book that looks at peasant organizing in these Mayan communities that eventually rise to become the basis of the Communist Party. And then, after the overthrow of Arbenz [the Guatemalan president], the Communist Party goes underground and continues to work. And what's interesting about it is that's not really the history of the Left that one gets when you study the history of Guatemala. When you study the history of the Left and the insurgency of Guatemala in the *I, Rigoberta Menchú* book, it tends to focus on the New Left, these new insurgencies in the 1970s—new guerilla organizations in the 1970s and the 1980s that were involved in interesting consciousness-raising and liberation theology. But there was this one area, leading up to this Panzós Massacre, where the Old Left, the Communist Party, still was very much influential. Part of that had to do with just the strength of the landed class in this region, which didn't allow any other kind of open political organization to take place. And I tried to use that book as a case study to make a broader argument about the Cold War and the importance of Guatemala in the unfolding of the Cold War. I wrote it right after 9/11, and I was trying to make an argument about the importance of militancy and militant political action in actually advancing democracy and actually advancing the liberalization of society. A lot of the kind of "pop isolationist theory" that emerged after 9/11 tended to draw an equation between political militancy and terror. So I was just trying to turn the tables around and look at how terror in Guatemala was actually an effect of a certain kind of democratic reform linked to neo-liberalism and the like. It was an interesting book to write; it was a very close study, on-the-ground study, of three, four generations of peasant organizing in this one area.

RC: *That brings up one of the things that's interesting about Guatemala. How something that was, almost, such a disaster, yet was viewed as such a success by the United States.*

GG: Yes. Eisenhower, how they turned Guatemala into a "showcase of democracy" with the overthrow in 1954 of Arbenz, this was consequential for a number of reasons. It was the CIA's first fully elaborated coup in which it mobilized all different aspects of the U.S. foreign policy to destabilize the country. The CIA was involved in the overthrow of Mossadegh in Iran the year before, but, you know, that was a very quick thing, and worked largely with the British. Guatemala was almost a year-long operation that drew from pop psychology and sociology in order to destabilize the country, for example, with, fake rumors and fake radio reports. It radicalized a whole generation of people, including Che Guevara, who was in Guatemala ministering as a socially aware doctor … And he has these great letters home; he talks about democracy in the air, and how you can breathe it in. And then, increasingly, he sees the manipulation of the institutions of political pluralism by the CIA. And he flees to Mexico after the coup. And that's where he meets Fidel Castro, and he becomes involved in the Cuban Revolution. And he repeatedly invokes Guatemala to justify the closing down of civil society in Cuba: "Cuba will not be Guatemala," he liked to say. The CIA, for its part, mis-recognized its own success in Guatemala. And the overthrow of Arbenz in 1954 becomes a model for the Bay of Pigs, which was a disaster, in Cuba. And that leads to further radicalization of the Left in Latin America. So you can see Guatemala as this very history-heavy moment that has ongoing repercussions.

RC: *Last question: why do you think that studying Latin America is important for people in the U.S.?*

GG: I think that Latin America has played an unacknowledged influential role in the creation of the United States in all sorts of ways. It's so important it's almost ignored. There's a weird psychological repression about it where it's so taken for granted, there's no need to actually talk about it. It's the region where economic elites first ventured abroad to link a certain form of Protestant capitalism with social reform, a linkage that continues to shape the way people tend to think about the world and how to bring about democratic reform elsewhere. Latin America is the place where the U.S. works out its legal and militaristic strategies. It's key in the formation of every political coalition that comes to power in the U.S. going back to James Monroe, to the Jacksonian period, to 1898, to the New Deal, to the New Right. It's deeply embedded in U.S. history. I think people need to learn how to talk about it and think about it beyond just [being] the place where the U.S. intervenes with less than fortunate outcomes.

Works Cited

Grandin, G. (2004). *The last colonial massacre: Latin America in the Cold War.* Chicago: University of Chicago Press.

Grandin, G. (2006). *Empire's workshop: Latin America, the United States, and the rise of the new imperialism.* New York, NY: Metropolitan Books.

Grandin, G., & Joseph, G. M. (Eds.) (2010). *A century of revolution: Insurgent and counterinsurgent violence during Latin America's long cold war.* Durham, NC: Duke University Press.

Menchú, R. (2010). *I, Rigoberta Menchú: An Indian woman in Guatamala.* London: Verso.

Stoll, D. (2007). *Rigoberta Menchú and the story of all poor Guatamalans.* Boulder, CO: Westview Press.

Essay: Struggling for Social Democracy: Latin American Visions and Cold War U.S. Resistance

By Diana B. Turk, Laura J. Dull, and Michael R. Stoll, with Brittany Rawson

It seems to me that Guatemala is going to be a source of Red infection throughout Central America, and the sooner we sterilize that source, the better.
(Senator Alexander Wiley of Wisconsin, 1954)

[W]e will, or we ought to be, committed to the principle that every sovereign nation has a right to determine for itself its own form of government.
(Senator William Langer of North Dakota, the sole dissenting vote on a resolution to interfere in Guatemala, 1954)

Our crime is our patriotic wish to advance, to progress, to win economic independence to match our political independence. We are condemned because we have given our peasant population land and rights.
(Jacobo Arbenz, just before a CIA-backed coup in 1954)

Support for military forces and intelligence units which engaged in violence and widespread repression was wrong and the United States must not repeat that mistake.

(President Clinton on the Arbenz coup, 1999)[1]

Many global and internal conflicts of the past century have been justified by the aggressor as either protecting or attacking a particular economic or political system. These campaigns are often portrayed as a fight between extremes: democracy versus totalitarianism, capitalism versus communism, imperialists versus anti-imperialists. As in all dichotomies, however, these stark contrasts mask complexities such as contradictory or overlapping practices (the U.S. government provides tax breaks for corporations, putting the lie to the notion of "free" markets), misleading claims (North Korea calls itself democratic), and variations among the systems (social democracy in Chile or one-party socialism in Cuba). Moreover, these polarizing words are often used to cover up other motivations for intervention or war, as when the U.S. supported the overthrow of Jacobo Arbenz in Guatemala in part to protect the powerful United Fruit Company. This is just one example of the many times that the U.S. government has assisted elite groups in purportedly anti-communist campaigns against peasants, Indians, and other disenfranchised groups in Latin America and the Caribbean (Saunders, 2007). In order for students to understand recent global history, they must enter this ideologically charged battleground and sort out the meanings of words like "communism" or "democracy," as well as recognize when and how these words themselves are used as weapons. In this unit on Latin American history, we asked students to do just this: to examine democracy and its variants in Latin America as a way of understanding the important role of this region in shaping global visions of government, equality, and justice.

It is no secret that the global history curriculum for secondary students is generously tipped toward Europe. Textbooks and curricula usually relegate Latin America to a few dishonorable mentions, mostly involving those instances in which the region has direct contact with Europe or the United States. The classical and post-classical Mesoamerican Empires, for example, are often footnotes in a study of the Age of Exploration in Europe. Typically, students spend a few days learning about the Incas, Mayans, and Aztecs before the focus shifts to the fall of these civilizations and then Latin America's role as colonial outpost for the European empires. Similarly, during two great periods of upheaval in Latin American history, the Bolivarian Revolutions of the early 19th century and the social revolutions of the 20th century, these regions are presented as oligarchic and prone to violence, settling for corrupted versions of Western political ideology, or in dire need of assistance from the West. Inevitably, simplistic explanations and curricular biases leave many secondary social studies students with unsophisticated understandings of recent Latin American history and the struggles over social democracy waged there.

Historical scholarship presents a very different view of Latin America and undermines some of the misconceptions and silences about the region and its historical figures in U.S. textbooks and curricula. Greg Grandin, the historian whose interview served as the basis for this chapter, challenges the idea that Latin America is characterized by "chronic violence," noting that in the past century, countries there have experienced less inter-state war, and fewer people killed, than those in Europe. Indeed, the violence in Latin America has tended to be directed at internal social movements and perpetrated by counterinsurgents often trained and supported by the Central Intelligence Agency (CIA): after 1958, "every Latin American military establishment except Cuba's received assistance from the United States, with the most repressive among them receiving the largest allocations" (Joseph, 2010, p. 405; see also Grandin, 2010, pp. 3–4). Grandin and other scholars also complicate the image of Latin American social movements as communist and therefore deeply dangerous to the U.S. and democracy. After World War II, the rise of anti-communism as a "global ideology capable of absorbing isolated local conflicts and projecting them into an international movement" provided justification for U.S. containment efforts in Latin America that often polarized conflicts there and narrowed the grounds for compromise (Grandin, 2010, p. 25). But it is misleading to label all the multiple efforts to overcome Latin America's colonial legacy of "inequitable and stunted development" as communist insurgencies (Joseph, 2010, p. 400). As Grandin (2004) explains, the Cold War in Latin America was not just about the "competing utopias" of communism and capitalism; rather, it was a clash over what democracy and "social citizenship" meant and the shapes they would take (p. 17). In fact, while there are variants of Marxism as in Cuba, Latin Americans made an early commitment to social democracy, reflected in Mexico's 1917 constitution that pre-dates those of Western Europe. Moreover, Grandin noted in the interview that "almost all of the rights that made it into the UN Declaration of Human Rights" came from Latin America and the Organization of American States (OAS) Declaration on the Rights and Duties of Man written in 1948.

Given that the concepts of "socialism" and "communism" still resonate in American political discourse as threats to freedom, the social studies educators and teacher involved in this chapter chose to focus their lessons on helping students untangle the meanings of political ideas deployed by diverse actors in recent Latin American history. The resulting unit involved students in comparing the Mexican constitution with the U.S. constitution and the French Declaration of the Rights of Man, to learn the multiple ways that democracy is defined in these documents; reading excerpts from Rigoberta Menchú's (2010) memoir to learn the causes and conditions of Guatemala's decades-long civil war; and complicating the anti-communist narrative of a newsreel about then-Vice President Nixon's visit to Caracas, Venezuela in 1958 by examining contemporary news sources and declassified government documents. These activities required students to reflect on what democracy means to them, to analyze the historical context for the beliefs of revolutionary groups, and to explain the ways in which social democracy in Latin America can offer a fundamental contrast to liberal democracy found in countries such as the United States. In addition, in learning how the U.S., allied with conservative and business elements in Latin America, framed leftist movements as "communist" in order to support interventions in Guatemala, Venezuela, and elsewhere, students encountered an historical context for ideological arguments at the heart of current political debates such as those over government-supported healthcare or "Obamacare" (e.g., Salsman, 2012) in the United States.

Social Democracy in Latin America

With the goal of designing an approach to teaching Latin America that would inspire youth to question traditional narratives about the past, our group turned to Greg Grandin, a professor of Latin American history at New York University. In addition to the interview he provided for this project, Grandin also shared recent scholarship (2004; 2006; 2010) and teaching materials on Latin America (n.d.). In his work on social movements, human rights, and U.S. foreign policy, Grandin argues for a re-envisioning of Latin America as the site of crucial debates about the meaning of democracy. To scholars of the region who have been preoccupied by "the fragility of democracy in Latin America," Grandin says:

> I think you have to explain the endurance or persistence [of social democratic ideals and movements]. That's the real historical question. That in the face of all of this violence and all this repression against democrats of all stripes, why does

that social democratic ideal not dissipate? It continues. And the persistence of that ideal, and of democracy understood not just as individual rights but some kind of social justice.

Central to Grandin's approach, then, is an examination of Latin America's contribution to social democracy, which he defined in his interview as the "protection or guarantees, not just of individual rights—the right to free speech, the right to religion—but social rights to education, to health care, to social security, and the right to unionize." As he noted, it would be "unthinkable having a constitution in Latin America that didn't guarantee social rights. Whether it is actually delivered upon and protected, whether the guarantee is actually fulfilled, is another question, but there's just a common-sense notion" of the importance of social as well as individual rights. In the U.S., by contrast, there are no social guarantees in our constitution, and America is "exceptional" among industrialized nations in that it lacks a strong labor or socialist party (Lipset, 1996). In addition, as a result of its emphasis on state services, Latin American democracy tends to be populist and direct, very different from the representative government more familiar to American students. This tension between forms of democracy has played a significant role in U.S./Latin American relations, especially during the Cold War, when U.S. interventions into Latin American politics were, according to Grandin, "overwhelmingly disastrous" and "egregious." In particular, Grandin pointed to the U.S. government's "morally bankrupt" support of a 1954 coup in Guatemala, in which the reformist, social democratic government of Jacobo Arbenz was overthrown in favor of a military dictatorship. This action represented "the CIA's first fully elaborated coup in which it mobilized all different aspects of U.S. foreign policy to destabilize a country" in order, allegedly, to "save" Guatemala from a perceived communist threat. For the most part, this intervention had the opposite effect of that claimed by the U.S., contributing to greater ideological conflict between the U.S. and Latin America and "radicalizing a whole generation of people," including Ernesto "Che" Guevara and Fidel Castro. The United States followed a similar pattern of supporting anti-democratic regimes in other countries in the region between the 1950s and 1990s, as in the Iran-Contra Affair in Nicaragua and President Ronald Reagan administration's support of Jean-Claude "Baby Doc" Duvalier in Haiti (see, for example, LaFeber, 1993).

U.S. willingness to support any efforts aimed at countering alleged communism helped Latin American elites justify and maintain their hold on power over the land and labor of marginalized populations like peasants, Indians, and workers through the use of terror, "disappearing" of opponents, and, in Guatemala, genocide (Grandin, 2011). In the words of the United Nations Commission for Historical Clarification, convened to investigate Guatemala's war,

> The state relied on the concept of an internal enemy to deliberately exaggerate the military threat of the insurgency. The inclusion of all opponents—whether pacifist or guerrilla, legal or illegal, communist or non-communist—under one label justified multiple and serious criminal acts [on the part of the state].
>
> (Grandin, 2011, p. 146)

Given this history of using particular words to heighten people's fears or mislead followers, it is no wonder that students and citizens struggle to differentiate among the wide varieties of political and economic systems in the world: communism in its ideal forms versus its devolution into dictatorships under Stalin and Castro; democracy linked to free market capitalism in the U.S. versus its social democratic variations in Western Europe and Brazil; and so on.

Grandin challenges educators and citizens to see the beliefs of Latin American revolutionaries and counter-revolutionaries as representing particular visions of democracy and the role of the state therein, created in dialogue with U.S. ideals and realities:

> You could almost think of the U.S.–Latin American relations over the last 200 years as a kind of imminent critique in which the U.S. and Latin America are fighting to define a shared set of nominally common values—democracy, republicanism, liberalism—but in very distinct ways. The U.S. is this kind of liberal, universalizing empire (for lack of a better word). Yet, often times [there has been] a gap between their actions and their ideals. Latin American nationalists defined themselves in between that gap, or identified that gap, and it allowed them to identify [themselves]. So the more individualistic the U.S. became, the more affirming of some kind of social democracy Latin Americans became.

This focus helps us to think about Latin America "beyond [being] just the place where the U.S. intervenes with less than fortunate outcomes," but rather as a pivotal site in the struggle over what democracy can be. Indeed, as a source for potentially more just alternatives than our current system marked by rising social inequality and poverty (Popper, 2011), there are rich avenues to explore with students in teaching about the recent history of Latin America.

Teaching Latin America—The "Forgotten" Region

Our first efforts at creating and teaching a unit on Latin America did not yield the kind of results we sought. We therefore decided to start over and form a new group to conceptualize and plan a different teaching unit. Our discussions centered on Grandin's argument that the Cold War in Latin America represented a clash over what "democracy" and "social citizenship" meant and the shapes they would take (Grandin, 2004, p. 17). We thus decided in this unit to explore the parameters of social democracy in Latin America, tracing its roots from the Mexican Constitution of 1917, through Guatemala's struggles over conceptions of democracy in the 1950s and subsequent decades, to the protests that met then-Vice President Nixon when he visited Caracas, Venezuela in 1958. For the culminating assignment of the unit, we designed a project that would require students to use the high-level historical-reasoning skill of perspective-taking (Davis, Yeager & Foster, 2001; Kohlmeier, 2006; Lee & Ashby, 2001; VanSledright, 2004, 2010; Wineburg, 2001) by putting themselves into the historical and cultural context of Latin America in the 1950s and rewriting the audio portion of a 1958 American newsreel from the perspective of either a Guatemalan or Venezuelan citizen.

Following a backwards planning model (Wiggins & McTighe, 2005), our group chose the following enduring understandings for students to gain from the unit (Chapter Resources I):

- The Mexican Constitution lays out a vision for democracy that is at odds in many ways with the version of democracy on which the United States was founded.
- The U.S. government and its people have often misunderstood the different ways citizens of Latin American countries have conceptualized "rights" and "freedoms," and there have been deep ramifications to these misunderstandings of social democracy in Latin America.
- Citizens of Latin American countries have paid an enormous price for supporting models of democracy that, while often more communal and more egalitarian than other forms of democracy, have differed from the model both practiced and promoted by the United States.

- Understanding the worldviews and meanings citizens of particular countries assigned to their everyday experiences requires a particular mindset that enables one to both step outside of one's own worldview and also take on the perspective of other historical characters, in a complex process called perspective-taking.

We then identified the following essential questions as useful ways to organize student learning through the unit:

- How does social democracy differ from individualist democracy?
- To what extent is one form of democracy more "pure" than the other?
- In what ways is social democracy similar to and different from communism?
- How and with what implications has the United States misunderstood social democracy, interpreting it as communism, in Latin America?
- How can students develop a sense of historical perspective-taking through a study of the ways citizens of different countries have conceptualized "rights" and "freedoms"?

Because our decision to rewrite the unit for Latin America came late in the school year, the planning group for this chapter ultimately included just one teacher, Brittany Rawson, who was teaching tenth grade global history at an urban high school in Brooklyn, NY. The group also included three social studies educators, Diana Turk of New York University, Laura Dull of the State University of New York at New Paltz, and Michael Stoll of William Jewell College, Liberty, Missouri. The unit on Latin America spanned six days of classes taught over two weeks, with either Diana or Laura observing and assisting Brittany in her classroom during many of the lessons. The time allotted for the unit was cut short by the end-of-year New York State Regents exams; in future teaching opportunities, we would wish for a seventh and perhaps an eighth day to do full justice to the learning experiences addressed in the following lessons.

"Social Democracy" in Latin America: Another Take on Democracy or Another Term for Communism?

Brittany Rawson taught tenth grade global history at the Dr. Susan S. McKinney Secondary School for the Arts in Brooklyn, NY. A white/Native American teacher who previously taught in another underprivileged setting not unlike her current school, Brittany was in her first year on the staff at McKinney, where she was responsible for teaching all global history classes to the nearly 90 sophomores enrolled in the school. McKinney is an under-resourced school with a largely black and Latino population; 71% of its students qualify for free or reduced lunch (Inside Schools, 2013). Brittany estimated that most of her students read several grade levels below their tenth grade placement. Based on their in-class performance and previous records of achievement, she projected that fewer than half would pass the state history tests required for graduation the first time they would take them.

Brittany exuded an easygoing yet commanding manner that enabled her to manage adeptly the challenges of teaching in this difficult setting, which included students who rarely came to class or who came very late, disrupting the flow of activities and requiring her to catch them up and integrate them into the discussion; audiovisual equipment that did not always work or that worked poorly; or an air conditioner that, when it worked, created so much noise it was hard to hear anything else over its hum. Brittany's passion for teaching history showed clearly, her voice rising with excitement and enthusiasm as she talked to the class, and her students—all of them minorities—responded to her with openness and appreciation. When she told them on one hot June day that she was going to steal an extra class session with them away from their Spanish teacher who should usually have them for a particular period on a Wednesday, they responded with pleasure. The students appeared happy to learn from the young Caucasian-looking woman with horn-rimmed glasses who dressed in slacks and flowered cardigans and wore her hair in a bun.

Drawing from Grandin's discussion about the central place social democracy has played in Latin American culture and recent history, we began the unit by introducing the students to the concept of social democracy and the ways that it both overlaps with and differs from communism and from other types of democracy, particularly the more individualist, market-driven form prevalent in the United States. Brittany's class had recently finished a unit on the French Declaration of the Rights of Man (1789), so she started the unit by juxtaposing that document, along with the U.S. Bill of Rights, against the Mexican Constitution of 1917. Brittany began the class by having the students define "communism" and "democracy," prompting them to recall previous learning on the different ways countries have chosen to organize their economic and political systems. Next, she led the class to recall their understandings of what communism looked like in the Soviet Union and the ways that an egalitarian economic system had morphed into a repressive regime, especially under Stalin. It was important, she felt, that students understand from the start how much could be at stake for individuals and communities under different political and economic structures.

Next, Brittany led the students through a document analysis activity, during which students rotated among five different stations, at each station analyzing excerpts from one of the three founding documents—the Mexican Constitution, the French Declaration of the Rights of Man, and the U.S. Bill of Rights. Using a grid to organize their analyses, the students determined which country the document was from, what arguments each excerpt was making, and the rights that were being protected in the excerpts they had read. For example, from the Mexican Constitution, the students examined the sections spelling out the State's obligation to

> contribute to better human relationships … together with respect for the dignity of the person and the integrity of the family, the conviction of the general interest of society, but also by the care which it devotes to the ideals of brotherhood and equality of rights of all.
>
> (Article 3)

and also the sections guaranteeing that minimum wages for all workers "be sufficient to satisfy the normal material, social, and cultural needs of the head of a family and to provide for the compulsory education of his children" and that farm workers should be entitled to "a minimum wage adequate to their needs" (Article 7). In addition, they examined sections of Article 7 that called for regular working hours, paid overtime, and the furnishing of "comfortable and hygienic living quarters" by employers for their employees.

From the Declaration of the Rights of Man, the students parsed through the fourth principle, focusing on the tenet that noted,

> Liberty consists in the freedom to do everything which injures no one else; hence, the exercise of the natural rights of each man has no limits except those which assure to the other members of the society the enjoyment of the same rights.

From the U.S. Bill of Rights, the students analyzed the first five amendments, namely: the right to free speech, the right to bear arms, the right not to have soldiers quartered in homes during peacetime, the right to avoid unreasonable searches and seizures, and finally, the right of the individual not to be compelled to serve as a witness against him- or herself.

Once the students had read and analyzed the three documents, Brittany then asked them to compare the different forms of government represented by each nation's founding documents. Drawing from what they saw as the rights outlined in the excerpts provided, the class arrived at definitions of two distinct forms of democracy: individualist democracy (France and the United States) and social democracy (Mexico). They then responded to a writing prompt that asked them to consider the ways that the latter was, in their view, similar to and different from communism. This complicated question pushed them to analyze critically the type of individualist democracy practiced in the United States and to realize that there were alternative forms of government that, while still democratic, had some facets in common with communism—for example, concern for the community and not just the individual.

Day Two of the unit began with reinforcement of the concepts addressed the day before. Brittany posed the essential question for the day, "Is social democracy communism?" and then broke it down to help the students make sense of their learning from the previous day: "How is social democracy similar to communism?" she asked. "How is social democracy different from Soviet-style communism?" Urging students to compare and contrast the rights of the 1917 Mexican Constitution with those addressed in the French Declaration of the Rights of Man and the U.S. Bill of Rights, Brittany generated a list on the board of the different rights that each founding document granted in the three nations and then asked students to consider how each overlapped with or differed from communism. For similarities between communism and social democracy, the students called out, "government involvement," "welfare system," "safety net," "minimum wage." For differences between the two, students offered, "social democracy has more individual rights such as freedom of speech," "it protects the community's rights but people still get to decide their own government," and "people still get to bear arms and have free speech in a social democracy, but they didn't in the Soviet Union." Brittany charted the students' responses, and the students took notes on their class handout (Chapter Resources II).

Once confident that the students understood how the three nations could conceptualize democracy so differently, Brittany offered the class an overview of Guatemala, showing where it was on the map and providing a brief explanation about its agriculture and its political structure leading up to the 1950s. She explained that by the 1950s, the United Fruit Company (later renamed the Chiquita Company) owned nearly half of the farmland in the nation and relied on Guatemalan products to satisfy the booming U.S. fruit market. When President Jacobo Arbenz Guzman, a liberal reformer elected in 1950, instituted land redistribution policies that favored the large peasant population but threatened the monopoly of United Fruit, the United States grew concerned, both because an American company was being threatened but also because the land redistribution policies looked to some, at least on the surface, suspiciously like communism. Brittany reminded the students about the international struggle then taking place between the capitalist United States and the communist Soviet Union. When she pointed out Guatemala's close proximity to the U.S. on the map, the students began to recognize why the United States would worry about a nation they perceived as being infiltrated by communists lying so close to U.S. borders. Brittany then explained how the CIA, fearful of Arbenz's motives, began to step up its engagement in Guatemalan affairs throughout the early 1950s, covertly orchestrating a coup d'état that overthrew Arbenz and installed the military leader Colonel Carlos Castillo Armas in 1954.

Brittany then gave a brief overview of events in Guatemala over the next several decades, including President Ronald Reagan's support in the 1980s of the military leader, General

Efrain Rios Montt, who in May, 2013 was convicted of genocide by an international court based on the mass violence he inflicted on the Mayan Indians and other native groups in Guatemala. Brittany then posed the question, "How much did the United States understand what was going on in Guatemala?" Cautioning the students that the material they would read next might be difficult and potentially upsetting, she turned the class's attention to the day's readings. *I, Rigoberta Menchú: An Indian Woman in Guatemala* (2010) is a "testimony" given by a Guatemalan peasant in the form of an oral history to the anthropologist Elisabeth Burgos-Debray. It was published in Spanish in 1983 and translated into English in 1984. Although much controversy surrounds Menchú's story in the wake of a study conducted by anthropologist David Stoll (1999), who found inconsistencies in her testimony when he dug further into her history, few argue with the notion that, as Greg Grandin argues in his book on Menchú, the narrative provides an accurate account of the brutality of the civil war in Guatemala (see Grandin, 2011).

In class, Brittany shared excerpts of *I, Rigoberta Menchú,* providing paragraph chunks of the text to her students on a left-hand column of the page and guiding questions, designed to help the class of largely struggling readers to make sense of the passages, on the right-hand side of the page (Chapter Resources II). The excerpts began benignly enough: "My name is Rigoberta Menchú. I am twenty-three years old. This is my testimony," but they continue into explanations of the social and cultural structures of the indigenous Guatemalan community to which Menchú belonged and then into graphic accounts of torture that her brothers faced in the hands of the death squads designed to hunt down those whom the government deemed a "bad influence" on the rest of the population. "At the beginning everybody works communally, clearing the bush in the mountains," Menchú recounted of her Guatemalan village.

> We work together: the women pulling out the small plants below and the men cutting down trees on the mountainside. When sowing time comes, the community meets to discuss how to share out the land—whether each one will have his own plot or if they will work collectively. Everyone joins the discussion. In my village, for example, we said it was up to all of us if we wanted our own plot or not. But we also decided to keep a common piece of land, shared by the whole community, so that if anyone was ill or injured, they would have food to eat.
>
> (2010, p. 64)

This communal way of life and the collective ways the villagers made decisions, especially regarding land usage, drew the attention of the military dictatorship then in power in Guatemala. By 1979, they had accused her family of being communists and of inciting rebellion among others in their village. In brutal detail, Menchú described the torture her younger brother faced in the hands of the Guatemalan military (see pp. 203–204). The students gasped in horror as they read the passages, some of them clutching their own bodies in protection, as one of their peers read aloud about how Menchú's brother had been tortured. As a stunned silence overtook the classroom, the student's voice recounted the horrors faced by a 16-year-old boy—the same age as most of the students in the class—whom the government accused of being a communist agitator. As the student finished the reading, Brittany showed a series of three photos: U.S. military advisors meeting with and training Guatemalan soldiers (National Security Archive, n.d.); Guatemalan soldiers executing suspected rebels in their own country (www.gwu.edu/~nsarchiv/NSAEBB/NSAEBB373/Eternal-Spring-117.jpg); and finally, a mass grave in Guatemala where those killed by the soldiers had been buried en masse (http://lens.blogs.nytimes.com/2011/11/03/in-a-fragile-nation-visible-realities/). The students then worked in small groups to answer the following questions:

1. Why would the [Guatemalan] government accuse Menchú's family of being communists?
2. Why would the government torture someone like Menchú's 16-year-old brother?
3. What was the U.S.'s relationship to the Guatemalan government?
4. If the Guatemalan government was torturing its own citizens, is the United States responsible in any way? Why?

After the students discussed the questions and wrote short responses in their groups, the class as a whole discussed their reactions to the Menchú reading, the graphic photos, and the question of U.S. culpability in the harm the Guatemalan government had wrought on its people. While the students seemed particularly horrified by the written accounts of the torture, some also seemed reluctant to accept that the United States would have supported a government that was torturing or killing its own citizens. "The U.S. knew what they would gain from supporting the Guatemalan government—power and fruit," one student said, while many nodded and called out in agreement. "But they may not have had the full information of what was really going on." "I don't think the United States understood the government of Guatemala," another responded. "Nor did they try to understand. The U.S. just supported [the] military dictatorship and that's what they went with." "The [United States] would [have] never of knew [sic] of [the torture]," another added, because "it's not like the general of Guatemala is going to tell the president of the United States that they are killing their own citizens." "But what if the CIA was training the Guatemalan government," another demanded in response, "wouldn't *they* have known?" "Yea, and isn't it the CIA's *job* to know what is going on?" yet another student noted. With nearly all the students in the class talking at once, the period ended, and Brittany assured the class they would resume the conversation the next day.

Brittany began the next class by asking the students to consider how different people could look at the same situation and arrive at different conclusions about it. As the "do now" for the day, she asked: "If you and a classmate (not a close friend—but someone you know from school) both witness a fight, why might you have a different explanation of what happened in the fight?" Next, she asked them: "If two historians are writing about the same event, why might they have different explanations of what happened?" After reviewing what they had learned about the genocide in Guatemala and particularly their discussion from the previous class about the extent to which the U.S. bore any blame for what had happened there, Brittany introduced the day's activity: to read and evaluate two opposing viewpoints published in the "Room for Debate" section of the *New York Times* on May 19, 2013. In that exchange, Greg Grandin, the historian who provided the interview for this chapter, and J. Michael Waller, provost of the Institute of World Politics in Washington DC, among other scholars, faced off on the question, "What Guilt Does the U.S. Bear in Guatemala?" As the *Times* framed the discussion:

> Guatemala's former dictator, General Efraín Ríos Montt, has been convicted of genocide in the slaughter of as many as 200,000 members of indigenous groups during the 1980s in a long bloody fight against the left. But little was said at the trial about U.S. involvement in Guatemala. A United Nations truth commission in 1999 said the United States bore much responsibility for advising, training, arming and financing the troops, even teaching torture, as part of the Reagan administration's

campaign against communism. What guilt does the United States bear in Guatemalan atrocities?

(Room for Debate, 2013)

In Brittany's words, "The question both of these historians are trying to answer is whether or not the United States is partially responsible for the genocide in Guatemala." She then directed the students to read the arguments posed by each Latin America scholar and, as a way of assessing and evaluating the different perspectives raised, to chart responses on a grid that asked them to explain:

1. Grandin's argument;
2. Waller's argument;
3. what I learned yesterday;
4. my opinion.

As the students sorted through Grandin's "Slaughter was part of Reagan's hard line" (2013) and then Waller's "Blaming the U.S. is easy propaganda" (2013), they struggled to reconcile the two arguments and to make sense of how two scholars, each of whom had dedicated much of his professional life to understanding Latin America, could so vehemently disagree on what had really happened there. As a result, the students' own debate from the day before, over what the United States did or should have known about the Guatemalan government's actions, took on particular salience and poignancy. Based on their reactions, one could "see" the students realizing, *no wonder we in this class can't agree on this; not even those who study this for a living can entirely agree on to what extent the U.S. bears blame!*

The next time the class met, Brittany turned the students' attention from Guatemala and the U.S. backing of the coup in 1954 and subsequent support for several decades of military dictatorships there to events in Venezuela in the late 1950s. After a quick review of what social democracy was and was not, she asked the class, "What motivated the United States to get involved in the politics of Latin America in the mid-20th century?" The students readily supplied responses, which Brittany charted on the board: to get resources such as fruit and other goods, fear that social democracy was actually another form of communism, and to prevent the Soviet Union from spreading communism to such close neighbors of the United States. Sensing that some of the students did not fully understand the fear many in the U.S. held of communism and the reach of the Soviet Union during the time period, Brittany reminded the class that the Soviet Union had developed its own nuclear bombs by the 1950s, and that, given its actions in other nations in Africa and Asia at the time, the United States had ample reason to be concerned that the Soviets were trying to win to their side smaller nations that then would pose a communist threat close to U.S. shores. At the same time, Brittany shared with the students the large role that Venezuela played by the late 1950s in supplying oil to the United States—an increasingly car-dependent nation—as a way of solidifying students' understanding of the political and economic motivations that prompted U.S. interest in Venezuelan affairs at the time. Once confident that her class understood the strategic context for U.S. concern with Venezuela in 1958, Brittany shared with her students a newsreel account of then-Vice President Richard Nixon's visit to Caracas in May, 1958 (Universal International News, 1958). This clip would serve as the springboard for the unit's culminating project: a challenge to students to re-write the audio portion of the newsreel from the perspective of either a Guatemalan or Venezuelan citizen who believed in social democracy rather than individualist democracy and who found U.S. involvement in Latin America problematic for political and economic—not to mention military—reasons.[2]

Vice President Nixon in Caracas: The Victim of a "Savage" Communist Mob or the Object of Student Protests against U.S. Interference in Venezuelan Economic Policies?

The newsreel cracks to life, an orchestra playing a triumphant march, while the words, "May 1958 *Nixon Ordeal:* Venezuela Mob, and Hero's Welcome Home" flash across the screen. The male narrator speaks in a serious yet confident tone to explain images of an airplane landing and then a smiling and waving couple appearing at the airplane door, with a crowd of men waving their arms and holding signs that read "Go Home Nixon" in the background:

> Vice President Nixon arrived in Venezuela—last stop on his South American tour. Awaiting him: Another of the well-planned campaigns of harassment that have marred every step of his way. But he and Mrs. Nixon arrived smiling, despite what has gone before, despite their knowledge they'll be targets for another communist-sparked onslaught.

The newsreel next depicts the Nixons and their party getting into cars—"closed cars, for the first time on this trip, a precaution that perhaps saved their lives [for] the Caracas siege exceeds their darkest expectations." As the film shows the cars stopping for traffic, "and the mob catches up! The mob attacks the car with stones and clubs," the narrator tells the audience. "Vice President and Mrs. Nixon are spat upon and reviled, while an inadequate police guard stands by, helplessly." An image of a car with a broken window appears on the screen, and the camera goes in for a close shot of the broken glass, as the narrator notes in alarmed tones, "The car itself testifies to the savagery of the mob." As the orchestra continues to play, the narrator next recounts the apologies given by the Venezuelan government, and Vice President Nixon's decision to return home the next day "with a heavy cordon of troops speeding their way." With "maximum security the order of the day, American marines have been rushed to nearby Caribbean bases in case Venezuela cannot keep order. But the leave taking went without incident," the narrator assures the audience, and Vice President and Mrs. Nixon return to Washington DC, where a crowd of nearly 10,000 cheering Americans welcome them home, and President Eisenhower himself is on hand to lead the ovation and extend his personal welcome to the Nixons. In a speech, Vice President Nixon assures the gathered crowd that despite what he and Mrs. Nixon had encountered, "in every country we visited, the majority of the people—the great majority in all walks of life—are friendly to the United States today." The newsreel ends on a triumphant note, with Americans assured that despite the "vehemence of the leftist attacks and communist agitators [who] betrayed themselves by their work," the United States remains liked and respected, and its government leaders capable of "making new friends" wherever they go, its military ready and waiting to restore order and security to any place where U.S. influence is threatened.

Brittany played the newsreel multiple times for the students, prompting them through the use of a grid to pick out "what I see" and "what I hear" in the clip and then put those two findings into dialogue. The class then discussed what they heard and saw in the clip and compared the images of a group gathered in protest, shouting and waving their arms, with the melodramatic voice-over recounting Vice President and Mrs. Nixon's efforts to avoid being harmed by the "savagery of the mob" that was there to "revile" them.

Next, the class examined three primary source documents related to the events to figure out what they thought actually happened during Nixon's visit to Caracas: A *Time Magazine* article from May 26, 1958, entitled "The Americas: The Guests of Venezuela," which recounted how "A pack of 200 students, skillfully whipped up by older men, hoisted bed sheets painted with the slogans of international communism, blew rubber Bronx-cheer whistles and shouted, 'Get out, Nixon!'"; an article from the *New York Times,* published May 16, 1958, which recounted the arrest of three men who were charged with conspiring to kidnap Vice President Nixon during his visit to Caracas ("Plot on Nixon Charged"); and finally, a now-declassified U.S. government document from May 14, 1958, titled "Background for Demonstrations in Caracas for Vice President Nixon," which states that while the demonstrations were "presumably organized and led by Communists," there was actually "little evidence to support this belief" and that evidence showed that "it is obvious that more non-Communists than Communists were in the crowds of students which carried on the demonstrations" (see Chapter Resources III for excerpts from the last document). This last document was the "smoking gun" for the students, because it showed that the U.S. State Department actually knew, even as it told a different public narrative, that there were more non-Communists than Communists involved in the protests and subsequent attack on Vice President Nixon's car in Caracas. Moreover, it suggested that the protesters were motivated not by communist agitators but by anger at the United States' support for the ex-dictator Perez Jimenez and other undemocratic Latin American leaders. This document, set against the others, would help the students understand how the "facts" can be shaped in multiple ways, depending on the perspective and goals of the authors. Thus, in analyzing the three documents, the students were instructed to pay particular attention to the *perspective* taken by each document's author. Once they had completed this exercise, the students would then write their own narration for the video, providing "the perspective of a Latin American citizen [either a Venezuelan reporter or a Guatemalan reporter who supports social democracy] on Nixon's visit to Caracas."

As the students tackled this complex assignment, it became clear to Brittany and Diana, who was observing and working with groups of students on the documents, that the students were having trouble jumping from an analysis of different documents and their perspectives on Nixon's visit to Caracas to a reconstruction of what a newsreel narrative would sound like from the perspective of a Latin American who was likely to be unfriendly to the U.S. and its actions in their countries. Having been taught critical reading skills throughout the year, the students were able to pick apart the perspectives offered in the three articles and make sense of what "spin" each author put on the events of May 1958: what in one document was clearly a group of "students" who were largely "non-Communists" could be presented in another document, written in a different place and for different purposes, as a "howling mob" that had been "whipped up" by Communist leaders. But students had trouble bringing the same critical evaluation skills to bear on the newsreel, as the film appeared to them to be providing just the "facts." Why was it, we wondered after class, that the students had no problem recognizing from their analysis of the documents that some within the U.S. might have a vested interest in how the events in Caracas should be framed for particular audiences, but when asked to rethink the audio track of the newsreel, they could not critically evaluate the video's narration that a "savage mob" of "Communists" had threatened the Nixons? Why did the students seem in some ways unable to realize that the newsreel *also* reflected a particular perspective on the events?

As we reflected on this situation, Brittany and Diana together concluded that the students, who had probably not been taught explicitly to analyze audiovisual offerings for argument, perspective, and bias, had come to the assignment with the understanding that an historical newsreel contains the "truth." Since social studies teachers often show documentaries as a way of showing "what really happened," students may not understand that a videotaped presentation, just like any other source, needs to be analyzed, contextualized, and evaluated. We realized in this case that we needed to step back and explicitly teach critical media-decoding skills, as we could not expect students to transfer their critical analysis of written materials to audiovisual sources.

For the next class session, then, Brittany started by asking her students what they thought the purpose of the news (television/radio/newspaper) was and why they thought people watched the news. The students called out their responses: the news "lets people know what's going on in the world." "For entertainment," another supplied. "You need to know what to look out for [as in dangers such as criminals or weather]," another student offered. Another student maintained that the news helps us "learn how we're better than others." Brittany next asked the students a question designed to get them to think about *perspective* as related to the news: "If two TV stations report on the same event, will their stories be exactly the same? Why or why not?" Easily, the students replied that different news stations would have different slants. "You mean when I watch the news, I might not get the truth?" Brittany asked. "Yes!" many replied. The news is "influenced by a political party," one student offered. "It's propaganda," agreed another. "Okay," Brittany said, "If news can be biased, then we need to analyze a news-clip from history for its agenda just the same as we do a current news-clip."

Brittany then led the students through a review of the four sources presented in the previous class session: the newsreel, the *Time Magazine* article, the article from the *New York Times,* and the U.S. government document. "Let's play 'one of these things is not like the other,'" Brittany said. "Which one is different? How would you categorize these documents?" Separating out the sources that were written for public/news purposes and the one written for a private/classified (government) purpose, the students began to sort through the four sources to pick out what they thought actually happened—*and from which perspective*—during Nixon's visit to Caracas in 1958. "What is a 'mob'?" Brittany asked. "What is the implication of using that word—particularly when combined with the word 'angry'? Are these the facts? Or is something else going on here?"

Charting students' responses on the board, Brittany led the class through the points of agreement and disagreement among the four sources:

Differences—news source	Similarities	Differences—government document
Communist	There was a crowd	Students
Angry mob	Someone threw a rock	More not-Communists than
Danger of assassination	U.S. military escorted Nixon	Communists
Military for protection	back to hotel	No evidence that it was
	Marines sent to Caribbean in case	communist led
	Venezuela could not keep order	No assassination attempt noted

Working carefully and deliberately through each of the sources achieved the desired purpose: the students' responses now showed that they understood the different ways that each was presenting information and for different purposes. "Where do you think the U.S. news organizations got their information on Venezuela from?" Brittany asked the students to consider. "What *perspective* might these sources have had?" The class next discussed why they thought the U.S. government might have given one perspective in the classified memo and another in more public venues: in other words, why the news would have been "shaped" in certain ways and for certain purposes. The students readily supplied reasons why they thought, given the historical context, that the U.S. government might have wanted to tell a story of a communist mob threatening Nixon, even if it were not the story that their classified document told: a tale of a communist mob threatening the Vice President would justify the U.S. being militarily involved in trying to enforce favorable (political and economic) policies to preserve its "friendship"—and indeed, its claim on natural resources in Latin American countries. Although at times the students conflated the reach of American capitalism in Guatemala via United Fruit with U.S. interest in Venezuelan oil, what resounded clearly from the discussion was that they now understood the dual prong of economic and political interests that propelled U.S. policies in the region in the 1950s. Fear of communism and desire for natural resources undergirded so much of U.S. involvement in Guatemala and Venezuela—as well as other nations—and these twin concerns provided justification for strong U.S. military presence and economic strong-arming in countries in the region. The fact that the U.S. so deeply misunderstood (or purposely mis-characterized) the political structures of the two countries, often mislabeling social democracies as communist, added fuel to the already smoldering fire.

Now the task of rewriting the narrative for the newsreel from the perspective of a Guatemalan or Venezuelan citizen made more sense. In groups, the students readily set to work, arguing about wording and checking back in their notes for accuracy. Brittany moved around the classroom from group to group, clarifying student questions and reminding them to consider the perspective of the new narrator (either Venezuelan or Guatemalan) whose words they were writing, and how these would differ from someone who was overtly pro-American. As the minutes ticked down on this last class of the year, Brittany once again showed the newsreel, but this time with the audio track turned off. As the picture played, the students read aloud their narratives one at a time. The newsreel still showed the same scenes but now "told" a different story. As one group narrated from the perspective of a Venezuelan:

> Vice President Nixon arrived in Venezuela today. As he got in a car, a crowd of Venezuelans gathered around the car. The citizens appeared to be angry, as they were throwing rocks at the car. The car was severely damaged. The Venezuelan leaders later apologized, yet the Vice President decided to cut the trip short anyway. The U.S. military escorted Vice President Nixon back to his plane. Vice President Nixon visited Venezuela as he was touring Latin America looking [to root out] communists.

Another group, writing from the perspective of a Guatemalan reporter, recounted similar events but provided the following explanation as well: "The protesters were against Nixon because he took their natural resources, and he was training their military to kill their own people." The newsreel—accompanied by revised audio tracks that both placed the U.S. involvement in Latin America in a more complicated light than the simplistic "desire for friendship" explanations of the original narration and refrained from using the terms "angry mob" and "communists"—left viewers with a much different impression of the events and the causes of the events surrounding Nixon's visit to Caracas in May 1958. Although none of the newly written narratives reached the truly anti-American angle that one might imagine a Guatemalan or Venezuelan adopting at the time period, the students' narrations clearly showed that they now understood how *perspective-taking* matters in historical inquiry.

Assessing the Unit: Where Latin America can Fit in a Test-Driven Curriculum

Because the unit on Latin America coincided with the last days of the school year, attendance—already a challenge across Brittany's entire school—fell sharply on the last day of class, with some students choosing not to attend class at all and others showing up with less than half the class period left. Still, in reflecting on how the lessons on Latin America had gone in her class, Brittany was struck by the extent of the students' interest in what they had studied and their curiosity about Latin America and its interactions and struggles with the United States since the middle of the 20th century. As the students learned the news that former Guatemalan dictator Efrain Rios Montt had been found guilty of genocide of nearly 2,000 indigenous Ixil Mayans during his rule in the early 1980s, their fascination with the country grew, as did their horror in learning the extent to which others, too, had experienced the terror of torture, such as those recounted in the *I, Rigoberta Menchú* reading in the decades following the CIA-orchestrated coup of 1954. As Brittany reflected later about her students' strong reactions to Menchú's testimony:

> I think sometimes people get the impression of teenagers that they are not shocked by violence, but these students were extremely shocked by the violence in Guatemala. And that is important. Urban kids can be so hardened to violence, but they were *shocked* by what they read. And I also think there is something to be said for the fact that we were reading it and not watching it in a documentary: reading it out loud in the classroom. I think you feel it more personally when you read it—and you [Diana] saw it—there they were, clutching themselves, and you can imagine it happening to yourselves, in some form or way.

Although when they began the unit, few of the students had any idea how to locate Guatemala on a map or knew to which area the term "Latin America" referred, by the end of the lessons, many expressed a strong interest in the region. Moreover, on the New York state global history and geography exam the following week when the students had to write essays on historical turning points or revolutions, many chose to write about events in Latin America, specifically Guatemala and Venezuela, going beyond the essay question's suggested topics of the Neolithic Revolution, the Industrial Revolution, the French Revolution, and the Protestant Reformation. One student compared the French Revolution, which she described as a government overthrow led by the people of France, to events in Guatemala, where she focused on the idea that a new government was more or less forced on them by a more powerful country. Others addressed the similarities between the CIA-sponsored coup d'état in Iran (the lessons for which serve as the focus of Chapter Seven in this volume) with similar efforts in Guatemala in the 1950s.

In reflecting back on the unit and its diverse learning experiences, the members of our planning group found satisfaction in the high-level of student engagement expressed during the lessons and the extent to which the majority of the class developed a clear understanding of historical perspective and the differing ways that countries in Latin America have conceptualized democracy. They also became aware of how the U.S., driven by the fears stirred up during the Cold War, has struggled with these varieties of social democracy that were, often unfairly, viewed as communist. In considering the unit's enduring understandings, we felt the students recognized that the Mexican Constitution of 1917 laid out a vision for democracy unlike those of the United States and France; certainly, the students came to appreciate the differences between notions of U.S. individualist democracy and Latin American social democracy. Through *I, Rigoberta Menchú* and additional documents about what the United Nations has called genocide in Guatemala, the students began to understand the enormous price some people in Latin America paid for supporting economic, social, and political principles that clashed with the economic, political, and social policies promoted by the U.S. Finally, through the content, skills, and attitudes they demonstrated in their culminating assignments, the students showed the extent to which they had developed the perspective-taking skills needed to put themselves into another person's shoes, drawing from that person's worldviews, in order to consider how he or she would interpret a particular series of events.

As in many learning experiences, we felt that students would have benefited from more time spent on the unit, particularly for the culminating project on rewriting the newsreel's narration. More transparency from the start about what it means to develop historical perspective-taking skills, as well as more explicit and intentional teaching of the critical decoding skills students need to analyze the argument and perspective inherent in a newsreel, would both strengthen the unit and make the culminating projects more powerful. Indeed, once we stepped back and provided more attention to media decoding, a decision that extended the unit by an additional day, we found that the students were much better able to grasp the diverse ways the events surrounding

Vice President Nixon's visit to Caracas might be "spun" by different authors for different purposes. As a follow-up to this unit, we believe that students would also benefit from further focus, however brief, on U.S.–Latin American relations in the 21st century. In that way, when Latin American leaders like the late President of Venezuela Hugo Chavez are charged as anti-American, students can be more alert to how labels are being used by leaders or the media as they seek to understand how various struggles are depicted and what issues—economic, political, human rights—are actually at stake in U.S. interactions with its southern neighbors.

For Brittany, as a global history teacher, working on this unit enabled her to access a whole region's history that she had previously neither studied much herself nor taught in any kind of a systematic way:

> This [material] was super new to me. I mean, I knew the United Fruit stuff, I knew the United states interfered in the region, but I didn't know a lot of what we read and what we looked at. [Without having been involved in this project], I think we would have done Cuba. Last year [when teaching this course], we did two days where we talked about Cuba, but not a lot of time spent on Latin America [more generally]. Which is sad, but it's also a reality, when you're preparing for the Regents. As a teacher it's easier to focus on the stuff I know really well, too, besides getting them ready for the Regents.

For her, access to the Grandin interview as well as to the materials surrounding Vice President Nixon's visit to Caracas proved stimulating and thoroughly changed the way she will teach Latin America in the future. Going forward, Brittany plans to teach this unit again, though next time she intends to place it earlier in the year, likely closer to the time that her class addresses the CIA-backed overthrow of the Iranian Premier Mohammed Mossadegh in 1953, so that her students can see the similarities between U.S.-sponsored events in Iran and those that took place shortly after in Guatemala. And she hopes, as do the other members of our planning group, that more global history teachers will be inspired by the Grandin interview and will make time and room in their schedules to teach the recent history of Latin America and the ways that its countries' political, economic, and social structures can help call into question otherwise taken-for-granted notions about what "democracy" means.

The more we can educate tomorrow's leaders about nations in which the democratic principles of freedom and equality can exist in harmony with fundamental social welfare rights and protections, the greater chance we have that our own nation and those we influence will someday move beyond the stark dichotomy of the thinking that says, *if it's not U.S.-exported individualist democracy, then it must be communism.* The greater chance we have, too, of living in a fairer and more egalitarian world where, as Senator Langer pointed out in evoking our own Declaration of Independence (chapter's opening quote), nations are free to determine the forms of governmental protections and ways of sharing land and resources that best serve their own people's needs and desires.

Notes

1   First, second, and last quotes are from a CIA report written by D. M. Barrett (2007), *Congress, the CIA, and Guatemala, 1954,* retrieved from www.cia.gov/library/center-for-the-study-of-intelligence/kent-csi/vol44no5/html/v44i5a03p.htm.

2   The back-story to how we came to know about this newsreel reveals much about the benefits of university–school partnerships: Robert Cohen, the author of this book who conducted the historian interviews, first encountered the newsreel at a lecture Greg Grandin gave on the history of the Cold War in Latin America. Cohen was gripped by the narrative's slant and immediately approached Grandin about the idea of using this source with students in middle and high school classrooms to critically interrogate

the Cold War narration of the news report. As a consequence of this discussion, Grandin put Cohen in touch with Alejandro Velasco, another professor at New York University, who had obtained formerly classified government documents that told a story very different from the one depicted in the newsreel. Velasco shared the documents with Cohen, and the seeds of this project were born. The authors would like to extend their deep thanks to Grandin and Velasco for sharing these exciting and largely heretofore unshared sources.

Works Cited

Davis, O. L., Jr., Yeager, E. A., & Foster, S. J. (2001). *Historical empathy and perspective taking in the social studies.* Boulder, CO: Rowman & Littlefield.

Grandin, G. (2004). *The last colonial massacre: Latin America in the Cold War.* Chicago: University of Chicago Press.

Grandin, G. (2006). *Empire's workshop: Latin America, the United States, and the rise of the new imperialism.* New York: Henry Holt & Co.

Grandin, G. (2010). Living in revolutionary time: Coming to terms with the violence of Latin America's long Cold War. In G. Grandin, & G. M. Joseph (Eds.), *A century of revolution: Insurgent and counter-insurgent violence during Latin America's long Cold War.* Durham, NC: Duke University Press.

Grandin, G. (2011). *Who is Rigoberta Menchú?* London: Verso.

Grandin, G. (2013, May 19). Slaughter was part of Reagan's hard line. *New York Times.* Retrieved from www.nytimes.com/roomfordebate/2013/05/19/what-guilt-does-the-us-bear-in-guatemala/guatemalan-slaughter-was-part-of-reagans-hard-line

Grandin, G. (n.d.). Teaching *Empire's Workshop.* Retrieved from greggrandin.com

Inside Schools. (2013). Dr. Susan S. McKinney Secondary School for the Arts. *Insideschools.* Retrieved from http://insideschools.org/high/browse/school/599

Joseph, G. M. (2010). Latin America's Cold War: A century of revolutionary process and U.S. power. In G. Grandin, & G. M. Joseph (Eds.), *A century of revolution: Insurgent and counter-insurgent violence during Latin America's long Cold War.* Durham, NC: Duke University Press.

Kohlmeier, J. (2006). "Couldn't she just leave?": The relationship between consistently using class discussions and the development of historical empathy in a 9th grade world history course. *Theory and Research in Social Education, 34*(1), 34–57.

LaFeber, W. (1993). *Inevitable revolutions: The United States in Central America.* New York: W.W. Norton and Company.

Lee, P. J., & Ashby, R. (2001). Empathy, perspective taking, and rational understanding. In O. L. Davis Jr., S. Foster, & E. Yeager (Eds.), *Historical empathy and perspective taking in the social studies.* Boulder, CO: Rowman & Littlefield.

Lipset, S. M. (1996). *American exceptionalism: A double-edged sword.* New York: W.W. Norton and Company.

Memo from Mr. Snow to Mr. Wardlaw. (1958, May 14). Background for Demonstrations in Caracas for Vice President Nixon. Declassified Government document.

Menchú, R. (2010). *I, Rigoberta Menchú: An Indian woman in Guatamala.* London: Verso.

Mexican Constitution. (1917). Retrieved from www.diputados.gob.mx/LeyesBiblio/ref/cpeum.htm

National Security Archive. (n.d.). The Guatemalan military: What the U.S. files reveal, volume II documents. In *National Security Archive Electronic Briefing Book No. 32.* Retrieved from www.gwu.edu/~nsarchiv/NSAEBB/NSAEBB32/vol2.html

Plot on Nixon Charged. (1958, May 16). *New York Times.* ProQuest Historical Newspapers New York Times (1851–2007) w/ Index (1851–1993), p. 10.

Popper, N. (2011, Dec. 5). OECD report cites increasing inequality in U.S. *Los Angeles Times.* Retrieved from http://latimesblogs.latimes.com/money_co/2011/12/income-inequality-rising-faster-in-us-than-other-developed-countries.html

Room for Debate. (2013, May 19). What guilt does the U.S. bear in Guatemala? *New York Times.* Retrieved from www.nytimes.com/roomfordebate/2013/05/19/what-guilt-does-the-us-bear-in-guatemala

Salsman, R. M. (2012, June 28). A finalized path to full, socialized medicine in the United States, thanks to conservatives. *Forbes.* Retrieved from www.forbes.com/sites/richardsalsman/2012/06/28/a-finalized-path-to-full-socialized-medicine-in-america-thanks-to-conservatives

Saunders, S. (2007, Oct. 24). CIA in South America. *Geopolitical Monitor.* Retrieved from www.geopolitical monitor.com/us-interventions-in-latin-american-021

Stoll, D. (1999). *Rigoberta Menchú and the story of all poor Guatamalans.* Boulder, CO: Westview Press.

The Americas: The Guests of Venezuela. (1958, May 26). *Time Magazine.* Retrieved from www.time.com/time/subscriber/article/0,33009,936915–2,00.html

Universal International News. (1958). *Nixon ordeal: Venezuela mob and hero's welcome home.* U.S.A. [Newsreel]. Retrieved from www.youtube.com/watch?v=nvigX1doz2U

U.S. Bill of Rights. Retrieved from www.archives.gov/exhibits/charters/bill_of_rights.html

VanSledright, B. (2004). What does it mean to think historically? … and how do you teach it? *Social Education, 68*(3), 230–233.

VanSledright, B. (2010). *The challenge of rethinking history education: On practices, theories, and policy.* New York: Routledge Press.

Waller, J. M. (2013, May 19). Blaming the U.S. is easy propaganda. *New York Times.* Retrieved from www.nytimes.com/roomfordebate/2013/05/19/what-guilt-does-the-us-bear-in-guatemala/blaming-the-us-for-guatemalan-deaths-is-easy-propaganda

Wiggins, G., & McTighe, J. (2005). *Understanding by design.* Upper Saddle River, NJ: Pearson Education Inc.

Wineburg, S. (2001). *Historical thinking and other unnatural acts: Charting the future of teaching the past (critical perspectives on the past).* Philadelphia, PA: Temple University Press.

CHAPTER RESOURCES

I. Unit Plan: Latin America

Common Core Standards

CCSS.ELA-Literacy.RH.9-10.1 Cite specific textual evidence to support analysis of primary and secondary sources, attending to such features as the date and origin of the information.

CCSS.ELA-Literacy.RH.9-10.2 Determine the central ideas or information of a primary or secondary source; provide an accurate summary of how key events or ideas develop over the course of the text.

CCSS.ELA-Literacy.RH.9-10.3 Analyze in detail a series of events described in a text; determine whether earlier events caused later ones or simply preceded them.

CCSS.ELA-Literacy.RH.9-10.4 Determine the meaning of words and phrases as they are used in a text, including vocabulary describing political, social, or economic aspects of history/social science.

CCSS.ELA-Literacy.RH.9-10.6 Compare the point of view of two or more authors for how they treat the same or similar topics, including which details they include and emphasize in their respective accounts.

CCSS.ELA-Literacy.RH.9-10.8 Assess the extent to which the reasoning and evidence in a text support the author's claims.

CCSS.ELA-Literacy.RH.9-10.9 Compare and contrast treatments of the same topic in several primary and secondary sources.

Essential Questions

- How does social democracy differ from individualist democracy?
- To what extent is one form of democracy more "pure" than the other?
- In what ways is social democracy similar to and different from communism?
- How and with what implications has the United States misunderstood social democracy, interpreting it as communism, in Latin America?
- How can students develop a sense of historical perspective-taking through a study of the ways citizens of different countries have conceptualized "rights" and "freedoms"?

Enduring Understandings

Students will understand that:

- The Mexican Constitution lays out a vision for democracy that is at odds in many ways with the version of democracy on which the United States was founded.
- The U.S. government and its people have often misunderstood the different ways citizens of Latin American countries have conceptualized "rights" and "freedoms," and there have been deep ramifications to these misunderstanding of social democracy in Latin America.
- Citizens of Latin American countries have paid an enormous price for supporting models of democracy that, while often more communal and more egalitarian than other forms of democracy, have differed from the model both practiced and promoted by the United States.
- Understanding the worldviews and meanings citizens of particular countries assigned to their everyday experiences requires a particular mindset that enables one to both step outside of one's own worldview and also take on the *perspective* of other historical characters, in a complex process called perspective-taking.

Culminating Assessment

Students will screen newsreel "Nixon in Caracas" and then write their own narration for the video, providing the perspective of a Latin American citizen (either a Venezuelan reporter or a Guatemalan reporter who supports social democracy) on Nixon's visit to Caracas.

II. Lesson Plans

Latin America: Day Two—Guatemala

Learning Objective

Students will be able to evaluate the American understanding (or misunderstanding) of social democracy in Guatemala.

Do Now

1. How is social democracy similar to communism?
2. How is social democracy different from Soviet-style communism?

Mini Lesson

Take Cornell Notes in your notebook.

Activity

The reading is an excerpt from a book written by a Guatemalan peasant and her experiences before, during and after the U.S. planned coup d'état in her country. Her book is called *I, Rigoberta Menchú*.

Reading

I, Rigoberta Menchú

My name is Rigoberta Menchú. I am twenty-three years old.

This is my testimony. I didn't learn it from a book and I didn't learn it alone. I'd like to stress that it's not only *my* life, it's also the testimony of my people. It's hard for me to remember everything that's happened to me in my life since there have been many very bad times but, yes, moments of joy as well. The important thing is that what has happened to me has happened to many other people too: My story is the story of all poor Guatemalans. My personal experience is the reality of a whole people.

At the beginning everybody works communally, clearing the bush in the mountains. How many years would that take one family? We work together: the women pulling out the small plants below and the men cutting down trees on the mountainside. When sowing time comes, the community meets to discuss how to share out the land—whether each one will have his own plot or if they will work collectively. Everyone joins the discussion. In my village, for example, we said it was up to all of us if we wanted our own plot or not. But we also decided to keep a common piece of land, shared by the whole community, so that if anyone was ill or injured, they would have food to eat. We worked in that way: each family with their own plot and a large piece of common land for emergencies in the community or in the family. It was mostly to help widows. Each day of the week, someone would go and work that common land.

Prompting Questions:

- *Why do you think the author is telling this story?*
- *How is what the author is describing similar to what we have learned about communism?*
- *How is this different from communism as we have learned about it?*

It was 1979, I remember that my younger brother died, the first person in my family to be tortured. He was sixteen years old. After the family's farewell, each of us went their own way: he stayed in the community since, as I said, he was the secretary of the community. He was the youngest of my brothers, though I have two little sisters who are younger. One of them went with my mother and the other stayed in the community, learning and training in self-defense. My mother, unable to find any other solution, had gone off somewhere else. My brothers too, because they were being hunted, and so as not to expose the community to danger … The thing is that the government put about this image of us, of our family, as if we were monsters, as if we were some kind of foreigners, aliens. The government called us communists and accused us of being a bad influence.

So, in order not to expose the community to danger, and to weed out this "bad influence," we had to go away to different places, but my younger brother stayed in the community.

Prompting Questions:

- *Why is community so important to Rigoberta Menchú?*
- *Why do you think the government accused Menchú's family of being communists?*
- *What do you think will happen to her younger brother?*

[They captured my brother] and took him to the camp, he was scarcely on his feet, he couldn't walk any more. And his face, he couldn't see any more, they'd even forced stones into his eyes, my brother's eyes. Once he arrived in the camp they inflicted terrible tortures on him to make him tell where the guerrilla fighters were and where his family was. What was he doing with the Bible, they wanted to know, why were the priests guerrillas? Straight away they talked of the Bible as if it were a subversive tract … They asked him what relationship the priests had with the guerrillas, what relationship the whole community had with the guerrillas.

Prompting Questions:

- *Why would the government torture someone like this?*
- *What was the U.S.'s relationship to the Guatemalan government?*

So they inflicted those dreadful tortures on him. Day and night they subjected him to terrible, terrible pain. They tied him up, they tied his testicles, my brother's sexual organs, they tied them behind with string and forced him to run. Well, he couldn't stand that, my little brother, he couldn't bear that awful pain and he cried out, he asked for mercy. And they left him in a well, I don't know what it's called, a hole with water and a bit of mud in it, they left him naked there all night. There were a lot of corpses there in the hole with him and he couldn't stand the smell of all those corpses. There were other people there who'd been tortured. He recognized several there who had been tortured. My brother was tortured for 16 more days. They cut off his fingernails, they cut off his fingers, they cut off his skin, they burned parts of his skin. Many of the wounds, the first ones, swelled and were infected. He stayed alive.

Prompting Questions:

- *If it was the Guatemalan government torturing its own citizens, is the United States responsible in any way?*
- *Why?*

Summary

Did the United States correctly understand the government of Guatemala? Why or why not? Use evidence from the reading to support your answer.

Latin America: Day Three—Guatemala

Learning Objective

Students will be able compare arguments about the role of the United States in the Guatemalan genocide.

Do Now

1. If you and a classmate (not a close friend, but someone you know from school) both witness a fight, why might you have a different explanation of what happened in the fight?
2. If two historians are writing about the same event, why might they have a different explanation of what happened?

Mini Lesson

Review: Genocide in Guatemala

Activity

The question both of these historians are trying to answer is whether or not the United States is partially responsible for the genocide in Guatemala. Please read through the two excerpts provided, paying careful attention to the arguments posed by the authors and the evidence they provide to support their arguments. After you have finished reading, the class as a whole will parse carefully through these excerpts to understand the positions of the two authors.

Reading

Slaughter was part of Reagan's hard line
Greg Grandin

> In 1966, the U.S. Army's *Handbook of Counterinsurgency Guidelines* summarized the results of a war game waged in a fictitious country unmistakably modeled on Guatemala. The rules allowed players to use "selective terror" but prohibited "mass terror." "Genocide," the guidelines stipulated, was "not an alternative."
>
> A decade and a half later, genocide was indeed an option in Guatemala, supported materially and morally by Ronald Reagan's White House. Reagan famously took a hard line in Central America, coming under strong criticism for supporting the contras in Nicaragua and financing counterinsurgency in El Salvador.
>
> The White House was less concerned with the massacres than with their effectiveness, or with countering the bad publicity.
>
> His administration's actions in Guatemala are less well known, but even before his 1980 election, two retired generals, who played prominent roles in Reagan's campaign, reportedly traveled to Central America and told Guatemalan officials that "Mr. Reagan recognizes that a good deal of dirty work has to be done."
>
> Once in office, Reagan continued to supply munitions and training to the Guatemalan army, despite a ban on military aid imposed by the Carter administration (existing contracts were exempt from the ban). And economic aid continued to flow, increasing to $104 million in 1986, from $11 million in 1980, nearly all of it going to the rural western highlands, where the Mayan victims of the genocide lived.
>
> This aid helped the Guatemalan military implement a key part of its counterinsurgency campaign: following the massacres, soldiers herded survivors into "model villages," detention camps really, where they used food and other material supplied by the U.S. Agency for International Development to establish control.

And Reagan was consistent in his moral backing for Guatemala's genocid-aires. On Dec. 5, 1982, for instance, he met with Rios Montt in Honduras and said he was "a man of great integrity" and "totally dedicated to democracy."

Just 10 days before this meeting, one declassified U.S. document reveals that the State Department had been informed of a "well-founded allegation of a large-scale killing of Indian men, women and children in a remote area by the Guatemalan army."

Other declassified documents reveal that the White House was less concerned with the massacres than with their effectiveness, or with countering the bad publicity stemming from reports of the atrocities.

The day after Reagan's endorsement, Guatemalan soldiers arrived at a village called Dos Erres and started killing. The slaughter went on for three days and by the time it was over at least 162 people, including many children, were dead.

Surely a nation so powerful that it can presume to debate the effectiveness of terror bears responsibility when terror in fact takes place.

Blaming the U.S. is easy propaganda
J. Michael Waller

The Rios Montt prosecution was less about justice and more about using the courts to wage political propaganda campaigns to settle old scores. Rios Montt's real crime was not genocide, according to prevailing logic, but his political beliefs. His polar opposite contemporaries in Central America will never be prosecuted because they were fighting for "progressive ideals."

For the same reason, the United States does not bear responsibility for any excesses in the Guatemalan civil war.

Few had clean hands in the battle over Central America in the 1980s. Why say only one side was villainous?

Let's take away the political labels and look objectively at the crimes. If Rios Montt is to be found guilty in 2013, for murders committed in the 1980s, then the current Nicaraguan president, Daniel Ortega, who led the dictatorial Sandinista junta during the bloody Nicaraguan civil war, and a contemporary of Rios Montt, should be tried on similar charges.

And if the United States is considered complicit in any crimes in Central America, that same justice should extend to the former Cuban dictator Fidel Castro and his brother and successor, Raul, who for decades ran the Cuban military. It was the Castro brothers, after all, who provided training and weapons for Ortega's murderous rule, and helped spread the leftist insurgency throughout Central America, which Rios Montt used to legitimize his actions.

Likewise, shouldn't former insurgents who committed war crimes in the 1980s also face justice?

Guerrilla leaders in El Salvador ordered assassination and urban terrorism in the 1980s, but now participate in its government. Should they not be tried for war crimes, too?

Ideally, yes. But what purpose would that serve, a generation after the fact? The success of El Salvador as a market economy and multiparty democracy rests on the very uncomfortable fact that, in exchange for peace and national reconciliation, a lot of bad guys had to go free.

As imperfect as the U.S.-backed amnesty-for-peace deals in Nicaragua and El Salvador were, they worked. As rewarding as it would be to see Ortega or Sanchez Ceren or Fidel Castro or U.S. officials share the fate of Rios Montt, it would not be in the interests of justice.

Grandin's Argument	Waller's Argument	What I learned yesterday	My Opinion
ex: Reagan broke rules to give the army of Guatemala weapons	ex: Both sides committed crimes	ex: U.S. sent the CIA to train soldiers in Guatemala	

III. Resource for Teaching Nixon in Caracas Newsreel

Declassified Government document, "Background for Demonstrations in Caracas for Vice President Nixon," May 14, 1958 (excerpt)

ARA—Mr. Snow   May 14, 1958

OSA—Mr. Wardlaw

Background for Demonstrations in Caracas Against Vice President Nixon.

The demonstrations upon the arrival of Vice President Nixon were presumably organized and led by Communists. So far, we have little concrete evidence to support this belief, but the similarity of the pattern of the unfriendly acts in Caracas with those on a much lesser scale in Lima, Bogota, and Montevideo, support a conclusion that they were master-minded by a single organization. The similarity consists of the display of the same types of placards with same mottoes in the various cities along the route, the same vehement hatred, and the same shouts of antagonism. Early reports are that the mobs in Caracas were composed of secondary and university students under the leadership of a few persons apparently of at least forty years of age who obviously were not ordinary students. All of this taken together makes reasonable the assumption that Communists were behind the Caracas disturbances.

However, it is also obvious that more non-Communists than Commu-nists were in the crowds of students which carried on the demonstration. We simply cannot assume that the great majority of students in Caracas are Communists for we have never had reports to this effect. According to infor-mation received from the Embassy today, the mobs constantly accused the United States of supporting dictators in Latin America. The mobs continually shouted about the admission into the United States of the ex-Dictator and the ex-Chief-of-Secret-Police, Perez Jiménez and Pedro Estrada, accusing us of sheltering these men. To a lesser extent the mobs referred to the deco-ration which we awarded Perez Jiménez in 1954. We were also accused of supporting Batista in Cuba, and of showing a predilection for dictators in general. Strangely enough, the mobs had little to say about petroleum restric-tions which had so disturbed the Venezuelan Government.

Certain developments springing from the Venezuelan Revolution of January 23, 1958, contributed to the extent and nature of the demonstration. The Caracas Police Force was completely dispersed by the Revolution. This meant that it was undoubtedly difficult for the Venezuelan Government to obtain advance information about the plans of the extremists. Moreover, it did not have a well organized, well trained body of police to deal with the mob. Reports indicate that the police disappeared when the Vice President's car was attacked. The Venezuelan Government has shown a reluctance to take a firm stand against the Communists, and may not have been inclined to take proper precautions to prevent the disturbance from being organized.

Four
The Middle East

Religion: Islamic History vs. Western Mythology

By Michael R. Stoll, with Melissa Mabry, Bradley Abel,
Rebecca Vercillo, and Paul Kelly

Framing the Questions: An Interview with Zachary Lockman,
conducted by Robert Cohen

Zachary Lockman is a professor of Middle Eastern and Islamic Studies and History at New York University. He received his Ph.D. from Harvard University. His books include *Workers on the Nile: Nationalism, Communism, and the Egyptian Working Class* (with Joel Beinin) (1987); *Workers and Working Classes in the Middle East: Struggles, Histories, and Historiographies* (1993); *Comrades and Enemies: Arab and Jewish Workers in Palestine, 1906—1948* (1996); and *Contending Visions of the Middle East: The History and Politics of Orientalism* (2004, 2009). Among his edited works and essays are *Intifada: The Palestinian Uprising against Israeli Occupation* (with Joel Beinin) (1989); "Railway Workers and Relational History: Arabs and Jews in British-Ruled Palestine" in *Comparative Studies in Society and History* (1993); "Imagining the Working Class: Culture, Nationalism and Class Formation in Egypt, 1899–1914" in *Poetics Today* (1994); "Arab Workers and Arab Nationalism in Palestine: A View from Below" in *Rethinking Nationalism in the Arab Middle East*, Eds. James Jankowski and Israel Gershoni (1997); and "Explorations in the Field: Lost Voices and Emerging Practices in Egypt, 1882–1914" in *Histories of the Modern Middle East: New Directions*, Eds. Israeli Gershoni, Hakan Erdem, and Ursula Wokoeck (2002). He served as president of the Middle East Studies Association in 2007and is currently a contributing editor of *Middle East Report*.

Robert Cohen: *Can you discuss the common misconceptions that Americans have about the Middle East?*

Zachary Lockman: In my experience, the biggest issue is not that students come into the classroom without ideas in their heads, but rather that they come in with a lot of ideas.

So, the first challenge is to deal with some of those ideas, which are often mistaken ideas about Islam in some general sense. When they think of the Middle East, they think of Islam. And they think of Islam in ways that have long roots in American society and culture, and Western society and culture generally, but are often very misleading. Islam seems to them deeply alien and, especially after September 11th, threatening and dangerous. They also understand Islam and Muslims very differently than they think of themselves as Christians or Jews or people they are more familiar with. Even East Asia and Hinduism don't have the same threatening value that Islam does. So they are often thinking about violence, fanaticism, and extremism. This is reinforced by all sorts of things in the popular culture going way back to the 19th century in this country and many centuries earlier in Europe. But it is also reinforced by all sorts of things that they see around them, including lots of academic work by people who have a lot of reputation and a lot of access and power and continue to propagate these kinds of notions.

So, often the first task is to try to deal with some of these very orientalist perceptions of the region as essentially Islamic in a very monolithic sense, and as radically different from us. That notion is very ingrained and is one of the fundamental building blocks of how we think about ourselves. High school kids don't think about this consciously, but I think that it is very deeply there. We are the West in some sense, and we trace our ancestry back to Europe—and then there is "them." This is a problem of course for many parts of the world. But, at least in the last couple of generations it has been particularly salient for the Middle East given the deep and often painful and violent entanglement of the United States with the Middle East. [With Muslims, the popular caricature is that] they are radically different from us, they are fanatical, they are extremists. They have these very strange notions. Islam worships a different god than Jews and Christians, and they are threatening. A lot of the first task is addressing those kinds of things and trying to talk about them or replace them with more useful notions or more accurate understandings of what Islam is about. And trying to frame things differently so that sense of alien-ness, of radical otherness and threat, can be talked about usefully.

RC: *Could you give an example? For example, if students see Islam as an alien and hostile influence or religion, how would you advise a high school teacher to address that coming in if the students have all these negative images, caricatures, or cartoonish images of Islam?*

ZL: Sure. There are all sorts of data. You can find lots of writing on this going back over a century and a half. And, there are a whole series of contemporary polls in the Muslim world showing that people [in Muslim countries] want to live in democratic societies as well. We don't want to throw out differences, of course. Some of these societies are quite conservative and patriarchal. There are real issues. But we have issues, too. People argue about and sometimes kill each other here over abortion. In other societies these things are often salient as well in different ways. Indonesia has had female leaders. Bangladesh, which is one of the largest Muslim countries—many of its political leaders have been women. It is a complicated, mixed picture. Just as you would not say that "all Christians are like this," and just as you would not explain the behavior of Christians today with reference to the Gospels, you can't do that for Muslims either. You try to convey that sense by showing a range of opinions and showing arguments, which have been ongoing from the beginning of time, about what the [Islamic] texts mean. You start with the same assumptions about Muslims and Islam as you do about Christianity, Jews, or with anything else, and show that there is a whole spectrum of opinion. And Muslims, like anybody else, are arguing over what they are and where they want to go, and what those texts mean. So there is a lot of material available in both historic documents and contemporary sources where people are having those debates.

RC: *It sounds as if teachers have to work toward teaching students not to judge Islam by stereotypes promoted by the media because of the "war on terror" and its focus on the most extreme, upsetting things. Yet, for many, such misleading media images seem like the only source that people have about Islam.*

ZL: Sure. I start my undergraduate courses by giving them some bad things to read so we can talk about them. I don't tell them "these are bad things," but I say "read these and tell me what you think about them." So, for example, [*New York Times* columnist] Thomas Friedman is always good for this. He is always a safe bet. Here is someone who is enormously powerful, right? He is seen as perhaps the leading commentator on foreign affairs for the last couple of decades. So here are two articles from op-ed pieces. I usually use "The World: A Dream-like Landscape, A Dream-like Reality" [Friedman, 1990]. It was written during the Gulf crisis in 1990. It is all about how radically different those places are. He uses this metaphor: "The symbol of the west is the cross where the symbol of the east, of Islam, is the crescent." First of all, what does it mean to say that the symbol of the west is the cross? [According to Friedman] we are rational because everything [we believe] is clearly delineated, whereas over there, it is like the desert. You never know what is going on. People say one thing, they mean another. They do one thing but there is a whole other agenda behind it. We are not like that. We basically say what we mean because the metaphor for our civilization is the cross. A lot of Jews might take issue with that, but let's leave that aside. The whole notion of this radical difference between "them" and "us"—we certainly don't say one thing and mean another. That's not conceivable. And he goes on like that. This gets published, and I think that a lot of people take it very, very seriously, this notion of radical difference as opposed to "let's look carefully at similarities, differences." And then [in class] we'll find out that we're not one thing and they're not one thing; there is not an "us" and a "them" in a useful sort of way. You know we could find lots of violent extremists here in the U.S., and we would find lots of people there in the Middle East who are very peaceable and so on.

Another classic piece is Thomas Friedman's, "Foreign Affairs: One Country Two Worlds" [Friedman, 2000]. He is traveling in Egypt, and he says, on the one hand, you have these high tech types—very modern—and then you have these peasants for whom nothing has changed in 2,000 years. Now, of course, anybody who knows anything about Egypt knows how radically everybody's life has changed in the last hundred years. Those peasants aren't living like their ancestors did in the time of the pharaohs. They have gone through land reform, political struggles, revolutionary regimes, and the reversal of land reforms under [Hosni] Mubarak and so on. This whole notion of two worlds, which is very similar to that radical distinction between them and us, the modern and the traditional—that is a very powerful metaphor. "We are modern but they are traditional which is why they do these strange and violent, fanatical things. Whereas we don't. We do modern things, right? And our intentions are good. And, we are guided by reason." These are very deeply embedded notions about how Americans see the world, although they don't help us understand very much. I often have people read these things and try to think about them. And, because students are primed to say, "Oh this is great, this is brilliant," you have to deal with that. But, if you push them and you say, "What does it mean to say the symbol of our civilization is the cross? And theirs is the crescent? What does that tell us really?" you can get something useful out of them.

Similarly, the classic article "The Roots of Muslim Rage" [Lewis, 1990] had enormous influence. Bernard Lewis, who is still referred to routinely in the *New York Times* as the leading scholar [of the Middle East], was invited to the White House right after September 11th and advocated the invasion of Iraq, among other things, as a response [to the terror attacks]. It is a great article because he is the one who invented the notion of the "clash of civilizations." The phrase is his actually. [Samuel] Huntington [1993] picked up on it and wrote his article shortly thereafter and turned it into a book. In this article, he says the "West has been in conflict with Islam for fourteen hundred years." And, the Gulf crisis and September 11th are the latest manifestations of this. But [Lewis's] notion of a West in conflict with Islam for 1,400 hundred years is deeply flawed. He says "Islam is a failed civilization and it failed to engage with modernity. Everything that has gone on is the result of the frustration of Muslims about their failure to engage properly with modernity. That is why they are enraged and why they do these violent things." He explains everything from the breakup of Yugoslavia and Kosovo to conflicts in Central Asia. Yet, if you look at any one of them, you can come up with much more complex historical things that go on rather than seeing them as the manifestation of these two civilizations in conflict, which Huntington then picks up and systematizes and takes further. But this kind of thinking is very deeply ingrained.

RC: *It sounds like what you are saying is that the Middle East is much more diverse and complex.*

ZL: Right. Looking at those societies, you find, of course, many different things going on. You find people fighting over different understandings of Islam. You find a lot of people who are as secular as you find in this society. Or they have relegated religion to the private domain. There is also more material now about everyday life sorts of things. There is a collection called *Struggle and Survival in the Modern Middle East* [Burke & Yaghoubian, 2005], which are very nice little portraits of people's lives and trajectories. That is one kind of material that can be used. There is [also] a lot of stuff published where people are arguing about "Who are we? What does it mean to be Islamic in this day and age? How do we take the powerful science and technology that the Europeans have and that they used to dominate us and do something with it? What do we throw out of our tradition? What do we keep of our tradition? What is authentic? What is not?" There are a lot of sources that could be used to get at some of these things.

RC: *People seem to look to "experts" on the Middle East, but those posing as experts sometimes turn out to have little expertise compared to scholars who seriously study the region. Do such supposed media experts writing about the Middle East really know something about the region? Do they speak Arabic? The media often seem to be recycling ideas about the region on a third-hand basis, without the expertise you see in Middle Eastern historical study or someone who studies the region in a serious way. I guess there are some exceptions, but this seems a serious problem.*

ZL: Sure. There are a lot of instant "experts" who don't know much about the region. They are talking heads or policy people. Bernard Lewis is an extremely erudite person. He knows Arabic and Persian and Turkish. So it is not just about language, it is also about one's frame. I don't doubt his erudition but I have some questions about how he frames things. Let's avoid those kinds of generalizations and essentializing about this part of the world and take things apart in the same way that we would want if someone was talking about our society. There is also a conflation of the Arab world with Islam. I think that people don't get that most Muslims live elsewhere [than the Middle East] or that Indonesia is the largest Muslim country in the world, by far, and it is a reasonably well-functioning democracy and an economic success story. It is not the same as Saudi Arabia. So again, trying to disaggregate in that sense.

RC: *I am also struck by the debates that are dominating the field. It seems so polarized that the two sides can barely even talk to each other—the whole debate about orientalism, for example. Could you describe some of the leading debates in this area?*

ZL: Well, I have to distinguish because when I started out in this field, a long time ago, it was still dominated by what you can call orientalist perceptions and modernization theory. The idea that we were modern and that America in the Eisenhower years was the pinnacle of modernity, and those other places were traditional and they were struggling to achieve modernity. This was applied to the rest of the world and informed American social science. But already in the late '60s, in the early '70s, there were challenges to that from all sorts of directions. Edward Said's [1979] critique of orientalism picked up on some of that and took it in its own direction. So I think in the academic and scholarly side of things this stuff is long gone. People are doing great work that isn't rooted in these kinds of perceptions and doing very careful historical, anthropological, sociological research. The problem is there is a dichotomy about what goes on in the world of scholarship and what goes on in the rest of the world where these kinds of things keep coming up again and get reproduced in part by America's involvement with the Middle East and the consequences of that. The scholarly literature has never been better in terms of the quality, the kinds of materials they use, the subtlety. The Middle East used to be kind of a backwater in academia compared to many other places. I think that is no longer the case.

RC: *Obviously, this is a big concern with teachers, but the revolts that happened in Egypt, Tunisia, Libya, the stirrings of dissent across the Middle East this past year [2011] were making headlines. Can you explain the roots of these revolts and what it tells us about the politics and societies of the Middle East? Can we talk about the Middle East without talking about the U.S.?*

ZL: One issue is that people think that those are crazy people out there who, for some reason, not only are busy fighting and killing each other, but they don't like us for some reason and on 9/11 did these terrible things to us. I think there is also very little understanding that the United States has been very deeply involved in this region, at least since the end of the World War II. The dominant outside power is the U.S. I don't think people have much notion of the scale of that involvement, but there are ways to get at that—for example, the role of the U.S. in overthrowing the government of Iran in 1953 and then re-imposing the Shah as absolute ruler. One can multiply these examples. Americans tend to think of themselves generally as innocent outsiders, only intervening for good purposes. But if you go back and look at the history, the U.S. has been supporting all sorts of regimes that do and profess things that are against the values that we like to think that we believe in. Saudi Arabia is perhaps the best case for this. It has been an American client state almost from day one, with the U.S. deeply involved. In the first Gulf crisis there were lots of commentators who said this was the first time that the U.S. had troops in Saudi Arabia. Yet there have been U.S. military bases going back to the 1950s in Saudi Arabia. So when things happen, like September 11th, it doesn't come out of nowhere. It comes out of a long history of involvement. And that then gets you into the question of making the distinction, which I think is hard for Americans, between explaining something and justifying something. That we need to explain where September 11th came from doesn't mean that it was a justifiable thing.

RC: *I remember very distinctly that people trying to explain the resentment of U.S. policy that paved the road to September 11th were attacked as if they were trying to justify those attacks.*

ZL: Right. People spend endless time trying to understand the Nazis. There are thousands of books and articles. I don't think any of them is trying to justify the Nazis but they are trying to explain where that came from. We are used to that in other realms. We find that acceptable. Nobody thinks we are justifying Hitler by explaining Hitler's psychology or the roots of why the Nazis were popular in Germany. The other piece of it is what goes on in that society. The standard of living for many Egyptians has dropped dramatically in the last 20 years. Egypt has followed the economic policies dictated by the International Monetary Fund and World Bank and it has led to widespread impoverishment. The percentage of people living on two dollars a day has risen dramatically in the last 20 years. And the government has pushed policies that led to rising unemployment, rolling back land reform that was instituted in the '50s under [Gamal Abdel] Nasser, which means that millions of rural households effectively lost their land. So there is a rising tide of social discontent, rising prices, labor activism.

RC: *On the Arab-Israeli dispute, I wonder how you handle teaching that here? What would you advise teachers about teaching that since it is so politically charged?*

ZL: That's a tricky one, although I think that it can be done. I teach an undergraduate survey course called "Palestine, Zionism, and Israel" pretty regularly. Students want to see [the Israeli–Palestinian conflict] as just crazy people who like killing each other for fun—not as a conflict which goes back 2,000 years. But the conflict is actually something that is very much about the history of the world in the last 100 or 150 years. It has some of the same causes as lots of other conflicts. It is not really just about religion. It is about nationalism and people struggling for control of the same land. I start by telling students that this is a sensitive issue, that people have strong feelings about this. You can have whatever feelings you like, but you need to be respectful of other students. You are welcome to make your argument but you also have to have something to back it up. It is not okay to say, "I feel this way because." You need to say why this has some basis in historical evidence or in your understanding of something. I try to set the ground rules early on. Then, I try to make it clear that [what I teach] is my interpretation, and I think it's the best interpretation that I could come up with. I'm prepared to defend it, because I think that it is better than other ones. But people will offer other ways of thinking about this and then we can sit down and compare them, and see what [evidence] they are based on. I try to help them understand why people in particular historical contexts thought as they did, responded as they did, did the kinds of things they did, so they can, in a sense, get inside people's heads—which isn't the same as thinking those things are politically or morally right. [Students] need to understand why the early Zionists or why Palestinians, or whoever it might be at a certain historical moment and specific context, responded the way that they did and how those things interacted to produce the history as it unfolded. I think it is possible to talk about [the conflict] in reasonable ways and help students understand that this is a very complex piece of history. But it is comprehensible. People are often afraid of this part of the world because it seems incomprehensible: "We don't understand why they are killing each other. It is just such a mess." Americans can make sense of baseball. They know the baseball statistics by heart, but somehow these other places seem just not understandable. So another point to make is that they aren't any less understandable or comprehensible than anything else. We can make sense of our own complex history; we can make sense of this part of the world, too.

RC: *I'd like to talk about the Middle East in comparison to other areas of the world. Most scholars who do global history like to look at regions comparatively and to think about interactions between different parts of the world. Do you think that is a useful frame? When you think of the Middle East are you struck by its similarity to other formerly colonized regions such as Latin America or Africa? Or does oil make the Middle East so distinctive that comparative history is less useful?*

ZL: There is certainly a lot of Middle East exceptionalism, where it has been treated as a little box, off by itself, governed by its own rules and strange ways and strange patterns. But we have to be very cautious about that. The Middle East is often used as a stand-in for the Muslim world generally. So again that issue needs to be addressed. That again gets us back to the images of the Middle East. People think about deserts and camels to this day. But Egypt today is predominantly an urban society for the first time in its history. Cairo is as big as New York. Most people live in big cities; they have big city problems. I would push in the direction of trying to look at similarities, common patterns, some of which are common to our own society or issues here as well.

RC: *The last question concerns sources for teaching the history of the Middle East.*

ZL: The Balfour Declaration is the promise to support the Zionist desire to create a national home for the Jews in Palestine. It is good to read because on the one hand it states, "we view favorably the establishment of a national home for the Jewish people," while on the other it says, "it being clearly understood that nothing shall be done which may prejudice the civil and religious rights of the existing non-Jewish communities in Palestine." How these two statements go together is a mystery. There is another great document by Balfour saying that we are going to basically ignore the wishes of the Arabs in Palestine's local population because they are not important and the aspirations of the Zionists are much more important. All the promises we made, we never intended to fulfill. We can't fulfill them all because they contradict each other. Blatant stuff. It's nice because it's a little moment in history when the fate of the region is decided, and what ends up happening is they divide it up between the British and French and imposed these colonial regimes, under a new form. So, these kinds of things can be read side by side. The last document is a little more controversial. This is Osama Bin Laden's first interview after September 11th. A Syrian born journalist, a Spanish national, interviewed him in October 2001, just to get his own words. This has to be handled very carefully so it doesn't seem like justification, but [it spells out] his argument. Bin Laden doesn't quite acknowledge being responsible for [the terror attack], but he says it's good and here's why. It isn't about, "We don't like your values, we want to kill off New York." It's about,

> You're attacking us, if you kill us we're going to kill you. If you stop killing us, we'll stop killing you. Your troops are in our country, and that has to end. You're propping up the Saudi monarchy, which is illegitimate ...
>
> (Lawrence, 2005)

so this is why this kind of thing is happening. It's—in his own voice—his explanation for why he's at war with the United States. It's not about values, even though he may not like our values; it's a political question.

Works Cited

Burke, E., & Yaghoubian, D. (2005). *Struggle and survival in the Middle East* (2nd ed.). Berkeley, CA: University of California Press.

Friedman, T. (1990, October 28). The world: A dream-like landscape, a dream-like reality. *New York Times*, Sec. 4, p. 3.

Friedman, T. (2000, January 28). Foreign affairs; One country: two worlds. *New York Times*, p. A23.

Huntington, S. (1993). The clash of civilizations. *Foreign Affairs* (Summer), 22–49.

Lawrence, B. (2005). *Messages to the world: The statements of Osama bin Laden.* London: Verso Books.

Lewis, B. (1990). The roots of Muslim rage. *The Atlantic* (September 1990), 47–60.

Said, E. (1979). *Orientalism.* New York: Vintage.

Essay: Religion: Islamic History vs. Western Mythology

By Michael R. Stoll, with Melissa Mabry, Bradley Abel, Rebecca Vercillo, and Paul Kelly

Over the past decade, no region of the world has occupied Americans' collective consciousness more than the Middle East. From the attacks of September 11, 2001 and the ensuing wars in Iraq and Afghanistan, to the Arab Spring of 2011, events in the area have dominated American foreign policy and media coverage. Despite this intense focus on the Middle East, many American students continue to misunderstand the region and its peoples. A National Geographic & Roper Public Affairs (2006) survey showed that more than two-thirds of Americans ages 18–24 could not locate Egypt, Indonesia, or Israel on a map. These same students demonstrated an ignorance of all non-Western cultures and religion, especially Islam: 48% of students thought that Islam was the dominant religion in India, and only 25% could name Indonesia as the country with the world's largest Muslim population. Moreover, only 28% of young Americans said it was "necessary" to know basic facts about foreign countries mentioned in the news. While American students have demonstrated such lack of knowledge of global geography and history time and time again (F. Hess, 2008; Paxton, 2003; Ravitch & Finn, 1987), this ignorance is especially striking, given global realities and the ongoing "War on Terror" initiated by the U.S. government after September 11th. Clearly, there are factors that prevent Americans from developing more accurate understandings of the Middle East and of Islam.

One explanation might be related to the ways in which the Islamic world is discussed in the social studies curriculum. While some authors of textbooks and curricula have made good efforts to address misconceptions about the region (e.g. WGBH Educational Foundation, 2002), most educational materials continue to present what textbook critic Gilbert Sewall (2008) calls "an incomplete and confected view of Islam" (p. 36). Critics from all sides agree that the history of Islam and the Middle East is poorly taught in social studies textbooks and curricular materials. Sewall contends that pressure from multiculturalists and pro-Muslim groups has led to intentional distortion or elimination of controversial topics that, he believes, gloss over "the ultimate dangers of Islamic militancy" (2008, p. 9). Douglass (2002) argues that textbooks create merely a "thumbnail sketch" of the region that "creates more stereotypes than useful understandings" (p. 33). In short, textbooks are not providing American students with sufficient understanding of Islam and its history in order to make sense of current events and their historical contexts.

It is likely that many of the misconceptions about the Middle East and Islam that students bring to school are also shaped by the students' own beliefs regarding religion and culture. When examining American public opinion on the Israeli–Palestinian peace process, recent polls showed that Americans' sympathies (overall tilted somewhat in support of the Israeli position) were strongly related to their religious affiliation and political leanings (Pew Research Center for the People & the Press, 2012). Moreover, intense media coverage of the Middle East during and since September 11, 2001 has exacerbated many of the stereotypes students already hold about the region and Islam. These stereotypes are connected to a long history of "Orientalism," scholar Edward Said's (1979) famed term for Eurocentric perspectives on Arabic cultures, and are often matched with equally virulent and misinformed anti-Western beliefs on the other side. Perhaps the most powerful and persistent of these misconceptions involves conceptualizing Islam as "some kind of monolith with a fixed anti-Western viewpoint," a view just as flawed as viewing all "Western" culture as a single entity (Commonwealth of Australia, 2001). Such beliefs are intensified by depictions of both cultures in the media. The political furor over George W. Bush's framing of the War on Terror as a "crusade" (Perez-Rivas, 2001) fanned the flames, and subsequent political discourse solidified in many minds the deeply religious nature of the conflict between the West and the Middle East. This context of ongoing misunderstanding, amidst a climate of heightened fear, must be acknowledged when developing projects aimed at educating citizens about the region.

This chapter documents the efforts of three teachers working with a scholar of modern Middle Eastern history, a social studies education researcher, and a social studies department head to address the knowledge gaps and biases of students in secondary global history and geography classes. Using a variety of primary and secondary sources as well as the knowledge and experience of group members, we designed and implemented several different learning experiences and curricular materials that we hoped would challenge students' existing perceptions of Islam and the Middle East. Students debated recent political flashpoints, including the controversy over the building of the Park 51 Mosque close to "Ground Zero" (the site of the fallen World Trade Center) in New York City and outrage over the publication of cartoons featuring the image of the Islamic prophet, Muhammad. Other students examined news articles, images, and videos featuring stories of everyday life in Islamic societies to empathize with individuals from different cultural perspectives. Finally, to learn the impact of history, geography, and culture on the Middle East today, some of our students focused on two document-based case studies, one on the Israeli–Palestinian conflict and the other comparing Islam's influence in modern Turkey with Iran's fundamentalist Islamic Republic since 1979. Through all of these activities, students learned the ways in which geography and religion shape identity for many in the Middle East, while also being exposed to the cultural diversity of the Islamic world. At the same time, our work demonstrated that some beliefs about the Middle East and Islam were hard to break and that teachers face significant challenges in teaching for empathy in the face of long-held stereotypes.

Misconceptions about Islam and the Middle East: An Historian's View

Professor Zachary Lockman's research and interview on the region provided a useful framework for the group's work on this project. Lockman, a scholar of Middle Eastern and Islamic Studies and History at New York University, has conducted extensive research on the society, culture, and politics of Egypt and Palestine. His most recent work focuses on the history and politics of orientalism as it relates to United States' foreign policy regarding the Middle East since 1945 (Lockman, 2009). For Lockman, the biggest issue in teaching the Middle East to American students is not their ignorance of the region, but rather the strength and amount of misleading and mistaken ideas they bring to class. Perhaps the most important of these ideas is the tendency for students to equate the Middle East with Islam, and for them to see all Middle Eastern history and culture as emerging from a single Islamic tradition. On the other hand, Lockman notes, Americans situate themselves as part of the "West," a "distinct civilization which has its own historical trajectory," rooted mainly in the history of Christian Europe. Seen through this historical perspective, Muslims have always been considered "deeply alien" and "threatening." Lockman argues that this notion of the West vs. the East is "very ingrained and is one of [the] fundamental building blocks" of American cultural identity, so much so that "students don't think about this consciously." A closer look at both the history of the West and the history of the Islamic world shows that there are not two distinct trajectories, but instead many examples of cultural interaction and shared heritage. For instance, Lockman argues, "you can't make sense of Medieval Europe without looking at Islam," since much of Greek culture had been preserved by Middle Eastern scholars before being reintroduced back into Western Europe during the Renaissance. In short, Lockman is concerned about a "very dichotomized way of looking at the world that doesn't really serve us" as historians, teachers, or students.

What is particularly troubling for Lockman is the fact that some leading academics have done their part to promulgate the "us versus them" viewpoint. For instance, historian and political commentator Bernard Lewis (1990) argued in a very influential article, "The Roots of Muslim Rage," that there has been a conflict between the Islam and the West since the founding of the religion, and that the growing fundamentalism in the Middle East can be explained by the region's failure to modernize along with the West. Similarly, *New York Times* columnist Thomas Friedman (1990) perpetuated the idea of a stark divide by using the symbols of the cross and crescent to represent Western and Middle Eastern societies, respectively, largely ignoring the complications of ascribing these symbols—and the meanings attached to them—to entire regions of people. To Lockman, these perspectives on the modern Middle East speak more often to political ideology than to deep historical study and "don't help us understand very much" about the complexities of the region. They are, however, "very powerful metaphors," and this makes them enticing, especially for politicians, pundits, and, indeed, students. Even though these perspectives are, in Lockman's words, "not very useful," they have become deeply embedded in any analysis of the Middle East. Therefore, he argues, students need to confront them directly by reading and unpacking sources like Friedman or Lewis, and, in doing so, it is likely they will confront their own conceptions of the region. As Lockman notes, "We need to take these things apart, then we'll find out that we're not one thing and they're not one thing."

These easy dichotomies must be overcome, because the realities of culture and politics in the Middle East are very complicated. For example, more Muslims live outside of the Middle East than in it, and the world's largest Muslim country, Indonesia, is a democracy with a growing capitalist economy. In addition, according to Lockman, while there are ways that Islam is central to the identities of most Middle Eastern people, there is a significant debate in the region about what it means to be Islamic in today's world. Lockman says that scholars and political figures alike are asking questions such as, "Who are we? What does it mean to be Islamic in this day and age? What do we keep of our tradition? What is authentic? What is not?" In fact, according to Lockman, we must be careful to avoid the "conflation of the Arab World with Islam," as clearly the connection between Islam and society is a "complicated, mixed picture." He points to Burke and Yaghoubian's (2005) collection of biographies of everyday people in the Middle East as an illustration of how Islam is only one of the many factors influencing daily life and cultural identity.

More nuanced perspectives on the Middle East have been promoted by scholars of the region for years. Lockman argues that a watershed moment was Said's (1979) critique of orientalism, which opened up studies of the Middle East to "very careful historical, anthropological, and sociological work" based not on top-down theorizing but instead on social historians' examination of daily life and culture. One concern for Lockman, however, is that these new trends in academia have not yet taken hold in the political and popular discourses surrounding the Middle East: "There is a dichotomy between what goes on in the world of scholarship and what goes on in the rest of the world." Moreover, Lockman states that there is still a stigma surrounding the study of September 11th that no longer exists around other horrific events such as the Holocaust. He posits that this trepidation on the part of historians to examine September 11th may be due to the fact that many Americans still see any attempt to explain the reasons for the attacks as somehow "sympathizing with terrorists," even though, as Lockman says, "[t]o explain where September 11th came from doesn't mean that it was a justifiable thing." In fact, teaching more about the causes of events like September 11th shows students that "it doesn't come out of nowhere. It comes out of a long history" of U.S. involvement in the region, including the use of military bases in Saudi Arabia since the 1950s and the overthrow of the government of Iran in 1953 in order to install the Shah as absolute ruler. These actions, as well as more recent events like the first Persian Gulf War, provide important historical context for September 11th, a context unfamiliar to many students. Lockman argues, and we agree, that education about the Middle East needs to change in order for students to think about this region in more complex ways.

Planning the Unit

The group of social studies educators involved in this project included two human geography teachers, Bradley Abel and Melissa Mabry; a global history teacher, Rebecca Vercillo; a social studies education researcher, Michael Stoll; and a social studies department head, Paul Kelly. The group met four times during the 2011–2012 school year, each time for roughly an hour of scholarly discussion and collaborative lesson planning. In between meetings, each teacher submitted reflections on source readings recommended by Lockman and generated lesson ideas. Each teacher then taught a unit of approximately 1–2 weeks in the spring of 2012 (one teacher also taught her lessons again in the Fall of 2012), allowing at least one of their human geography or global history courses to be observed by the department head and social studies education scholar. These observational data, as well as teachers' written reflections and students' written work, provided fodder for rich debriefing sessions among all participants after each teacher had taught his or her unit.

The group members taught their lessons at John Hersey High School (JHHS), a large comprehensive high school in the northwest suburbs of Chicago. The school serves mainly middle class students and is generally regarded as among the top high schools in Illinois. On the most recent state tests, over 80% of students met or exceeded standards, and the average ACT score of students at the school is higher than the state average. While the school is roughly 75% white, it does have significant Hispanic (13%) and Asian (8%) minorities. Roughly 13% of students at the school are eligible for free or reduced lunch, a number that is below the state norm of 21% (Illinois State Board of Education, 2012). Although the group did not survey the religious beliefs of the students involved in this project, community demographics indicate that the vast majority of students come from Christian or Jewish backgrounds, although there were also some students of Islamic faith. While the majority of students have traditionally been successful at JHHS, in recent years the school has made "college readiness" a goal for all students and a subject of teachers' professional development. At the time of this research, the school was implementing several aggressive interventions targeting "at risk" students, including an increased emphasis on reading and writing skills.

The teachers involved in this project were all veteran educators who have been teaching for between 5 and 15 years, all with distinguished teaching records. All of the teachers emphasize literacy and document analysis in their classes every day, a commitment reflected in the lessons they developed and implemented for this project. The teachers eagerly volunteered for this project because of its use of innovative history scholarship on a challenging teaching topic and the opportunity to collaborate with other educators. Our group was fortunate to have the support of building administration as well as the participation of the social studies department head.

During the time of this project, both Bradley and Melissa taught courses in human geography to mostly ninth grade students of varying skill levels. Their course, while covering all the themes of a traditional geography course, utilized a case study approach to analyze current events around the globe. Both teachers had committed to integrating argumentative writing skills into their courses as part of the school-wide emphasis on college readiness. Melissa explained her course goal as getting students "to leave my course with a broader understanding of the world and current events and with the skills to be able to participate in them as active citizens." After spending time in Israel, Bradley had come to "understand first-hand the toll the Israeli–Palestinian conflict has taken on ordinary people." He hoped to heighten students' awareness of the different and often difficult conditions that shape life in other places.

A third teacher, Rebecca, taught tenth grade world history, a broad survey course designed to integrate world history content with literacy skills development. Given that Rebecca planned to open her course with this unit, she hoped to design "activities that would illustrate for students the relevance of history and culture as they relate to current events," a theme she would revisit throughout the course. Like Melissa and Bradley, she also incorporated primary source document analysis and argumentative writing into this unit as an introduction to the skills her students would be developing throughout the year.

How Should We Approach the Middle East?

The group began its work particularly motivated by the opportunity to learn more about the Middle East and address what everyone admitted was a relatively weak spot in their teaching. Immediately, we found the Lockman interview and source materials to be sweeping in scope and conceptually complex. This made for some very fruitful and at times politically charged dialogues amongst group members, but it also presented a challenge in terms of relating the material to the abilities and interests of ninth and tenth grade students. Lockman's criticisms of traditional approaches to the Middle East resonated with the teachers, all of whom admitted to framing their teaching of the Middle East at least partly in orientalist or "us versus them" terms. Rebecca, in particular, indicated that she was unhappy with teaching the "Islamic world" in terms of its achievements merely to contrast them with those of the "Western world." Melissa and Bradley were similarly interested in finding ways to make their comparative study of world religions less prone to broad stereotypes.

Eventually, we settled on what seemed to be main theme in the Lockman interview and other readings: *much of what Americans know about the Middle East, and Islam in particular, is based on misunderstandings that have deep roots in culture, religion, and history.* As the United States continues to diversify through immigration, and the world reacts to increasing globalization, American students' understandings of other cultures and the religious differences that have led to conflicts have never been more important. The teachers expressed frustration with how little their students really knew about the world's diversity, current events, and geography, noting that, all too frequently, for example, their students associate all Muslims with terrorism. These were the kinds of troubling misconceptions we hoped—and felt a moral responsibility—to correct.

After making a list of the various ways in which their students misunderstood Islam and the Middle East, the planning group focused on tackling two key ideas. First, we decided to confront head on students' beliefs about Islam and its relationships to the cultures of Middle Eastern societies. Since, as Lockman argues, Western students often conflate political issues and cultural values when discussing Islam, we developed our first set of essential questions to attack this problem: Is Islam merely a religion? Or, is it a political concept? Or, finally, is it set of social structures? We felt that this question would provide students with an engaging framework for learning about Islam and applying their knowledge to current global events. But we felt that this question on its own was not enough to overcome the "us versus them" dichotomies that Lockman discussed. Islam is not the same everywhere, nor is culture the same throughout the Middle East. To help disrupt this notion of a monolithic culture, we developed develop a second set of essential questions: why do "they" hate "us"? Is this even a valid question? Who are "they," historically and culturally? And, by extension, who are "we"? What makes the answers to these questions so complicated?

To answer these questions, we planned to push students to think in sophisticated ways about potentially controversial issues. The teachers were invigorated by this challenge, as they believed that controversial issues are the backbone of engaging social studies courses (D. Hess, 2008). Unfortunately, secondary students are rarely asked to grapple with contentious topics, and many struggle to thoughtfully engage perspectives that may differ from their own. As Melissa observed, many of her students "come with the opinions of their parents and have not been exposed to both sides of every argument. Others come totally oblivious to national and world affairs. I want them to understand another viewpoint, even if they don't agree." Requiring students to debate different sides of an argument meant that they needed exposure to, and practice examining, multiple perspectives. Toward this end, the group decided to focus on ways students might be able to empathize with everyday people from the Middle East. Such an approach involved identifying compelling personal stories and struggles and providing opportunities for students to consider the historical, cultural, and social contexts of those individuals or groups (Levesque, 2008). In addition, since controversial subjects require adequate historical and analytical evidence to justify perspectives, the teachers planned to incorporate historical thinking practices such as document analysis and evidence collection skills (see Holt, 1990; Lesh, 2011; Wineburg, 2001). In this effort, they were supported by a department-wide emphasis on using primary and secondary source documents to enhance the intellectual sophistication of student arguments and enable deeper engagement with the past.

Given our focus on historical thinking skills and perspective-taking, it seemed logical to examine a few historical cases in depth rather than attempt a survey of the entire Middle East. Melissa and Bradley chose to focus on the Israeli–Palestinian conflict because of its central place in U.S. foreign policy and global media coverage as well as its linkages to questions of religious, ethnic, and national identity. As Melissa explained, this topic delivered "the biggest bang for the buck":

> The problems and conflicts that have been occurring in the Middle East for several years have shaped world and U.S. politics on a yearly basis. Our foreign policy is often dictated by what is going on there, and that is one of the reasons why I think it is so crucial for students to be exposed to this information.

The topic also aligned well with the core course theme of identity, a theme that Bradley argued was particularly salient for his students:

> Our ninth graders are trying to figure out their own identity and who they are. The identity conflict between Israelis and Palestinians allows the students to take a look at

a biblical, historical, and political conflict, and understand how identity, and a sense of who you are, can lead to something so big as what is going on in the Middle East.

On the other hand, the global history teacher, Rebecca, decided to take a comparative approach that examined the relationship between Islam, politics, and recent relations with the United States, using Iran and Turkey as her case studies. This approach allowed her to "dispel typical notions or stereotypes about the Middle East" by confronting students with "what they think they know about Islam." The contrast of Iran with Turkey, in particular, provided a useful opportunity for guided discovery learning, an instructional model in which students must decide what evidence serves as examples or non-examples of a given concept, in this case Islamic identity (Eggen & Kauchak, 2012). It also allowed Rebecca to use the unit as a preview of upcoming historical events in other contexts, including the Age of Imperialism, the World Wars, and the Cold War.

The Middle East in the Classrooms

At first glance, the group's challenge to collaboratively design learning activities for use in both geography and world history courses seemed daunting. Indeed, the idiosyncrasies of each course and teacher meant that the learning activities would not be the same across all classes involved in the project (Chapter Resources I, III). At the same time, though, there was a strong group consensus that all activities should adhere to the framework discussed above and should be designed collaboratively. This meant that teachers designed and helped implement learning activities for classes other than their own. It also meant that the geography classes would be infused with a good deal of recent world history content, and vice versa, thereby broadening the approaches of all the teachers involved.

The Geography Classes

We broke the geography unit into three distinct, week-long sections, each with its own "big idea." The first part began with a discussion of contemporary issues regarding religion as a way both to "hook" students into a study of the modern Middle East and to bring out some important student misconceptions about religion and Islam in particular. The students took a survey of religious beliefs (Chapter Resources V), and then discussed their answers in small-group settings that rotated every two minutes, thereby gathering a variety of student perspectives. After the groupwork, the teachers conducted whole-class discussions of the surveys, with the caveat that students were not allowed to share their own perspectives. Rather, each student was required to discuss what they found interesting about other students' responses. The next day, students took a similar anticipatory survey (Chapter Resources V) entitled "How much do you know about the separation of Church and State?" These two surveys and introductory discussions led to the first big idea for the unit: what should be the role of governments in issues of religion? Bradley and Melissa asked their students to brainstorm responses to this question, which they then shared with the class. These responses, posted on the wall, were re-visited as students read articles on recent political controversies involving Islam: the building of an Islamic Cultural Center on a site near the fallen World Trade Center in New York City (Murphy, 2010); the decision by Lowe's, the home improvement store, to pull its ads from the reality show, *All-American Muslim* (Ng, 2011); the controversial publishing in Denmark of cartoons featuring the prophet Muhammad (e.g. Sullivan, 2006); and France's decision to ban the wearing of religious symbols in school (e.g. Sciolino, 2004). Using these articles as well as their own examples, students gathered evidence to either support or refute the following thesis statement: "It is morally appropriate for governments and political figures to become involved in religious matters." This thesis (or its antithesis) was the subject of an informal classroom debate.

The second part of the unit focused on using various media tools to depict the major beliefs and practices of Islam, with a special emphasis on what the teachers termed "myth-bashing," the direct confrontation of student misconceptions with vivid images of reality (Chapter Resources II). Students answered a series of fact-based questions about Islam and Islamic culture before examining a series of images depicting Islamic culture around the world as well as images of Islamic women from countries in Africa and the Middle East. Some of these images depicted everyday women in "traditional garb" such as burqas, while others depicted less stereotypical images such as Muslim women athletes, Saudi women demonstrating for the right to drive, and protests against religious discrimination in the United States. Students also watched two short video clips from a series entitled "Faith and Fear: Islam in America" (ABC News, 2010), one of which featured a teen roundtable on Islam. The final activity entailed the creation of a "perceptual map" of the Middle East using Geographic Information Systems (GIS), in which the students compared their ideas about Islamic culture and the geography of the Middle East with the realities presented by demographic and geographic data. After these activities, students wrote reflections answering the following question: "How does your initial perception of Islam and the Islamic world differ from the realities presented in these activities?"

After a test on the main concepts and beliefs of Islam, the teachers moved to the final part, a focus on the Israeli–Palestinian conflict. In order to emphasize the controversial nature of the conflict, we decided that students would have to "take sides" and support their position with evidence. Ultimately, we settled on two main idea statements for students to defend or refute: "Palestinians have hurt their chances at becoming a country" and "Israelis are making it hard for Palestinians to ever have a country." The majority of the week's activities centered around students analyzing documents supplied by the teachers and collecting evidence either for or against each statement, as well as evidence that pointed in other directions. Using an evidence collection template (Chapter Resources VI), students participated in a series of document analysis activities related to six "sticking points" we identified as essential to understanding the conflict:

1.   the Israeli occupation of the West Bank;
2.   the future of Palestinian refugees and prisoners;
3.   the future of Israeli settlements in the West Bank;
4.   the Israeli security fence/wall being built;
5.   the future of Jerusalem;
6.   extremism on both sides.

In addition to excerpts from primary source materials such as the Balfour Declaration, the Hamas Covenant, and mid-19th century Zionist pamphlets, teachers provided students with news articles (Tolan, 2006; Woodward, 2000) and map-based sources (A land divided, 2002). These documents were carefully chosen to represent a variety of perspectives on the six sticking points as well as give students relevant background information on the conflict.

The unit culminated with an event that the group called a "forum" on the Israeli–Palestinian conflict, to which geography and other classes were invited. The forum consisted of an hour-long debate between two teachers. With Melissa acting as moderator, Bradley took on the Israeli perspective, while social studies department head Paul argued the Palestinian side. The students were presented with both sides of the debate beforehand in the form of teacher-written essays on the topic (Chapter Resources VII), and each of the six major sticking points was highlighted during the debate. Each teacher emphasized his point of view using dramatic performance, images, video clips, and humor. What began as a formal debate with each teacher giving a 10-minute presentation developed into a back-and-forth discussion about which group has a rightful claim to the land. After the forum, teachers directed students to write about what they viewed as the main forces shaping Palestinian and Israeli identities and provide evidence in support of one of the two main idea statements. A debriefing activity the next day included a discussion of these prompts as well as student reflection on the actions that should be taken to solve the "identity crisis" between the Israelis and Palestinians.

The World History Class

Similar to the units designed for Melissa and Bradley's classes, the learning activities for Rebecca's world history class took a three-part approach, moving from student misconceptions about Islam to historical case studies. Because this unit was taught at the beginning of the school year, the group decided that debate might not yet be appropriate for students who were still unfamiliar with each other and the teacher. Given that Rebecca had less time to spend on the topic than the other teachers, her unit focused on skills development with one summative assessment, a thesis supported by evidence on the question: "How would you describe the modern Middle East?"

Rebecca began her unit by asking students this very question. She instructed students to locate Turkey and Iran on a map and to speculate on what these countries might be like based on their geography. She then asked students to work in groups to create a wall chart contrasting the cultural, geographic, and political characteristics of these Middle Eastern countries with Europe and the United States. Students were encouraged not to filter responses, but to list, based on their own experiences and prior knowledge, as many things as possible for later class discussion. Once the groups finished their work, each shared some of their contrasts with the rest of the class. Other groups were invited to comment on, agree with, or dispute the information presented. Rebecca also asked them to consider whether these perceptions were accurate for the entire Middle East.

Following this discussion, students analyzed two Middle Eastern societies in depth: Iran and Turkey. These nations were chosen for their distinctive cultures as well as their recent cultural and political trajectories. Both nations also experienced revolutionary upheavals in the 20th century—Turkey in 1923 and Iran in 1979—which continue to shape their cultural and political identity in modern times. The task at hand for students was to connect contemporary descriptions of each nation to these watershed events and to compare and contrast the two nations' subsequent histories. To achieve this objective, Rebecca directed students to read a section in their textbook (Bentley & Ziegler, 2010) about the political, social, and cultural characteristics of Iran since 1979 and Turkey since 1923. For further context, students viewed excerpts from the graphic novel *Persepolis* (Satrapi, 2003) and conducted guided internet research on Turkish cultural characteristics. Students used the evidence gathered from these sources to complete an evidence collection assignment (see Chapter Resources VIII), which would then be used as the foundation for an in-class discussion. This assignment, similar to ones used by Melissa and Bradley, required students to act as social scientists and historians by collecting evidence from a variety of sources in order to develop an argument.

Following the evidence collection activities and assessment, the class reviewed the differences they had uncovered in their research on the two nations. Students' overwhelming response was that while Iran and Turkey had some similarities, mostly stemming from their shared Islamic heritage, the two countries differed significantly in terms of political structures and cultural traditions. To push their thinking, Rebecca then asked, "Why are Turkey and Iran so different despite being so geographically close and sharing the same religion?" (Chapter Resources IV.) To answer this question, students examined a set of primary and secondary source documents from the Turkish independence movement of 1923 led by Mustafa Kemal Atatürk and the 1979 Islamic Revolution of Ayatollah Ruhollah Khomeini. These documents included speeches, news articles, images, and maps that revealed multiple reasons for the different political and cultural paths of each country since their respective revolutions. Students analyzed these documents using historical thinking skills in a document-based question (DBQ) format (Chapter Resources III), which they would then consult for their final essay assessment.

The final learning activity in the unit involved comparing the Islamic Revolution in Iran to the radical fundamentalist movements in other parts of the Middle East such as the Taliban and al Qaeda. In a gallery walk format, pairs of students viewed images from the Iranian Revolution and Taliban rule in Afghanistan and read excerpts of statements by Osama bin Laden (Lawrence, 2005). Rebecca instructed students to discuss the similarities and differences in these documents. The ensuing class discussion centered on the themes of, and contexts for, fundamentalist Islamism and its relationship to the U.S. For example, Rebecca pointed out that unlike with Iran, Turkey's relations with the West have been friendly—indeed the United States considers Turkey an ally, and Turkish membership in the European Union is under discussion.

Students spent the final day of the unit writing an argumentative essay in response to the question, "How would you describe the modern Middle East?" Given the complexity of this task, Rebecca intentionally left the prompt open-ended and subjective. She expected that in writing their essays, students would explain their positions with evidence they had already gathered in their evidence collection templates, the gallery walk, and research on the differences between Turkey and Iran since their revolutions. The educator group intended to compare student responses on this essay to their initial statements at the beginning of the unit to see where and how student views might have changed.

Moving Beyond "Us" and "Them"?

The collegial atmosphere within the planning group extended to its observation and data collection process. At least one group member other than the teacher of record observed each learning activity in both the geography and world history courses. Observers often sat in on student groups and engaged students directly when comments or thoughts needed explanation or further development. In observing each class period, we paid particular attention to the ways in which students referred to the Middle East or Islam, the misconceptions students articulated, and the evidence students used to support their arguments during discussions. We found that the quality of student discussion was mixed, as the misconceptions they held seemed to be so entrenched. We were pleased, however, that by the end of the units in all three classes, students' beliefs about the modern Middle East and Islam did seem more nuanced, and discussions grew more sophisticated.

In both the geography and world history lessons, the clearest evidence of student misconceptions came at the beginning of the units, when teachers elicited students' prior understandings of Islam and the Middle East. In the geography classes, the introductory discussions on religion were very engaging, with high-levels of student participation and active facilitation on the part of teachers, whose role was to clarify student comments or ask follow-up questions such as "Why do you feel this way?" or "What makes you think that?" The anticipatory surveys on religion and ensuing discussion indicated that a majority of students held several misconceptions in common. For instance, most students did not believe that Muslims worshipped the same God as Christians and Jews, even when corrected by Muslim students in the class. Conversely, some students discussed the Christian "trinity" and ascribed a similar structure to Islam. In addition, a majority of students seemed unclear about the relationship between religion and politics in the United States. They were surprised to learn that despite the large role that religion seems to play in American politics today, the Constitution never refers to any deity. They were also surprised that many lawsuits in U.S. history involving religion and the public sphere were intra-faith controversies brought up by Christians, not by atheists or non-Christians.

In Rebecca's introductory brainstorming sessions, the world history students articulated potent stereotypes, making references such as "full of Arabs," "terrorism," "that head thing … I don't know what it's called," "Egypt," and "spicy food" to describe the Middle East. Our group anticipated that peers within the class would correct the misconceptions of others, so we had advised Rebecca not to intervene during this discussion. However, students did not step in as we had expected. In the few instances when students did try to correct others, their "corrections" came out as flawed as their classmates' original statements. Assertions like, "Egypt isn't Arab, it's Hindu!" and "Iran hates us because we killed Osama [bin Laden]" were peppered throughout the discussions. Overall, it appeared that most students came with ideas about the Middle East that reflected an error-laden and clearly orientalist perspective toward culture.

Based on these initial experiences, it became clear to the teachers that student prejudices posed a large challenge to the goals of the project. The group felt that is was important to, as Melissa put it, "get their thoughts out in the open where the class can unpack them," but in early discussions, this unpacking did not seem to be happening. Subsequent activities, based on contemporary and historical case studies, were more successful at promoting constructive dialogue because they provided a common context for students and grounded the discussion in concrete situations instead of generic stereotypes. In particular, discussions of current events seemed to provide students with the right mix of controversial topics for fostering debate and real-life stories with which they could empathize (D. Hess, 2008).

In the geography classes, the news articles regarding religious controversies led to animated discussions. Some students argued that *All-American Muslim* was "just a reality show" and not controversial at all, meaning that Lowe's and others were just "Muslim bashers." Other students praised Lowe's for "taking a stand for traditional values." Some simply stated, "It's a free country." Responses were similarly divided when it came to the French ban on wearing religious symbols in schools. Many students thought that France had gone too far, which led both classes to a discussion of religious freedom in America. Some students thought that "there should be some limits when it comes to religion," while others countered that "the government is not allowed to set limits" and therefore there should be no boundaries to religious freedom. The teachers were much happier with the quality of dialogue surrounding the current events controversies, and observers noted that the lively class discussions featured students directly responding to each other's points rather than simply sharing their own ideas.

Surprisingly, there was much less debate in the classroom when discussing the Park 51 Mosque and its construction so close to Ground Zero. Perhaps this was due to students' belief that "diversity of viewpoints and religions is a good thing" for American society. In Melissa's class, an overwhelming majority of students accepted one student's premise that "inter-faith dialogue is the key to changing the reality that Muslims in America are treated and thought of differently." But debate might have been avoided because there was a real possibility of students offending each other. Two Muslim students in Melissa's class gave personal examples of their "different treatment," including experiences in airports and stores, as a rationale for building the center. A Muslim student in Bradley's class spoke of similar experiences with his family. These personal stories spurred further questions by their classmates, and the teachers found themselves wanting to validate—and even highlight—the views of the Muslim students without putting these students "on the spot" in the midst of a politically charged discussion. The non-Muslim students in the class remained respectful, but they did not challenge their Muslim counterparts in the same ways they had challenged each other when debating other controversies. At any rate, the lack of debate indicates that there might have been a silencing effect (see Weis & Fine, 1993) that inhibited students from sharing many details about their ethnic or religious identities. Indeed, after this activity, this small group of Muslim students did not make any further personal contributions to discussions again, and their future participation in class largely blended into that of the other students. Still, Melissa and Bradley felt that this discussion was worthwhile because of the questions it elicited from students.

While promoting in-class debate helped students reflect on their notions about Muslims, providing map-based sources allowed students to construct new, fact-based understandings of the Middle East. In every class, students demonstrated limited knowledge of the region's geography but readily admitted their ignorance and, in most instances, quickly reframed their understandings when given materials that enabled them to do so. In Bradley's class, students were shocked by the relative lack of overlap between their "perceptual maps" and the reality of the Middle East as presented to them in the GIS activity. In particular, students thought most Muslims lived in Saudi Arabia and were surprised to see that there were multiple countries with larger Muslim populations. In addition, most students' perceptual maps rarely matched those of students sitting next to them, leading to dialogues between students about their misconceptions. In Rebecca's class, students used "hot and sandy" and "camels" to describe the region physically, and could not locate Iran or Turkey on a map. There was surprise that the nations actually shared a border. This led some students to believe that the nations were culturally and politically similar, but this notion was quickly abandoned upon further research. When Rebecca began contrasting the concept of "empire" with that of "nation," students appeared to have some difficulty grasping the differences. Until she showed them a map of the Ottoman Empire superimposed on the modern Middle East, there was little recognition among students of the myriad cultures, languages, and ethnicities contained within that mammoth geopolitical entity. Following this, there was a greater understanding in the class about the importance of national identity in both Iran and Turkey. Moreover, the use of maps in class greatly helped enhance student understandings of the Israeli–Palestinian conflict. Teachers were able to show students why issues like the location of Israeli settlements in the West Bank and the proximity of holy sites such as the Dome of the Rock and the Wailing Wall have made a two-state solution difficult. Observers often saw students pointing to or talking about maps of the region. Indeed, the most sophisticated arguments made by students regarding the "sticking points" of the conflict revolved around land. Later assessments by the teachers confirmed this anecdotal evidence: student knowledge of the geography of the Middle East greatly improved as a result of these lessons.

The use of images and video also proved to be an important factor in promoting student thinking on controversial issues. Melissa dedicated a large part of one of her lessons to the differences in women's rights across Islamic countries. To do so, she used images and documentaries to illustrate the wide variation across the region in dress (e.g., differences between the burqa and hijab), access to education, and full citizenship rights. While analyzing images of Turkish culture, one group of students argued that, at least in some cities, "Turkey looks just like America!" In giving examples of dress and freedoms for women during discussions, the group drew from the images they had seen. Short video clips had a similar effect on students in that personal stories from the films resonated in later class discussions in ways that other texts did not. Some students shuddered in horror at the screen when a Christian pastor's teenage son told a Muslim teen that he was going to hell. Depictions of Palestinian refugee camps reduced a few students to tears. The observers agreed that the emotional realism and complexity of the images and films were powerful rejoinders to the stereotypes students held about Muslims living in the Middle East.

The forum on the Israeli–Palestinian conflict appeared to provide the most powerful opportunity for student immersion in multiple perspectives about the Middle East. The students clearly relished the passionate, back-and-forth debate, even though most were not convinced by either side. After the teachers finished their prepared statements and students were allowed to ask questions, students challenged each debate participant to defend his perspective. Students asked complex questions such as "Why are you justifying terrorism?" (to the Palestinian side) and "How can a country that believes in the sanctity of property steal territory from those who rightfully own it?" (to the Israeli side). Student comments expressed sympathy with the Israeli perspective on some points, such as the need for security ("if Hamas went away, there'd be no need for aggression [from Israel]"), and with the Palestinian perspective on others, such as the illegality of Israeli settlements in the West Bank ("of course you [Israel] can do whatever you want when you are supported unconditionally by America"). As the forum ended and students were urged to attend their next class, a group of roughly 20 students stayed behind and continued discussing the issues with each other and the teachers. Both Melissa and Bradley needed to use an entire class period the next day to analyze the debate, and Bradley heard from more than one student that the forum "brought the conflict to life." Based on the teachers' experiences and student feedback, the project group considered the forum to be its most successful learning activity. By modeling respectful disagreement about a heated issue, the debate affirmed Thomas E. Kelly's (1986) contention that social studies teachers should adopt a position of "committed impartiality"—that is, they "should state rather than conceal their own views on controversial topics" while at the same time "insuring that competing perspectives receive a fair hearing through critical discourse" (p. 130).

Our whole group met following the lessons to share the results of the students' written work and changes in student thinking regarding Islam and the Middle East. Bradley and Melissa were particularly eager to share their students' papers from their unit on the Israeli–Palestinian conflict. One of the biggest surprises was the subtlety of students' arguments. Given the enthusiasm with which the students participated in the forum and the rather dogmatic approach of the two debaters, we expected to read similarly opinionated essays from the students. Yet the majority of students, rather than taking a clear side in the issue, wrote as if they were members of the United Nations trying to resolve this thorny conflict. One student wrote, "the question of who is wrong and who is right is not the right question to ask, because this is a complex issue with no 'correct' answer." Essays like this one demonstrated sophisticated understandings of the political and cultural realities of the region. One student remarked that the conflict is "really about Israelis versus Israelis and Palestinians versus Palestinians," and that "a solution will not occur until both sides contain the extremists." Another student stated that "Palestinians and Israelis have so much in common," and "that peace will come when they want it to come." In addition to the debate, the teachers also credited the extensive evidence collection activities for the depth and precision of thought demonstrated in the essays. Indeed, many students displayed a range of analytical skills, reaching conclusions rooted primarily in textual and documentary evidence rather than presuppositions and opinions. For example, a student who initially wrote that "Israel should let Palestine be a country because there would be less fighting that way" later strengthened his position by adding evidence such as, "The pattern of Israeli aggression against Palestinians includes the building of the settlements across the Green Line, the so-called security wall, and constant checkpoints." Melissa and Bradley were very pleased to note that, overall, student writing had substantially improved.

As in the geography classes, Rebecca's world history students clearly understood that there are very separate and distinct cultures in the Middle East. In their essays, a vast majority of students responded in one of two ways. Most students took a comparative approach in discussing what they had learned about the modern Middle East, which is not surprising given the course focus. These students used thesis statements that stressed both the similar Islamic heritage of Iran and Turkey as well as the nations' distinct histories, cultures, and political structures. For instance, one student explained that "Turkey and Iran are both republics, yet differences exist in terms of the political leadership of each nation, particularly in its relationship to Islam." Rebecca was thrilled to encounter such nuanced thinking so early in the school year. Other students responded to the prompt by drawing conceptual distinctions between Islam and Islamic fundamentalism. These students tried to clear up some common misconceptions about the faith and people who practice the faith, arguing that Americans view the Middle East from a completely westernized perspective. One student's thesis statement read, "While it is true that the majority of the Middle East is Islamic, we need to remember that there are differences between fundamentalists and average Muslims." With respect to both types of responses, we were pleased to see a "correction" to a few of the misconceptions that had emerged in earlier class discussions.

Concluding Thoughts

The educators in our group entered this project knowing that the Middle East and religion—and in particular Islam, which is often associated with terrorism—can be tough topics to discuss with 14- and 15-year-olds. Nonetheless, we believed that teachers have a responsibility to teach controversial issues. Perhaps the greatest challenge for the teachers was the tension between wanting to appear "neutral" or "objective" while recognizing their own biases and perspectives on the issue. The teachers were passionate about topics like the Israeli–Palestinian conflict and Islamic fundamentalism, and this made it difficult to present all sides of the issues from a completely non-biased perspective. For the most part, the teachers heeded Lockman's advice to make the unit less about defending or supporting particular views and more about modeling how students can and should develop their own sophisticated perspectives on complex issues. In fact, without initially naming it as such, our group of teachers had adopted a stance of committed impartiality (Kelly, 1986). Rather than hiding their own views on the Israel-Palestinian conflict, for instance, the debaters laid them bare, opened them up to analysis and criticism, and challenged students to do the same through the evidence collection and argument development activities. In this way, the teachers allowed themselves to be participants in democratic discourse on controversial issues without losing their authority as teachers (D. Hess, 2008). At the same time, the learning experiences in this unit were highly engaging because they allowed students to participate in the discourse along with the teachers, a process which required them to develop their own informed perspectives based on evidence and analysis, not conjecture and stereotypes.

Yet troubling notions about the Middle East and Islam proved persistent. One of our goals was to show students that the world does not conform to easy stereotypes: Arabs are not always terrorists, and women can be and are leaders of majority-Muslim nations. The learning activities in this unit proved fairly successful in confronting such stereotypes, because they tended to be based on a lack of knowledge that was easily corrected. However, some of the students' beliefs and values were more difficult to complicate. For instance, while students may have understood conceptually that it is possible for a Muslim to be an outstanding American citizen, there was still a tendency for some to identify Muslims as anti-American. Moreover, at the end of the unit, some students still could not separate their understandings of the Islamic religion from the words and actions of Islamic fundamentalists. Many students' comments included the terms "us" and "them," even after discussing the limitations of such dichotomies. Suggestions like "nuking" the Palestinians, even if made in jest and certainly not mainstream among students, expressed the limits of students' worldviews. Such deeply held, and perhaps unconscious, beliefs are hard to change. While units like ours certainly help, there is much more work to do.

Rather than being wary about teaching controversial subjects, however, these realities energized the group and reinforced for us the value of thoughtful teaching methods in social studies classes. Being innovative in this case meant getting "back to the basics" of the discipline. Reading about and discussing recent events made learning about different parts of the world relevant in ways that textbooks and primary source materials cannot always do. In addition, new chapters are added every day to the long-standing cultural conflicts that were the subject of this unit. Students could not help but hear about political controversies and hate crimes, and they brought their questions, efforts to understand, and opinions about these to each lesson. It was empowering for teachers to see their students gain a broader understanding of what was happening around the world, but it was also stimulating for the teachers, who were learning right alongside the students.

While knowledge of current events is crucial, it is not the only requirement for an informed perspective. Primary and secondary source analysis and evidence collection skills remain important to learning about the past and the present. The group's efforts demonstrate that regular practice in historical thinking facilitates student understanding. By categorizing and analyzing documents in open-ended critical reading exercises, students not only began to re-consider their misguided beliefs regarding the Middle East and its diverse cultures, but they also could hone the skill of gleaning relevant and applicable evidence from challenging texts in order to construct evidence-based, historical arguments. As students sat side by side with their peers of all academic levels and critically analyzed issues of major global consequence, a spirit of academic community emerged. It is our hope that these students will continue to cultivate rational thought about global issues and empathy toward others as they enter our diverse and complicated global society.

Works Cited

ABC News. (2010). Faith and fear: Islam in America. *ABC News* report. Retrieved from http://abcnews.go.com

A land divided. (2002, March 15). A land divided. *Time, 159.*

Bentley, J., & Ziegler H. (2010). *Traditions and encounters: A global perspective on the past* (5th ed.). Columbus, OH: McGraw-Hill Education.

Burke, E., & Yaghoubian, D. (2005). *Struggle and survival in the Middle East* (2nd ed.). Berkeley, CA: University of California Press.

Commonwealth of Australia. (2001). Mutual misperceptions: The historical context of Muslim-Western relations. *Current Issues Brief, No. 7.* Canberra, Australia: Department of Parliamentary Library.

Douglass, S. (2002). Teaching about religion. *Educational Leadership, 60*(2), 32–36.

Eggen, P., & Kauchak, D. (2012). *Strategies and models for teachers: Teaching content and thinking skills* (6th ed.). Boston, MA: Pearson.

Friedman, T. (1990, October 28). The world: A dream-like landscape, a dream-like reality. *New York Times,* Sec. 4, p. 3.

Friedman, T. (2000, January 28). Foreign affairs; One country: two worlds. *New York Times,* p. A23.

Hess, D. (2008). Controversial issues and democratic discourse. In L. Levstik, & C. Tyson (Eds.), *Handbook of research in social studies education* (pp. 124–136). New York: Routledge.

Hess, F. (2008). *Still at risk: What students don't know, even now.* Washington, DC: Common Core.

Holt, T. (1990). *Thinking historically: Narrative, imagination, and understanding.* New York: College Board.

Huntington, S. (1993). The clash of civilizations. *Foreign Affairs* (Summer), 22–49.

Illinois State Board of Education. (2012). School report card: John Hersey High School. Retrieved from www.isbe.net

Kelly, T. E. (1986). Discussing controversial issues: Four perspectives on the teacher's role. *Theory and Research in Social Education XIV*(2), 113–138.

Lawrence, B. (2005). *Messages to the world: The statements of Osama bin Laden.* London: Verso Books.

Lesh, B. (2011). *Why won't you just tell us the answer? Teaching historical thinking in grades 7–12.* Portland, ME: Stenhouse.

Levesque, S. (2008). *Thinking historically: Educating students for the twenty-first century.* Toronto, Canada: University of Toronto Press.

Lewis, B. (1990). The roots of Muslim rage. *The Atlantic* (September), 47–60.

Lockman, Z. (2009). *Contending visions of the Middle East: The history and politics of Orientalism* (2nd ed.). Cambridge, UK: Cambridge University Press.

Murphy, D. (2010, August 20). Is Ground Zero mosque part of culture war or symbol of tolerance? *Christian Science Monitor.* Retrieved from www.csmonitor.com

National Geographic & Roper Public Affairs. (2006). *Final report: National Geographic–Roper Public Affairs 2006 geography literacy study.* Washington, DC: National Geographic Society.

Ng, C. (2011). Lowe's backlash: Conservative Christian group behind ad pullout not backing down. *ABCNews.com.* Retrieved from http://abcnews.go.com

Paxton, R. J. (2003). Don't know much about history—never did. *Phi Delta Kappan, 85*(4), 264–273.

Perez-Rivas, M. (2001, September 16). Bush vows to rid the world of "evil doers." *CNN.com.* Retrieved from http://edition.cnn.com/2001/US/09/16/gen.bush.terrorism [full text of speech can be found at http://georgewbush-whitehouse.archives.gov]

Pew Research Center for the People & the Press (2011, September 20). Palestinian statehood: Mixed views, low visibility. Retrieved from www.people-press.org/2011/09/20/palestinian-statehood-mixed-views-low-visibility

Ravitch, D., & Finn, C. (1987). *What do our 17-year-olds know? A report on the first national assessment of history and literature.* New York: Harper & Row.

Said, E. (1979). *Orientalism.* New York: Vintage.

Satrapi, M. (2003). *Persepolis.* New York: Pantheon.

Sciolino, E. (2004, February 11). French assembly votes to ban religious symbols in schools. *New York Times.* Retrieved from www.nytimes.com

Sewall, G. T. (2008). *Islam in the classroom: What the textbooks tell us.* New York: American Textbook Council. Retrieved from www.historytextbooks.org/islamreport.pdf

Sullivan, A. (2006, February 7). Your taboo, not mine. *Time.* Retrieved from www.time.com

Tolan, S. (2006, May 21). Refusing to see the other side of the story. *Chicago Tribune.* Retrieved from http://articles.chicagotribune.com

Weis, L., & Fine, M. (Eds.). (1993). *Beyond silenced voices: Class, race, and gender in United States schools.* Albany, NY: SUNY Press.

WGBH Educational Foundation. (2002). Global connections: the Middle East. Retrieved from www.pbs.org/wgbh/globalconnections/mideast/index.html

Wiggins, G., & McTighe, J. (2005). *Understanding by design* (expanded 2nd ed.). Alexandria, VA: Association for Supervision and Curriculum Development.

Wineburg, S. (2001). *Historical thinking and other unnatural acts.* Philadelphia: Temple University Press.

Woodward, K. (2000, July 23). Jerusalem: A city that echoes eternity. *Newsweek.* Retrieved from www.thedailybeast.com/newsweek

CHAPTER RESOURCES

I. Unit Plan: Middle East, Geography (Melissa and Bradley)

Common Core Standards

CCSS.ELA-Literacy.RH.9-10.1 Cite specific textual evidence to support analysis of primary and secondary sources, attending to such features as the date and origin of the information.

CCSS.ELA-Literacy.WHST.9-10.1a: Introduce precise claim(s), distinguish the claim(s) from alternate or opposing claims, and create an organization that establishes clear relationships among the claim(s), counterclaims, reasons, and evidence.

Essential Questions

- Is Islam merely a religion? Or, is it a political concept? Or, finally, is it a set of social structures?
- Why do "they" hate "us"? Is this even a valid question? Who are "they," historically and culturally? And, by extension, who are "we"? What makes the answers to these questions so complicated?

Enduring Understandings

Students will understand that:
- The Islamic world consists of diverse societies and cultures.
- Many commonly held beliefs about Islam and the Middle East are based in misconceptions or limited understandings of the region and its people.
- The differences between the "Islamic world" and the "West" are due to historical, cultural, religious, and geographic factors.
- There are many historical and contemporary causes of the Israeli–Palestinian conflict, including Israeli occupation of the West Bank, the future of Palestinian refugees and prisoners, the future of Israeli settlements in the West Bank, the Israeli security wall, the future of Jerusalem, and extremism on both sides.

Culminating Assessment

Each student will write an argumentative essay referencing the main "sticking points" of the Israeli–Palestinian conflict and defending one of the following thesis statements:

a) Palestinians have hurt their chances at becoming a country.
b) Israelis are making it hard for Palestinians to ever have a country.

Selected Learning Activities

Lesson 1: Students will take anticipatory surveys of student beliefs and knowledge about the role of religion in political and social life (Chapter Resources V). The results of these surveys will be discussed by students in small groups that rotate every two minutes. After this "lightning round," there will be a whole-class discussion in which students are not allowed to share their own perspectives—instead, they must only discuss what they have heard from others. Responses will be written on posters on the wall and left there to be edited throughout the unit.

Lesson 2: Students will read articles on recent political controversies involving Islam and find evidence to support or refute the following thesis statement: "It is morally appropriate for governments and political figures to become involved in religious matters." Student evidence will be used in an informal class debate. Students will read articles such as:

- "Your taboo, not mine" (Sullivan, 2006);
- "Is Ground Zero mosque part of culture war or symbol of tolerance?" (Murphy, 2010);
- "French assembly votes to ban religious symbols in schools" (Sciolino, 2004);
- "Lowe's backlash: Conservative Christian group behind ad pullout not backing down" (Ng, 2011).

Lesson 3: Students will take a short pre-assessment on knowledge of Islam and the Islamic world. They will then learn facts about and examine various images depicting the beliefs and practice of Islam around the world. Students will write reflections on these facts and images responding to the following question: "How does your initial perception of Islam and the Islamic World differ from the realities presented in these activities?" (see Chapter Resources III).

Lesson 4: In groups, students will analyze documents on the historical and current Israeli–Palestinian conflict and collect evidence in support of one of the following thesis statements: a) "Palestinians have hurt their chances at becoming a country"; or b) "Israelis are making it hard for Palestinians to ever have a country."

Using the evidence collection template (Chapter Resources VI), students will search for evidence tied to six "sticking points":

- Israeli occupation of the West Bank;
- the future of Palestinian refugees and prisoners;
- the future of Israeli settlement in the West Bank;
- the Israeli security fence/wall;
- the future of Jerusalem;
- extremism/terrorism on both sides.

Historical and current events sources will include:

- The Balfour Declaration (http://avalon.law.yale.edu/20th_century/balfour.asp);
- Hamas Covenant (http://avalon.law.yale.edu/20th_century/hamas.asp);
- 19th Century Zionist Pamphlets (www.fordham.edu/Halsall/jewish/jewishsbook.asp);
- "Jerusalem: A City that echoes eternity" (Woodward, 2000);
- "Refusing to see the other side of the story" (Tolan, 2006);
- "A land divided" (*Time,* 2002).

Lesson 5: Students will read background essays on the Israeli–Palestinian conflict (Chapter Resources VII) and participate in a class forum. Students will witness a debate between two teachers, one presenting the "Israeli perspective" and the other presenting the "Palestinian perspective." Following the debate, students will be given an opportunity to ask questions of the presenters. Students will then use the knowledge gained from the forum as well as their examination of historical and contemporary documents to write an argumentative essay (see above).

II. Lesson Plan III: Changing Perceptions of the Islamic World

Aim: Who are "they" (Muslims) historically and culturally? Who are "we"?

Objectives: Students will understand that many commonly held beliefs about Islam and the Middle East are based on misconceptions or limited understandings of the region and its people

Do Now: Students will begin by writing on the following prompt: "When you think of the Middle East, what images come to mind? List at least three." Students will share their answers with partners.

Activity: Students will complete a K-W-L chart on Islam and the Islamic world. Students will use the results of the opening discussion as well as their own prior knowledge to write what they know and believe about Islam and the Islamic world as well as any questions they have about Islam. Students will share what they have written with a partner before discussing with the whole-class. The teacher will solicit student responses but will not correct student misconceptions or answer student questions. Students will then learn facts about and examine various images depicting the beliefs and practice of Islam around the world. Students will take notes on these facts and images on their K-W-L charts, especially focusing on new ideas or ways their understandings of Islam and the Islamic world have changed.

Resources used here will include:

1. Video excerpts from "Faith and Fear: Islam in America" (ABC News, 2010). Students will view the video excerpts depicting the experiences of Muslims in America and contrast this with their prior statements about Islam.

2. Teacher will display images of Islamic culture, including depictions of Islamic women from around the world.

   (www.pbs.org/pov/thelightinhereyes/photo_gallery_background.php?photo=3#.Um3eKRYmTdk)

   Students will discuss the very different portrayals of Muslim women and how they differ depending on the culture they are from.

3. GIS Perceptual Map Activity

   a) Students will go to: http://cascourses.uoregon.edu/geog610wp/hgia/geography/ch2/index.html and click on "Activity 1: Mapping Culture Regions (Middle East)." A blank map of the general area of the Middle East will appear on the screen. Students will trace a boundary around what they consider to be the cultural boundaries of the Middle East. When they are finished they will save this as their "Initial View."

   b) Students will overlay their "Initial View" with the GIS data maps presented on the website. Students should compare the cultural, social, and geographic data on the region with their conception of the Middle East in their "Initial View," and write a response to the following prompt: "Which three overlays best correspond to the map you drew of the Middle East? Why do you believe each of these layers represents the Middle East?"

c) Students will turn on all three chosen GIS map layers at the same time. Regions that overlap will be progressively shaded, with the darkest shading indicating areas where all three layers overlap. Students will write in response to the following prompt: "How does your initial perception of the region differ from this composite view? What have you learned about what constitutes the Middle East?"

Closure: Students will write a short exit slip reflection, responding to the following question: "How does your initial perception of Islam and the Islamic World differ from the realities presented in these activities?"

Homework: Students will begin reading about the conflict that defines the Middle East more than any other: the Israeli–Palestinian conflict. Students will revisit the GIS activity to predict the ways in which the differences between Israelis and Palestinians are as much cultural as they are due to geography.

III. Unit Plan: Middle East, World History (Rebecca)

Common Core Standards

CCSS.ELA-Literacy.RH.9-10.1 Cite specific textual evidence to support analysis of primary and secondary sources, attending to such features as the date and origin of the information.

CCSS.ELA-Literacy.WHST.9-10.1a: Introduce precise claim(s), distinguish the claim(s) from alternate or opposing claims, and create an organization that establishes clear relationships among the claim(s), counterclaims, reasons, and evidence.

CCSS.ELA-Literacy.RH.9-10.2: Determine the central ideas or information of a primary or secondary source; provide an accurate summary of how key events or ideas develop over the course of the text.

Essential Questions

- Is Islam merely a religion? Or, is it a political concept? Or, finally, is it a set of social structures?
- Why do "they" hate "us"? Is this even a valid question? Who are "they," historically and culturally? And, by extension, who are "we"? What makes the answers to these questions so complicated?

Enduring Understandings

Students will understand that:

- The Islamic world consists of diverse societies and cultures.
- Many commonly held beliefs about Islam and the Middle East are based in misconceptions or limited understandings of the region and its people.
- The differences between the "Islamic world" and the "West" are due to historical, cultural, religious, and geographic factors.
- The two major revolutions in the modern Middle East, the Turkish Revolution in 1923 and the Iranian Revolution of 1979, represent different approaches to the role of Islam in Middle Eastern society and government.
- Islamic fundamentalist movements around the world share ideological similarities.

Culminating Assessment

During class and using any notes collected during the unit, students will write a well-developed, argumentative essay response to the following prompt:

How would you describe the modern Middle East? Explain by giving details on the politics and culture of different Middle Eastern societies, including Iran and Turkey.

Selected Learning Activities

Lesson 1: Based on their prior knowledge, students will create a wall chart contrasting the geographic, cultural, and political characteristics of the Middle East with the "West" (Europe and the United States). Pairs of students will be given a writing utensil and asked to write whatever comes to mind in these three categories. After all student groups have posted their information, the teacher will lead a whole-class discussion to review and clarify the class understandings of the Middle East. This wall chart will be revised as students learn about the Middle East.

Lesson 2: Students will work in groups to complete an evidence collection activity on the culture, social structures, and political structures of Iran and Turkey (Chapter Resources VIII). Students will use their textbooks as well as internet sources and excerpts from the novel *Persepolis* (Satrapi, 2003). This evidence will be used in responding to a series of prompts comparing and contrasting Iran and Turkey in these areas. The activity will conclude with a whole-class discussion on the questions: *Which nation is more representative of the modern Middle East, Iran or Turkey? Why do you think this?* Students will compare the evidence collected here with the wall chart they previously created (see above), and revise the chart to incorporate their new learning.

Lesson 3: Students will analyze primary source materials comparing and contrasting the Iranian Revolution in 1979 with the Turkish Revolution in 1923 in a document-based question (DBQ) format (see Lesson Plan 3: Comparing and Contrasting the Iranian and Turkish Revolutions, Chapter Resources IV).

Lesson 4: In pairs, students will participate in a gallery walk which presents primary sources comparing the Islamic Revolution in Iran to radical fundamentalist movements in other parts of the region such as the Taliban in Afghanistan and al Qaeda. Students will make notes on the similarities and differences between these depictions of fundamentalism, and their connection to the United States' relationship to the Middle East. Following the gallery walk, students will gather as a class to discuss the documents and develop a class definition for, and examples of, Islamic fundamentalism.

IV. Lesson Plan III: Comparing and Contrasting the Iranian and Turkish Revolutions

Aim: Why are Turkey and Iran so different today despite being so geographically close and sharing the same religion?

Objectives: Students will understand that the two major revolutions in the modern Middle East, the Turkish Revolution in 1923 and the Iranian Revolution of 1979, represent different approaches to the role of Islam in Middle Eastern society and government.

Do Now: Students will begin class with a "whip" review of their knowledge of Iran and Turkey today. Each student, in rapid succession, will share one piece of information about the culture, social structures, and political structure of Iran or Turkey from his/her evidence collection template from the previous lesson. The teacher will then ask students to consider how Iran and Turkey got to be the way they are today.

Activity: The teacher will explain to students that today's activity will center on two turning points in recent Middle Eastern history, the Islamic Revolution in 1979 and the Turkish Revolution in 1923. These revolutions had very different goals and outcomes and were significant in determining the current culture, social structures, and political structures of each nation. In order to learn more about the revolutions, students will analyze primary source materials comparing and contrasting the two revolutions in a document-based question (DBQ) format.

In pairs, students will complete a guided historical thinking activity and analysis questions to examine each document and discuss the ways they might be used as evidence for a response to the following prompt: *Compare and contrast the revolutions of Turkey in 1923 and Iran in 1979 in terms of their cultural and political goals.* To answer this prompt, students will complete a Historical Argument Template which asks them to reword the prompt into their own words (task analysis); find three (3) different points of comparison/contrast between Iran and Turkey (topic grouping); and list evidence from the documents to support their topics (evidence collection).

Historical Argument Development Template

PROMPT: *Compare and contrast the revolutions of Turkey in 1923 and Iran in 1979 in terms of their cultural and political goals.*		TASK ANALYSIS: (What is this prompt asking me to do?)		
1st point of comparison/ contrast:		2nd point of comparison/ contrast:		3rd point of comparison/ contrast:
Document Evidence (Cite document #s):		Document Evidence (Cite document #s):		Document Evidence (Cite document #s):
THESIS STATEMENT:				

Sample Document #1

Background: In a speech delivered in 1927, Ataturk explained and justified his policies as founder of modern Turkey.

(www.fordham.edu/halsall/mod/modsbook54.asp)

Analysis Questions:

- Why did Ataturk say he abolished the caliphate?
- What additional actions did he take to remove Islam from a public or political role in the new Turkish state?

- What can you *infer* was Ataturk's view of Islam?
- After reading the last paragraph of his speech, what is Ataturk trying to achieve for Turkey?

Sample Document #2

Background: An Islamic Revolution in Iran brought to power in 1979 a government committed to the thorough Islamization of public life. The revolution had been inspired and led by Supreme Leader Ayatollah Khomeini, an Iranian religious scholar, who was adamantly against the regime of the Shah. This document provides the flavor for Khomeini's thinking.

(www.fordham.edu/halsall/mod/modsbook54.asp)

Analysis Questions:

- According to Khomeini, who are the enemies of Islam? What did they do to become enemies?
- What aspects of public and social life under the Shah does Khomeini criticize?
- What kind of rule does Khomeini see for Iran? How is this rule different from what you would see in the United States or Europe?

Sample Document #3

Background of picture: The Iranian regime celebrates Revolution Day today in the streets of Tehran.

(http://news.bbc.co.uk/2/hi/in_depth/7856172.stm)

Analysis Questions:
- What can you tell about the POV (Point of View) of the people in the picture? What makes you think that?
- How do these celebrations reflect the values of the Iranian Revolution from 1979?

Closure: Each student will write his/her thesis statement on the whiteboard in the front of class. Teacher will lead discussion on student responses to the prompt, probing students for specific evidence from the documents when possible.

Homework: Students will use the evidence from these documents and previous lessons to prepare to write an in-class essay on the following prompt: *How would you describe the modern Middle East? Explain by giving details on the politics and culture of different Middle Eastern societies, including Iran and Turkey.*

V. Anticipatory Surveys

Survey of Religious Beliefs

Directions: Answer the following questions as honestly as you can. Express your own personal beliefs concerning religion and your experience. Circle the appropriate number on the 5-point scale in response to each question (5 means yes, very much, 3 is neutral, 1 means no, not at all).

5	4	3	2	1	1. Do you think religion is less important among young people today than it was when your parents were teenagers?
5	4	3	2	1	2. Do your religious beliefs agree with those of your parents?
5	4	3	2	1	3. Should organized religions become involved in political issues, such as war or the presidential campaign and election?
5	4	3	2	1	4. Have organized religions helped to improve relations between people of different races or faiths?
5	4	3	2	1	5. Should the religions make dietary (food) laws for their followers?
5	4	3	2	1	6. Should prayers be a part of public school activities?
5	4	3	2	1	7. Should the words "In God We Trust" be on U.S. currency?
5	4	3	2	1	8. Should the words "under God" be a part of the Pledge of Allegiance?
5	4	3	2	1	9. Do you think that organized religion plays an important and valuable role in the world today?
5	4	3	2	1	10. Would people's behavior get worse if no one believed in God?
5	4	3	2	1	11. Do you believe that the goodness/badness of any action depends on the circumstances (for example, stealing or killing is not always wrong)?
5	4	3	2	1	12. Is prayer a worthwhile activity?
5	4	3	2	1	13. Do you believe that when a Muslim speaks of "Allah" and a Jew speaks of "Yahweh" and a Hindu speaks of "Brahman" and a Christian speaks of the "Trinity" that they are all speaking about the same entity?
5	4	3	2	1	14. Do you think all religions are equally true and worthwhile?
5	4	3	2	1	15. Do you feel that you must obey the teachings of your religion, even if they do not agree with your personal beliefs?
5	4	3	2	1	16. Would you approve of your son/daughter holding and publicly displaying religious beliefs which do not agree with yours?
5	4	3	2	1	17. Would your parents care if you dated/married someone of a different faith?

Survey on Separation of Church and State

How much do you know about the separation of Church and State?

1. How many times does the word "God" appear in the Constitution?

2. The pledge of allegiance, first published in 1892, has included the words "under God" since ...

  a) 1892   b) 1914   c) 1942   d) 1952

3. In 1890, Bible reading was outlawed from Wisconsin schools. Who was responsible?

  a) a Lutheran family   c) an atheist family

  b) a Roman Catholic family   d) a Jewish family

4. True or False? There has never been a Catholic President.

5. What motto is found on U.S. currency?

6. Intelligent design has been proposed as an alternative to teaching what?

7. True or False? There have been laws requiring schools to display the 10 Commandments.

8. What is the fastest growing religion in the United States?

VI. Evidence Collection Template: Israeli–Palestinian Conflict

Main Idea Statement #1: Palestinians have hurt their own chances at becoming a country.

Evidence A:		Sticking Point:
How does this evidence support the main idea?		
Evidence B:		Sticking Point:
How does this evidence support the main idea?		
[Additional evidence statements as needed]		

Main Idea Statement #2: Israelis are making it hard for Palestine to ever become a country.

Evidence A:		Sticking Point:
How does this evidence support the main idea?		
Evidence B:		Sticking Point:
How does this evidence support the main idea?		
[Additional evidence statements as needed]		

VII. Teacher Essays on the Israeli–Palestinian Conflict

The Israeli–Palestinian Conflict: The Israeli Perspective

The Israeli–Palestinian conflict is one of massive importance to the world. It has at times undoubtedly brought out the worst in its conflicting adversaries, the primarily Jewish state of Israel and the as yet unborn state of "Palestine," with its Muslim Arab majority. The frustration and hardship produced by this conflict have led world leaders to seek a peaceful solution that is acceptable to both Israelis and Palestinians. This has proven extremely difficult. Historically, anti-Semitism (the common term for anti-Jewish sentiment) has frequently resulted in the persecution of Jews in many world areas, with the German Holocaust serving as the pinnacle of hatred. In the minds of many Israeli leaders, therefore, a peaceful solution must serve the goals and needs of the Israeli population. The state of Israel has had and will likely continue to have difficulty in compromising with the Arab world to end the Middle East conflict because of a constant fear for its survival and security. This fear stems directly from the aftermath of the original creation of the modern state of Israel, and has only intensified as the conflict has spread outside of Israel's borders and involved neighboring countries as well. Currently, there are several "sticking points" that prevent peace. The historical legacy has drastically impacted the current mindset of the Israeli government, and indeed has created an environment in which Israelis believe that their very identities are threatened.

From its inception, the nation of Israel has feared for its very survival. In 1948, the weakened British Empire turned over control of the geographic region historically known as "Palestine" to the United Nations (UN). The UN "partitioned," or divided, Palestine into two separate regions that were to organize themselves into "states" (nations). One of the new "states" contained a population dominated by a specific cultural group of Muslim Arabs who called themselves "Palestinians." Palestinians had lived in the area for centuries under the rule of the Ottoman Empire (which was eliminated by the 1920s) and the British Empire (from 1919 to 1948). The other new "state" contained a majority Jewish population, consisting largely of 20th century settlers from Europe hoping to establish a Jewish homeland that had not existed since biblical times (a belief known as *Zionism*). This ancient history of Jews (ancient Hebrews) in the region, coupled with the world's legacy of anti-Semitism, led to a desire on the part of Jews in the region to create a permanent Jewish homeland called Israel. When Israel was created as an independent nation in 1948, its Arab neighbors—Egypt, Lebanon, Syria, Jordan, and Iraq, furious at the perceived intrusion of a large Jewish population—immediately declared war on the infant nation. Israel defeated the invading nations, and for security purposes, annexed significant parts of the area that was to have become the Arab Palestinian state. The remaining areas wound up "in limbo," and no Arab state was ever created. Jordan occupied an area that has come to be known as the "West Bank." Egypt occupied an area that came to be known as the "Gaza Strip." The 1948 partition and the resulting military conflict played a major role in creating Israel's perceived need for security. Its policies have thus been driven by a desire to protect itself, both from internal and external threats.

A second historical example of Israel's security goals in action is an event known as the "Six Day War." In 1967, fearing an impending attack by its Arab neighbors, Israel launched a "preemptive" attack against Egypt, Jordan, and Syria. This short but very successful conflict resulted in Israel's occupation of the West Bank, Gaza Strip, and the Golan Heights (a hilly region on the Syrian border). Israel currently refers to the areas as the "administered territories." Defying a UN Resolution (Number 242) calling for Israel's withdrawal from these areas, the Israeli government insists that it must maintain control over significant portions of the West Bank and Gaza Strip. Without control over these areas, Israel claims it will be unable to adequately defend itself, both from its potentially hostile neighbors and Palestinian militants who coordinate violent attacks from towns and camps in the regions. Once again, from its perspective, the Israeli government was forced to take drastic action, even defying world opinion, to ensure its survival and provide its citizenry with security. However, far from ensuring a peaceful existence, Israel's actions have contributed to problems that have lingered until the present day.

Israel's desire for security has led to one of today's most contentious issues. In the late 1970s, the Israeli government began to establish "settlements," or colonies, of Jewish residents in the West Bank and Gaza Strip. World opinion, as displayed in the Fourth Geneva Convention, forbids building on occupied land. The Israeli government has taken the stance that since there was no permanent sovereign Palestinian state at the time, there is no reason why these should not be built. Additionally, Israelis on the right, who wish to take a hard line with the Palestinians, have claimed that the land rightfully belongs to Israel anyway, thus nullifying any Palestinian claims of "illegal occupation." Since the earliest settlements began, over 300,000 Israelis have moved into the West Bank and Gaza. They are strategically placed to provide security to Israel as well as to prevent a contiguous Palestinian state. Critics of current Israeli Prime Minister Ariel Sharon accuse him of intentionally placing Israelis in key areas, including rural lands which cut Palestinian territory in two, and suburban areas which surround and isolate key Palestinian cities. Defying the criticism, Sharon and other Israeli leaders insist that their only motive is the safety and security of the Israeli population. This massive stumbling block to peace has arisen, from the Israeli perspective, only because of a demonstrated need for self-preservation.

Yet another issue fundamental to the problem is that of Palestinian refugees and prisoners. As a result of the 1948 war, millions of Palestinian Arabs were displaced from their homes. Additionally, thousands of Palestinian "militants" are currently incarcerated by Israeli authorities as a result of Israeli crackdowns on terrorism and protest. Israel's stance on these issues is clear. If it were to allow all Palestinian refugees (as well as their extended families) to return to the West Bank, Gaza Strip, and even modern Israel, a Jewish Israel may no longer exist. Such a large population shift would, from Israel's perspective, threaten the security and very survival of Israel. If prisoners (some of whom are indeed terrorists) were released in large numbers, there is a very realistic fear that terror attacks would not merely continue, but intensify. While Israel freed 334 prisoners in 2003, it is assumed that few, if any, of the several thousand remaining will be released. For security purposes, Israel feels that its stance must follow a hard line. Granting Palestinian refugees the "right of return," as it is called, threatens the Jewish identity of Israel; freeing prisoners threatens the safety of the populace. Once again, Israel's policy decisions are based on its desire to ensure the security of its people.

Perhaps the most ideologically contentious issue of all is that of Jerusalem, the capital of Israel as well as Palestine. The city of Jerusalem is holy to both Jews and Muslims. Israel believes that the survival of its identity as a Jewish homeland is threatened unless it can fully possess and control the holy city. Currently, the western portion of the city is completely under the control of Israel, while East Jerusalem (which holds many holy sites) is traditionally the Arab area. Few Israelis venture into the eastern half of the city, which is poorly maintained by the Israeli government. After the Six Day War of 1967, Israel seized East Jerusalem from Jordan, and despite UN resolutions instructing Israel to withdraw, Israel insists that Jerusalem is its "eternal, undivided capital." Driven by a need for survival and security, Israel has cut East Jerusalem off from the rest of the West Bank. It has encouraged settlements that surround the city and it has annexed lands around the city, causing confusion regarding the real boundaries of Jerusalem, making it nearly impossible for Jerusalem to ever become the capital of a Palestinian state. Rather than compromising on this issue, the Israeli government has made self-preservation its primary goal.

The final and, in many ways, the most frustrating issue that complicates the Israeli–Palestinian conflict is the problem of extremism. While there are many Israelis who strive for peace and desire an end to the conflict with the Arab world, there are others who consistently oppose peace efforts. In the modern world, images of terrorists perpetuate stereotypes regarding Arabs and the religion of Islam. Seldom, however, are the victors of conflict portrayed as extremists. In Israel, there are many who oppose compromise with Palestinians, as well as the rest of the Arab world, on the grounds that any compromise threatens the existence and security of Israel. Whether the issue is settlements, refugees, Jerusalem, or a controversial 310-mile "separation wall" currently being built along the West Bank, Israeli extremists threaten the peace process due to their beliefs and fears. One strikingly tragic example is the assassination of Israeli Prime Minister Itzak Rabin in 1995. Rabin was the architect of peace agreements with Palestinian leaders. Conservative Israelis, fearing changes and compromise with those they viewed as terrorists, opposed Rabin's policies. Finally, an Israeli radical (not a Palestinian terrorist) murdered the Israeli Prime Minister. Events such as these demonstrate the profound difficulty in achieving peace in Israel/Palestine. Acting on what they believe is best for Israel's future, extremists have done their best to derail the peace process. A few years ago, Prime Minister Ariel Sharon led a removal of the entire Israeli presence from the Gaza Strip, while permanently solidifying its position in West Bank settlements. Despite the fact that this move may have protected Israeli civilians and soldiers alike, extremists, including those from Sharon's own party, opposed this action, feeling that Israel must not give in to Palestinians at all.

The Israeli–Palestinian conflict is clearly one of great complexity and frustration. While numerous peace efforts have been made, the conflict drags on and on. What makes this conflict so frustrating is that compromise has become quite difficult. As long as the state of Israel feels that its security and even survival are threatened, it will continue to act in ways that anger Palestinians. From its first armed conflict in 1948, to the Six Day War of 1967, to the modern settlements, refugees, and Jerusalem problem, Israel has constantly faced what it perceives as a noble uphill struggle for its identity. While it seems as though the entire world yearns for Middle East peace, it has remained an elusive goal.

The Israeli–Palestinian Conflict: The Palestinian Perspective

The Israeli–Palestinian conflict is one of massive importance to the world. It has at times undoubtedly brought out the worst in its conflicting adversaries, the primarily Jewish state of Israel and the as yet unborn state of "Palestine," with its Muslim Arab majority. The frustration and hardship produced by this conflict have led world leaders to seek a peaceful solution that is acceptable to both Israelis and Palestinians. This has proven extremely difficult. Palestinians, angry with the Israeli government, have not always sought a peaceful reconciliation with Israel. Because they feel they have been denied a viable, autonomous Palestinian state, Palestinian Arabs have resisted compromise with the state of

Israel. This resistance, due to a feeling of "second-class citizenship," originated in the 1948 creation of Israel itself, continued as Israel's territory increased, and is today embodied in several "sticking points" that threaten the Middle East peace process. Historical and current Israeli actions are interpreted by Palestinians as heavy-handed and unfair.

The very creation of the nation of Israel was and remains controversial in the minds of Palestinian Arabs. In 1948, the weakened British Empire turned over control of the geographic region historically known as "Palestine" to the United Nations (UN). The UN "partitioned," or divided, Palestine into two separate regions that were to organize themselves into "states" (nations). One of the new "states" contained a population dominated by a specific cultural group of Muslim Arabs who called themselves "Palestinians." Palestinians had lived in the area for centuries under the rule of the Ottoman Empire (which was eliminated by the 1920s) and the British Empire (from 1919 to 1948). They refused to accept the terms of the partition, which they viewed as unfair. The other new "state" contained a majority Jewish population, consisting largely of 20th century settlers from Europe hoping to establish a Jewish homeland that had not existed since biblical times (a belief known as *Zionism*). This ancient history of Jews (ancient Hebrews) in the region, coupled with the world's legacy of anti-Semitism, led to a desire on the part of Jews in the region to create a permanent Jewish homeland called Israel. Clearly, however, the "giving away" of Arab land in 1948 was deemed unacceptable by most Arabs, even those who peacefully coexisted with Jewish residents prior to the partition. Thus, when Israel was created as an independent nation in 1948, its Arab neighbors—Egypt, Lebanon, Syria, Jordan, and Iraq—furious at the perceived intrusion of a large Jewish population, immediately declared war on the infant nation. Israel defeated the invading nations, and for security purposes, annexed significant parts of the area that was to have become the Arab Palestinian state. The remaining areas wound up "in limbo," and no Arab state was ever created. Jordan occupied an area that has come to be known as the "West Bank." Egypt occupied an area that came to be known as the "Gaza Strip." No state called "Palestine" was thus created. Thus, it is safe to say that initially, the very creation of Israel itself was the root of Palestinian hostility.

From the Arab perspective, Israel's later actions further exacerbated the situation, threatening the future of Palestine. In 1967, fearing an impending attack by its Arab neighbors, Israel launched a "preemptive" attack against Egypt, Jordan, and Syria. The attack was a massive Israeli success. This short conflict, known as the Six Day War, resulted in Israel's occupation of the West Bank, Gaza Strip and the Golan Heights (a hilly region on the Syrian border). Defying a UN Resolution (Number 242) calling for Israel's withdrawal from these areas, the Israeli government insists that it must maintain control over significant portions of the West Bank and Gaza Strip. Palestinians refer to these as the "occupied territories," and see Israel's actions as a direct attack on the autonomy of Palestinian Arabs. Partially due to Israel's success, the major point of contention between Israel and the Arab world was no longer whether or not Israel should exist, but what the future "Palestine" would look like. Thus, Israel's military victory and subsequent occupation of what was to become the state of Palestine perpetuated the Palestinian belief that peace with the Israeli government could result in great loss of land and power.

Already feeling like prisoners in their own homeland, Palestinians grew angrier still in the years following the Six Day War. In the late 1970s, the Israeli government began to establish "settlements," or colonies, of Jewish residents in the West Bank and Gaza Strip. To protect the settlers, Israel has also deployed troops to the sites. Palestinians view Israel's settlement-building as an intentional choice meant to prevent a realistic, viable Palestinian state. To support this, they point to the locations of these settlements. Often placed between key Arab cities, the settlements prevent convenient travel and communication, frequently forcing innocent Palestinians to pass through Israeli military checkpoints to attend work or school. World opinion, as displayed in the Fourth Geneva Convention, forbids building on occupied land. Despite this, the Israeli government continued to build new settlements, as well as additions to existing settlements, bringing the current number of Israeli settlers to over 300,000. As long as the settlements remain in the West Bank and Gaza Strip, Palestinians are likely to feel that their sovereignty is threatened, and are quite unlikely to seek compromise with the Israeli government.

Yet another issue fundamental to the problem is that of Palestinian refugees and prisoners. As a result of the 1948 war, millions of Palestinian Arabs were displaced from their homes. Palestinian leaders stress the "right of return" when negotiating the refugee issue. They feel that since Israel unfairly expelled Arabs from Israel, as well as the West Bank and Gaza Strip, the return of those refugees and their families is the only fair response. Clearly, the Israeli government wishes to prevent their return, but Palestinians appeal to fairness when pursuing this issue. The second issue is that of prisoners. Thousands of Palestinian "militants" are currently incarcerated by Israeli authorities as a result of Israeli crackdowns on terrorism and protest. From the Palestinian perspective, the Israeli justice system unfairly punishes thousands of Palestinians for the violent actions of a few. Despite the release of 334 prisoners in 2003, Palestinians believe that Israeli officials are not doing enough. Besides, they claim, Palestinians would not have to commit militant acts were it not for the oppression of the Israeli government. In the minds of many Palestinians, these assumptions add up to the conclusion that Israel will never allow them to be more than second-class citizens. This mindset leads many Palestinians to forsake any hope or desire for compromise.

Perhaps the most ideologically contentious issue of all is that of Jerusalem, the capital of Israel as well as Palestine. The city of Jerusalem is holy to both Jews and Muslims. Palestinians believe that Jerusalem will be the capital of a future Palestinian state. Currently, the western portion of the city is completely under the control of Israel, while East Jerusalem (which holds many holy sites, including the site where Muslims believe the Prophet Muhammad ascended to heaven) is traditionally the Arab area. Few Israelis venture into the eastern half of the city, which is poorly maintained by the Israeli government. After the Six Day War of 1967, Israel seized East Jerusalem from Jordan, and despite UN resolutions instructing Israel to withdraw, Israel insists that Jerusalem is its "eternal, undivided capital." It has encouraged settlements that surround the city and it has annexed lands around the city, causing confusion regarding the real boundaries of Jerusalem. These settlements and annexations make it nearly impossible for Jerusalem to ever become the capital of a Palestinian state. Nonetheless, frustrated Palestinians continually bring up the issue during peace talks. A successful compromise on Jerusalem remains elusive.

The final and, in many ways, the most frustrating issue that complicates the Israeli–Palestinian conflict is the problem of extremism. While there are many Palestinians who strive for peace and desire an end to the conflict with Israel, there are others who consistently oppose peace efforts. In the modern world, images of terrorists perpetuate stereotypes regarding Arabs and the religion of Islam. This is primarily a result of the actions of a relatively small number of radicals who threaten the peace process. Some of these radicals are Palestinian attackers and suicide bombers. When the second *intifada* (uprising) against the Israeli government began in September 2000 (the first occurred in 1987), attacks on Israeli targets in Israel itself as well as the West Bank and Gaza Strip became frequent and intense. Because unemployment and poverty rates are huge in the West Bank and Gaza Strip, many Palestinians feel an increasing sense of desperation, and have consequently supported a more radical stance. Sadly, many Palestinians have turned to Hamas, a terrorist group based in the Gaza Strip, to lead the way to Palestinian autonomy. As long as extremist groups like Hamas and Islamic Jihad have the ability to recruit members and terrorize, the peace process will never move substantially forward.

Recent events suggest that the Palestinian reliance on extremism could continue. In 2005, Israel decided to withdraw completely from the Gaza Strip, removing its settlements and its military presence. Despite the fact that some believe this choice could lead to peace, Palestinian extremists, including Hamas, have boldly claimed that it was terror itself that drove the Israelis to exit the Gaza Strip. This unsettling conclusion may embolden Palestinian extremists to take their doctrine of brutality to new heights within Israel and the West Bank. At the very least, it has given Hamas something that it views as a precedent for future actions.

The Israeli–Palestinian conflict is clearly one of great complexity and frustration. While numerous peace efforts have been made, the conflict drags on and on. What makes this conflict so frustrating is that compromise has become quite difficult. As long as Palestinians feel that Israel is preventing them from possessing a realistic, sovereign Palestine, difficulties will remain. From the first armed conflict in 1948, to the Six Day War of 1967, to the modern settlements, refugees, and Jerusalem problem, Palestinians and the Arab world have constantly faced what they perceive as a noble uphill struggle. While it seems as though the entire world yearns for Middle East peace, it has remained an elusive goal.

VIII. Evidence Collection Assignment: Iran and Turkey

World History—Evidence Gathering Activity: Iran and Turkey

Goal: Today, we are going to explore the ever-changing nature of the Middle East by dispelling current stereotypes and understandings we may have of the region and studying more in depth about the modern-day states of Turkey and Iran and how their cultures today have their roots in history.

Part I—Research
Read the section on Turkey and Iran in your textbook and create a list of characteristics of each country with respect to the themes of geography we have discussed so far: social structure, political structure, and culture.

Then visit the following sites to gain more information on the two nations:

- CIA World Factbook

  www.cia.gov/library/publications/the-world-factbook/index.html

- Turkish Cultural Foundation

  www.turkishculturalfoundation.org

- Iranian Cultural & Information Center

  http://tehran.stanford.edu

	Turkey	Iran
Social Structure		
Political Structure		
Culture		

Part II—Document Analysis

Background: *Persepolis* is an autobiographical graphic novel by Marjane Satrapi that follows a young girl as she comes of age against the backdrop of the Iranian Revolution. Look at the excerpts of the book provided to you and answer the following questions with your partner:

1. Is this source a primary or secondary source? Why?
2. Did you find anything interesting about these images or anything that reflects the ideas we have been discussing in class?
3. What is the message that the author/director is portraying in these images?
4. What can you tell about the author's point of view on the role of Islam in society? How does she feel about Western ideals?

Part III—Thesis Statement Creation

Using what you now know about Turkey and Iran from the documents, pictures, and sources, create a thesis statement that answers each of the following prompts. For each thesis statement, provide at least two pieces of evidence to support it.

Prompt #1: Compare and contrast the social structure, political structure, and culture of Iran with those of the United States.

Prompt #2: Discuss two ways in which Turkey has embraced Western culture, while still maintaining its own cultural identity.

Prompt #3: Analyze factors, both historical and modern, that have created cultural, social, or political distinctions between Iran and Turkey.

Prompt #4: Discuss the role of Islam in Iranian and Turkish culture today.

Big Picture Question (for discussion following activity)

Which nation, Iran or Turkey, is more representative of the modern Middle East? Why do you think this?

Five
The Soviet Union and Eastern Europe

Clashing Ideologies: Consumer Culture and the Fall of Communism

By Diana B. Turk, with Allyson Candia and Abby Rennert

Framing the Questions: An Interview with Stephen Kotkin, conducted by Robert Cohen

Stephen Kotkin is the John P. Birkelund Professor in History and International Affairs and the Vice Dean of the Woodrow Wilson School for Public and International Affairs at Princeton. He received his Ph.D. from the University of California, Berkeley in 1988. He is the author of several books, including: *Steeltown, USSR: Soviet Society in the Gorbachev Era* (1993); *Magnetic Mountain: Stalinism as a Civilization* (1995); *Armageddon Averted: The Soviet Collapse* (2008); and *Uncivil Society: 1989 and the Implosion of Communist Establishments,* with a contribution by Jan Gross (2009). His edited and co-authored volumes include *Mongolia in the 20th Century: Land-locked Cosmopolitan* (with Bruce Elleman) (1999); *Political Corruption in Transition: A Skeptic's Handbook* (with András Sajó) (2002); *The Cultural Gradient: The Transmission of Ideas in Europe, 1789–1991* (with Catherine Evtuhov) (2003); *Korea at the Center: Dynamics of Regionalism in Northeast Asia* (with Charles Armstrong, Gil Rozman, and Sam Kim) (2005); and *China's Borders and Beijing's Power: Twenty Neighbors in Asia* (with Bruce Elleman and Clive Schofield) (2012). He served on the core editorial committee of *World Politics* from 2004 to 2010 and was a member of the editorial board at Princeton University Press from 2003 to 2007. He is currently writing a book on dictatorship and power entitled *Stalin's World.*

Robert Cohen: *I think a good place to start off with is what would you say are the biggest misconceptions that Americans tend to have about the Soviet Union, and Eastern Europe, and generally the history you study?*

Stephen Kotkin: The most important thing to understand about the Soviet Union and communism is that it was in a relationship with the capitalist world. There's nothing more important than that. This means that the entire fate of the Soviet Union was dependent on the reality and the image of capitalism. So during the interwar years—between World War I and World War II, during the Great Depression—capitalism's reality and image were strikingly bad. Tens of millions of people were unemployed, and yet the entire world was also divided into colonies among a handful of European countries. The Soviet Union built this socialist system, this crazy socialist system, during this low point of the capitalist world, and so many people who might have questioned Soviet realities looked and gave them the benefit of the doubt because of the relation to capitalism.

But in the wake of World War II, the world outside's story changed on them. They kind of got the rug pulled out from under them. Stalin anticipated another "great depression," because that's what capitalism did: it de-stabilized itself through these big, great depressions. Truman, I think, anticipated a big great depression after World War II. But it turned out that after World War II, the capitalist system had its greatest decades ever. Between the 1940s and the 1970s, the capitalist system had a boom that was absolutely unprecedented. Moreover, it was a middle class boom. It was not just the kind of boom that we have today. It was not a plutocratic boom; it was not a Gilded Age boom. It was a Levittown, middle class, homeownership, spread-the-wealth boom. Between the 1940s and 1973, West Germany grew more than 10% per year in GDP. West Germany was the China of its day. Japan was equally spectacular.

That boom in the capitalist world combined with the change to democracy, [and that] combined with the fact that Germany was no longer a fascist dictatorship, and Japan was no longer a militarist dictatorship. Instead, they were rule of law democracies having this fantastic economic boom spreading to the middle class. And finally, the United States was fully engaged in the international system, in a way that it had never been before, following World War II. It didn't withdraw this time. So, all of this changed the rules of the game on the Soviet Union.

And the Soviet Union was doing fine. It had recovered from the devastation of World War II. Most of World War II was fought on Soviet soil and Chinese soil. They were the two big losers. Of the 55 million people killed in World War II, 27 million were Soviet inhabitants, and about 10 to 13 million were Chinese. So you have close to 40 million of the 55 million World War II deaths: the Soviet Union and China. That's where the war was fought. The Soviet Union had one-third of its GDP wiped out—but they recovered, they reconstructed—and they did extremely well. The problem for the Soviet Union wasn't that it was doing poorly: it was that it was in this competition, and in the competition it was losing, or falling farther behind. No matter how many apartments they built, no matter how many sausages they produced, no matter how many things that they changed in the parameters of measuring standard of living and daily life, they were not West Germany; they were not Japan; they were not the United States; they were not Italy; they were not Britain; they were not France. And so they were crushed—in a "daily life" competition—a competition of standard of living and daily life. They were crushed in the post-World War II period. This is by far the most important thing to understand about the trajectory of communism.

RC: *And do you think that Americans understand that? Or do you think it's almost refracted through U.S. Cold War ideology and a kind of triumphalism implying that the Soviet Union fell because of America's resolve to win the Cold War arms race?*

SK: We have a focus on the military. We think the military competition destroyed them. That's exactly wrong. Their military was quite sophisticated, and they did a good job. The military industry in the Soviet Union was the best-performing sector in the whole Soviet economy. They had rockets, they had tanks; they had everything you could possibly need: Nuclear weapons, chemical weapons, biological weapons. *And* they were able to carry that burden: it did *not* produce social unrest. So here's a place that was armed to the teeth and was good at military production. That was the thing they were best at. The problem was they were no longer fighting German tanks. It wasn't, you know, the Battle of Kursk, with the Nazi tanks on the one side and the Soviet tanks on the other. It was the battle of the silk stockings. It was the battle of the department store. It was the battle of the grocery store. It was the battle of the ethnic restaurants. It was the battle of daily life, and they had no answers in the battle of daily life.

This is the strangest and most important thing. We think we crushed them militarily. But they went toe to toe with us militarily, all the way to the end, and then some. Today the Russian military industry is *still* highly productive. They still have big weapons merchants in the international market. That's the thing that they didn't lose. They lost the "daily life" competition.

Now, we certainly give ourselves too much credit for the fact that the Soviet Union collapsed. And that's for the following reason: just because you lose doesn't mean you have to concede. Just because the other side has won doesn't mean you're going to give up. The thing that's most important to understand about why the Soviet Union gave up is not just that they lost the competition— this was something that they felt, over time, more and more—but so what? Maybe capitalism would go into a great depression at some point. Maybe Soviet fortunes would improve vis-à-vis the capitalist world. Just because you're crushed in a competition—there might be another quarter, another half-time you can play.

But what happened was this: in 1985, the generation of the 1960s came to power in the Soviet Union—the generation of people who thought they could reinvent the world. Who thought that they could produce the socialism that the Soviet Union always promised but was never able to realize. And so Mikhail Gorbachev and his whole generation of 1960s Party officials, they were true believers in a better path to socialism, which they thought was inherent somewhere in the Revolution but had been lost somewhere along the way. And so they began a reform of the system to make the system live up to its ideals.

And this had happened before in Eastern Europe. It had happened, for example, in Hungary and Poland in 1956, in Czechoslovakia in 1968. And each time it happened, something funny was the result. Instead of a reformed socialist system, the system began to liquidate, like quicksand. Give people a little bit of freedom, and it turns out, they want all of it. Take some censorship away, that is to say—relax censorship, and they want no censorship. Allow some political organization, and they want alternative political parties. Allow some market relations in the economy, and an economy based on planning begins to disintegrate. And so each time there had been an attempt to get to this reformed socialism, this idea that there was a better form of socialism in the Revolution—each time that had been tried it had produced, essentially, all liquidation. The system began to unravel, like you pull a thread out of a sweater until the entire wool is now just one big long thread, instead of a sweater.

And so in 1985 this attempted idealist reform came to power and peacefully, unintentionally but peacefully, liquidated the Soviet system. This was a colossal surprise, because no dictatorships, superpowers, *ever* walk away from power. Even though they thought that the other side had the upper hand, they still had the 40,000 nuclear weapons, 40,000 tons of chemical weapons, and a biological weapons program that the CIA didn't know about. And they didn't use any of it. They didn't use it for blackmail purposes; they didn't use it to bring the world down with them. They just quietly, unintentionally undid their system, and then let it fall. Once it was in the free-fall, they didn't try to prop it back up. So while the outside-world competition was the critical factor, for the fact that socialism existed only as the antidote to capitalism, and if it wasn't better than capitalism it had no reason to exist, the internal critical factor of why it went peacefully, and why it went when it went, which was in the late 1980s, is because this generation of 1960s people, like Mikhail Gorbachev, came to power. So, he pulled the system down trying to make it compete better with the capitalist world.

RC: *That generation, when you think about what happened in the 1980s, versus Hungary in 1956 or Czechoslovakia in 1968—why, do you think, this generation responded differently? In other words, that there wasn't this clamp-down by the Soviet regime? Do you think by that time, the regime's leaders knew the Soviet system wasn't working and became demoralized?*

SK: Yes, demoralized … Think of it this way. The Soviet conservatives were right. They kept saying that reform was dangerous. That liberalization of the system was a bad idea. And we had to be tough, that we had to be sort of neo-Stalinist. We had to take a hard line against dissent. We shouldn't allow any tinkering or reform with the system, because it endangers the system as a whole. That was the lesson they drew from 1956 in Hungary. That was the lesson they drew from 1968 in Czechoslovakia. But the conservatives were not the full story. There was this generation of liberalizers, especially these 1960s-types, who felt that they could have a Prague Spring in the Soviet Union like Czechoslovakia had in 1968. And that it wasn't that the system was vulnerable to self-liquidation, it was that the conservatives blocked a real reform, and a real reform would work if it was just given a chance. And so, "Sure, we could relax things a little bit. After all, we have 300 million people, mostly loyal, and the system employs just about every single person; there's no unemployment. And we had economic growth every year except a couple of years like 1979 and 1980, when it dipped below, GDP dropped those two years." And so they were confident that the system was fixable and that it wouldn't be completely destabilized if they attempted the reforms that had been attempted in Hungary in 1956 and Czechoslovakia in 1968. And the conservatives warned them that "You don't know what you're doing. We're going to get in trouble."

Mikhail Suslov, who was in charge of ideology during the whole Brezhnev period, when he would receive the scientists and the writers and the others, they would say, "Why can't we relax censorship a little bit? Why can't we just loosen up a little bit? Let's just allow our people to breathe? Let scientists do science, let the artists do art." "Well, as soon as I lift censorship, who's going to send the tanks to Moscow?" That was his rhetorical answer to that. Because when they had lifted censorship in Hungary in 1956 and in Czechoslovakia in 1968, the whole system completely fell apart, and Moscow had had to send the tanks in. And he felt that if they lifted censorship domestically there'd be nobody, as it were, to send the tanks in.

Now it was a little bit of a surprise, after Gorbachev and the liberalizers, trying to improve the socialist system, after they'd destabilized it, there was a little bit of a surprise that there was no crackdown. That the conservatives didn't kick Gorbachev out and, instead, re-impose order, the way that it had happened in 1956 in Hungary, in 1968 in Czechoslovakia. And the answer to that failure of the crackdown, in the late 1980s, has to do in part with the demoralization that you were talking about.

As time went on—not just in the '50s and the '60s, but by the time they got to the late '80s—there was deep and profound demoralization in the ranks of the privileged classes in the Soviet Union as well as Eastern Europe. They were living in a capitalist world. They were saying that the capitalist world was exploitation, but their most coveted goods were all those capitalist goods. Their suits were made in the capitalist world. They wanted videos from the capitalist world—all of which was prohibited to the rest of the population, but was accessible to them, as members of the elite. So they lived in an anti-capitalist system, supposedly, but they coveted every single thing they could get their hands on that was capitalist. And their kids were the same way: the kids of the elite wanted jeans. And they didn't want to work in the Party or the trade unions—they wanted to be Soviet trade representative in Greece, or in the U.K.—somewhere else where it was nice to live.

And so by the late '80s, you did have demoralization within the elites. But further, in addition to that, you had the fact that Gorbachev didn't fully understand that there were no Gorbachevs in Eastern Europe. And that if they tried to liberalize the system, Eastern Europe was particularly vulnerable, because they lived right in front of that capitalist store window. They saw that capitalism every day. And the idea that they would find some type of stable, improved socialism in the teeth of the capitalist competition in Eastern Europe was perhaps the most utopian aspect of the Gorbachev reforms. And Eastern Europe just crashed in a matter of months when Gorbachev refused to send in the tanks, when he repealed the so-called Brezhnev Doctrine, which meant the right to interfere, to uphold the socialist system, with force. He repealed that Brezhnev Doctrine; nobody believed him, but then he didn't send the tanks in 1989, and Eastern Europe collapsed. And that really undid the possibility of a kind of counter-revolution or re-imposition of the system to get rid of the reformers and to hold on, the way they had tried it in decades earlier.

The reform coalition when it started in 1985 was not a single person and not a single group. The military wanted the reform because they wanted better competition with the capitalist world. The KGB wanted the reform because they wanted better competition with the capitalist world. And then a whole bunch of idealists wanted the reform because they wanted an improved socialism to live up to its promises and its ideals, to what they saw as the original 1917 ideals.

Socialism was supposed to be better that capitalism; what was the point? If capitalism was free and socialism was un-free, how was socialism better? If capitalism had a high standard of living and socialism had a low standard of living, what was the point of having socialism, why wouldn't they just have capitalism? If capitalism was superior, both morally or politically and economically, socialism was doomed. And so there was an imperative, a political moral imperative and an economic imperative, and then, for the military, KGB, there was a geopolitical imperative, to re-energize the system. Now, it wasn't a kind of ruthless, *realpolitik* realist re-energizing of the system. They didn't say, "Oh, forget about socialist economics. We'll do a capitalist economy but we'll clamp down and hold power," the way Deng Xiaoping did in the Chinese case. It wasn't just a retrenchment to cut costs because they were overextended. It was an extremely idealistic reform of the system from top to bottom, elections to Communist Party positions, reinvigorating the Soviets. It was *not* something that was forced on them. It was something that they themselves felt needed to be done because of external pressure from the capitalist world, but primarily because of a vision of fixing the system and living up to its ideals.

Now, in the reform coalition you had a tremendous number of people who had been reformers under Khrushchev, who—during the Khrushchev de-Stalinization, during the opening-up of the system; after Stalin died in 1953; after Khrushchev's 1956 so-called "secret speech" at the 20th Party congress, saying that Stalin had committed numerous crimes, arresting and executing innocent people on a grand scale, in the hundreds of thousands of executions and in the millions in the arrests—after these people had experienced the reform attempts of the late 1950s and early 1960s, they were still in the system. And when the conservatives removed Khrushchev in 1964 and ended some of the reforms that he had tried, and went back a little bit on the de-Stalinization, and re-imposed greater censorship—when all of that happened, these people didn't emigrate; they stayed within the Soviet Union. And they came to power again, in their minds, when Gorbachev came to power. And so they were going to have a second chance. A second chance at the Khrushchev-era reforms, a Soviet-style Prague Spring, when they would get it right this time.

So, not everyone was an idealist. But we underestimate the tremendous amount of idealism prevalent, inside the Soviet system, in the 1980s when Gorbachev came to power. That didn't mean they knew what they were doing. They were improvising and feeling their way. They didn't have a model for a stable, reformed socialist system: it was something they were groping for. But nonetheless, they were willing to try. And they were in this coalition with the geopolitical side, with the military and the KGB.

RC: *The thing about Stalinism as discussed in your book is that you did connect it, on some level, with a utopian ideal. It seems that there's a certain kind of idealism to Stalininism that did have the ability to attract many people.*

SK: One of the things that we have difficulty understanding is that violence can be popular. When the Soviet Union arrested enemies, when it used violence against people who were supposedly against the system, when it rounded up oppositionists, when it rounded up alleged or accused spies, this was not necessarily unpopular. People believed that there was class struggle, that there were enemies, that the international bourgeoisie and its agents inside the Soviet Union were against the Soviet system; that was true. And they believed it was widespread; that was a little bit less true. And if it was rooted out, that was a good thing. And so violence against class enemies, using force on behalf of a cause—if you believe the cause is just, you might also believe that the means could be any and all, in order to make sure that you don't let the cause down.

That doesn't mean that everyone liked the purges and the violence and the arrests—of course not. Many people, in fact, gave up their allegiance to the system because of the violence. Many people were put off tremendously by the purges and the mass violence. However, not everybody was put off by the violence. This is true in Nazi Germany, it's true in Japan; it's true in many authoritarian regimes. Authoritarianism can also be popular. It can be popular on a nationalist basis; it can be popular on a class basis.

And so we need to look at the Stalinist system in that light. Not meaning that *everyone* supported it, not meaning that everyone had a choice—because the idea of "support" in an authoritarian regime is complicated; you don't really have a free choice. You're more complicit in a regime like the Stalinist regime than you support it because you can't just say, "Okay, I won't support it," and survive that. You can try to be neutral, you can try to withdraw, you can try to go into some kind of internal emigration to avoid being supportive of the system in public—so it's more like complicity than support, but many people are complicit out of ideological conviction.

Now, having said that, one of the things that's observable about communism which is different, is that there is "The God That Failed" phenomenon. People who are disillusioned can only be disillusioned if they had illusions in the first place. People who believe nothing are never disillusioned: they're just cynics. So what you see in the Soviet case, and this is throughout all the communist countries, is people having a trajectory of acquiring convictions, or acquiring belief in the system, and then losing those convictions and losing that belief in the system. For some, it was, for example, the purge trials, in 1936 and 1937 and 1938. For others it was the Hitler–Stalin pact in 1939. For others it was the secret speech with Khrushchev, revealing Stalin's crimes (to those who still didn't know) in 1956. For others it was the intervention in Hungary in 1956 or the intervention in Czechoslovakia in 1968.

For different people, there were different moments of disillusionment. For some it was only the revelations of *glasnost* under Gorbachev, in the late 1980s and early 1990s, when they found out just how well people lived, how high their standard of living was in the capitalist world, compared with the socialist world. Some people were disillusioned and others were still gaining their convictions. Many people in Poland in 1956 were losing any illusions about the system, but many people inside the Soviet Union were only acquiring them, because of Khrushchev's secret speech and the idea that, "Hey, there were crimes, but maybe we can get socialism right the next time, or a second time, or a second chance." So the illusion–disillusion, or conviction–loss-of-conviction trajectory, is not linear. It's not just up and down for all people at the same time. But that trajectory of up and down at some point, of conviction and loss of conviction, is true across the entire 11 time zones of the Soviet Union, throughout Eastern Europe, and throughout all of the communist satellites.

Communism is different in that it elicited belief and it profoundly disillusioned people. When you have an ideology you're susceptible. The ideology can empower you, it can give more power to the system because you have a lot of true believers, but it's also a point of vulnerability if those believers should ever become disillusioned, which of course was the case. At different times and different places for different people, but a similar process of disillusionment, at some point, for some reason.

RC: *What do you think about the comparison between Stalinism and Nazism? How does that work as a comparison?*

SK: There's a certain similarity in obvious ways: one-party systems, use of violence for political ends, many people killed—in the millions. But the similarities are actually not that great. Imagine this: imagine that Hitler decides at some point that he's going to murder *all* Nazi provincial rulers, he's going to murder all loyal Nazi diplomats. He's going to murder all the generals at the top of the *Wehrmacht.* He's going to execute them, all of them, or almost all of them, by the tens of thousands, if not the hundreds of thousands. He's going to execute the Gestapo heads. He's going to do all of this, he's going to murder all loyal Nazi elites who came to power with him, in the party, police, army, and the foreign affairs ministry. And he's going to accuse them all of being spies for the other side. And they're going to publicly confess to having been spies for the other side. And the populace is going to more or less buy that they were spies for the other side. So that everybody who comes to power in the Nazi revolution with Hitler "worked for the other side." And 1.7 million of them are going to be arrested, and 700,000 of them are going to be executed. It's just impossible to imagine, that Hitler would do that—or that he could have done that, and that the German people would have accepted that. But that's what Stalin did. He murdered his own party, he murdered his own army, he murdered his own police, he murdered his own foreign affairs commissar, or ministry. And he murdered them, accusing them of being spies for the opposite side, and they publicly confessed (usually after torture, but nonetheless they went public and confessed) and the populace to a very great degree accepted that there were such spies and there was such treason and sabotage domestically. That's just very, very different. The Soviet and the German systems were different.

The people who did local histories of Nazi towns, after 1945, they went back to Germany, and they interviewed survivors of the Nazi regime. And they were able to interview not just Nazi officials, who had survived their own regime, but they were able to interview Social Democrats, and Communists. German Social Democrats and Communists, supposedly the biggest enemies to the Nazi regime; they were alive after 1945 in many of these communities and were interviewed. If you went to the Soviet Union to interview people, as I did, forget about opposition to the Communist regime, they were all dead and buried. Or they had been sent to the Gulag; that is, the labor camp system. But even the loyalists were gone. Even the regime's own people were not there to be interviewed. This is a very different dynamic. So while there are certain similarities in structure—one-party systems, use of political violence, leader cult, Hitler and Stalin, there are these similarities; but I also see tremendous differences that make the two systems ultimately not the same thing.

RC: *How do you account for the difference, and for what you describe about Stalin; is there a way to explain all that?*

SC: Well, the Nazi thing is about the Jews. It's about German nationalism, and it's about exterminating, eradicating the Jewish community from their midst. It's about racial purity. And so its enemies are very different. When they can, they go after the Jews, and they exterminate them. They conquer these other countries, and one of the first things they do is not just exploit the raw materials and exploit the local population as forced labor, but they put the Jews on trains and send them to gas chambers. The Soviet Union is not a racial utopia. It's not there to eradicate Jews. The Soviet Union is, instead, to build a new world, *not* on the basis of Russian nationalism, or anti-Semitism, Jewish eradication, but on the basis of anti-capitalism. And so, that dynamic produces a different kind of enemy. But it also produces a different type of belief system in the masses or in the wider population. That's one of the big differences: that Nazi violence is violence on behalf of a racial community, and Soviet violence is violence on behalf of overcoming capitalism and building a supposedly better socialist world.

But there's another difference, besides that big difference, that's really, really important. And that is that the Soviet case was not genocidal on purpose. People write today a lot about Stalin's genocides, about the equivalent, or even the greater, number of people murdered by Stalin. It's now an extremely popular topic. Genocide is now an extremely widespread popular topic of investigation. In part because of what we lived through in Rwanda, but in part because people now have more information about what happened in the Soviet Union since it collapsed, and some (but not all) of the archives are opened up. The Soviet Union didn't kill people to kill them. The Soviet Union killed people to build a better world, which meant that if you eradicated people, it was not because they were necessarily part of a single group. This is hard for people to understand.

We also see that, with the *kulaks,* Stalin sought to impose control over the countryside so that the cities and the army would never run out of grain. He also thought he could industrialize agriculture. So between industrialization of agriculture and state control, we had what we call "collectivization." It's actually a misnomer. Now once these supposedly richer peasants [*kulaks*] were deported from the villages, as part of the drive to impose control over the villages—they were deported into Siberia and the Far East, from villages all across the Soviet Union—once they were deported, the question came up of, "Okay, what happens to their children? Are their children automatically enemies of the Soviet Union, because they were born to parents who were accused of being rich, or *kulaks?*" And the answer was complicated. Why should the children not be given the opportunity to work for a living and to prove their loyalty to the Soviet Union? And so in fact, the children were more or less amnestied. This does *not* justify the deportation of several million people to faraway wastes because they were accused of being rich peasants, when in fact many of them had no more than one or two cows—and some of them had no cows, but they were accused of being a *kulak,* and that was it—this does not justify that type of action by the state. But it's interesting to see the Soviet regime wrestling with the children of these people: were they by definition evil because they were descended from those who were enemies? Or could they somehow be contributing, positive citizens, inhabitants of the Soviet Union? This is a little bit different, in my view, from the Nazi regime.

RC: *It's not about biological racism, is what you're saying.*

SK: Correct. A Jew is a Jew is a Jew, and that's it, and their children, and everything else, and it's something that behavior cannot change. You cannot be loyal, no matter how hard you try to be a loyal Jew, you are a Jew for the Nazis, and therefore you are supposed to be eradicated, removed from the community in order for the German race, the German nation, to survive. That kind of eradication looks similar to the Soviet's, though, because so many millions of people die in the Soviet Union. And there were so many deportations, and deportations of whole nations, like the Koreans from the Soviet Far East, or the Chechens, who were accused of collaboration under German occupation in World War II. And when the Soviets swoop back in, the Chechens are deported en masse. It looks similar to the Nazi regime, but in my view there are crucial differences.

RC: *Regarding the fall of the Soviet system, your book* Uncivil Society *[2009] was surprising in that it challenged the popular view that when we looked on TV and saw the masses of crowds out there in 1989, people would say, "Well, this was a popular revolution, it was brought down by the masses of people in motion." But it seems you were saying something different, that while those crowds were significant, what was more significant was the relatively passive response of that political class, the elite class. It's quite different from looking at the media, and getting the impression that the system fell because there was this insurgency. I wonder if you could just say something about that.*

SK: Well, what's revolution? What do we think revolution is? We have this sense that revolution is when people go out in the streets, like they did recently in Egypt. They protested in the central square of the capital: Tahrir Square in Cairo. And they were brave, and they didn't run away when the tanks or the guns came out, and they toppled the regime. Now, were the people in Tiananmen Square in June 1989 in China less brave than the people in Eastern Europe in 1989? Were those three million people in Tehran in the summer of 2009 less brave than the people in Eastern Europe in 1989? The answer is, of course not. They're not less brave. Revolution—the answer to the question of what is revolution has to be sought outside the streets. It has to be sought in elite politics—in elite demoralization or in the elite willpower. And, of course, in the elite's ability to hold on because of the international system.

RC: *So there are bottom-up and top-down views of revolution, and it's a mistake to just look at such events from the one vantage point rather than both?*

SK: In some cases there's nothing in the streets, there's no revolution in the streets whatsoever. There are no uprisings, there are no demonstrations, and systems topple. They topple because the elite loses its willpower or its belief in the system's viability. Or because one faction of the elite is ambitious and pushes aside another faction. Now sometimes elite demoralization is caused by street demonstrations and the bravery of the crowds. Sometimes the bravery of the crowds has a very big effect on the elite politics. But in the end, revolutions begin and end, in the political system itself, in the inside.

When addressing Eastern Europe in 1989, I introduce political economy, that is to say, the economic performance of the socialist regimes, vis-à-vis capitalism, in a predominantly capitalist world. That's a very important variable that's usually overlooked. I also introduce elites' understanding of the system's viability—what you had earlier called "demoralization," and I agree that that's the right term. How much did they believe their systems remained viable, their systems had a future, that they themselves still had a future in these systems? And of course the Gorbachev factor, where he refused to use Soviet force to uphold the Eastern European communist regimes, and he dissuaded and tried to inhibit the East Europeans themselves from using force to uphold, their own force, their own armies, to uphold these Eastern European communist regimes. So, you have a kind of political economy lost to capitalism, crushed by capitalism and daily life, elite demoralization, and removal of the Soviet backstop—and then the people come out into the streets.

The people don't come out into the streets very early; they come out quite late in the game. Moreover, when the people come out into the streets, it's not clear what they want. Some people want, for example, just more food. And some want, for example, just to be able to travel to West Germany to see it, to go through the Wall and come back, maybe not to emigrate. Some people, of course, want freedom. And they want a better way of life which looks more like the capitalist way of life, both politically and economically. However, the East German regime plans a crackdown in October of 1989, in the city of Leipzig, when there are about 70,000 people marching for peace, in a so-called peace demonstration after Mass on Monday night. And they do it week after week, every Monday night. Had the East German regime cracked down successfully in Leipzig in October of 1989, I'm not sure the Wall would have fallen. When these regimes show their teeth, and they succeed in showing their teeth, they can override discontent and demonstrations.

Let's remember that in 1980–1981, Solidarity—an independent [Polish] trade union, which had 10 million members, and existed for 18 months of freedom—there was a crackdown in December of 1981, and 5,000 to 6,000 Solidarity activists were arrested in a single night, and Solidarity was driven underground, and the regime put the genie back in the bottle and held power from 1981 through 1989. And Solidarity was not a spent force; it was still underground—but it was nothing like it had been at its height in 1980–1981 when it had the 10 million members. The problem for the Polish regime was it was still broke and its economy was still nonperforming, and then Gorbachev removed the Soviet backstop. So, the success of the crackdown in December of 1981 was very impressive, except there was no political, economic program to make the crackdown stick, so they could revive the economy and they could win people's loyalty, the way that had happened in China after the Tiananmen Square crackdown in June of 1989. There was no follow-through in the Polish case to re-energize and make the system dynamic.

But the crackdown was very impressive and bought a lot of time. And had there been a successful crackdown in East Germany in October 1989, maybe that regime would have bought some time. Maybe not. We'll never know. But the fact that there was no crackdown emboldened the people in the streets. When regimes are supposed to be authoritarian, and they fail to crack down against a challenge, many people who were afraid to challenge it lose their fear. And you can go from 70,000 people in the streets to 300,000 or a million in a very short period of time. Kind of like a bank run. And that's what happened to these regimes in 1989.

Work Cited

Kotkin, S. (2009). *Uncivil society: 1989 and the implosion of the communist establishment.* New York: The Modern Library.

Essay: Clashing Ideologies: Consumer Culture and the Fall of Communism

By Diana B. Turk, with Allyson Candia and Abby Rennert

> In Europe and America, there's a growing feeling of hysteria/ Conditioned to respond to all the threats/ In the rhetorical speeches of the Soviets/ Mr. Khrushchev said we will bury you/ I don't subscribe to this point of view/ It would be such an ignorant thing to do/ If the Russians love their children too.
>
> Sting, "Russians," from *Dream of the Blue Turtles* (1985)

When the musician Sting released his poignant song "Russians" in 1985, the United States and the Soviet Union had been embroiled for four decades in the political and military stand-off of the Cold War. For Americans of a certain age, this song gave voice to the nagging sense of unease felt by many: that at any moment, the Soviets might launch a rocket at the U.S. or one of its allies, President Ronald Reagan would order a massive retaliation, and the world as we knew it would cease to exist. This scenario was painted in brutal detail by the 1983 made-for-television movie *The Day After,* which attracted more than 100 million viewers and provoked countless community and town hall discussions about the horrors of nuclear war. While the threat of nuclear war and its devastating aftermath gripped the popular imagination, President Reagan and his military allies, especially Defense Secretary Caspar Weinberger, launched a massive military build-up designed to challenge what they saw as the Soviet "military machine" of the Cold War (Hoffman, 2009). The revival of the B-1 bomber program, the deployment of the Pershing II missile in West Germany, the proposal of the Strategic Defense Initiative—the so-called "Star Wars" program, which aimed to use outer space stations for defense against Soviet missiles—all contributed to an enormous increase in the U.S. military budget (Hoffman, 2009; Schrecker, 2004). "Victory through Strength" served as the American administration's motto during the mid-to-late 1980s, and by the time the Berlin Wall fell in 1989 and the Soviet Union collapsed two years later, the image of President Reagan as Cold Warrior who had stared down and defeated the Soviets through U.S. military might was cemented in the popular imagination. According to conservative thinker Richard Perle, "'The collapse of the Soviet Empire in Eastern Europe is in large measure a result of the postwar strength and determination of the alliance of Western democracies'" (Schrecker, 2004, p. 2). According to Cold War historian Ellen Schrecker, the idea that "[c]ommunism's failure was America's success" quickly became a truism within the American political and socio-cultural landscape:

> That the denizens of Eastern Europe and the former Soviet Union might also have had a hand in the process rarely figures in the story. Instead, [in this view] it was the strategic resourcefulness of the American government, the technological dynamism of the American economy, and the moral and cultural superiority of the American system that simply (but peacefully) overwhelmed the backward tyrants of Moscow. Outside of the Left and a handful of academics, few even question the notion that America "won" the Cold War.
>
> (Schrecker, 2004, p. 2)

But according to Princeton University Professor of Russian History Stephen Kotkin, the fall of the Soviet Union came not because the United States beat the U.S.S.R. in an arms race, but rather because the Soviet Union lost the "battle of everyday life." "We have a focus on the military," Kotkin noted, when asked about why the Cold War ended:

> We think the military competition destroyed them, [but] that's exactly wrong ... The military industry in the Soviet Union was the best-performing sector in the whole Soviet economy. They had rockets, they had tanks; they had everything you could possibly need: Nuclear weapons, chemical weapons, biological weapons. *And* they were able to carry that burden: it did *not* produce social unrest. So here's a place that was armed to the teeth and was good at military production. That was the thing they were best at. The problem was they were no longer fighting German tanks. It wasn't, you know, the Battle of Kursk, with the Nazi tanks on the one side and the Soviet tanks on the other.

It was the battle of the silk stockings. It was the battle of the department store. It was the battle of the grocery store. It was the battle of the ethnic restaurants. It was the battle of daily life, and they had no answers in the battle of daily life.

Rather than being a case of Reagan and the United States *winning* the Cold War, the Soviet Union, according to Kotkin, essentially *lost* the stand-off, due to the fact that its citizens—especially the elite, who, in their travels abroad were able to see how those in the Western world lived—wanted material goods that were unavailable inside Soviet borders. "We think we crushed them militarily," Kotkin argued,

> But they went toe-to-toe with us militarily, all the way to the end, and then some. Today the Russian military industry is *still* highly productive. They still have big weapons merchants in the international market. That's the thing that they didn't lose. They lost the "daily life" competition.

Indeed, as Kotkin noted, by the 1950s and 1960s,

> there was deep and profound demoralization in the ranks of the privileged classes in the Soviet Union as well as Eastern Europe. They were living in a capitalist world. They [communist leaders] were saying that the capitalist world was exploitation, but their [elites'] most coveted goods were all those capitalist goods. Their suits were made in the capitalist world. They wanted videos from the capitalist world—all of which was prohibited to the rest of the population, but was accessible to them, as members of the elite. So they lived in an anti-capitalist system, supposedly, but they coveted every single thing they could get their hands on that was capitalist. And their kids were the same way: the kids of the elite wanted jeans. And they didn't want to work in the party or the trade unions—they wanted to be Soviet trade representative in Greece, or in the U.K.—somewhere else where it was nice to live.

Further, the citizens of the Eastern European countries had even more sense of what they were missing by living under communism rather than capitalism. Eastern Europeans were "particularly vulnerable," according to Kotkin, "because they lived right in front of that capitalist store window. They saw that capitalism every day." Once the Soviet leader Mikhail Gorbachev instituted the economic reforms known as *perestroika* and the political reforms known as *glasnost,* those living under Soviet rule in Eastern Europe, who saw what they were missing through the chain link fences dividing them from the capitalist countries of Western Europe, began to agitate for more freedoms and greater liberalization of economic control: "Socialism was supposed to be better that capitalism," Kotkin explained. "If capitalism was free and socialism was un-free, how was socialism better? If capitalism had a high standard of living and socialism had a low standard of living, what was the point of having socialism?" And when Gorbachev refused to send in tanks to quell rising unrest, the Soviet Union simply crumpled. "The idea that they would find some type of stable, improved socialism in the teeth of the capitalist competition in Eastern Europe was perhaps the most utopian aspect of the Gorbachev reforms," Kotkin argued. "Eastern Europe just crashed in a matter of months when Gorbachev refused to send in the tanks, when he repealed the so-called Brezhnev Doctrine, which meant the right to interfere, to uphold the socialist system, with force."

The most important thing to understand about the communist Soviet Union, according to Kotkin, was that it formed and existed entirely in relation to capitalism:

[T]he entire fate of the Soviet Union was dependent on the reality and the image of capitalism. So during the interwar years—between World War I and World War II, during the Great Depression—capitalism's reality and image were strikingly bad. Tens of millions of people were unemployed … The Soviet Union built this socialist system … during this low point of the capitalist world, and so many people who might have questioned Soviet realities looked and gave them the benefit of the doubt because of the relation to capitalism.

But in the wake of World War II, the world outside's story changed on them. They kind of got the rug pulled out from under them. Stalin anticipated another "great depression," because that's what capitalism did: it de-stabilized itself through these big, great depressions. [President Harry] Truman, I think, anticipated a big great depression after World War II. But it turned out that after World War II, the capitalist system had its greatest decades ever. Between the 1940s and the 1970s, the capitalist system had a boom that was absolutely unprecedented. Moreover, it was a middle class boom. It was not just the kind of boom that we have today. It was not a plutocratic boom; it was not a Gilded Age boom. It was a Levittown, middle class, homeownership, spread-the-wealth boom. Between the 1940s and 1973, West Germany grew more than 10% per year in GDP. West Germany was the China of its day. Japan was equally spectacular.

That boom in the capitalist world, combined with the change to democracy, combined with the fact that Germany was no longer a fascist dictatorship, and Japan was no longer a militarist dictatorship. Instead, they were rule of law democracies having this fantastic economic boom spreading to the middle class. And finally, the United States was fully engaged in the international system, in a way that it had never been before, following World War II. It didn't withdraw this time. So, all of this changed the rules of the game on the Soviet Union.

When viewed alone and not in comparison to the capitalist West, the Soviet Union was doing well, especially given what it had lost during World War II. As Kotkin argued:

Most of World War II was fought on Soviet soil and Chinese soil. They were the two big losers. Of the 55 million people killed in World War II, 27 million were Soviet inhabitants, and about 10 to 13 million were Chinese … That's where the war was fought. The Soviet Union had one-third of its GDP wiped out—but they recovered, they reconstructed—and they did extremely well. The problem for the Soviet Union wasn't that it was doing poorly: it was that it was in this competition, and in the competition it was losing, or falling farther behind. No matter how many apartments they built, no matter how many sausages they produced, no matter how many things that they changed in the parameters of measuring standard of living and daily life, they were not West Germany; they were not Japan; they were not the United States; they were not Italy; they were not Britain; they were not France. And so they were crushed—in a "daily life" competition—a competition of standard of living and daily life.

Far from losing a military battle with the U.S., then, as the Cold War story is often told in American popular culture and in American classrooms, the Soviet Union was doing fine militarily. Instead, it lost the "daily life" competition. Soviet General Secretary Mikhail Gorbachev essentially undid the entire communist market structure by allowing, through a loosening of market rule, the Eastern bloc citizens to get a taste of what they were missing all those years under communist rule. And once they had a glimpse of what capitalism potentially offered, there was no going back: "And so in 1985, this attempted idealist reform came to power and peacefully—unintentionally, but peacefully—liquidated the Soviet system." Of course, as Kotkin noted, this total *undoing* of the Soviet structure—as opposed to loosening it—was both unexpected and unprecedented:

> This was a colossal surprise, because no dictatorships, superpowers, *ever* walk away from power. Even though they thought that the other side had the upper hand, they still had the 40,000 nuclear weapons, 40,000 tons of chemical weapons, and a biological weapons program that the CIA didn't know about. And they didn't use any of it. They didn't use it for blackmail purposes; they didn't use it to bring the world down with them. They just quietly, unintentionally undid their system, and then let it fall.

For the Soviet Union, then, it was not the military run-up that brought down its political and economic structure; it was the greater exposure its citizens had to the standard of living of capitalist neighbors that brought people to the streets and to the gates to the West. The Soviet Union fell because its citizens wanted jeans and CDs.

Understanding the Cold War through a "Material Culture" Lens

For history and social studies teachers, the U.S.S.R.–U.S. stand-off in many ways defines the 20th century in both the U.S. and global history curricula. In fact, in order to understand freedom movements, rights movements, changes in work and industry, struggles over resources, and many other events and trends of this time, it is essential to understand the ways in which the Cold War "camped" nations big and small around the world into opposing blocs, and then how and why this stand-off dissipated as it did in the early 1990s. As teachers fascinated by the Cold War, the group who came together to re-think teaching this era found ourselves gripped by Kotkin's arguments regarding the important role that "the daily life competition" played in the fall of the Soviet Union, especially since the story of the Cold War that we had learned as Americans coming of age in the 1980s and 1990s was one of U.S. military prowess. All of us found Kotkin's arguments about the unraveling of the communist bloc compelling, and given his focus on the "things of everyday life," it made sense to us to consider incorporating material culture—essentially, an analysis of *things*—into the teaching unit we would develop.

Material culture is an approach to the thinking, learning, and doing of history that incorporates an analysis of things—the "stuff" of everyday life (Glassie, 1999). As historical archeologist James Deetz noted, material culture consists of "that segment of our physical environment which we modify according to culturally dictated behavior" (1996, p. 35). Considering "culture" to include the concepts, beliefs, and values we use to understand and interpret the world around us and to determine how to act appropriately within it, material culture entails the *physical* by-product of those actions: "the things to which groups assign meanings that are culturally specific and, indeed, culturally relative. Any object that has been manipulated by humans thus falls under the broad mantle of material culture" (Turk, 2006, p. 51). Of course, not all objects convey meaning or "signify" to quite the same extent (Prown & Haltman, 2000, p. 2). Items that pose central connections to certain facets of what pre-eminent material culturist Jules Prown referred to as "fundamental human experience"—including polarities of life/death, power/lack of control, security/

danger, desire/frustration, freedom/constraint—tend to be those that hold the best potential for rich analysis using a material culture lens (Prown & Haltman, 2000, pp. 2–3; Turk, 2006, p. 51). As Turk (2006) noted in her article on ways to use material culture in the study and teaching of history, "Carefully chosen items can serve as important windows into the cultures that made, used, and saved them" (p. 51). But how do we *work* with objects in order for them to be able to serve as evidence in an historical inquiry? Analyzing and making sense of an object's history (when, where, who, how saved, and why?), its material (made of what? what ingredients were needed to make it?), its construction (what tools and technologies were needed?), its design (what plans and underlying ideas and theories went into creating it?), its function (both intended and unintended uses), and its implications and meanings (how did it shape or affect the world in which it was made and used?) can help those who want to use a material culture approach to make as much meaning as possible of an object within an historical or anthropological context. Objects do not stand alone as "markers" of historical meaning, just as we do not ask a single primary source document to stand alone for a particular era or historical trend. Therefore, it is always necessary to put an object into "conversation" with other sources, to explore links, connections, disruptions, and the ways the object does or does not "signify" the culture(s) that made and/or used it (Pershey, 1998; Turk, 2006, p. 51).

All of us who worked on this unit immediately grasped the incredible potential of material culture to introduce students to the power and cultural importance of *things,* as in how the "stuff of everyday life" (Deetz, 1996) shaped the course of Cold War history. Our group consisted of two teachers: Allyson Candia, a 28-year-old white woman with five years of teaching experience, who spent her first two years as a teacher at a high school in the Bronx and currently was focusing on tenth grade global history at the High School for Environmental Studies on the west side of Manhattan; and Abby Rennert, an eighth year teacher in her early thirties, working with sixth grade English Language Arts (ELA) and social studies classes in the South Bronx. In addition, Diana Turk, a social studies education professor with a background in both American history and anthropology, led the group. Drawing from Kotkin's arguments and our sense of the important role played by material goods—especially, the comparison between U.S. goods and Soviet goods, as well as ordinary Soviet citizens' desires for more and better choices of goods as the 20th century progressed—we drew from Wiggins and McTighe's (2005) backwards planning approach and crafted the following essential questions to frame our unit on the Cold War of the 1950s through the late 1980s:

- How does the type of government countries choose shape their histories?
- How does access to "stuff" contribute to the rise and fall of nations in the 20th century?
- What was daily life like for ordinary people in the Soviet Union during the post-World War II period through the 1980s?
- How did the experiences of ordinary Soviet citizens differ from those of ordinary middle class Americans during the same time period?
- Why did the Soviet Union collapse?
- What role did the U.S. play in the fall of the Soviet Union and what other factors also played important roles?
- To what extent was the Cold War fought through material goods?

Through creating learning experiences to provide students with the content and skills needed to respond to these essential questions in complex and multifaceted ways, we hoped students would leave our unit with the following enduring understandings:

- The U.S.S.R. collapsed due to losing the "daily life" competition with the West and not because of military weakness vis à vis the U.S.

- Although the U.S. painted the U.S.S.R. as "backwards" in Cold War rhetoric, in the years following World War II, in which the Soviet Union saw the loss of millions of its citizens as well as one-third of its GDP, the U.S.S.R. actually surpassed most nations militarily and in terms of space exploration, as well as in terms of the production of daily goods. It was simply *in comparison with* the capitalist United States that the U.S.S.R. did not seem to measure up.
- A major reason the U.S.S.R. broke up was because elites who had been abroad wanted the same access to goods and choice of goods that they saw available to citizens of other nations.

And for Allyson, working with tenth graders:

- Opening up markets in the Soviet Union in the 1980s caused it to collapse, whereas in China, the authoritarian regime stayed strong due to differences in how the respective governments exerted power: in China, the government tightened individual freedoms and beliefs and sent in tanks to quash democracy movements, even while opening the markets to consumer products, while in the Soviet Union, idealist reformers such as Gorbachev believed that they could open things up economically without losing control, ultimately refusing to call in tanks against their own people.

In addition to the identified content and attitudinal outcomes for the lessons, we also planned the Cold War unit with the conscious pedagogical goal of using interdisciplinary approaches as well as innovative methods and materials to reach students with varying learning styles and differing reading levels (Chapter Resources I).

Teaching and Learning the Cold War in Diverse Classroom Contexts

As a high school teacher working in a New York State Regents-based school, Allyson is under a great deal of pressure to prepare her students not only to pass her class but also to succeed on the state-wide, high-stakes exam that determines diploma status for graduating students. While she has flexibility in choosing resources for her units of study, Allyson feels a strong sense of responsibility to focus on those areas broadly examined and most frequently addressed on the Regents exam. Abby, on the other hand, has more flexibility in choosing her history and social studies curricula—but less time than Allyson to focus on history or social studies in her largely English language arts (ELA)-based classes. As a middle school ELA teacher who is responsible for weaving social studies into the curriculum, she is not required to prepare her students for a high-stakes history exam. The pressures she experiences are around focusing more of her time on enhancing student literacy. Indeed, Abby's primary responsibility entails preparing her students for the yearly mandated ELA tests. This exam determines not only individual student performance but also the entire school's performance under No Child Left Behind and, with the recent transition to performance-based evaluations in New York, Abby's own assessment as a teacher. Thus, any time spent on history or social studies is time not spent on ELA; Abby must therefore believe deeply in and be able to justify—to herself, her school administration, and her students' parents—the value of any history- or social studies-based unit that she chooses to teach in her classroom.

Given the two teachers' very different needs and pressures, we chose as a group to determine some broad parameters and key foci for our unit, and then to allow the teachers to develop lessons and choose materials as they saw fit. Due to strong group dynamics and a shared interest in using a multi-modal approach to teaching and learning, in the end the two teachers relied on the same sets of materials while choosing to introduce the unit to their students in different ways. The rest of this chapter will provide descriptions and analyses of the Cold War units that both teachers taught as well as discussion of the ways their students grappled with and ultimately processed the learning experiences.

Teaching the Cold War—Allyson Introduces the Unit

Allyson teaches global history at the New York City High School for Environmental Studies (HSES), a well-established, theme-based school with 1,394 students. HSES is a diverse school in the truest sense, with a population that is roughly 57% Hispanic, 17% Asian, 15% black, and 11% white; 56% of students qualify for free or reduced lunch. By most measures HSES is a successful school, graduating 82% of its students after four years and 87.5% after six years. Only 7.4% of the students qualify as English Language Learners, and only 12.9% require special education services—numbers far below the norm in New York City public schools (New York City Department of Education, 2013). Eighty-one percent of HSES' graduates go on to either two- or four-year colleges (Inside Schools, 2013a).

Allyson's teaching experience shows in the ease and fluidity with which she moves through a class of 30 students. She has a friendly and approachable yet no-nonsense air about her, and the students—a mix of mostly black and Latino students, with a handful of Caucasians and Asians—respond easily to her, calling her by her name, Ms. Candia, rather than the generic "Miss" that is so common in public school classrooms throughout New York City. The room in which she teaches is wide and sunny, with plenty of room for the students' desks and ample wall space to show off student work. A section of wall entitled "Ms. Candia's Super Stars" displays several pieces of truly impressive work. According to Allyson, not just "the best" but "the best for particular students" gets displayed on this board. Other sections of the room feature write-ups of class and school goals, the latter focusing on raising credit accumulation, graduation rates, and attendance over the previous year's already high numbers.

On the warm spring day of the visit to her classroom, Allyson and her students were reveling in the air conditioning that was finally cooling the room after days of extreme heat. As the students began to file into the classroom, Allyson greeted them by calling, "Guys, get a do-now at the door." Most of the students found seats and began to unpack their books and get ready for class, though a few continued to mill around, making jokes and otherwise distracting their classmates. After a minute or so, Allyson called, "Faces up here," and all except one student found seats and began to attend to the day's "do-now" work. The one student who did not respond required more effort from Allyson. She told him, "You are not acting like an adult today, so I need to treat you like a little kid," and she walked him to a seat away from where his friends were sitting. Despite muttering about feeling "like an orphan, all the way over here," the boy settled himself down and joined the rest of the class in getting to work. Throughout the nearly hour-long period, Allyson alternated between leading the class from the front of the room and moving around the classroom to answer students' questions and prompting individuals or groups to provide better or more detailed responses on their extensive, content-heavy worksheets. At one point, in response to a student's teasing, Allyson joked in return, "You know I love you all—except one." As she said this, she turned dramatically, with a smile, toward the boy who had acted out earlier, obviously joking with him—and he in return smiled back, clearly not offended by her joke.

Allyson launched her unit with a lesson focused around the question, "How did the Cold War lead to tensions between the two superpowers?" She began the day by challenging the students to imagine that they were leaders of a great superpower, one of two in the world, and to consider the kinds of advice their advisors might give them in order to keep the balance of power in their favor, gain as many allies as possible, and woo additional support from as-yet unallied nations in Africa, Asia, and Central and South America. Would their advisors recommend sending troops into the smaller countries? Providing economic aid? Joining an alliance with other nations? She encouraged the students to consider the potential outcomes of these different scenarios—and used their responses as previews of what happened in the post-World War II period.

Next, Allyson paired the students to review what they remembered about communism, social-ism, capitalism, and democracy—the political and economic ideologies that would serve as the back-drop for the students' study of everyday life during the Cold War. Once the students had generated some ideas, Allyson gave her students an excerpt from the interview with Russian historian Stephen Kotkin that helped frame the economic contexts of the Cold War period. This excerpt focused on how the post-World War II boom in Western countries surprised Stalin and other proponents of communism by in essence "pulling out the rug" from under the Soviets. Through analysis of this excerpt, Allyson began to establish for her students the struggle between Soviet communism and U.S. capitalism during the post-World War II period—of nations adopting not only differing ideolo-gies and approaches, but wielding these *in opposition* to one another. Bringing these understandings to bear on Winston Churchill's "Iron Curtain" speech of March 5, 1946, Allyson and her students continued to explore what they saw as a stark contrast between the Western and the Soviet, the capi-talist and the socialist—and U.S. Cold War rhetoric of "the free" versus "the oppressed."

The next day began with a repeat of the leader-and-his-or-her-advisors exercise, but this time related specifically to Korea and Vietnam. After watching two short BrainPOP documentaries (BrainPOP, 2013) related to the Korean and Vietnam Wars, Allyson prompted her students to make sense of what unfolded through a series of questions designed to tease out what it was about Korea and Vietnam, two small and seemingly unimportant nations, that made them so significant to the two Cold War superpowers. "What is a proxy war?" Allyson asked her students. "Why were American lawmakers so afraid of Vietnam becoming communist?" The students completed Venn diagrams to help them identify the struggles over ideology and economics that defined the Cold War stand-off between the U.S. and the Soviet Union, while keeping in mind the question, "How might being caught in a struggle between superpowers affect a developing nation?"

Allyson's class next turned to an examination of political cartoons related to the Truman Doc-trine, the Marshall Plan, and the Berlin Airlift, asking: what were the purposes of each of these programs? How might the propaganda surrounding them reveal the U.S.'s conception of itself as liberator? How might this conception be different if viewed from the perspective of the Sovi-ets? Through such questions, Allyson challenged her students to think about the ways stories differ when told from differing sides: how did the U.S. depict communism in its publications? Conversely, how might the Soviets have depicted capitalism in their own political cartoons? This exercise required the students to practice the critical thinking skill of perspective-taking, which served as good warm-up for what was next to come.

At the end of this lesson, Allyson assigned her students a second excerpt from the Kotkin interview. This one posited that rather than the U.S. *winning* a military stand-off against the Soviet Union, as many in the U.S. tend to believe, in fact the Cold War ended because the Soviet Union *lost* the battle of daily life. With this text, Allyson moved the unit from an interesting but some-what predictable analysis of the economic and political contexts of the Cold War into something entirely unexpected for a high school classroom: for the rest of the unit, the class would focus on an investigation of everyday life for ordinary Soviet citizens as opposed to their ordinary (middle class) American counterparts, and how the desire for *stuff,* as Kotkin argued, could have brought down a world Superpower like the Soviet Union.

Abby Introduces the Unit

Like Allyson, Abby Rennert has a wonderful rapport with her students at the Knowledge and Power Preparatory Academy (KAPPA)/MS 215 in the South Bronx. KAPPA enrolls 405 students in a highly structured, academically oriented program that was originally modeled after the successful KIPP (Knowledge is Power Program) Academy Charter Schools. KAPPA boasts an attendance rate of 95.4%, which is much higher than one might expect given its demographics: 87% of its students qualify for free or reduced lunch, 13.3% of its students are English Language Learners, 44% of KAPPA's students are black, while 47% are Hispanic, and an additional 7% are Asian. The school lists 1% of its students as white, but on the day of a visit to the school, one observer saw no white faces at all, except among the teachers (Inside Schools, 2013b).

Abby's classroom bubbles with energy, but the students—all in uniform—are extremely cooperative and polite. As Abby enters the classroom, a spirited group of 25 sixth graders, 15 of them boys, eagerly await her attention. The students are all young people of color: most of African or West Indian descent, with a handful of Latino children present as well. Two of the ten girls wore headscarves that day. A small and slim white woman, Abby taught for two years in another challenging urban middle school setting, prior to coming to KAPPA, where she has now taught for six years. This school is a comfortable setting for her, and Abby is clearly liked and respected by the students who gather around her both before and after class, and also by her colleagues who pop by in their non-teaching periods.

On a hot day in June, all of the children in the class were dressed in their "gym day" clothes—navy sweatpants and navy shirts emblazoned with the KAPPA Middle School logo—rather than their usual uniform. Despite the heat and the summer-vacation-is-near feel in the air, the students sat with rapt attention as Abby introduced the unit on the Cold War, their eyes following her as she moved around the room. Whenever she posed a question, numerous hands waved in the air, and some students even called out, "Ohhh, Ms. Rennert." When she did call on a student to speak, the eyes of the others moved directly to him or her, giving the speaker their full attention. Few of the students interrupted either Abby or each other during the period. At one point, she asked a slumping student who looked ready for sleep to "please sit up now," but aside from this, Abby's students required little behavior management. Indeed, the classroom hummed along at an unusually high-level of engagement and focus for a middle school setting.

Rather than starting, as Allyson did, with the many political and military events and struggles that challenged U.S.–Soviet relations during the 1950s and 1960s, Abby began the unit for her sixth graders with an explicit focus on what different economic and political structures meant: "How does a capitalist economy differ from a communist economy?" she asked her students in the unit's first lesson. "How does democracy differ from socialism?" Abby drew up a series of vocabulary words for her students and provided definitions for each: Communism, Socialism, Democracy, Capitalism, Totalitarianism, and Imperialism. Once the students had basic definitions as well as some understanding for each word, Abby asked them to consider the effects of a centralized economy: what might be the pros and cons of a communist approach? The students next discussed which economic approach—capitalism or communism—they considered to be fairer. Initially, most of the students chose capitalism as the fairer approach, a response that was perhaps not so surprising given that they were in an American classroom. Abby complicated their initial reactions, however, by playing a game in which some students won and others lost. She gave the students the opportunity to choose whether or not she should take back the winners' points and redistribute them equally to the whole-class, so that each student would have an equal number of points. Many of the students, particularly those who had fewer points at the end of the game, now chose redistribution—an approach more in line with communism. This led to a lively discussion about the pros and cons of capitalism and communism—an especially compelling topic for discussion among students whose own families' social and economic positions have for the most part not made them "winners" in the American capitalist game.

To further set the groundwork for the unit, the next day Abby turned to a quick study of World War I and its aftermath and to World War II and the concept of "Superpowers" that arose after the war. She explained how two allies from World War II, the U.S. and the U.S.S.R., became such bitter enemies only a few years later. To ensure that her students had an understanding of the basic terms needed for their study, Abby provided them with another list of vocabulary words and their definitions: Cold War, Arms Race, Containment, Red Scare, Proxy War, SALT I and SALT II, and *glasnost* and *perestroika*. She also gave them short readings on the political and military challenges faced by the U.S. and the Soviet Union with scaffolded reading comprehension questions and lists of the allies and enemies of each of the two superpowers. Students then grappled with the reasons why certain countries feared others during the Cold War by writing their answers to the follow-ing prompts: "How do you think the non-communist countries felt about the spread of commu-nism?" and "How might a country's attitude toward communism affect its decisions (consider trade, alliances, and immigration)?" Through these activities, Abby sought to ensure that students had a basic grasp of the Cold War political struggles and relevant terminology so that they could make sense of Kotkin's argument about why the Soviet Union fell. Abby used the same quotes Allyson had used with her tenth grade students, and her students worked from similar worksheets and other materials, with additional modifications related to their grade level.

Teaching and Learning about the Cold War through the Lens of Material Culture

After laying a strong foundation for the significant events and players in the Cold War, both teachers now turned their students' attention to the essential question, "To what extent was the Cold War fought through material goods?" To give their classes a sense of what life may have felt like for ordinary Soviet citizens during the post-World War II "boom" time in the U.S., both Abby and Allyson showed short clips from the Robin Williams comedy, *Moscow on the Hudson*. Allyson contextualized the movie by explaining that, prior to the 1980s, the emphasis of the Soviet Union's Five-Year Plans was on heavy industry, an outcome of which included scarcity of consumer goods. In the first clip, Robin Williams' character, Vladimir Ivanoff, waits in line for shoes, only to find, upon reaching the front, that they have no shoes in his size—or even close to his size—and that his limit on shoes is two, although he needs three pairs. Without complaining, Vladimir hands over his coupons and sets out to wait in yet another line. He asks someone what they are waiting for, and the reply is that the line is either for toilet paper or chickens. No one in line can tell him, and the impli-cation is clear: they do not know what they are waiting for, yet they have no choice but to wait; their need is great, whether it be for food or for basic necessities. The line stretches way down the street and around the corner, and, as the snow falls, Vladimir has to pull up his collar against the wind.

In the next scene that both teachers showed their students, Robin Williams' character is now touring New York City, having arrived as part of a traveling circus. On the last stop of their tour, the Soviet group is taken to visit the department store Bloomingdale's. No sooner does the bus door open, than the visiting Russians descend on the store, grabbing any blue jeans they can see, with a particular interest in anything designer. Once again, the implication is clear: here in the U.S. there is plenty; here there is freedom to grab. Rushing from department to department, the Russians pile their arms with stuff. From this scene, the basic theme of Kotkin's interview becomes clear: the Russians, like their American counterparts, want stuff. The downfall of the Soviet Union will take place in the men's department at Bloomingdale's—not on the battlefield.

However, another scene from the movie that the teachers showed suggests a more complicated take on the "desire for stuff" theme. After his defection to the U.S., Robin Williams' character goes to a grocery store to buy coffee. He asks where the coffee line is, and is told that there is no line: he may go choose whatever he wants from the coffee aisle. He finds the aisle for coffee, only to become completely overwhelmed by the range of choices: Taster's Choice, Maxwell House, Nescafé, Chock full O' Nuts. Unable to make a decision, Vladimir literally breaks down on the floor. It turns out that choice can induce paralysis—one of the downsides to the market-based system in the U.S.

The movie clips served as a perfect segue for Allyson, the high school teacher, to introduce her students to the 1959 "Kitchen Wars," the debate that took place between Richard Nixon, then-Vice President of the United States, and Nikita Khrushchev, the Soviet leader. This debate strongly underscores Kotkin's thesis about these nations' conflicts over the provision of consumer goods during the Cold War. In pairs, Allyson's tenth grade students acted out the following script:

1959: Khrushchev and Nixon have War of Words

Setting	Soviet leader Nikita Khrushchev and U.S. Vice President Richard Nixon have had a tense exchange of words about the benefits of communism versus capitalism. This was the latest and most public of a series of impromptu debates between the two leaders which started yesterday on Mr. Nixon's arrival in the U.S.S.R. at the start of his 11-day visit. This time, the two men were touring the American trade exhibition in Moscow's Sokolniki Park ahead of its opening that evening. They stopped in front of a mock-up American kitchen displaying the latest gadgets—washing machines, toasters, and juicers. *[Both men enter kitchen in the American exhibit.]*
Nixon	I want to show you this kitchen. It is like those of our houses in California. *[Nixon points to dishwasher.]*
Khrushchev	We have such things.
Nixon	This is our newest model. This is the kind which is built in thousands of units for direct installations in the houses. In America, we like to make life easier for women …
Khrushchev	Your capitalistic attitude toward women does not occur under communism.
Nixon	I think that this attitude toward women is universal. What we want to do is make life more easy for our housewives …
Nixon	This house can be bought for $14,000, and most American [veterans from World War II] can buy a home in the bracket of $10,000 to $15,000. Let me give you an example that you can appreciate. Our steel workers, as you know, are now on strike. But any steel worker could buy this house. They earn $3 an hour. This house costs about $100 a month to buy on a contract running 25 to 30 years.
Khrushchev	We have steel workers and peasants who can afford to spend $14,000 for a house. Your American houses are built to last only 20 years so builders could sell new houses at the end. We build firmly. We build for our children and grandchildren.
Nixon	American houses last for more than 20 years, but, even so, after 20 years, many Americans want a new house or a new kitchen. Their kitchen is obsolete by that time … The American system is designed to take new inventions and new techniques.

Khrushchev	This theory does not hold water. Some things never get out of date—houses, for instance, and furniture, furnishings—perhaps—but not houses. I have read much about America and American houses, and I do not think that this exhibit and what you say is strictly accurate.
Nixon	Well, um …
Khrushchev	I hope I have not insulted you.
Nixon	I have been insulted by experts. Everything we say [on the other hand] is in good humor. Always speak frankly [truthfully].
Khrushchev	The Americans have created their own image of the Soviet man. But he is not as you think. You think the Russian people will be dumbfounded to see these things, but the fact is that newly built Russian houses have all this equipment right now.
Nixon	Yes, but …
Khrushchev	In Russia, all you have to do to get a house is to be born in the Soviet Union. You are entitled to housing … In America, if you don't have a dollar you have a right to choose between sleeping in a house or on the pavement. Yet you say we are the slave to communism.
Nixon	I appreciate that you are very articulate and energetic …
Khrushchev	Energetic is not the same thing as wise.
Nixon	If you were in the Senate, we would call you a filibusterer. You—[*Khrushchev interrupts*]—do all the talking and don't let anyone else talk. This exhibit was not designed to astound but to interest. Diversity, the right to choose, the fact that we have 1,000 builders building 1,000 different houses is the most important thing. We don't have one decision made at the top by one government official. This is the difference.
Khrushchev	On politics, we will never agree with you. For instance, [Statesman Anastas] Mikoyan likes very peppery soup. I do not. But this does not mean that we do not get along.
Nixon	You can learn from us, and we can learn from you. There must be a free exchange. Let the people choose the kind of house, the kind of soup, the kind of ideas that they want.
Khrushchev	You Americans expect that the Soviet people will be amazed. It is not so. We have all these things in our new flats.
Nixon	We do not claim to astonish the Soviet people. We hope to show our right to choose. We do not wish to have decisions made at the top by government officials who say that all homes should be built in the same way.

After discussing this role-play exercise and script, along with the worldviews and arguments of the two men, Allyson left her students with the question, "To what extent was the Cold War fought through material goods?" The next day, they would engage in a material culture analysis to learn firsthand what the battle of "stuff" was really about. Abby's class did not perform the kitchen debates, instead spending the entire period discussing and analyzing the *Moscow on the Hudson* clips in preparation for the material culture activity that would come next.

A Material Culture Exercise—Student Learning in the Cold War Unit

The students in both classes arrived to the next lesson to find posters tacked to the walls around the room. On one side, large images depicted shiny, "modern" American kitchens, as captured in the advertisements shown in magazines and journals of the 1950s and early 1960s. On the other side of the room, posters made from the grainy black and white photographs of the same era displayed images of small and dingy Soviet kitchens. The contrast between the two sets of images was striking.

In warm-up exercises designed to get students thinking about what an analysis of consumer goods can reveal about a particular culture, Abby and Allyson asked their students to think about an object they owned that held special meaning for them and what this object might "tell" others about them. The students shared their responses, which focused on toys in the younger class and on ipods and phones in the older group, and discussed how objects might "signify" certain things to others and thus have meanings beyond just their literal purposes. Next, the teachers led their students through guided practice of how to thoroughly examine an everyday object, looking at something in their classroom. As Abby put it to her sixth graders, "Pretend that we've just arrived in the classroom as time travelers from the year 3012. You are all archeologists and are amazed by all the unusual objects in this room. One item in particular really interests you. You have never seen such an item, and figuring out the significance of this item is incredibly important to your understanding of the year 2012. You must follow certain steps in your research." The teachers guided students first to *describe* the item they had selected, paying careful attention to its color, size, creation, and ingredients. Secondly, they had the students *identify* their objects by considering what the item looked like and what they thought it might have been used for. The students next *evaluated* their object, considering the attention the creator might have placed on beauty (aesthetics) and trying to determine its relative value and cost. In the next step, the students *analyzed* their objects, asking who might have made it and for what reasons, and what some of the intended and unintended functions of the item might have been. Finally, the teachers prompted their students to *interpret* the object, by thinking about what meanings the object might have carried within the culture(s) that made and used it, in what ways this object might have affected people's lives, and why the object might have mattered historically and culturally.

Once the students had practiced doing material culture analysis using these steps drawn from Turk (2006), the two teachers turned their students' attention to the objects shown in the posters on the walls and asked them to analyze one object each in the Soviet and U.S. kitchens:

1. Describe the item that you chose from the pictures of a Soviet or American kitchen. Describe its size, color (or what you think its color may have been), what the object is made of, how "complicated" or "simple" the object is in terms of how it was made, what tools might have been needed to make it, whether it is hand-made or machine-made, etc.
2. Identify the item. What does it look like? What do you think it might have been meant for? What might it have been used for? Can you think of other possible uses?
3. Evaluate the item. This is your chance to "judge" it. Is it a cheap item or expensive? Is it one-of-a-kind or one of many? Does it look like it is effective at what it is meant to do? Is it valuable? Has someone tried to make it beautiful or is it just a "working" item? What else can you say to evaluate it?
4. Analyze the item culturally. Who do you think made the item? For whose use? What do you think was the intended function of the item (what it was made to do)? What do you think were some unintended functions of the item—in other words, can you imagine the item being used in ways that its maker didn't plan for? If so, how?
5. Contextualize the item, or think about it in relation to the other sources we have studied. Consider the readings you have done or film clips you have viewed that might help you make sense of this item and what it might have meant for the culture that made and used it. Think about how those other sources might help you make sense of what this item meant.

6.   Interpret the item. What do you think it might have meant to the culture that created
      and used this item to have it exist? How did it change people's lives? Why might this item
      matter? What does it tell us about history and culture? Think about the analysis you have
      done above and what other materials you have looked at that might help you make sense of
      this item and its meaning within the culture that made and used it.

Through this exercise, students worked to understand, for example, what the image of a basic
sink and single-burner stove in the Soviet kitchen, or the shiny American refrigerator and toaster
oven, might have signified to middle class Americans as well as to Soviet citizens, who may have
seen these latter items at the American trade exhibition in Moscow where the "kitchen debates"
took place. The students also considered what themes emerged from their analyses of the items
and what the objects suggested about American and Soviet culture during the late 1950s and
early 1960s (Chapter Resources II and III).

   The written work and in-class discussions in both classes showed that the use of material
culture analysis helped students to see and feel the differences in daily life for (most) Americans
and (most) Soviets at the time. For example, one student in Allyson's class summarized how
the examination of material objects could reveal important facets about American and Soviet
cultures:

> All of the items are basically used for the same purpose, whether it's an American item
> or Soviet item. America gave the option to choose the brand/style of an item, while
> the Soviet people were simply supplied with whatever the Soviet Union distributed.
> American culture believed that life should be made easier by using different items and
> objects, while the Soviet Union did not invest in such technology. The Soviet Union did
> not support technological advancement in consumer products.

In another piece of writing, the same student provided additional interpretation:

> The lack of consumer goods in the Soviet Union affected the way people live[d] under
> communist rule. Soviet people were unable to choose goods that were available in other
> countries. They were restricted from options and were not caught up with the rest of the
> world technology-wise. The United States had made the lives of its people … easier, by
> the availability of different products.

Another student in Allyson's class wrote a similar analysis, noting,

> The Cold War was the "battle of daily life." Americans won because of its [sic] capital-
> istic form of government, versus the Soviet Union's communist form of government.
> Americans had hundreds of choices, while the Soviets were forced to use whatever
> they were given.

A third student wrote,

> American objects seemed to have a better quality and variety to offer. Because Amer-
> ica was so industrialized and had a system to capitalizing [sic] to support them, they
> are able to acquire new up-to-date technology and various varieties in foods and appli-
> ances. Because the Soviet Union was a communist society, there were not many
> varieties offered to the people at all.

After analyzing the objects in U.S. and Soviet kitchens and what meanings these may have held for citizens of each country, another student in Allyson's class concluded,

> The people in the communist nations wanted consumer goods like the people in the capitalist nations had. They wanted … toasters and small things that would affect their daily lives. The communist countries could not keep their people happy or provide for their basic needs.

Through class discussion about the kinds of objects contained in the U.S. and Soviet kitchens, the students in Allyson's class came to understand that "basic needs" were exactly what the Soviets *did* provide, whereas American consumer culture sought to create deeper "needs" than just the basics among its middle class inhabitants. Indeed, this discussion thread allowed the class to step back and consider the ways the pictures themselves—those of the American kitchens being glossy advertisements whereas the Soviet pictures were black and white photos of actual kitchens— painted a juxtaposition that itself needed a critical lens in order to keep the class from slipping into naive acceptance of the narrative of capitalism = plenty vs. communism = need that was so prevalent in U.S. propaganda from the Cold War era. Through carefully structured discussions that pushed the students to determine objects' *intended functions*—how they worked and what they worked for—as well as their *unintended functions*—the meanings they signified and the connotations they prompted—Allyson was able to ensure that her students understood how the Cold War represented a battle over "everyday life"—and how those objects could be put into "conversation" with other Cold War sources to illustrate deeply what communism and capitalism really meant to everyday people who lived in each society.

The students in Abby's sixth grade class also derived important understandings from their examination of the Cold War kitchens. Asked to compare a photograph of a smiling American woman in an attractive dress using a shiny toaster oven complete with multiple dials and settings (www.todayifoundout.com/wp-content/uploads/2010/08/micro1.jpg) to an image of an unsmiling Russian woman dressed in an apron with only a knife and pot as the tools in her basic kitchen (http://henrikduncker.com/blog/wp-content/uploads/duncker-kitchen-work.jpg),[1] Abby's students quickly noted the differences between the depictions. As one put it, "The woman in America is having fun. Also she likes and enjoys her job. And she enjoys being in America. On the other hand, the other woman [in the Russian kitchen] looks disappointed. She looks like tragedy." Other students characterized the Soviet kitchens as "old," "cheap," and as containing "not much technology," as opposed to the "shiny," "advanced," and "fun" U.S. kitchen. But in a compelling discussion that followed their analyses of the kitchen images, the students in Abby's class invoked issues of class and race by comparing the humble American kitchens of their own recently-arrived immigrant families with the Soviet kitchens of the 1950s and 1960s. Their circumstances of course complicated the simplistic dichotomy—seen in the movie *Moscow on the Hudson* as well as in Cold War era U.S. propaganda—of America as new, shiny, and technologically complex and the Soviet Union as basic, simple, and dingy. Certainly, the students recognized that for most middle class (especially white) Americans during the Cold War era, this distinction in access to goods and new technologies *did* lead to increased ease in their everyday activities as compared with those who lived in the U.S.S.R. Indeed, even while the students' families may not have access even today to the range and choice of appliances shown in the "modern" American kitchens of the 1950s and 1960s, they recognized the differences in *possibility*. In other words, while acknowledging the downsides of capitalism, where not everyone can afford the newest and best technologies, Abby's sixth grade students were still able to understand why those who lived in the Soviet Union would have wanted what they saw in capitalist countries, and how this "desire for stuff" might have brought Soviet citizens to the streets in protest. As one of Abby's students put it, in a sentiment echoed by many of her peers, "Well, they [Soviet citizens] wanted resources and freedom of stuff … They wanted variety [in] there [sic] daily life."

Still, when asked to evaluate in which economy they would prefer to live, many of Abby's students remained true to their sentiments after the redistribution game, providing critiques of capitalism as they now understood it: "[I would prefer] communism," one wrote, "because of economy [sic] let every one get equal wealth better than capitalism where every one competes for money." Another student agreed, noting that under communism, citizens "are entitled to free health care, free education (including university), child care, and a system that protects citizens from poverty and hunger." Some of their classmates disagreed, favoring a capitalist system because, "The democratic government and the capitalism economy is the most fair. Choosing your own government executive is way better … Having a capitalist economy is better because people earn money that they worked for." While in this statement, the student conflated the political concept of democracy with the economic concept of capitalism, rather than treating them as separate ideologies, overall, Abby's students' analysis of the kitchen objects helped them to recognize the different systems adopted by the U.S. and Soviet Union during the Cold War and to see Kotkin's everyday life battle argument firsthand. Moreover, this exercise provoked a sophisticated critique of capitalism based on students' own lived experience and their understandings of race and class in America—a stance that might not otherwise have been possible in a sixth grade class.

Teacher Reflections on Teaching the Cold War through a Lens of Material Culture

Given the powerful extent to which their students engaged with the unit's concepts and activities, both Allyson and Abby reported strongly positive impressions of the Cold War unit. Allyson stated,

> Overall, the unit went really well. The different activities throughout the unit gave it a lot of variety, and taking some time to think about how historians think [in reference to the Kotkin interview and to material culture as an approach] was really useful.

She was very enthusiastic about the use of material culture analysis, as this represented a new and different way of thinking and learning about history for her students:

> We had a long discussion in that class about how historians get their information and about the different types of fields in the social sciences, and we talked about archeologists and anthropologists and how they use material culture to inform what they do, so I thought that talking about social studies in that context and applying it to what historians know and other fields in the social sciences was really useful.

For her, the unit's multimodal approach to teaching and learning brought exciting and innovative lenses through which her students could grasp the larger messages and historical questions of the Cold War:

> The unit included really a lot of different activities, and every day was something different, so the students were challenged and engaged constantly. They loved the

media, they loved *Moscow on the Hudson,* they actually loved the song "Russians"—I mean, they loved it, we did a whole analysis of "Russians." It was a very potent song. I gave them the lyrics, and we did a soapstone [an analytical tool that considers Speaker, Occasion, Audience, Purpose, Subject, Tone] analysis of it … So I really felt that the unit touched on all the different interests that they have: there was music, there was a movie—I showed them the actual Kitchen Debates at one point, and they were really into that as well, they thought Khrushchev was hilarious, and they *got* it. I think at the end of the unit, more than just remembering the facts, they *got* this whole idea that the Soviet people wanted material goods and that that was what it really boiled down to, that it was this conflict between material goods in the West and the Soviet Union's repression under communism and not getting that *stuff,* so I think that they got the big idea and that they will remember it. I actually was talking with the students just the other day [two months after the Cold War unit], talking about communism in China, and how China opened up its markets and how it still maintained communism at the upper levels of government, and one of the kids in the class remarked, "Like in the Soviet Union, where they didn't have jeans and stuff" … [A]nd in the essays they wrote, they made some of those connections, and I think just understanding that, helped them retain a lot of the little "facts"—the facts kind of hang onto those big ideas.

Abby, too, found the varied sources and approaches used in the unit to be one of its key strengths. The Kotkin interview had proved challenging for her sixth graders to process and understand, even when broken down into short chunks. But, according to Abby, the clips from *Moscow on the Hudson*

really helped [the students] understand the interview and really helped bring home the idea of communism, whereas if they hadn't had that visual aid, they would have struggled so much more with what that means, because if I tell them it's about communism, it's not the same as seeing the visual images of communism. And that helped them pull the right information [from the interview].

Both teachers deeply appreciated how the Kotkin interview allowed them to plan deeper and richer units than they would otherwise have done. In addition, they were pleased at how their classes had engaged with the excerpts presented to them. As Allyson stated,

The historian interview was really useful, because it gave me as a teacher a lens to enter planning the unit. A lot of times, when I'm planning a unit, if I'm going in with fresh eyes and asking, what is the best way to frame this unit, I need a good way in, so it was really useful to have that interview with the historian. I also think that sometimes history teachers look at the content as a whole and think, "how can I teach these facts and how does the textbook break it up, like the sections of the textbook and how can I break it up?" and I do that all the time, you know, "I have to get through this unit and how do I do it," but I thought reading the interview with Kotkin really gave the unit a trajectory; it gave it a narrative, and it gave me a storyline kind of to give them, a lens. And something that they cared about too, because it was so relatable: everybody wants stuff and everybody, you know, especially teenagers, they really latched onto that idea of not having the ability to go from store to store and pick out what they wanted, and so we kept coming back to that throughout the unit, and also that idea of, this people as being so alien to Americans, I think especially though looking at the song, that there was almost a fear there, that they really got it—they're not so alien at all. But going back to the interview, for planning I think it made it very, very useful, that it gave it a structure and an intent.

For Abby, the interview's content and argument gave her a sense of confidence in teaching what was, for her and for her students, essentially new material:

I was apprehensive teaching the content because I hadn't done it before … I guess I was intimidated as to how much the students could understood being sixth graders, but that part of it went better than I thought it would. So the interview gave me the entry point that the students could access the information. And I think we framed a lot of where we were going with the unit around [Kotkin's] ideas.

Indeed, for the students as well as for the teachers, the interview provoked a deeper and richer sense of the history. "The students took it really seriously," Allyson noted, stressing in her tone the key points she was trying to make, "They were aware that it was an interview by a *historian*, an *expert* in the field *right now*, and what people in *college* were reading." Allyson highlighted the concepts that she felt really mattered to her students: "So framed like that, the students took it seriously … This was somebody who is working today and his *perspective* on *history*. And the students got a lot from it. Just using those little chunks of it framed the whole unit." In Abby's class too, the interview provided a framework for the students to make sense of the material:

I think as far as breaking down the interview and really reflecting on it, I had some students who got it like this (*snap*), and then there were others who I wish we had had more time for discussion to make sure that everyone truly understood what was being said in the interview. But, many students just got it—and what was good, too, was that it wasn't my go-to students who necessarily had the insights. [The interview] helped them get the main points.

For both teachers, the inclusion of material culture analysis as a methodology proved exciting and challenging, and they felt it warranted more time in their classes. Allyson said,

I would definitely keep the lesson on material culture … I would do [it] over the course of two days, getting deep into the material culture. I would also introduce the material culture method earlier in the year so they were used to the questions. This was a way of thinking, and it took time. I could see nuggets of understanding, little light bulbs going off.

For Abby too, the material culture analysis proved exciting. For her students especially, who may have struggled with reading and comprehending traditional texts, looking at images of objects allowed them to access meanings they may otherwise have missed. In both classrooms, the focus on everyday life, rather than on the abstract politics of the Cold War or the economic systems that characterized the two superpowers, brought the unit home to the students in very personal and understandable ways. "Looking at it in terms of everyday objects is so useful and made the unit real to them and made it personal," Allyson said.

> A lot of times this is what is missing in history and social studies classes, which is why kids *hate* them, because it's all of these people who they have no relationship to, but when they were looking at the kitchens, they were like, "Oh, look at this compared to that, that's whack." And they came up with some very interesting insights. They really picked up on that the Soviet advertisements were the same thing repeated over and over again—why? And really getting into why would the Soviet advertisement be, "buy one vacuum cleaner," and why would the American one be, "buy *this* specific vacuum cleaner."

As a middle school humanities teacher, a key aspect of the unit that particularly excited Abby was its alignment to the Common Core Standards. Because the unit used "textual analysis" as a central teaching tool, requiring students to read, interpret, analyze, compare, and evaluate multiple texts including object images, and then asked them to write about these interpretive steps, the Cold War unit offers an example of how Common Core Standards can be met through a well planned and well executed history unit. Common Core Reading Standards 1, 2, and 3 for grades 5–6, for example, call for students to: "cite specific textual evidence to support analysis of primary and secondary sources," "determine the central ideas or information of a primary or secondary source," and "provide an accurate summary of the source distinct from prior knowledge or opinions." Standards related to integration of texts with knowledge and ideas call for students to: "Integrate visual information (e.g., charts, graphs, photographs, videos, or maps) with other information in print and digital texts," "Distinguish among fact, opinion, and reasoned judgment in a text," and "Analyze the relationship between a primary and secondary source on the same topic" (New York State Education Department, 2013). Certainly, our Cold War unit challenged students to perform each of these tasks in addition to many others. For Abby, this alignment with the Common Core Standards proved important to her teaching and helpful in keeping a focus on social studies even in her ELA classroom: "The unit was very Common Core aligned," she noted, "And so much in line with what we're doing, with critical thinking, with the cultural analysis part." As a result, working on this unit contributed to Abby's own professional development by offering her a model of how to make a unit both historically rich and focused on ELA and Common Core Standards. She noted:

> I have never done anything like this before, especially long term. I have been aware of the [backwards planning model] but hadn't used it before, and I'm now shifting all units into this, because it aligns better with Common Core. This was the first time I had been forced to think about it more in depth. Common Core, starting with standards and then building units around tasks, really works here. Just using the textbook … doesn't target questions that I want to forefront, but doing it this way, with the handouts and the visuals, it really helped. I never had guidelines, with looking at a document and an image and really think[ing] about it piece by piece. If I had approached the Cold War on my own, I don't know what I would have done. My reference for this material was college, and then it was through a different lens.

For both teachers, keeping the focus on everyday life in the Soviet Union provided a fresh approach to Cold War history, which can often become American-centered even when taught in a global history class. As Abby put it,

> Looking at the unit the way we did, not so much from the American perspective—
> we didn't spend time thinking about what it meant for America. Sometimes when
> you do hear about the Cold War, it's how did America respond? But here it was
> what did it mean for those living in the Soviet Union during the Cold War? And that
> was good.

Every unit, no matter how successful, has its elements that need revision. For both teachers, the element of time—wanting more time to go deeper, to discuss longer, to explain further—weighed heavily. And because they chose to teach through the innovative approach of material culture, which neither had tried before, this sense of needing more time was particularly pressing. While both teachers largely followed Turk's (2006) steps for teaching history with and through objects in the kitchen images lesson, they found that students struggled to analyze so many objects in one sitting. Turk recommends deep rather than broad analysis: honing in on just one or two objects and then putting these into conversation with other sources about and from the era. Therefore, when teaching the unit again, both teachers plan to spend more time on the *method* of material culture, as well as an examination of just one or two images, rather than trying look at multiple images in the same lesson. For Abby, spending more time practicing interpretation of material culture would have helped her students make deeper meaning of the analysis of the Soviet and American kitchens:

> Focusing the unit around material culture was important and really worth it, but I
> intend to give it more time next year. With material culture analysis, they needed
> more guidance of what each step really meant, so I need to break it down better
> next time.

Both teachers also plan to introduce material culture earlier in the year and to use it in other units as well, so by the time they get to the Cold War, which is usually taught in the spring, their students will have hopefully developed some facility in analyzing and deriving historical meaning from object images.

Concluding Thoughts

Overall, the two teachers felt a strong sense of success regarding the unit: "I would teach it identically and would definitely use the interview again," Allyson concluded. "I think it was a really successful unit." The group planning process also worked well for her, which surprised her. "I tend to plan on my own, lock myself in a room and get it done," she said.

> This process was really successful for me. I think that this went really well. Sometimes
> when teachers plan together, they come up with one document, but everyone's teach-
> ing styles are different. So here, it was really helpful to have our ideas but then to be
> allowed to work with things myself and make it work for me. Sharing materials, such
> as primary sources and different media, and brainstorming ideas, in addition to using
> the Kotkin article, and then together, after we read it, bringing it out all together, it was
> really jumping out, so I think that doing the shared essential questions and the shared
> enduring understandings gave me the freedom as well as the knowledge to run with
> [the unit].

For Abby, too, the process of working together, of parsing through the interview and then planning together, bore important—and lasting—fruit:

> If I had gone to teach the Cold War on my own, framing it would have been intimidating to the point where I think I would have probably just walked away from it. I wouldn't have known how to approach it, wouldn't have had the resources to teach. But doing this project, I got the ideas for the resources, material analysis and interview, and I know I wouldn't have thought to have used these.

According to both teachers, the strong foundation of the Kotkin interview, along with the group approach to planning, gave them the depth of understanding and the courage to explore teaching paths that they might not have considered or felt comfortable taking. In a real sense, this made the unit as well as the experience especially effective and important.

Equally important is the extent to which students are able to answer the essential questions that drive the unit and thus show mastery of its enduring understandings. In this case, the students in both classes left the unit understanding how a nation's form of government—especially as illustrated in the stark differences between the U.S. and U.S.S.R. during the Cold War era—would fundamentally shape the lives and experiences of its inhabitants. Through their introduction to material culture as an interpretive lens and through their analysis of the Kotkin interview (and the dramatic reading and examination of the Nixon–Khrushchev Kitchen Debate in Allyson's class), the students came to understand the ways the Cold War was fought through material goods. By analyzing Cold War kitchen-related objects in addition to other primary and secondary sources on the topic, the students came to understand what daily life was like for ordinary people in the Soviet Union and for ordinary people in the U.S. during the same period. Bringing in their own experiences, the sixth grade students complicated the dichotomy of capitalism equating with plenty vs. communism equating with need and offered heartfelt critiques to an economic system (capitalism) that many in the U.S. simply take for granted as "right." And finally, the unit's thesis that, as Kotkin argued, the U.S.S.R. collapsed due to losing the "daily life" competition, allowed the classes to go beyond the simplistic narrative of America as the "winner" of the Cold War by virtue of its superior military. Developing an understanding of how nations rise and fall, and appreciating that change can come due to internal, social factors and not just at the hand of military foes, are essential concepts for students to grasp. Learning how a people's desire for blue jeans—or toasters or refrigerators or other material objects—can bring down as vast and powerful an empire as the Soviet Union shows in a very real way both the power of ordinary people and the power of that very human desire for "stuff."

Note

1   Although the teachers used this image in their lessons as an example of a woman in a Soviet era kitchen, later research revealed that the picture dated from the 2000s in Russia, not from the 1950s Soviet Union. Nevertheless it depicted a kitchen that was most certainly from the Soviet era.

Works Cited

BrainPOP. (2013). Retrieved from www.brainpop.com
Deetz, J. (1996). *In small things forgotten: An archeology of early American life.* New York: Doubleday.
Ferry, K. (2011). *The 1950s kitchen.* Oxford: Shire Library.
Glassie, H. (1999). *Material culture.* Bloomington and Indianapolis, IN: Indiana University.
Hoffman, D. (2009). *The dead hand: The untold story of the Cold War arms race and its dangerous legacy.* New York: Doubleday.

Inside Schools (2013a). High School for Environmental Studies. *Insideschools.* Retrieved from http://insideschools.org/high/browse/school/81

Inside Schools (2013b). Kappa Middle School. *Insideschools.* Retrieved from http://insideschools.org/middle/browse/school/375

Mazursky, P., Taylor, G., & Guzman, P. (Producers), & Mazursky, P. (Director). (1984). *Moscow on the Hudson* [Motion picture]. United States: Sony Pictures.

New York City Department of Education. (2013). *Office of English Language Learners 2013 demographic report.* NYC Department of Education. Retrieved from http://schools.nyc.gov/NR/rdonlyres/FD5EB945–5C27–44F8-BE4B-E4C65D7176F8/0/2013DemographicReport_june2013_revised.pdf

New York State Education Department. (2013). *Common Core 9–12 Social Studies Framework.* New York State Education Department. Retrieved from www.engageny.org/sites/default/files/resource/attachments/ss-framework-9–12.pdf

Pershey, E. J. (1998). Handling history: Using material culture to create new perspectives on the role of technology in society. *The OAH Magazine of History, 12*(2), 18–24.

Prown, J. D., & Haltman, K. (Eds.). (2000). *American artifacts: Essays in material culture.* East Lansing, MI: Michigan State University.

Schrecker, E. (Ed.). (2004). *Cold War triumphalism: The misuse of history after the fall of communism.* New York and London: The New Press.

Turk, D. (2006). What can a hot comb (or other objects) tell us about history? Using material culture to complicate the history we teach and learn. *The OAH Magazine of History, 20*(1), 50–53.

Wiggins, G., & McTighe, J. (2005). *Understanding by design.* Alexandria, VA: Association for Supervision and Curriculum Development (ASCD).

Works Consulted

Carbone, C. (2011). Staging the kitchen debate: How Sputnik got normalized in the United States. In R. Oldenziel & K. Zachmann, K. (Eds.), *Cold War kitchen: Americanization, technology, and European users.* Cambridge, MA: MIT Press.

Hume, E. (Writer), & Meyer, N. (Director). (1983). *The day after.* New York: American Broadcasting Company.

Kotkin, S. (2009). *Uncivil society: 1989 and the implosion of the communist establishment.* New York: The Modern Library.

Oldenziel, R., & Zachmann, K. (2011). *Cold War kitchen: Americanization, technology, and European users.* Cambridge, MA: MIT Press.

Reid, S. E. (2009). Happy housewarming: Moving into Khrushchev-era apartments. In M. Balina & E. A. Dobrenko (Eds.), *Happiness Soviet style.* London: Anthem Press.

Reid, S. E. (2011). Our kitchen is just as good: Soviet responses to the American kitchen. In R. Oldenziel, R. & K. Zachmann, K. (Eds.), *Cold War kitchen: Americanization, technology, and European users.* Cambridge, MA: MIT Press.

CHAPTER RESOURCES

I. Unit Plan: Cold War

Common Core Standards

Sixth Grade Class

CCSS.ELA-Literacy.RH.6-8.1 Cite specific textual evidence to support analysis of primary and secondary sources.

CCSS.ELA-Literacy.RH.6-8.2 Determine the central ideas or information of a primary or secondary source; provide an accurate summary of the source distinct from prior knowledge or opinions.

CCSS.ELA-Literacy.RH.6-8.4 Determine the meaning of words and phrases as they are used in a text, including vocabulary specific to domains related to history/social studies.

CCSS.ELA-Literacy.RH.6-8.5 Describe how a text presents information (e.g., sequentially, comparatively, causally).

CCSS.ELA-Literacy.RH.6-8.6 Identify aspects of a text that reveal an author's point of view or purpose (e.g., loaded language, inclusion or avoidance of particular facts).

CCSS.ELA-Literacy.RH.6-8.7 Integrate visual information (e.g., in charts, graphs, photographs, videos, or maps) with other information in print and digital texts.

CCSS.ELA-Literacy.RH.6-8.8 Distinguish among fact, opinion, and reasoned judgment in a text.

CCSS.ELA-Literacy.RH.6-8.9 Analyze the relationship between a primary and secondary source on the same topic.

Tenth Grade Class

CCSS.ELA-Literacy.RH.9-10.1 Cite specific textual evidence to support analysis of primary and secondary sources, attending to such features as the date and origin of the information.

CCSS.ELA-Literacy.RH.9-10.2 Determine the central ideas or information of a primary or secondary source; provide an accurate summary of how key events or ideas develop over the course of the text.

CCSS.ELA-Literacy.RH.9-10.3 Analyze in detail a series of events described in a text; determine whether earlier events caused later ones or simply preceded them.

CCSS.ELA-Literacy.RH.9-10.4 Determine the meaning of words and phrases as they are used in a text, including vocabulary describing political, social, or economic aspects of history/social science.

CCSS.ELA-Literacy.RH.9-10.6 Compare the point of view of two or more authors for how they treat the same or similar topics, including which details they include and emphasize in their respective accounts.

CCSS.ELA-Literacy.RH.9-10.8 Assess the extent to which the reasoning and evidence in a text support the author's claims.

CCSS.ELA-Literacy.RH.9-10.9 Compare and contrast treatments of the same topic in several primary and secondary sources.

Essential Questions

- How does the type of government countries choose shape their histories?
- How does access to "stuff" contribute to the rise and fall of nations in the 20th century?
- What was daily life like for ordinary people in the Soviet Union during the post-World War II period through the 1980s?
- How did the experiences of ordinary Soviet citizens differ from those of ordinary middle class Americans during the same time period?
- Why did the Soviet Union collapse?
- What role did the U.S. play in the fall of the Soviet Union and what other factors also played important roles?
- To what extent was the Cold War fought through material goods?

Enduring Understandings

Students will understand that:

- The U.S.S.R. collapsed due to losing the "daily life" competition with the West and not because of military weakness vis-à-vis the U.S.
- Although the U.S. painted the U.S.S.R. as "backwards" in Cold War rhetoric, in the years following World War II, in which the Soviet Union saw the loss of millions of its citizens as well as one-third of its GDP, the U.S.S.R. actually surpassed most nations militarily and in terms of space exploration, as well as in terms of the production of daily goods. It was simply *in comparison with* the capitalistic United States that the U.S.S.R. did not seem to measure up.
- A major reason the U.S.S.R. broke up was because elites who had been abroad wanted the same access to goods and choice of goods that they saw available to citizens of other nations.
- Opening up markets in the Soviet Union in the 1980s caused it to collapse, whereas in China, the authoritarian regime stayed strong due to differences in how the respective governments exerted power: in China, the government tightened individual freedoms and beliefs and sent in tanks to quash democracy movements, even while opening the markets to consumer products, while in the Soviet Union, idealist reformers such as Gorbachev believed that they could open things up economically without losing control, ultimately refusing to call in tanks against their own people.

Culminating Assessment

Students will conduct material culture analysis on images of objects and appliances from kitchens in the U.S.S.R. and the United States during the Cold War era. Students will build written and oral arguments about the two cultures at the time, their citizens, and their citizens' levels of happiness with their countries' economic structures based on these analyses. Students will interpret the meaning of objects and how the objects signified certain realities about U.S. and U.S.S.R. economic structures using a variety of additional sources, including documents, photographs, and audiovisual sources.

II. Lesson Plan: The Cold War and the Kitchen (Tenth Grade Global History Class)

Aim: How did availability of consumer goods affect the Cold War?

Objectives:

- Students will understand that the U.S.S.R. collapsed due to losing the "daily life" competition with the West and not because of military weakness vis-à-vis the U.S.
- Students will understand that major reason the U.S.S.R. broke up was because elites who had been abroad wanted the same access to goods and choice of goods that they saw available to citizens of other nations.
- Students will understand the history and significance of the Kitchen Debates.
- Students will learn to analyze material objects according to carefully articulated steps.

Do now: What can consumer goods tell us about a culture? Think about something that you own that could tell someone from the future something unique about our culture. Draw a picture of it, then explain what that object would tell someone from the future about kids living in New York City in 2014.

	_____
	_____
	_____
	_____
	_____

Activity (partner work): You and your partner are from the year 3014. You are archeologists, and have discovered a very unusual object on one of your digs. You have never seen such an item, and figuring out the significance of this item is incredibly important to your understanding of the year 2014. You must follow certain steps in your research. Examine the item, and do the following steps.

1. *Describe* the item that you see. Describe its size, color, what the object is made of, how "complicated" or "simple" the object is in terms of how it was made, what tools might have been needed to make it, whether it is hand-made or machine-made, etc.
2. *Identify* the item. What does it look like? What do you think it might have been meant for? What might it have been used for? Can you think of other possible uses?
3. *Evaluate* the item. This is your chance to "judge" it. Is it a cheap item or expensive? Is it one-of-a-kind or one of many? Does it look like it is effective at what it is meant to do? Is it valuable? Has someone tried to make it beautiful or is it just a "working" item? What else can you say to evaluate it?
4. *Analyze the item culturally.* Who do you think made the item? For whose use? What do you think was the intended function of the item (what it was made to do)? What do you think were some unintended functions of the item—in other

words, can you imagine the item being used in ways that its maker didn't plan for? If so, how?

5. *Interpret* the item. What do you think it might have meant to the culture that created and used this item to have it exist? How did it change people's lives? Why might this item matter historically and culturally? This is the "so what" question so think about what analysis you have done above and what other materials you have looked at that might help you make sense of this item and its meaning within the culture that made and used it.

Classwork (steps for analyzing material objects): Do the following steps for *each separate item.*

1. *Describe* an item that you see in the pictures of either the Soviet or American kitchens. Describe its size, color, what the object is made of, how "complicated" or "simple" the object is in terms of how it was made, what tools might have been needed to make it, whether it is hand-made or machine-made, etc.

Item 1:	Item 2:	Item 3:

2. *Identify* the item. What does it look like? What do you think it might have been meant for? What it might have been used for? Can you think of other possible uses?

Item 1:	Item 2:	Item 3:

3. *Evaluate* the item. This is your chance to "judge" it. Is it a cheap item or expensive? Is it one-of-a-kind or one of many? Does it look like it is effective at what it is meant to do? Is it valuable? Has someone tried to make it beautiful or is it just a "working" item? What else can you say to evaluate it?

Item 1:	Item 2:	Item 3:

4. *Analyze the item culturally.* Who do you think made the item? For whose use? What do you think was the intended function of the item (what it was made to do)? What do you think were some unintended functions of the item—in other words, can you imagine the item being used in ways that its maker didn't plan for? If so, how?

Item 1:	Item 2:	Item 3:

5. *Contextualize* the item, or put it into "conversation" with other sources. What readings have you done, transcripts have you analyzed, materials have you seen, or film clips have you viewed that might help you make sense of this item and what might it have meant for the culture that made and used it? This is your chance to put the item "into dialogue" with other sources and think about how those other sources might help you make sense of what this item meant.

Item 1:	Item 2:	Item 3:

6. *Interpret* the item. What do you think it might have meant to the culture that created and used this item to have it exist? How did it change people's lives? Why might this item matter historically and culturally? This is the "so what" question so think about what analysis you have done above and what other materials you have looked at that might help you make sense of this item and its meaning within the culture that made and used it.

Item 1:	Item 2:	Item 3:

Closure (independent work): Once you have analyzed two or more objects, what themes do you see among the items and their meanings (what do they have in common?) What larger assumptions or statements can you make about American culture or Soviet culture during the 1950s and early 1960s based on your analysis of these items? In other words, what's the *big* idea?

III. Lesson Plan: The Cold War and the Kitchen (Sixth Grade Humanities Class)

Aim: What caused communism to fail in the U.S.S.R.?

Objectives:

- Students will understand that the U.S.S.R. collapsed due to losing the "daily life" competition with the West and not because of military weakness vis-à-vis the U.S.
- Students will understand that major reason the U.S.S.R. broke up was because elites who had been abroad wanted the same access to goods and choice of goods that they saw available to citizens of other nations.
- Students will understand the history and significance of the Kitchen Debates.
- Students will learn to analyze material objects according to carefully articulated steps.

Do Now: Think back to the interactive map that showed the spread of communism. Is Russia still a communist country today? Circle one answer: Yes   No

If yes, why do you think communism lasted? If no, why do you think communism failed?

Activity: Student will read aloud (in turns) and take notes on the following excerpt from Stephen Kotkin Interview—Spring 2011:

> We [the United States] have a focus on the military. We think the military competition destroyed them. That's exactly wrong. Their military was quite sophisticated, and they did a good job. The military industry in the Soviet Union was the best-performing sector in the whole Soviet economy. They had rockets, they had tanks; they had everything you could possibly need. Nuclear weapons, chemical weapons, biological weapons. *And* they were able to carry that burden: it did *not* produce social unrest. So here's a place that was armed to the teeth and was good at military production. That was the thing they were best at. The problem was they were no longer fighting German tanks. It wasn't, you know, the Battle of Kursk, with the Nazi tanks on the one side and the Soviet tanks on the other. It was the battle of the silk stockings. It was the battle of the department store. It was the battle of the grocery store. It was the battle of the ethnic restaurants. It was the battle of daily life, and they had no answers in the battle of daily life.
>
> This is the strangest and most important thing. We think we crushed them militarily. But they went toe-to-toe with us militarily, all the way to the end, and then some. Today the Russian military industry is still highly productive. They still have big weapons (merchants) in the international market. That's the thing that they didn't lose. They lost the "daily life" competition.

After the class has read and analyzed the excerpts from the Kotkin interview, students will respond to the following questions:

1. In what way is the typical American understanding of the eventual destruction of the Soviet Union wrong?
2. What was the real battle between the Soviet Union and the United States, according to the interview? Explain your answer.

Closure: Answer the question: What happens when people are not satisfied with their lives?

Homework: Respond in a well-written paragraph to the following questions:

How do you think current citizens of the United States would feel about communism? Could it ever work in the United States? Why or why not?

Six
War Crimes in the 20th Century

War Crimes in Global Perspective: From the Eastern Front to No Gun Ri

By Stacie Brensilver Berman and Robert Cohen, with Michael Catelli and Josef Donnelly

Framing the Questions: An Interview with Mary Nolan and Marilyn Young, conducted by Robert Cohen

Mary (Molly) Nolan holds the Lillian Vernon Professorship for Teaching Excellence in the Department of History at New York University. She received her Ph.D. from Columbia University, where she trained as a Modern German historian. Her publications include *Social Democracy and Society: Working-class Radicalism in Düsseldorf, 1890–1920* (1981); *Visions of Modernity: American Business and the Modernization of Germany* (1994); and, most recently, *The Transatlantic Century: Europe and America, 1890–2010* (2012). She is co-editor of *Crimes of War: Guilt and Denial in the Twentieth Century* (with Omer Bartov and Atina Grossman) (2002) and *The University against Itself: The NYU Strike and the Future of the Academic Workplace* (with Monika Kraus, Michael Palm, and Andrew Ross) (2008). She also publishes on the politics of Holocaust and World War II memory in Germany, including "Air wars, memory wars" in *Central European History* (March 2005) as well as on anti-Americanism and Americanization in Europe and American anti-Europeanism. She is on the editorial boards of *International Labor and Working-class History* and *Politics and Society*.

Marilyn Young's biography can be found in Chapter Seven.

Robert Cohen: *Molly, even though your historical scholarship focuses primarily on Germany, you chose in* Crimes of War [2003] *to explore the history of war crimes from a comparative perspective, with chapters not only on German but also American as well as Japanese war crimes. How do you find it helpful to view the history of war crimes comparatively? Can you offer us a working definition of war crimes? And, why is it important for American teachers and students to study this history?*

Mary Nolan: Let me start first with a working definition of war crimes. It's a very capacious and sometimes unclear category but it refers to violations of what have come to be established in international law as the rules of war. War crimes can entail everything from the mistreatment, humiliation, and forced labor of civilians through mass forced migration, the abuse of prisoners of war, on up through genocide.

The real expansion of crimes of war, which include genocide and crimes against humanity when they are committed in the context of a war, came in the wake of World War II. What constituted war crimes was laid out in part in the Nuremberg Trials and in part in the Tokyo Trials—both of these for leaders of the Nazi and the Japanese militarist regimes. And then they were codified more fully in the genocide convention at the UN and the convention on torture. The U.S. has signed on to all of these international conventions: the Geneva Conventions, the genocide convention, the convention against torture. So, these are international laws that we acknowledge. So, it is very important for Americans to look at how these laws came into being, where they have been violated, including by the U.S.

RC: *So thinking about it comparatively is a must because it seems like the attempt to outlaw war crimes started out as an international movement.*

MN: It started out as an international project. So to understand how war crimes came to be defined and how certain and not all war crimes get prosecuted, one needs to look comparatively. But I think that there are deeper reasons why one needs to look at war crimes comparatively. No nation wants to acknowledge that its military has committed war crimes, that its government may have sanctioned the commission of war crimes. It's almost as though by definition every country says, "War crimes are what somebody else does, not what we do." So one needs to look comparatively to see … who is doing what? And, what are the myriad ways in which these actions are very similar?

RC: *It seems, then that the nation state is an obstacle to understanding this, and you have to transcend it in order to be able to push through all these rationalizations that grow out of nationalism.*

MN: Yes, absolutely. I think that the other reason why you need to look comparatively has to do with the history of the Holocaust … that this is the benchmark for the worst of war crimes against humanity that can be committed. So there is always a tendency, in fact, to look comparatively and to say, "Well, how is it similar to and different from [the Holocaust]?" And, I think one wants to make comparisons … not to say "Is it as bad?" But to look at the different ways in which a variety of war crimes, crimes against humanity, and genocide committed in war occur and are equally bad.

RC: *It seems as if forgetting is as important a part of the history of war crimes as remembering … A crimes of war conference that was supposed to accompany a German exhibit in New York on the Wehrmacht's—that is, the German Army's—war crimes in World War II was cancelled because the exhibit caused outrage in Germany. A similar pattern of forgetting seems to have occurred, on a smaller scale, yet still a gruesome war crime that the U.S. forces committed in Korea at No Gun Ri … How do we account for this massive historical amnesia? Does it derive from a national defense mechanism that is global in scale? And, for teachers who may not know this history, can you summarize the involvement of the Wehrmacht in war crimes on the Eastern Front? Marilyn, on the U.S. military can you describe what happened at No Gun Ri? I don't think many Americans know about this history.*

MN: The Germans in post-World War II West Germany, which is held up as the model country for remembering the crimes it committed, didn't want to acknowledge *massive* participation in war crimes. It acknowledged horrible crimes had been committed in the name of the German nation. ... There was a tendency to say, "Okay, it was the top Nazi leadership, it's the SS [schutzstaffel] who perpetrated the Holocaust and war crimes, but the *Wehrmacht,* these millions of German soldiers who fought on the Eastern Front were innocent" ...

When the *Wehrmacht* went into the Soviet Union in June of 1941, it went in having been issued the infamous Commissar Order, which said that the rules of humanity and international law don't apply because we don't expect Russians to adhere to them; therefore, any kind of leniency or respect for international law is out of place. Do what you wish with people labeled as political commissars ... When most people think of the Holocaust, they think of the kind of industrialized mass killing in places like Auschwitz. In fact, half of the Jews who were killed were killed outside of the camps by the *Wehrmacht,* by SS units, and then by reserve police battalions, rounding up and shooting, killing in a face-to-face kind of way. In addition, when the *Wehrmacht* went into the Soviet Union, it captured over five and a half million Soviet POWs [prisoners-of-war]. It had made no preparations for treating, feeding, caring for them, and over 3 million of them died.

And what is interesting is that when the exhibit [on the *Wehrmacht*] was up, reactions to the exhibit were very divided. There were families that donated to the organizers of the exhibit these photos albums, photos that were sent back from the Eastern Front by soldiers there, and the wives and families or the soldiers when they returned had meticulously compiled these, which were a mixture of photos from the Russian countryside, kind of war tourism, photos of humiliating Jews, sometimes photos of hangings. They are quite astonishing documents.

RC: *[Marilyn Young,] can you describe what happened at No Gun Ri, because I think teachers would not have heard of the war crimes that occurred there?*

Marilyn Young: No Gun Ri is the name of a village. And [the No Gun Ri war crimes] occurred early in the war. The American forces were retreating very rapidly and in hot pursuit, they were, of North Koreans ... The difficulties were, there are refugees running away from the fighting and then there is this army coming at you, and you're retreating. The orders were to keep the refugees from infiltrating American lines. They had to stay where they were. On the other hand, they are fleeing fighting. There are fire fights going on everywhere. The Americans tell one set of refugees from this place, "Go stay over there. You are going to be safe over there." And they [refugees] listen. They just go. And they hide and they wait. And then all of sudden [the U.S. forces] open up on them, and kill large numbers of these villagers where they were supposed to be.

Now, why that happened is very, very confusing. A bad order? People not knowing who was there? You could say fog of war. But, you have to say something else. Why didn't they know? Somebody told them to move there; somebody said "fire on them." And, nothing, absolutely nothing ever came of this. The villagers, the survivors, tried to bring charges long after the war. South Korea is very prosperous, an American ally. And, they try to bring charges before the South Korean government. And they fail, over and over again.

But the thing about No Gun Ri is that like My Lai, it was not singular. Not at all. There were refugees fleeing across a bridge. The order comes to bomb the bridge and the pilot flying over said, "There are people on it." And, the answer is, "Bomb the bridge" so advancing enemy soldiers can't get across it. So, they bomb the bridge. And then the order comes to strafe the river, which is frozen. So they do. There were atrocities in Korea—and one has to say they were on both sides: the North Koreans committed atrocities and the South Koreans committed atrocities watched over by Americans who didn't commit them themselves but knew they were happening.

The Korean War was three years, so it was far more concentrated than Vietnam, which takes place over a much more extended period of time. The city of Seoul changed hands many times. At one point it is in the hands of the Americans and the South Koreans. But, it had recently been in the hands of the North Koreans. The South Koreans round up very large numbers of people that they suspect were friendly with the Northern occupiers. A huge number, well over a thousand. And they start to systematically kill them. British soldiers hear of this, and they race to make it stop. And, they actually literally turn their guns and they say, "This is not going to happen." American soldiers who were there too didn't behave that way for whatever reason. There is an article on Korea … by John Osborne, titled "Men at War: The Ugly War," published in *Time Magazine* (Aug. 21, 1950), [describing these events].

MN: This is one of the things that made the *Wehrmacht* exhibit so powerful and so deeply upsetting to Germans and Austrians. Seeing it made clear exactly what you were saying about No Gun Ri and My Lai. These were not aberrations. These were an everyday part of those wars. What the *Wehrmacht* exhibit did was to follow three *Wehrmacht* Army units via photographs as one went into the Ukraine, one into Belarus, and one south into Serbia. And the photos were compiled from official propaganda photos and the snapshots taken by ordinary soldiers.

RC: *Marilyn, because No Gun Ri has been forgotten by the public both in the 1950s and 1990s, what do you think teachers could do to push back a bit? To show this is something that is important to think about?*

MY: It is important for people to understand that the Korean War did not begin in June 25, 1950 but that there had been a low level civil war going on for several years before that … What happens in June is that the civil war becomes internationalized. It had been a civil war, now it is totally international. American troops are there. American troops are there after doing very pleasant occupation duty in Japan. Many of them are very ill trained. For many, this is their first combat experience … The fighting is very intense at this point because the North Korean Army does look like it is going to push [south quickly]. The South Korean Army fades away, it is nothing. And the Americans are in this little pocket, at the bottom of the peninsula, where they hold on. So you have this retreat all the way down from the 38th parallel, fighting the whole way. And the fighting is, as a reporter from *Time* put it, "savage." And an intensity and a savagery that he had not ever seen before, because, he says, this is a war, among the people and, to some extent, he is careful here, against them. In this period, when No Gun Ri took place, there was guerrilla warfare, like Vietnam. Now, it ends, it is wiped out. But there was. And it was not Northern infiltrators. There were Southerners involved in it.

Robert Lifton[2005] said about the Vietnam War, and I think that you can say it about any civil war in which foreign powers intervene, that it is an atrocity-producing situation. I think that is right. It is a situation in which atrocities are absolutely inevitable.

MN: There are four kinds of reasons that people give to exonerate or dismiss the war crimes and atrocities that occur. One is, well, you on the other side did it too. Or you did it first, and we are only responding. The third is, it is necessary because the other side behaves so badly. In the case of Korea, the North Koreans, we knew that they were going to be so awful. So we had to do this, and make sure that they didn't. Or, as your last example suggests: looking back, in retrospect, it turned out okay so it didn't matter.

But either international law always applies or international law is meaningless. You cannot decide whether you are going to let it apply or whether there are excuses or not. You cannot say,

"Yes, we did something bad, but somebody else did something bad." It is, "We did something bad, and they did something bad too."

MY: There is absolutely no way to know, and in fact, it would seem to me that it would be much easier to make the argument against it. If you feel by and large, on the whole, that the Korean War ended well for the South Korean people … Not for the Korean people as a whole because Korea was leveled but for some numbers of South Koreans. There is no connection between that fact and the commission of atrocities. None. Absolutely zero. That is one thing. … There is no way that these war crimes, as far as I can see, in any way, contribute to a military victory. They are the outcome of fighting war to begin with. So, that is the first level. That war has unforeseen outcomes, both on the ground in terms of great battles, but also for individuals … I do not believe that it [war] is impossible without vast war crimes. If you felt that war is a crime, and I often do, that is one thing. But that's sort of fruitless because then you are saying that, "I can't even think about this. Since war is a crime, forget it, then I am not going to even think about this [issue of war crimes]." Since war exists, and I do want to think about it [war crimes], and I want to think about ways in which there are kinds of rules which people know about and if they're violated, they will be liable, then take responsibility. This doesn't seem to me a bad thing. Some people think that it makes war more easy or more likely. I don't believe that.

MN: The extent to which it [war crimes as unlawful] is taken seriously is reflected in the lengths to which governments try to say that, "Yes we knew these laws exist but this is a special case."

RC: *The thing that is striking about this is the parallels to what we discussed earlier regarding the rationalizing of Nazi war crimes in World War II. When it comes to rationalizing war crimes it does not seem to matter whether a nation is a representative democracy like the U.S. or a tyrannical dictatorship like Nazi Germany. There are such similarities in the way they justify their abuses, and that is a challenge to the whole idea of American exceptionalism … Many people in the U.S. would be offended: How can you compare the Attorney General of the U.S., a democratic country, to the Nazi officials in Germany who produced the Commissar Memorandum justifying war crimes on the Eastern Front? And yet there seem to be these parallels.*

MN: Yes, they are very similar in structure. And it is this: "Yes, we will acknowledge international law. We will say rules of war are a good thing to have. But we're going to tell you why we're a special case, and we can violate them with impunity in this case." The fact that they take them seriously enough [to make formal arguments for exceptions to these rules] is something to build on. Like Marilyn, I agree it would be better if there were no wars, vastly better, but since there are wars and are likely to be in the foreseeable future, then it's important to look at how one might regulate them, or punish the most egregious war crimes.

RC: *Marilyn, in teaching No Gun Ri, would it make sense to teach its history together with My Lai? My Lai is often seen as this big exception, an aberration, almost an unprecedented one, in the American way of war. No Gun Ri calls that into question. I mean, it is commonly assumed that My Lai was the result of exhausted men losing control, not part of a larger pattern. And by making it seem so aberrational, Americans evade the larger question of war crimes, and there is no sense, as there was in post-World War II Germany, that we need to come to grips with this criminality in our history. So putting the two U.S. atrocities in these wars in Asia together seems to offer a way to show that even in these two very different American wars in different eras, we have U.S. war* *crimes and need to ask why these occur, why no one has been punished for them, and why they are almost purged from American memory. So putting these two events together is a way of saying, "Hey, maybe these are not some little exception but are actually an important part of the history of American warfare."*

MY: I think that would work very well. I think that you would have to say, though, in terms of My Lai, that numbers of people didn't follow orders. And I think that's crucial to say. There are two ways that students in my experience respond to this. One thing students say is, "We don't know how we would have acted in that circumstance. They're our age. They get this order. Their buddies have been killed the day before and the day before. And they've been given this big thing: going into enemy territory. How would we respond?" But then you have to say, "Why did these guys [some of the soldiers present at My Lai] refuse? Why do you think you would be the one who would look straight in the eyes of a 12-year-old—10-year-old—two-year-old child and shoot him in the head?"

RC: *And the U.S. helicopter pilot who saw what was going on and landed at My Lai and tried to stop the mass murder …*

MY: Hugh Thompson. He was there and tried to stop it. But so did Michael Bernhardt. And that's another very good film you can show. It's about 20 minutes. It's called *Interviews with My Lai Veterans* [Strick, 1971]. It was made relatively close to the trial. There were a number of rapes. There is one point when the unseen voice of the interviewer asks one of these guys, "Were there rapes?" And you can see him remembering and then saying "No." But there were 20 rapes. They also sat along the side and ate lunch. It's a wonderful interview because in it, you see people, two people saying, "No, I didn't do it." And then there is a follow-up film 20 years later, *Four Hours in My Lai* [Sim, 1989], which is a full scale [documentary], there you see these guys 20 years later.

. . .

RC: *How would you respond to those who use comparisons in a distorted way to rationalize war crimes by arguing, for example, that the Germans may have committed war crimes on the Eastern Front but that is because the Russians were so bad? How do you respond to the argument that says that not only did the Russians commit war crimes but that the Soviet threat in a way caused the war and these German crimes in the first place? This is an increasingly popular argument with some sectors of the German public.*

MN: Yes, and many argue that the Americans were also very bad. Since 2000 there has been a lot of attention to the air war, the bombing of German cities, which did cause incredible destruction, although the death tolls compared to what the Germans did on the Eastern Front were relatively low. It was about 500,000 or 600,000 Germans who were killed in the bombings. But it was a violation of international law to bomb civilians.

RC: *How does this death toll from the Allied bombings compare with those killed by the Germans on the Eastern Front?*

MN: Well, you have in the Holocaust nine million. The death toll in the Soviet Union in World War II is now estimated to be 27 [or] 28 million. It was a very different kind of war across Europe than the American Second World War, which is imagined as "the good war," in which the Americans heroically came in and won the war, in their view. Europeans view it quite differently.

But to get back to your question about comparison, comparison is useful less to say who is worse as a perpetrator or who suffered most as a victim than to understand in the 20th century, and now into the 21st century, the prevalence of very brutal wars in which civilians account for the overwhelming majority of casualties, and in which war crimes and crimes against humanity proliferate. This not something exceptional. This kind of warfare is absolutely central to the last hundred years of history. If we want to understand that history, if we want to understand how politics and society have been shaped, we have to accord this a central role … Indeed it is doubtful that genocide on the scale in which it occurred could have occurred outside of these total wars, wars that either mobilized an entire society in very brutal civil wars that followed on American bombing, as in the case of Cambodia, or European-wide wars as World War II was, where the Holocaust occurred.

RC: *That seems a really important point for teachers: that war is not just about battles, [but] that you need to connect the history of genocide and war crimes with the history of war. So what we're saying may seem unpleasant for peace loving teachers who loathe war and don't enjoy teaching about it: that we have to move war and its social consequences to the center of the history curriculum for the 20th and thus far for the 21st century as well. Do you think that's right?*

MN: I think one absolutely has to. My guess is although I don't know the high school history curriculum in the Soviet Union and now Russia or in Germany, certainly the war and the Holocaust both feature prominently for Europeans because both World War I and World War II had such an enormous impact on society. There's no way to teach 20th century history without featuring it prominently.

MY: I think here they teach World War II for sure and that's about it, really. And that's also the same. World War II made America what it is, prosperous, more important, the leader, the revival of Europe, all of that …

MN: And because war was never fought on American soil since the Civil War, the potential value of adhering to international law and avoiding war crimes is not an everyday fact of life: your father, your uncle, your grandfather didn't perpetrate war crimes. Your grandmother, your wife, your sister didn't suffer them.

RC: *That seems a big part of the problem: here in the U.S. there's almost a triumphalist narrative about war. [Historian Eric] Hobsbawm, at the start of his global history of the 20th century (1994) has all these quotes by Europeans, filled with pathos, who view the 20th century in tragic terms as a century dominated by horrible wars and brutality … That's not how Americans tend to view the 20th century at all—and not how they view war. And maybe that is something that history teachers in the U.S. need to push back on, connecting the history of war with genocide and war crimes.*

MN: And that you see the Holocaust as actually being enabled by, and integrally related to, World War II. There's a way in which the Holocaust gets inserted into the history of anti-Semitism and persecution of the Jews, and it goes on in a world of German government boycotts and *Kristallnacht* and then the camps, and the war is ignored. The Holocaust began when the *Wehrmacht* went in and started rounding up and shooting.

MY: I think you can say that the Holocaust as the extermination of European Jewry would not have occurred without the war. It is absolutely key to the war. It is not something that they say, "Oh, let's have a war so we can kill all the Jews." That was not the chronology.

RC: *Could you walk us through the primary sources that you selected for our teachers to use as they teach about the history of war crimes? Starting, Molly, with that order of the Germans near the start of the war to disregard the rules of war.*

MN: The Commissar Order, which was issued on June 6, 1941, from the Führer Headquarters, that is to say Hitler's Headquarters, was transmitted to all the officers of the *Wehrmacht*, which was getting ready to invade the Soviet Union. So the reason that I think this is really important is that it lays out very clearly the determination not to abide by any of the rules of war. It singles out civilians as key people who will be attacked. Not just soldiers. We are talking about political commissars, not members of the Red Army. And it suspends all need to detain, charge, try, and treat with any judicial procedures whatsoever. It sets the context and gives a very sweeping permission for the fighting of war outside the rules of war.

[And from the Eastern Front,] I have photographs. These are from the book, the German title was, *War of Annihilation* [in English, *The German Army and Genocide* (Hamburg Institute, 1999)]. The English catalogue was going to accompany the exhibit that never opened in New York City. And the photographs that are useful to look at are ones which are part of a series of photographs of the humiliation of Jewish forced laborers. These are photographs that were taken by the propaganda company and by individual soldiers. They documented what were clear violations of the rules of war. That you singled out a particular ethnic group, that you employed civilians as forced laborers, that you humiliate and degrade them.

The second set of photos are of the innumerable civilians who were hung. Those not shot immediately were hung in order to try to, in the eyes of the *Wehrmacht*, be an example against any kind of local resistance. And, these photos, there are hundreds of them, this is a very small selection of them.

RC: *What would you say, if you could talk to a teacher about why it is important to talk about this issue of war crimes and genocide and study war—and again, I think there is a reluctance to deal with these things. It is not really in the curriculum in the way that either of you are talking about. What would you say to them about why it is important to study this history in a comparative context?*

MN: As I said earlier, because war and war crimes are such an important part of the history of the last hundred years. And, because they are teaching American boys and girls who may well find themselves fighting in wars where the dangers of their being asked to commit war crimes or tempted to commit war crimes will be very great. And it is very important to have thought in advance about the last hundred years of war and what war crimes are, about why they happen, and who says yes and who says no.

MY: I think that you could say in 1945 there wasn't an American, an ordinary American alive, who thought that the United States would be involved in war again. And in five years the U.S. was involved in war again. And then at the end of that war there was no one who thought they would be involved in another war in 10 years or less. And they were. And, at the end of that war, no one thought there would be another one. And within years you had a string of little ones. And then Gulf War I. Now Gulf War II [the war in Iraq] and Afghanistan. So, war has been a constant component of the lives of Americans since 1945. And since they are likely to live into a century of ongoing war in which the U.S. is involved in war, it is well to know the history of what has happened before.

MN: Yet another reason is that Americans pride themselves, rightly or wrongly, as having been in the forefront, being a real leader in the post-World War II effort to define human rights. And from the 1970s and on, to really push human rights, and yet war crimes and crimes against humanity have continued. And the U.S. has expressed increasing ambivalence about adhering to those human rights as defined in international law. That is a paradox that really needs to be analyzed and discussed at length, particularly since we continue to incarcerate who we define as illegal combatants at Guantanamo. The torture memos are still on the books justifying a variety of behaviors that others justly condemn.

MY: I think that it would be interesting for a history class … to read about who proposed the international criminal court, who signed onto it. And what are the reasons that the United States has not. Since the U.S. regularly charges other with crimes of war it would just be interesting to see why they are so reluctant to participate.

Works Cited

Bartov, O., Grossman, A., & Nolan, M. (Eds.). (2003). *Crimes of war: Guilt and denial in the twentieth century*. New York: The New Press.

Hamburg Institute. (1999). *The German Army and genocide: Crimes against war prisoners, Jews, and other civilians in the East, 1939–1944*. New York: The New Press.

Hobsbawm, E. (1994). *The age of extremes: A history of the world, 1914–1991*. New York: Vintage Books.

Lifton, R. J. (2005). *Home from the war: Learning from Vietnam veterans*. New York: Other Press.

Osborne, J. (1950, Aug 21). Men at war: The ugly war. *Time Magazine*.

Sim, K. (Director). (1989). *Four hours in My Lai* [Motion Picture].

Strick, J. (Director). (1971). *Interviews with My Lai veterans* [Motion Picture].

Framing the Questions: An Interview with Charles Hanley, conducted by Robert Cohen

Charles J. Hanley graduated from St. Bonaventure University in 1968 and joined the Associated Press (AP) in Albany, NY the same year. He served as a U.S. Army journalist in South Carolina and Vietnam in 1969–1970. He resumed his work at the AP upon his return, later becoming a political correspondent and then bureau news editor. He was AP assistant managing editor and deputy managing editor in 1987–92. Until his retirement in 2011, Hanley served as a special correspondent with the Associated Press International Desk in New York. He has covered six wars over 30 years and reported from more than 70 countries. He is the author, with Martha Mendoza and Sang-Hun Choe, of *The Bridge at No Gun Ri: A Hidden Nightmare from the Korean War* (2001), based on their investigative reporting on the massacre at No Gun Ri, for which they won a Pulitzer Prize.

Robert Cohen: *Interview with Charles Hanley in New York City on April 11, 2011 about No Gun Ri and the documents surrounding that massacre.*

Charles Hanley: I'll begin at the beginning by telling you that the survivors first went public …well, they tried to go public actually, in 1960, long ago. But that was a brief period of democratization in Korea. And then [South Korean dictator] Park Chung Hee took over, and everything was quashed.

RC: *And during the pre-sixties period it was too repressive in South Korea for the No Gun Ri story to be discussed, they were U.S. allies and so the government there would not want this mentioned?*

CH: One of the survivors would have a couple of drinks and start talking about it. And he would hear the next day from the police … He would just talk to the neighbors, whoever would be in town at a bar or whatever. I don't know. The police would come to call on him to tell him, "You better stop talking about this." That is the 1950s and the 1960s.

But by the mid-1990s, because of the liberalizing of South Korea, the survivors of No Gun Ri were again able to begin filing petitions. And in conjunction with that, the leader of the survivors, Chung Eon-yong, the former policeman who lost two children and whose wife was badly wounded at No Gun Ri, he wrote a book that was published as a novel. That was the only way he could get it published. But, it was a book describing No Gun Ri, using factual information. It was called *Do You Know Our Agony?* That's the usual English translation. It was not published in English.

At that point, Sang-Hun Choe at the AP [Associated Press] Bureau in Seoul, who was a new correspondent there, wanted to write about these accusations. That was 1994. He was not allowed to by the editors at the AP.

In late 1997, he brought it up again. I won't go into all the circumstances, but they were more favorable, and he was able to go ahead and write a piece about the allegations. That piece arrived at AP in New York and was suppressed. At least it got out in Seoul but the New York foreign desk and others in the leadership at the AP decided that they didn't want to publish it. He was not told why.

But luckily one of the [AP] editors in New York said, "Well, at least we should try to check it out on the U.S. side and see if we can find the soldiers involved." And so then Kevin Noblet—he was the deputy editor at AP—he tried to get the Washington Bureau to work on it. And they eventually refused and just said they weren't interested. So then luckily, he thought of our investigative team, which was called the Special Assignment team, and the editor, Bob Port, immediately recognized this as an important story. And he put his little team to work on it.

They began by finding the documents. Well, they actually began because the U.S. Army contended there were these series of petitions presented by the survivors, culminating with a claim filed with the compensation commission … I forget the full name of it. It is sort of a bi-national thing compensating for military damage for maneuvers and all these sorts of things or any damage under the SOFA, the Status of Forces Agreement. They filed this formal claim and the U.S. military responded by saying that "there is no evidence that the First Cavalry division was in that area at the time, as you claim." They also—actually it was an earlier claim, but they said, "This would have been connected by a combat activity and therefore the U.S. government is not liable." There are U.S. court decisions over the years that say this. Finally that claim was rejected, simply on statute of limitations. Time had run out.

The first story we wrote was a fairly brief story about the rejection of the claim. But finally, this thing had gotten onto the wire. Meantime, Bob Port's people, namely Randy Herschaft, the researcher, and Martha Mendoza, the reporter, were working on it. Randy's first discovery was a very simple one, online, going to the official Army history of the war [Appleman, 1961]: finding that the First Cav was indeed in the area at that time.

And so, once you see this, that they are lying, as a journalist, you have an obligation to follow up on this. So Randy was sent down to Washington, and he began digging up these documents. There were only a couple, initially, that we found, shooting the refugees, shooting the civilians. Then Martha and Randy did this remarkable thing. Well, mostly Martha—of wallpapering the walls of the Special Assignment team office with these topographical maps from 1950 … Half a century later, you could still get copies of this, so Martha put up seven or eight of these, one for each day in late July 1950. And, she and Randy began collecting all of the coordinate reports from all of the units. They were usually reporting in twice a day, their coordinates after [they] were moving around the front. And then she took little stickers, and every day, they were full of these different colored stickers for different units to show the movement of who was where when. And that's when I came back, and I got involved.

And I went up to their office, and I saw this, and I just couldn't believe my eyes. I said, "Martha, this is amazing! How have you done this?" So she and I began to focus and try to figure out which units and then we narrowed it down, and narrowed it down …

It was the 34th [phone] call [to potential sources] Martha found a guy who talked about civilians being shot, refugees being shot under a bridge. A couple of calls later I got a guy who talked about it. So we knew [it was] the second battalion of the Seventh Cav that did this …

It turned out it was the whole battalion that knew about it. Anyway, so we finally figured out what platoon it was and focused on those guys … And it was simply a case of these guys on one side of the Pacific describing in detail the same event that these Koreans were telling us in the same detail: tunnel under the bridge, the babies screaming, the bodies piling up in the entrances to the tunnels because people were trying to protect themselves so they were piling up bodies there …

So [initially] we had really just a few documents, but they were very damning documents. We took that Kean, the General [William B.] Kean document [Chapter Resources VII], saying "treat civilians as enemies" up to West Point to a military lawyer Gary Solis, who was … teaching a course on military law, law of war, and we showed him the Kean [document], and he couldn't believe his eyes. He said that he had never heard of anything like this—except for the Indian Wars there had never been a document like this.

RC: *Can you describe the Kean letter?*

CH: The Kean memo said "treat civilians as enemies." It is a very brief memo that went to his division. General Kean was the commanding general of the 25th Infantry Division that was right next door to the First Cav. He said that "Korean police have been directed to remove all civilians from the area between the blue lines shown on the attached overlay, and report when the evacuation has been accomplished. All civilians seen in this area are to be considered as enemies and act accordingly." Now the Army investigative report subsequently from 2001 claimed that "Well, Kean didn't say to shoot them." You know, "treat them as enemy," but he didn't say to shoot them. I think they said, "He must have meant that they should be arrested." Well, I don't think so because this was passed along, this was the follow-up log: "Commanding General Kean directed we notify the chief of police that all civilians moving around in the combat zone will be considered as unfriendly and shot." This is their transmission down the line of the order.

So, yes, we had few documents but they were very, very damning. And basically unprecedented. And, that's all we needed. We said that we had three pillars. We had the Koreans, the Americans, and the documents that showed that these orders were flying around. Three legs to a stool or whatever. And so, it was all very hard work done in April, May, June of 1998. Then in July I wrote the story. I did all the writing, and in late July, we had a meeting with quite a number of people, 10 or 12 people, photos were involved, with the executive editor, Bill Ahearn. And, Ahearn started bringing up objections, including "the AP doesn't break news." You could just see that they were nervous as hell about this story. Of course, the initial story had been killed, had been spiked, months earlier. "The AP doesn't break news. It's okay to shoot civilians during wartime." These are just some of the quotes that I remember from the meeting, etc, etc. Just very, very defensive and in any event … but, not telling, not saying that we aren't going to publish this …

We refused to take "no" for an answer, basically. Just to give you an idea: we were forbidden to deal with our TV people. And, the AP has [had a] very large TV operation since the mid-1990s, but based in London, run by Brits. These guys knew if I talked to our Brits about the story, the Brits would go crazy. So they forbade us to deal with the Brits on television. All kinds of people we couldn't talk to. We couldn't talk to our graphic people, we couldn't talk to anybody. Martha and I had planned to go to Korea. At the last minute that was canceled. It was quite an agonizing experience personally for all of us …

We continued interviewing, finding new leads, and discovering more of what we find in the book [2001]. The blowing up of the bridge, the killing of hundreds of refugees on the bridge, the air strafing, other incidents of strafing of refugee columns, etc. So, we are developing all of these things. We are also getting to know the GIs, the veterans better, our No Gun Ri veterans, much better, re-interviewing them, visiting them. And, learning more about, one of the big themes of the book is PTSD [post-traumatic stress syndrome], and the haunting of these men and obviously the Korean survivors as well. And learning how many of them had ghosts visiting them all their lives, how many were on VA programs for PTSD, taking drugs, etc.

And there was even a case when Martha stopped by … [to interview] one fellow in the hospital in South Carolina, and this was finally when we got TV on board. She and TV went down there to interview another veteran in South Carolina. And she stopped by the hospital to see this one fellow and he said, "Well, you know, it seems that I have been cured"—he had some sort of brain tumor—"and I know why I have been cured because I finally talked about No Gun Ri." And, "You've got to get that story out." The guys all knew that we were having this problem. And they wanted this story out. They needed to get this thing off their chests.

Finally, in March of 1999, we were summoned into the executive editor's office—my two editors and me, Port and Kevin Noblet and me. And Ahearn and the executive editor told us, "We've made a decision. We're not going to publish this story." And, my editors were just kind of dumbstruck. And I finally piped up and said, "What are the reasons? Why?" And he said, "Well, this story has a prosecutorial tone to it. And number two, there is material in the GI interviews that should be in the story and is not in the story."

It was too controversial, too explosive. The AP historically had always been a conservative—small c—conservative, journalism organization. And, they just wanted nothing to do with it. Well … I had said months earlier, "We've got to play hard ball with these guys." I wasn't going to let this thing get [suppressed], be part of suppressing of a My Lai. I told him that. I told Ahearn, "This is a My Lai, you can't suppress it, period." So Port had been trying to play nice with him but eventually what I did, I managed to get word around the industry about what was happening. And they [AP] started hearing back.

The important thing here is that the AP is unique in being a cooperative, a non-profit cooperative, owned by America's newspapers. So when the owners starting calling up and saying, "What is going on? We hear that you are suppressing this My Lai-type story." Then they realized that they had been caught, they had no choice …

RC: *It speaks to an unwillingness to confront war crimes.*

CH: Oh, yeah, and it still goes on. Anyway, it is important for people to understand that the process at the AP was not all very smooth. But eventually we did get published. And you know, at that point, it still came down to, we have the basic documents but by then we had also developed the air strafing story. And, we had those documents.

We realized that we'd gotten the makings of a separate story here just on the air strafings. And that was based largely on the documents. And then we tracked down (these mission reports have the pilots' names on them) … some of them. They were somewhat helpful. They were, of course, all officers. When we were doing our interviewing on No Gun Ri, I told Martha and Randy that we're going to save the officers for last, because I knew that the [enlisted] men would be more honest [than their commanders]. I wanted to be able to confront the officers with what we had learned from the men. With the Air Force pilots, they're all officers so you've got to start with them and end with them. And they weren't as forthcoming as some of the enlisted men in the Army were with us. But we got plenty. And, then meantime Sang-Hun was tracking down the victims, survivors of these strafing attacks by U.S. air planes.

RC: *Could you describe the events at No Gun Ri as you see it, based on all these different sources?*

CH: Well, it began with the lack of preparation of the troops that were sent in with the North Korean invasion. The U.S. simply sent over constabulary type troops from Japan to try to shore up the South Koreans. They didn't have sufficient training … They didn't get any training in handling civilians. And then they show up in Korea … So that's the situation, the context of the whole situation. Then the villagers, who were later slaughtered, were chased from their homes by American troops for reasons that still remain unclear. But there was general confusion within the American ranks about how to deal with civilians. Should they stay put? In some cases they were told to stay put, in some cases they were told to go north, in some cases they were told to head south. In this case they were forced out of their villages and made to head south. And they ran into the second battalion of the Seventh Cavalry regiment.

Meantime, stories had flown all over the war front about North Korean guerrillas infiltrating via refugee groups. This was a very heavy rumor over the war front, and yet when you look at the documents, at the record, there are very, very few cases documented of such a thing. It is a typical situation at a warfront where these rumors get out of hand. And so the men grew afraid of all Koreans. And here they were faced with this large group of Koreans coming down the road … So these orders were flying around, and on the morning of July 26, 1950, there was a general order from the Eighth Army, which was the overall command, telling all units not to let refugees cross the line.

And we interviewed early on in the No Gun Ri work … a man, a retired colonel, who was a lieutenant at No Gun Ri, and he told us that he remembered that order and what do you do if they [the Korean civilians] keep coming? He said, "We had to shoot them to stop them." Now this particular officer claimed that the shooting didn't last very long and also that he left the scene, and he didn't know what happened later. Now you know there is all this sort of dissembling, particularly among the officers. So that order, that general order, came down from the Eighth Army.

This large group of refugees is coming down the railroad tracks, walking down the railroad tracks towards the Seventh Cav unit, and suddenly they are attacked. Actually they're not moving. They are sitting having lunch on the tracks, and they are suddenly attacked from the air by apparently two war planes, rockets, strafing bombs. We are not quite sure of all the ordinance that were involved. And many of them were killed.

They end up—the survivors end up—in the tunnel under the railroad overpass at No Gun Ri. And then over three days these ground troops of the second battalion, Seventh Cav continue firing into the tunnel to kill them all. They do kill practically all of them in the process. And most of them were women and children and others were old men, many of them.

RC: *And that's the thing that distinguished this from My Lai, how long it lasted, which surprised me a lot since this happened over the course of three days.*

CH: And that's why the U.S. Army investigative report claims [are not credible], they actually used the words "not deliberate," which simply defies the English language and common sense. It lasted three days. There were no ceasefire orders. They knew these were civilians, and it certainly was deliberate. And then this unit got the order to retreat further, and they simply left them behind, and the North Koreans discovered all the bodies. Apparently there were about 20 to 30, mostly children, who survived under the piles of bodies. And that was about it. But this policy of firing upon refugees and not letting them through the lines persisted for months in the Korean theater. The strafings continued from the air.

As a result of our reporting in September 1999, within weeks people started coming forward and filing petitions with the South Korean Defense Department about similar incidents. And by early 2000, we counted 60 some-odd complaints, and I think this was a major driving force behind the establishment of the Truth and Reconciliation Commission in Korea in 2005. By the time that they started collecting claims themselves, they counted 200 incidents—what they called civilian massacres by the U.S. military.

RC: *Do you know, did the military eventually do something to stop these attacks on civilians?*

CH: Well, the course of the war had a lot to do with that. Because the Americans then went into North Korea, which is another obscured landscape of killings that have to be much worse than what happened in South Korea. And, we have men in fact telling us, you know, we would talk to them about the whole war, they would tell us about No Gun Ri, and then they would say things like, "Well, it was even worse up in North Korea, what was done." One, I remember, he told me, he said, "Did you ever hear about the Nanking Massacre in China?" I said, "Sure." He said, "This was worse than that."

RC: *Following up on the issue of denial: so you have AP being so unwilling initially to have the story come out, and then you have the U.S. Army response, the report, this Army investigation, and that seems to just be an exercise in denial as well.*

CH: Actually it was not directly from [President Bill] Clinton, but it was directly from the Defense Secretary [William] Cohen. He ordered the Army investigation, and the Army Inspector General was put in charge of the investigation.

We were out in the morning papers. The next day, Cohen ordered an investigation. It was clear from the journalism that this was a pretty open and shut case. They didn't need to look any further to order up an investigation. And [the South Koreans] wanted to do a fully joint investigation— in other words, jointly interrogate witnesses. [But] the Americans wouldn't allow that … The Koreans wanted to join the investigation, and the Americans would not go along with that and so, separate investigations were conducted. And subsequently, as I noted in the *Critical Asian Studies* article [2010], the U.S. Army investigators deceived the Korean government about a number of things: the existence of documents, the non-existence of documents, and such. And testimony.

RC: *I know that you wrote about the John Muccio letter [Chapter Resources VI] in the* New York Times. *Maybe you could describe that a little?*

CH: That is very key and easy enough to explain. The night before the No Gun Ri Massacre began—and by the way, I think that I will start calling it a massacre. We were forbidden to call it a massacre in the copy that we put out. And, in fact, when we won the Pulitzer Prize, Lou Baccardi was there as the AP was reporting the Pulitzer awards, and the Pulitzer citation referred to it as a massacre—and he had them strike that word out from the citation. In other words, we didn't quote the Pulitzer.

RC: *What did they call it?*

CH: A killing. We usually called it a killing, a refugee killing. But, the day before, the evening before the killings began or the massacre at No Gun Ri, there was a high-level meeting, behind the front, of U.S. military, the U.S. embassy, and Korean civilian officials to discuss what to do about refugees. The next morning, the order, the written order, came down from Eighth Army to stop all refugee movements across the lines. But meantime that next morning, [Muccio], the U.S. ambassador to Korea, who was not himself in that meeting the evening before, his number two was there. But [after] he got a report, obviously from his number two, the U.S. Ambassador John Jay Muccio sent a letter to Dean Rusk who was then the Assistant Secretary of State for Asia, East Asian, saying that at this meeting, last evening, "It was agreed upon to fire on civilians that approach American lines. First a warning shot and then if they continue advancing they will be fired upon." And, Muccio advised Rusk that "I thought I should tell you about it because it may cause repercussions in the United States if this gets out, etc."

The letter was not reported, was not acknowledged, in the 2001 U.S. Army investigative report of No Gun Ri. This letter, obviously, is critical evidence in this case. [But] we hadn't seen it. In late 2005, Sahr Conway-Lanz, a historian from Harvard who had done Ph.D. work in this general area, reported in a journal of diplomatic history the existence of the letter. And he then called me up and told me about this. We had not perused enough of State Department files to have found this. Then, we went and got ourselves—not relying upon him, we got our own copy of it—and we were able to report it. This was in 2006. We reported on the existence of the Muccio letter and asked the Pentagon why this was not in the [U.S. Army investigative] report [on No Gun Ri]. They would not address our question directly. The Pentagon simply said, in effect, "We did the best job we could. We checked everything we could"—something to that effect.

The South Korean government, then learning about the Muccio letter, presumably from the AP report, wanted to know why it wasn't in the report. At that point, we learned the South Korean government was told that yes, the Pentagon investigators had seen the letter, but they didn't use it for whatever reason, whatever excuse they gave the South Koreans at that point. We then contacted the Pentagon again and got the excuse that they did not report the existence of the letter because they did not think that it was relevant to the No Gun Ri case—which of course is total irrationality.

This is a very good example of the kind of whitewash and cover-up that the U.S. Army investigation amounted to. There are many other examples of other documents—and documents that were misrepresented in a couple of cases. They had to be reported by the Pentagon report, they had to be acknowledged because—this is very interesting—of an inter-service business. It is very clear this is the reason because Air Force researchers turned up the Turner Rogers memo in which the number two Air Force guy in Korea wrote to the number one Air Force guy saying, "We should stop strafing refugees. The Army's got us strafing refugees. We shouldn't be doing it."

It appears to me that the Air Force realized that the Army was going to suppress this document [Chapter Resources V]. The Air Force looks relatively better because of this document, because [it shows that unlike the Army], they didn't want to strafe refugees. The Army was making them do this. And so it was in the Air Force's interest to leak this document, which they did to CBS News. This was in the middle of 2000, during the middle of the investigation by the Army. It was leaked to CBS News. Again we went and got the document on our own.

So the Army then had to acknowledge the existence of the document. It had been reported in the press, but what they did was they did not reproduce the document. They did not reproduce any document. This is an important point: in their 300-page report, they did not reproduce a single document. I think that if they reproduced an innocuous document, it would be obvious that they weren't reproducing an important document. So they didn't reproduce any.

They denied the existence of mission reports of the Air Force's 35th Fighter Bomber squadron, incriminating mission reports about attacking refugees. [In] the Army report, which is very sloppy and very clumsy in many ways, you could find internal evidence … that they had the mission reports of the 35th squadron. But then they told the South Koreans that they didn't exist. We learned that from the South Koreans. And when you look at the list in the back of the report of the documents shared with the South Koreans, the 35th squadron is not there. And yet in the body of the report the Army investigators in effect forgot to erase the references to the 35th squadron reports. So the internal evidence is clear that they had the reports. Not only that, but the AP had the reports. So we knew these existed. And these were very incriminating reports, and yet this prevented the South Koreans from coming to very hard conclusions about the strafing of refugees by the U.S. Air Force.

As important was a series of 10 or 12 orders handed down by generals and colonels in the August–September–October period of 1950, in which they very directly and blatantly ordered the shooting of refugees just indiscriminately, things like an order from a regimental commander which said, "Shoot all refugees coming across the river." General [Hobart R.] Gay who was the commander of the First Cav division, which was responsible for No Gun Ri later, sending down an order saying that refugees are "fair game." And on and on, these sorts of documents that were suppressed. We discovered—our AP researcher Randy Herschaft found—that the Army investigators, the Army researchers, and historians found these documents when they did their research for the No Gun Ri investigation and underlined, asterisked, and put arrows showing these salient points, which was so relevant to this whole No Gun Ri business, and yet somewhere up the line in the investigation these documents were suppressed. They were not reported or acknowledged in the No Gun Ri report.

RC: *And there is no way to find out who was responsible for doing that and why …*

CH: Number one, we are talking about Pandora's box. There has never been an apology for My Lai. Certainly there has never been an apology for No Gun Ri. And if you start apologizing and acknowledging liability, presenting compensation, then you have a Pandora's box situation. In Vietnam, Korea, you name it. The U.S. never apologized and never paid compensation.

It is pretty much a mystery to me [as to who turned the U.S. Army investigation into a whitewash]. We have never learned whose hand really stopped this. I do get a sense—see [Lieutenant-General Michael] Ackerman, for example, with the Muccio letter—I do believe in my exchange with him about the Muccio letter, I sensed that he honestly was surprised by this. That he never knew about it. One interesting thing is when they released the investigative report in January 2001, I was on leave, but I came back to the AP to go to Washington for the investigative report release with a couple of colleagues. And we were called in. They did it late, I guess it was a Thursday, not Friday. I always thought it was a Friday, in typical fashion, you know you release the bad news on a Friday afternoon. But they released it in a very strange way. You got the report and within a half hour you had a news conference on it so that people, journalists, couldn't have possibly read the report and understood it by the time that you have the news conference.

And in between they had a background briefing for just a very few of us with General Ackerman. But he was sitting here. I'm sitting there. We were at a big table, a couple of his officers are here. And then [there] was a row of a couple of colonels, JAG [Judge Advocate General's Corps, legal advisors] colonels, behind him over here. Ackerman was just not helpful at all, although he did acknowledge that they hadn't found the Seventh Cav log.

That log is so important to this whole story. That is where the orders and the information would have been about the killings. And it is missing from the National Archives. And I said, "Did you ever find the Seventh Cav log?" "No, we didn't." So they were well aware of the importance of it. And what happened to it? "Well, you know, somebody said there was a fire," some bullshit. Then finally we were so exasperated, I said, "General Ackerman, was anything wrong done at No Gun Ri?" Meaning, I don't know how I quite phrased it, but meaning morally, legally, a mistake by somebody. "Was something wrong done?" And he started answering in a fairly honest way and one of the lawyers jumped up behind him and said, "No!" He simply said "no" and stopped him from going on.

RC: *What was your reaction when you first encountered the Muccio letter?*

CH: I was stunned actually. Sahr Conway-Lanz, the historian, he was living in New York at the time, and he came over to my apartment, and we looked it all over and talked about it. I was quite amazed as you would be. Through this whole thing, you can't imagine … how amazing that you would have someone on the phone, and they would start talking about, early on, when we're really getting to the bottom of this, and here I'm the guy who said that we will never get to the bottom of this, and here they are blurting it out because they want to get it off their chest. There was one very interesting, not No Gun Ri but I don't know if you read about the blowing up of the bridge over the [Nakdong River]. It's an episode in the book [2001]. And it was in our follow-up journalism thing, not No Gun Ri. The Americans and the South Koreans are retreating farther, and they are retreating farther across the Nakdong to form the Pusan perimeter, which finally held out against the North Koreans. But there were two bridges over the Nakdong. Now in our reporting on No Gun Ri, we learned about the blowing of one bridge at a place called Waegwan because it is just mentioned very briefly in the official Army history [1961] because General Gay, First Cav division gave the order to blow the bridge with refugees on it. That was in the official Army history, which wasn't published until 1960 and got no attention. It is just one paragraph of General Gay telling the Army historian, "I had no choice, I had to do this. I blew up the refugees."

But Randy and I knew there was another bridge, and so we had a hunch that that bridge was also blown up that day. And we went into the files. We found an AP story of the blowing up of that bridge, that second bridge on August 2, I think, 1950. The AP story was by Hal Boyle, who was one of the great AP journalists—he was a Pulitzer Prize winner from World War II. And here he was in Korea, reporting on the Korean War. And he reported that refugees had been coming across the bridge, lots of refugees, hundreds and hundreds of refugees. And that an engineer officer ran out and fired his pistol off into the air to chase them back and then the bridge was blown up. So the implication was that they chased the refugees off the bridge.

Well, in that story, they quote a guy, Corporal Rudy Giannelli from the Bronx. He was the colonel's driver. And the colonel told him, "Go talk to the two journalists and tell them what happened." And so they have a couple of quotes from Giannelli. We tracked down Giannelli, and we said, "Do you remember that day?" He was in Florida, I've got him on the telephone, I asked, "Do you remember that day?" He said, "Do I remember that day? It was the worst day of my life. All those poor people. We blew up all those poor people." I couldn't believe it. This was just a hunch that we were working on. And sure enough, he tells me everything that he remembers about the steel flying and the bodies and the water buffalo flying, blowing off into the river. I think there were, probably had to be, at least 500 people blown up on that bridge.

RC: *I guess the rebuttal to the way that we talk about war crimes is the relativist claim, "Oh, everybody does it," The South Koreans were brutal to their own civilians, and that the North Koreans were brutal to the South Koreans.*

CH: Yes, so there is brutality without racial difference. There is certainly that but there is certainly brutality because of race. What's often pointed to, of course, is the difference between America's Pacific war and America's European war in the treatment of civilians and bombing and the atomic bombing, etc.

RC: *Do you think that you and your team of reporters, having done more than anyone to bring the story of the No Gun Ri massacre, that the story you broke is having any effect? In the face of all this denial and amnesia about this, do you have any kind of hope at all that No Gun Ri will register in the American memory? Or is this whole pattern of denial and the refusal to engage with the history of this war crime just too pervasive?*

CH: You are right. Of course it was important to get it on the record for those who care. And, in journalism, particularly in the AP, the saving grace is knowing that in a country of 300 million—the world is so many billion—you are always going to have a hell of a lot of people who are interested in this stuff and will take it and take it on board and make it part of their own knowledge of history.

Works Cited

Appleman, R. E. (1961). *South to the Naktong, North to the Yalu: United States Army in the Korean War.* Washington D.C.: Center of Military History/United States Army.
Hanley, C. (2010). No Gun Ri. *Critical Asian Studies, 42*(4), 589–622.
Hanley, C., Choe, S., & Mendoza, M. (2001). *The bridge at No Gun Ri: A hidden nightmare from the Korean war.* New York: Henry Holt and Co Publishing.

Essay: War Crimes in Global Perspective: From the Eastern Front to No Gun Ri

By Stacie Brensilver Berman and Robert Cohen, with Michael Catelli and Josef Donnelly

At its best, modern global history offers a path beyond parochialism and national chauvinism, enabling students to view their society critically by assessing it comparatively in relation to the larger world. It can be a sobering experience for students raised on politicians' platitudes about the U.S. as the greatest nation on earth to test such nationalistic assumptions via real data from across the globe. This is why, for instance, the Nobel Prize winning economist Joseph E. Stiglitz, in *The Price of Inequality,* used a comparative lens to shock Americans out of their complacency. Stiglitz (2012) offered data showing that in such pivotal areas as social mobility, poverty rates, infant mortality, educational attainment and life expectancy, the U.S. lags behind other nations: "once account is taken of inequality, the United States is ranked twenty-third, behind all the European countries" based on the United Nations Development Program's (UNDP) measure of human development (p. 22). Taking a cross-national perspective, then, a whole range of questions emerges about how and why social inequity expands and why it varies from nation to nation.

A comparative framework is every bit as illuminating when applied to the history of war and war crimes, since it forces us to see beyond nationalistic assumptions of American innocence and to ask where and when U.S. war-making has resembled that of other nations whose armed forces have committed war crimes. Teaching the history of war crimes, the subject of this chapter, is a challenging task precisely because questioning such nationalistic assumptions can be politically sensitive, causing cognitive dissidence among students raised on heroic images of the U.S. armed forces. But for teachers in the U.S.—the sole military superpower and one that has largely been at war since the start of this century—teaching students the history of war and war crimes is an essential act of civic education, and doing so via comparative history offers us the opportunity to push beyond the mantra of American exceptionalism.

Since war crimes have been defined and outlawed via international conventions and law, it is a subject that must be viewed comparatively. Not just Americans but most peoples across the globe tend to fall into nationalistic forms of denial where their own war crimes are concerned, a tendency that can only be countered by an international perspective and strengthening individual awareness of standards of international law. As Mary Nolan, an historian of Germany whose interview was a starting point for the unit described in this chapter, explained:

> To understand how war crimes came to be defined and how certain [but] not all war crimes get prosecuted, one needs to look comparatively. But I think that there are deeper reasons why one needs to look at war crimes comparatively. No nation wants to acknowledge that its military has committed war crimes, that its government may have sanctioned the commission of war crimes. It's almost as though by definition every country says, "War crimes are what somebody else does, not what we do." So one needs to look comparatively to see … who is doing what? And, what are the myriad ways in which these actions are very similar?

Nolan pointed out that ultimately, all war crimes are judged comparatively since they are viewed in relation to the Holocaust, which she calls "the benchmark for the worst of war crimes against humanity that can be committed." Indeed, the first thing that comes to mind when one hears the term "war crimes" is, as Nolan suggested, Nazi Germany's extermination of millions of Jews during World War II. Holocaust education is now a mandated part of public education, and the tragedy perpetrated by the Nazis has also been brought to the forefront of popular imagination through Holocaust museums in New York, Washington, D.C., and Israel, and in major feature and documentary films. While students' knowledge of the Holocaust has the potential to serve as a useful starting point for grappling with the difficult subject of war crimes, it is also true that the unbelievable scale of the Nazi nightmare is so unique that in our schools it is not always linked to immediate roots in war itself. That is, as Nolan argued, one can focus so much on the debate about the deep roots of the Holocaust in the long history of European anti-Semitism or the tragic, human cost of genocide that one almost forgets that what made the Holocaust possible was a *world war*. So the first step in promoting deeper learning about war crimes is to remind students of three crucial points: Hitler's war of aggression and the international violence of world war laid the foundation for the Holocaust; this tragedy is at the heart of the history of war and war crimes in the 20th century; and the Holocaust, as the most massive of war crimes, offers us a moral, legal, and historical framework for analyzing other war crimes in contemporary global history.

Confronting America's Dark Past

Although the study of war crimes in recent global history can begin with the Holocaust, it must not end there. Otherwise students would be left with the mistaken impression that crimes of war are merely some very rare aberration—and one that is unique to totalitarian states. In addition to approaching war crimes issues more comprehensively and globally, students need to explore the painful fact that sometimes even the armed forces of democratic powers, including the United States, commit these atrocities. This means not only looking at the relatively well-known war crime committed by U.S. troops in My Lai during the Vietnam War—when U.S. troops murdered hundreds of unarmed civilians, including women and children—but also lesser-known massacres committed by both sides in the Korean War, firebombing during World War II, and 21st century violations in Middle East wars. As an example, the U.S. reacted with horror to the aerial bombing of civilians by the Nazis in Spain during the 1930s—a reaction paralleled in Picasso's great anti-war painting "Guernica." But during World War II, still fondly remembered by many Americans as "The Good War," the U.S. would itself engage in such bombings in Dresden, Tokyo, and other major cities of the Axis powers. In the documentary film *The Fog of War* (2003), former U.S. Secretary of Defense Robert McNamara acknowledged that, had the U.S. lost World War II, he and other planners of the bombings might well have been tried on war crimes charges on account of the massive civilian deaths wrought by this air assault. Clearly, then, war crimes and crimes against humanity are not always committed by people whom Americans commonly acknowledge as evil or the "bad guys."

With this in mind, the teaching group assembled for this chapter planned to use a comparative framework to help students arrive at a working definition of war crimes and to identify the common patterns as well as the differences that emerged from the war crimes being examined. This approach seemed promising to all three high school teachers in our group, Josef, Stacie, and Michael, even though they worked in diverse educational environments that ranged from high-needs, inner city schools to high performing urban and suburban schools. We also agreed that the lessons would center on primary sources that were accessible and well suited to understanding each discrete episode as well as larger patterns in the history of war crimes.

To start our unit, we shared with young people the definition of war crimes established by the Charter of the International Tribunal at Nuremburg in 1945. They defined war crimes as:

> murder, ill-treatment or deportation to slave labor or for any other purpose of civilian population of or in occupied territory, murder or ill-treatment of prisoners of war or persons on the seas, killing of hostages, plunder of public or private property, wanton destruction of cities, towns, or villages, or devastation not justified by military necessity.

Armed with this knowledge, students could better contextualize atrocities about which they may have previously learned, such as the conditions at the Andersonville Prison during the U.S. Civil War and the Bataan Death March in the Pacific War of World War II. Once students understood what war crimes are, their frequency, and the way they touch all involved, they would be ready to engage with the focus of our unit: a comparison of war crimes of American soldiers at No Gun Ri in the Korean War, often described as the "forgotten war," with another case of war crimes, such as those committed by the *Wehrmacht*—the non-SS German Army—in the Soviet Union during World War II. As one of the teachers involved in our group reflected,

> Yes, we know Hitler and Himmler were evil and were responsible for many deaths, but it is not the only example of war crimes that should be examined. What No Gun Ri represented for me was a chance to examine war crimes committed by "the good guys," by the democratic nation everyone wants to emulate. This, for me, was an excellent opportunity to challenge students' preconceived notions of who commits and who doesn't commit war crimes.

Interviews with Mary Nolan and Marilyn Young, historians of Europe and Asia, respectively, and with journalist Charles Hanley, who won a Pulitzer Prize for his work uncovering the massacre of Korean civilians by U.S. troops at No Gun Ri, provided a powerful foundation for our unit. Nolan and Young discussed the pervasiveness of war crimes, the inherent connection between the mass violence of war and crimes against humanity, and nations' denial about their armed forces engaging in such criminality. Nolan also discussed the uses and misuses of comparative history to understand the nature of modern warfare and war crimes:

> [C]omparison is useful less to say who is worse as a perpetrator or who suffered most as a victim than to understand in the 20th century, and now into the 21st century, the prevalence of very brutal wars in which civilians account for the overwhelming majority of casualties, and in which war crimes and crimes against humanity proliferate. This is not something exceptional. This kind of warfare is absolutely central to the last hundred years of history. If we want to understand that history, if we want to understand how politics and society have been shaped, we have to accord this a central role.

Nolan spoke specifically about the Commissar Order (Von Brauchitsch, 1941) issued from Hitler's Headquarters at the start of the Nazi invasion of the U.S.S.R., "which said that the rules of humanity and international law don't apply because we don't expect Russians to adhere to them; therefore, any kind of leniency or respect for international law is out of place." This became a license for mass murder of civilians on the Eastern Front, most prominently Jews and Communists, by the regular German Army, the *Wehrmacht*. So it was not merely the sadistic, specialized SS forces, traditionally associated with Nazi war crimes, who committed massive atrocities, but even the regular German Army perpetrated these crimes.

While this information on Germany was potentially groundbreaking for students, the scholar's perspectives on Korea were even more so, since the topic receives so little coverage in the standard middle and high school curriculum in the United States. The Korean War's origins are indeed poorly understood and its war crimes, which were little reported in the U.S., have long been forgotten here. As Marilyn Young explained:

> It is important for people to understand that the Korean War did not begin in June 25, 1950, but that there had been a low level civil war going on for several years before that ... So first the war, it has to be said, [came] at this moment of decolonization. Korea had been a Japanese colony. After the [Second World] War, Korea is supposedly independent but it is under two military regimes, the Soviets, north of the 38th parallel and the Americans, south of the 38th parallel. There were supposed to be elections for unification in a single government. But there is ongoing, low level civil war. What happens in June is that the civil war becomes internationalized.

To help account for the eruption of war crimes in this Korean conflict, Young cited Lifton's (2005) point that any civil war in which foreign powers intervene is "an atrocity-producing situation." The American soldiers sent to fight in Korea, many of whom expected to serve in postwar Japan, found themselves in an untenable situation in which they did not understand the language, culture, or guerrilla warfare around them. According to Young, the tragic events at No Gun Ri evolved from these circumstances. Nolan suggested that the moral descent into war criminality in Korea did not register in any deep or lasting way with U.S. commanders or the public, owing to a common pattern of rationalizing that civilian deaths were a regrettable but inevitable part of the massive violence that characterizes modern warfare:

> There are four kinds of reasons that people give to exonerate or dismiss the war crimes and atrocities that occur. One is, well, you on the other side did it too. Or you did it first, and we are only responding. The third is, it is necessary because the other side behaves so badly. In the case of Korea, the North Koreans, we knew that they were going to be so awful. So we had to do this, and make sure that they didn't. Or, as your last example suggests: looking back, in retrospect, it turned out okay so it didn't matter.

Young and Nolan urged teachers and students to critically interrogate such rationalizations. Speaking of Korea and No Gun Ri, Young concluded, "There is no way that these war crimes, as far as I can see, in any way, contribute to a military victory. They are the outcome of fighting war to begin with."

It took almost a half century for the American public to learn of the No Gun Ri Massacre of 1950, in which U.S. war planes and ground troops fired upon and killed hundreds of Korean civilians. The teachers in our group thought that in designing lessons on No Gun Ri, this long-term pattern of denial—including the U.S. Armed Forces covering up the No Gun Ri Massacre and similar repression of the truth in South Korea for the sake of its alliance with Cold War America—was itself a topic that demanded attention in their classrooms. Indeed, the story of how a massacre committed by U.S. troops in 1950 finally came to light via newspaper exposés written by an international team of investigative reporters in the 1990s reads like a detective story. Only in this case, the "detective story" was not only true and dramatic but carried with it a powerful historical lesson about how difficult it is to get even a democratic nation to own up to its dark past.

This is what made our interview with journalist Charles Hanley so fascinating. Hanley's team of investigative reporters uncovered the events at No Gun Ri in 1999, and their reports on the massacre, published by the AP, not only made headlines nationally and internationally but were of such historical significance that they won a Pulitzer Prize. Hanley spoke of the correlation between versions of the No Gun Ri story told by Korean and American witnesses. Both verified the horrible atrocities described in "damning" but previously classified U.S. military and State Department documents Hanley and his team discovered:

> It was simply a case of these guys on one side of the Pacific describing in detail the same event that these Koreans were telling us in the same detail: tunnel under the bridge, the babies screaming, the bodies piling up in the entrances to the tunnels because people were trying to protect themselves so they were piling up bodies there.

Hanley called his evidence "three pillars," meaning he had testimony from Koreans and Americans as well as U.S. government documents. Finding the information and writing the report, however, was only half the battle, as the AP at first refused to publish this explosive story, doing so only under pressure from others in the industry who heard rumblings of the story. Of the No Gun Ri Massacre itself, Hanley explained:

> It began with the lack of preparation of the troops that were sent in with the North Korean invasion … There was general confusion within the American ranks about how to deal with civilians … Meantime, [inaccurate] stories had flown all over the war front about North Korean guerrillas infiltrating via refugee groups … This large group of refugees is coming down the railroad tracks, walking down the railroad tracks towards the Seventh Cav unit, and suddenly they are attacked. Actually they're not moving. They are sitting

having lunch on the tracks, and they are suddenly attacked from the air by apparently two war planes, rockets, strafing bombs … And many of them were killed. They end up—the survivors end up—in the tunnel under the railroad overpass at No Gun Ri. And then over three days these ground troops of the second battalion, Seventh Cav continue firing into the tunnel to kill them all. They do kill practically all of them in the process. And most of them were women and children and others were old men, many of them.

This is shocking information about a war that receives little attention. It is certainly a revelation of which the vast majority of Americans are still unaware. We tend to think that our enemies, or at least those that we consider evil, are the only people capable of willingly murdering innocents. While students might be able to grapple with the knowledge of another country committing such acts, it will likely be as incomprehensible to teenagers as it is to many adults that those we are taught to respect could be guilty of this type of slaughter. That is why this topic must be placed in context and taught carefully and intentionally.

A key question that emerges when examining U.S. war-making and war crimes in comparative perspective is whether America's geographical advantage (the two oceans that shield it from the battlefields of Europe and Asia) ironically leaves Americans peculiarly ill equipped to come to grips with the tragic aspects of modern warfare. As Nolan noted, U.S. ideas on war and intervention differ from those of Europeans because most Americans have not seen war's effects up close:

I think that if you have experienced war in your own country, if you are living with the ongoing reminders of the wars you have fought, whether you have won or you have lost, you are much more wary about these kinds of interventions.

Nolan and Young both cited what they see as American's current popular image of Vietnam veterans as victims, regardless of the war crimes some committed, as symptomatic of the unreflective perspective on war that prevails in the U.S. Hanley focused on the U.S. Army's cover-up of No Gun Ri, the U.S. news media's initial refusal to print the story, and the language used by people in power when they speak of "the killing," rather than war crimes, to illustrate a similar problem with how an American public infatuated with the U.S. military and its prowess has great difficulty facing the whole issue of U.S. war criminality. Nolan concurred that there is reluctance in the U.S. to think about war crimes, especially those in which American soldiers are implicated. But Young insists that it is one of the key responsibilities of history teachers and historians to teach Americans to confront the history of U.S. war-making and war crimes, since wars have been so central to recent U.S. history:

War has been a constant component of the lives of Americans since 1945. And since they [our students] are likely to live into a century of ongoing war in which the U.S. is involved … it is well to know the history of what has happened before

in a way that does not airbrush out the history of atrocities that accompany such massive violence.

A Comparative Unit on War Crimes
Designing a Unit for Diverse Environments

The teachers who came together to create and teach this unit brought with them varying levels of experience, from a first year teacher to a 10-year veteran, and they taught in vastly different educational settings. Among the challenges in planning the unit, then, were the divergent populations and environments for which the three teachers had to tailor their lessons. With the mentoring of historian and social studies professor Robert Cohen, the teachers created a unit cohesive in its purpose and overall direction, yet adaptable so that each teacher could implement lessons in his or her own way.

Josef, a first year teacher, teaches at an international school in an urban environment. Recent immigrants dominate the population of 393 students. The vast majority of students, 77.5%, are from low income households. Sixty-nine percent of students are Latino, with small percentages of white and African American students. Many of the students in Josef's ninth and tenth grade classes are "off track" and therefore older than the typical freshmen and sophomores. Since 89.5% are English Language Learners (Inside Schools, 2012a), Josef has to devote a great deal of time to developing vocabulary and building context. Josef's classes are one hour each and meet every day, providing students with consistency throughout their studies. Students sit at tables with three other peers, a set-up that facilitates group work but also increases the likelihood of distractions. Josef is therefore very vigilant about classroom management.

To teach this unit, Stacie, an experienced social studies teacher turned doctoral student, returned to the classroom at the large urban high school where she had previously taught. Stacie's school is the opposite of Josef's in many ways: the school is larger, with more than 4,000 students, only 9.1% of whom are English Language Learners. In addition, only 28.5% of the diverse population of students comes from low income households, and twice as many students as at Josef's school go to college upon graduation (Inside Schools, 2012b). The school is arts oriented, with students able to audition for spots in the music, theater, and fine arts programs. Student artwork covers the halls, and display cases highlight student achievements such as the national champion chess team and state champion "We the People" and Virtual Enterprise teams. Unlike others in the group who implemented the curriculum in ninth grade classes, Stacie brought her lesson into an eleventh grade Advanced Placement class. The class consisted of 45 students seated at desks arranged in an arc. The desks move easily to accommodate group work and differentiated activities when necessary. The school runs on a different schedule every day, with classes meeting from 50 minutes to an hour, four times a week. On the day that Stacie taught the war crimes lesson, the period was 55 minutes.

Michael's students are traditional ninth graders at a suburban school. The total enrollment is 1,150, 92.3% of whom are white, with only 1.3% qualifying as low income. There is a 12.5:1 student/teacher ratio (Local Schools Directory, 2012), which is drastically different from the more crowded classes in which Josef and Stacie taught their lessons. Michael's students' desks are arranged in traditional rows, with students often turning to classmates adjacent to them in cooperative learning activities. Michael's chronological approach to history meant that he introduced the unit while teaching World War II, leading his students in a discussion of war crimes and returning to it during a unit on the Cold War when he reached the 1950s. Michael spent three days on the unit, with each class period lasting 40 minutes.

This teaching group established common goals and outcomes in the form of essential questions and enduring understandings (Chapter Resources I), as discussed in Grant Wiggins and Jay McTighe's (2005) *Understanding by Design*. The essential questions were:

- To what extent are war crimes an inevitable part of war?
- To what extent is there a distinction between war and war crimes?
- Should all war crimes be measured relative to the Holocaust? Why or why not?
- Who should be held accountable for war crimes—nations or soldiers—and to what extent?
- Why is it more acceptable to blame certain groups, like the SS, for war crimes than others, like the *Wehrmacht*?

Once we had established the questions, we chose the following enduring understandings as our deep learning goals for the students:

- The definition of war crimes is expansive and it has great moral, political, and historical significance.
- Actions taken on Germany's Eastern Front, in Korea, and in Vietnam should be classified as war crimes.
- Perceptions of the war and of the enemy influence the way governments and people perceive war crimes. This often hampers international organizations' ability to hold nations accountable for these crimes against humanity.
- There is an inherent link between war and war crimes, with war providing cover for the crimes that soldiers and nations commit against civilians.
- The myth that only evil nations and governments commit war crimes is just that; in reality, all nations have committed war crimes at some point in their history.

We believed that it would be nearly impossible for students to grasp the magnitude of the war crimes, their continuing effects, and their relevance today without a firm understanding of what makes something a war crime. That is why we started the unit with a discussion of the Nuremburg definition of war crimes cited above. We then asked students to determine whether or not particular events counted as war crimes, and how these crimes were viewed by citizens within and outside of those countries. We hoped that understanding the concept of war crimes in relation to specific cases would increase the applicability of the unit by enabling students to identify and evaluate other instances of war crimes in the past and the present.

Moral Responsibility and Controversy in Teaching about War Crimes

The teachers were energized by the new history they learned through the interviews with Hanley, Nolan, and Young. They had never read about No Gun Ri and the Commissar Order in their prior studies nor had they engaged in comparative historical analysis of war and war crimes discussed here. They were eager to share this new knowledge with their students through lessons that could involve them in active learning using the primary source documents that Hanley, Nolan, and Young provided. The Nolan–Young and Hanley interviews respectively provided us with two rarely discussed, little known topics: the *Wehrmacht*'s actions on the Eastern Front during World War II and the massacre at No Gun Ri in Korea. Both events invite inquiry and interesting comparisons using our essential questions: they took place during wars, No Gun Ri involved countries not usually associated with committing such horrors, and the nations responsible continue to shy away from acknowledging their guilt. In the German case, there has been a tendency to blame war crimes on smaller, elite Nazi military units such as the SS rather than on the regular army, a tendency that exonerates ordinary German soldiers from involvement in massive war crimes. The Commissar Order and emerging records of mass *Wehrmacht* atrocities on the Eastern Front, however, challenge this view. Both cases fit into established global and U.S. history curricula. By evaluating and comparing the Eastern Front atrocities by German soldiers in World War II with U.S. troop actions at No Gun Ri, students could begin to problematize the simplistic American memory of its troops being the "good guys" in the Korean War.

In addition to the *Wehrmacht* case, we discussed the strengths and challenges of juxtaposing other events with No Gun Ri: the My Lai Massacre, often taught as an isolated incident but shown by No Gun Ri to be more common than people think; the Bataan Death March and Rape of Nanking, which would incorporate World War II into the unit; and instances from other time periods, as in Columbus's massacre of Arawaks revealed in Bartolomé de las

Casas's journals. In the end, since we believed it would be interesting to explore various paths in answering our essential questions, each of the teachers selected different cases for comparison. Beyond these pedagogical considerations, we needed to tackle the moral issues that arise from a unit on war crimes that force us to probe the nature of war itself. Many fictional depictions celebrate combat as glorious and heroic. Media-saturated students, immersed in film, television, and video game versions of war, don't often see the other side, in which soldiers act dishonorably, large swaths of land are destroyed, and innocent people die. Debunking such myths and including the underside of war are important steps to take before deep discussions of wars' meanings can begin.

Accountability, responsibility, and blame inevitably enter the conversation when discussing the history of war crimes—and this obviously invites controversy. It is likely that sensitivities will be stirred when probing the history of war crimes committed by the U.S. military with students, often brought up to revere the military, confronting such questions as "Who should be held accountable for war crimes—nations or soldiers—and to what extent?" We thought that such issues are best addressed by exploring such questions on a comparative basis, enabling students to probe war crimes initially by looking abroad and then returning home. For example, the German case introduces students to the way nations shy away from the tough questions on war crimes, by asking, "Why was it more acceptable in Germany to blame the SS for war crimes, but to be in denial about the crimes of more common soldiers in the *Wehrmacht?*" Germany's recent reticence to address the *Wehrmacht*'s culpability (see for example, Bartov, Grossmann, & Nolan, 2002) mirrors President Clinton's tepid apology (in which there was no admission regarding war crimes) for the No Gun Ri tragedy almost 50 years after the fact (see Clinton, 2001; Kempster, 2001).

Teachers seeking to bring 21st century information on U.S. war crimes into this unit could generate further controversy when asking students about recent symbols of military misconduct like those at Abu Ghraib. Therefore, a major aspect of our discussion and planning focused on how to teach in ways that respect and reflect the delicate nature of a unit that challenges our students and our country's nationalistic assumptions. To cope with and address these concerns, we sought to have students examine and break down their preconceived notions about war and situate the war crimes in their time. We also struggled with the ethical aspect of what we would teach, as the moral weight of the war crimes issue is far heavier than in most other historical topics introduced in the classroom. We agreed to integrate questions of morality into our individually planned units, fostering important discussion that resonates today.

Planning and Teaching War Crimes

The distinct needs of the students in our diverse classrooms led us to work out the details of what we would bring into the classroom on our own, while adhering to the larger framework we created in our group. We were fortunate to have access to extraordinary primary sources, including photographs of *Wehrmacht* war crimes and "war tourism" from the Eastern Front in World War II (Browning, 1992; Hamburg Institute, 1999) and recently declassified military documents, courtesy of Charles Hanley, who gathered this information as part of his research on the No Gun Ri story (2001; 2010). All of us tapped into these sources and modified them as needed in our classes. We also had the benefit of meeting with two of our interviewees, Molly Nolan and Charles Hanley, who provided us with valuable insight into how they believed these topics should be taught. We were able to incorporate their advice and the additional sources they provided for us into the lessons.

Teachers' Lesson Plans

For Josef, building his students' vocabulary was the first step. He started with terms integral to the eras, such as *communist* and *refugees,* and then moved on to the bureaucratic terms that students would encounter in the government documents—*military memoranda, directives, correspondence.* At Josef's school, teachers rely on activity guides that, as he explained, "weave content and English language building activities." Josef intended for his students to act as historians in their quest to answer the essential questions, and he needed to facilitate their comprehension to allow that to happen. His planning, therefore, integrated previously successful strategies including dictation, in which students listen to a passage and discuss its central themes, and scaffolding, where students read complex, jargon-filled documents, write down facts about the document, and then draw conclusions based on what they read and their classmates' inferences. Through these strategies, Josef hoped that his students would be able to assess the origins, character, and meaning of war crimes and whether or not such acts are an inevitable aspect of warfare. Josef also chose to compare the events at No Gun Ri to the harm inflicted on Native Americans by Columbus and his subordinates. Josef completed the Columbus unit just prior to beginning the war crimes unit, and having already introduced Bartolomé de las Casas's journals, decided to have his students draw connections between that piece of writing and the journalistic coverage of No Gun Ri. For Josef's students, relating two units taught in sequence was especially useful.

With only one day to devote to the topic, Stacie opted to focus primarily on No Gun Ri, eliciting points of comparison from the students throughout the course of the lesson. Unlike the other teachers, Stacie taught this lesson (Chapter Resources II) near the end of the school year after the class had a good overall grasp of the state-mandated curriculum in U.S. history—a curriculum that did not include mention of No Gun Ri. The students' knowledge base as eleventh graders in an Advanced Placement history class meant that Stacie could count on them to make connections and think about the issues in ways that the other teachers could not. Stacie therefore opted to begin with a contemporary example, a discussion of Seymour Hersh's 2004 *New Yorker* article on Abu Ghraib. She then moved on to a more general discussion of war crimes to yield a student-generated definition of war crimes that they could draw upon to identify examples and explain why those events qualified as war crimes. The majority of the lesson would be devoted to students taking on the role of journalists "discovering" the events of No Gun Ri—using the actual U.S. government documents on the massacre that Hanley's team of investigative reporters uncovered—and the U.S. Army cover-up that followed. Students would then determine whether or not No Gun Ri could be classified as a war crime according to their definition and compare it with the others they had mentioned previously. After completing this work, students were asked to address the essential question: "Are war crimes an inevitable part of war?"

Michael chose to teach parts of the unit at several intervals over the course of the semester, keeping the thread running between units on World War II and the Cold War. He introduced the concept of war crimes and worked with students to arrive at a definition of the term while he taught World War II. He used that to segue into a discussion of *Wehrmacht's* brutal violence on the Eastern Front and whether or not the *Wehrmacht* committed war crimes, without making any other points of comparison. He later returned to the theme of war crimes during his lessons on the Cold War, spending two days on the Korean War and No Gun Ri. Michael divided these lessons into one predominantly focused on the origins and significance of the Korean War and another on the events of No Gun Ri and President Clinton's apology almost 50 years later. Michael emphasized the essential questions pertaining to accountability and blame, based on the precept that students would have more interest in learning about the events from the point of view of the near-present. Michael planned to have his students work in groups to evaluate the documents and decide the issue of blame in addition to determining the appropriateness of Clinton's very limited apology (2001). He then planned to bring the conversation full circle, addressing the issue of responsibility as applied to the actions of the *Wehrmacht.*

While the details and strategies differed, there were commonalities among the three teachers' approaches. All three teachers adhered, albeit in different ways, to the comparative element of the unit. All utilized a variety of rich primary sources, including and going beyond the government documents supplied by Charles Hanley. Each of the teachers emphasized writing skills, from note taking while reading the documents to reflecting on the essential questions and thinking deeply about these topics in groups and on their own. Although the lessons at times departed from the planned structure, the teachers ultimately fostered the enduring understandings upon which we collectively agreed.

Students Learn about War Crimes

By virtue of the distinct lesson plans, teaching styles, and school environments in which we taught the War Crimes unit, students' experiences differed widely. There were basic differences, such as the amount of time each class spent on the unit, to more complex variations, including the ways in which we asked students to synthesize information. Given these differences, which are likely to be mirrored in the diverse experiences of teachers reading this chapter, it seems useful to consider separately the experiences of each teacher with his or her own unit and students.

Josef's meticulously planned activity guide is a wealth of resources and tasks, including maps, images, primary source documents, secondary source materials, information on Charles Hanley, and cause and effect charts. It builds map skills, requires students to understand the geography of Korea and the surrounding region, scaffolds vocabulary while teaching students how to use context clues, builds reading comprehension, and asks students to interpret visual aids. It also spells out the questions on which the unit was predicated:

- Are war crimes an inevitable part of war?
- Who should be held accountable for war crimes—nations or soldiers—and to what extent?
- How did Charles Hanley change the public's perception about United States' involvement in the Korean War?

Josef ultimately deviated from relying strictly on this packet, realizing that, in order to complete the unit before the school year ended, he needed to devote a majority of the class's time to analyzing the primary documents. Josef introduced the unit with a lesson on the Korean War, utilizing the skill building aspects of his activity guide. Then he devoted four class periods to dissecting and analyzing the documents. He began by displaying the following questions on a Smartboard for the entire class to answer:

- What is a refugee?
- What was the Cold War?
- What was the reason for having a military checkpoint at No Gun Ri?

Josef then related student answers to each of the documents, taking time to have students work on them in groups before reconvening to analyze them together. In this way, he noted, "the students unpacked the perspective of United States Army officials as well as government officials." He also used common threads to help students make connections and tie together what they learned, opening students' eyes to the idea that the "good guys" are not always innocent of brutality and wrongdoing.

Josef also took the extraordinary step of inviting Charles Hanley into his class to discuss his discovery of the massacre at No Gun Ri and the Army's cover up, and to answer students' questions about the events and his own role.[1] Josef informed his classes that the unit would culminate with Hanley's appearance, so this provided additional motivation to engage in the material so as to be prepared for this event. As Josef stated,

> Having an actual journalist, or in this case I would refer to Mr. Hanley as an historian, really contextualized the event. The fact that the actual person who investigated the event and who the students studied in detail [came to speak to them] gave relevance to the event.

Hanley began by showing a clip from a powerful BBC documentary, *Kill 'Em All: American War Crimes in Korea* (Williams & Roberts, 2002), telling students before the viewing that the confluence of poorly trained, misinformed, mismanaged American soldiers and Korean civilians attempting to move away from the dictatorship in the North led to the massacre at No Gun Ri. Hearing the man who uncovered the massacre explain it in a clear, relatable manner added to the already enormous impact of the video. Following this, Hanley went into detail about his process in discovering the event, a story that fascinated the students. He then took student questions, which reflected the deep knowledge they had already learned: "Why does the U.S. fight if it's not their war?" "Were you afraid of retaliation for revealing the story?" "Why do you want people to know the Army committed a crime?" "Do you feel like a hero?" To this latter question, Hanley replied that in this situation, "Heroes are the soldiers who were there and talked about their experiences." According to Josef, "History became tangible and interesting for the students, which helped close the unit on No Gun Ri."

In Stacie's one-day lesson (Chapter Resources II), the students took on the role of investigative journalists, analyzing one document at a time, recording their interpretation on organizational grids, and drawing conclusions about what happened at No Gun Ri based on the information that they culled from synthesizing the documents. After beginning with Abu Ghraib, Stacie's students evaluated the definition of war crimes established by the Nuremberg Convention in 1945, which they interpreted as: "intolerable acts, possibly justified by war"; "violations of human rights during war"; and "unjustified crimes against civilians." Students also immersed themselves in a discussion of why an international tribunal would attempt to prohibit such actions, and why war becomes a breeding ground for actions labeled as "war crimes." Many debated the tendency to hold the vanquished, but not the victors, accountable for these actions and thought that all nations, regardless of whether they win or lose, should be held responsible for war crimes. In this discussion, one student made a historical connection to the "War Guilt Clause" in the Treaty of Versailles. The students identified links between war and war crimes, including the way in which international attention on war provides cover for a nation's other actions. Students also discussed the increased paranoia that comes with war, which they cited as the reason behind Japanese internment, an unpunished U.S. war crime in their opinion.

After building this conceptual framework, the class broke into 12 groups (three sets of four groups), and each group received one document. For homework the night before, the students had read a *Time* magazine article from 1950 entitled "Men at War, the Ugly War" (Osborne), that Professor Young had recommended, so they came into the lesson with knowledge of the events at No Gun Ri. Before analyzing the documents, each group started with a discussion of this article to ensure that all participants understood what happened in Korea and at No Gun Ri. All of the documents detailed what U.S. State Department and military officials referred to as the "refugee problem," including the Army's official orders to restrict refugees' movements and use force against them when U.S. military forces deemed it necessary. Each group selected one member who would be the "source," traveling to other groups to share what they learned from their document. The sources went from group to group imparting information, while the "journalists" were instructed to question the "source" until they were confident they had uncovered all they needed to know about each document and could put the pieces of the puzzle together. Students entered all of the information they gathered on organizational grids, which prompted them to draw conclusions based on what they gathered. The following concluding questions were designed to push the students toward answering the essential questions, particularly the aim of the lesson, "Are war crimes an inevitable part of war?":

- Based on your findings, what was the U.S. Army's official position on treatment of civilians during the Korean War?
- Would you characterize these actions as war crimes?
- What should the U.S. government do with this information?
- Who should be held accountable?
- How should this be presented to the American people?

Time constraints prevented a full debrief of the activity and the lesson, but as the class came to a close, students overwhelmingly declared that they believed the events at No Gun Ri should be classified as war crimes because "civilians were the target, not simply collateral damage." The assessment brought the closure that the lesson did not. Using their organizational grids, each student fulfilled his or her journalistic role by writing a newspaper article revealing the Army's actions in Korea in July 1950. Their articles addressed the question of inevitability and compared No Gun Ri with other war crimes and crimes against humanity, mostly citing the My Lai Massacre that would occur 18 years later. These writing assignments illustrate profound engagement with the essential questions, as students concisely and analytically discussed the U.S. Army's actions and cogently addressed their larger implications regarding the history of war crimes (examples in Chapter Resources III).

Michael's students began the unit with a complex discussion of war crimes related to the *Wehrmacht*'s slaughter of Soviet civilians. He opened class with a series of scaffolded questions, first asking students, "What are war crimes?" and distinguishing between crimes and war crimes, specifically. He then asked his students to provide general examples of actions that might be categorized as war crimes and, finally, prompted students to name specific events that fit their definition. Students considered these questions in groups, with the class reuniting to share their answers. Michael's ninth grade students had some difficulty arriving at a concrete definition for war crimes, and he had to stop the discussion to differentiate between war crimes and crimes against humanity: students needed to understand that to classify actions as war crimes, they must happen *in the context of war.* By the end of the discussion, students could deftly identify recent acts and historical examples of war crimes, including the use of mustard gas in the trenches during World War I. Having established this foundation, the remainder of the lesson focused on Operation Barbarossa and the *Wehrmacht*'s actions on the Eastern Front, including the Commissar Order officially sanctioning the murder of Soviet prisoners of war. The short span of Michael's class period meant that the end of the lesson was rushed, but students left with the idea that the *Wehrmacht,* German soldiers, and not just the SS and other elite Nazi forces, committed atrocities on a mass scale.

A little over a month later, Michael returned to the topic of war crimes during his unit on the Cold War. He delivered a mini-lecture introducing the Korean War and the issues that led to it, questioned the class for comprehension, and then proceeded to review the concept of war crimes. Michael asked, "What falls into that category (war crimes)?" One student responded,

"Actions that are not authorized," and after Michael pushed back, another replied, "[Action that] violates rules of engagement." Using this as an opportunity, Michael reminded the class that the *Wehrmacht*'s actions were, in fact, authorized, and then segued into No Gun Ri. The class read a short excerpt from the 1950 *Time* magazine article (Osborne), reflecting on what it said about the significance of fighting an idea and how that creates a different kind of enemy. Michael once again broke students into groups to read and analyze documents on the U.S. regarding Korean civilians using the following questions:

- Summarize in your own words the policy that the United States adopted toward refugees in the Korean War. Do you think this is a fair policy?
- Why might American forces adopt this policy toward Southern Korean refugees?
- What events might happen because of this?

Michael moved through the room as the class worked, resolving vocabulary-related issues and assisting students who struggled with understanding the documents and their meanings.

The following day, the class focused on firsthand accounts of No Gun Ri via testimony from U.S. soldiers and Korean survivors, asking, "How do soldiers talk about what happened and why?" Next, Michael brought up President Bill Clinton's statement from 2001, in which he said, "On behalf of the United States of America, I deeply regret that Korean civilians lost their lives at No Gun Ri in late July, 1950" (Chapter Resources IV). Michael led his class in a discussion of accountability and blame and asked, "Is this an apology or does it fall short?" Students determined that Clinton's "apology," in which he never actually apologized, was unsatisfactory. Some said it was too short, others felt it was too late, while still others countered that it simply wasn't Clinton's responsibility. Michael concluded the unit by bringing the class back to the ideas of inevitability and blame, as well as a nation's level of responsibility for atrocities that, unfortunately, are all too common among nations.

Although each teacher implemented the unit in a way that he or she believed would yield optimal results for students, all of the students read and assessed the same documents, modified to meet their needs. These included the Eighth Cavalry Regiment's itinerary, with references to restricting refugee movement; a July 25, 1950 memo to General Timberlake of the Air Force with the subject "Policy on Strafing Civilian Refugees" (Chapter Resources V); a letter to Dean Rusk from July 26, 1950, relating the steps taken by the U.S. Army to impose a curfew on South Korean civilians with the use of force as a consequence for disobeying (Chapter Resources VI); and a July 27, 1950 order to consider all civilians as "enemies" and have "action taken accordingly" (Chapter Resources VII). Together, these documents built the case that soldiers committed war crimes during the Korean War with high ranking officers directing them to do so. Josef and Michael also showed their students a 16-minute clip of the BBC documentary entitled *Kill 'Em All: American War Crimes in Korea* (Williams & Roberts, 2002) in which South Koreans speak emotionally of losing parents and loved ones at No Gun Ri, some of whom died protecting the survivors from the attacks. In the video, U.S. soldiers speak of the nightmares and overwhelming guilt they continue to feel from their role in the massacre. Both classes sat rapt listening to the testimony from both sides, with the video providing a personal element that no document could. All of the teachers relied, at least in part, on cooperative learning techniques, encouraging and empowering students to begin to comprehend and interpret information on their own, with the teacher providing assistance when necessary.

The important work of Nolan, Young, and Hanley provided the pivotal materials, stories, and courage to bring this unit and its essential questions into our classrooms. We know about war crimes on the Eastern Front in World War II, at No Gun Ri, and elsewhere, because a brave person or group of people acted on what they knew to expose these tragedies. Although students traveled different paths, they ultimately reached the same destination through the unified focus on the essential questions: that is, they got a taste of that experience of exposure and truth-telling that Hanley so vividly described—and realized that war crimes are not simply committed by citizens of distant lands.

Students Respond to Essential Questions

In each class, students responded to teachers' inquiries, challenged each other to think profoundly during group work, actively sought teachers' help with comprehension and context, and reacted positively when teachers pushed them to dig deeper. We hoped that the enthusiasm and interest they had shown in these activities would translate into thoughtful and well-supported answers to the provocative essential questions. Happily, students in all three classes formed cogent answers to many of the questions posed at the start of the unit. For example, Josef recounted that a majority of his students, after learning about the plight of the Arawaks and the massacre at No Gun Ri, answered the question, "To what extent are war crimes an inevitable part of war?" with a resounding "Yes!" One student wrote in her activity guide that the violence and death associated with war inevitably leads to war crimes. Stacie's students, too, decided that war crimes are unavoidable for multiple reasons, although some believed that such horrors are a conscious choice on soldiers' parts and could be prevented if people's morals were intact. Their insights included:

- in times of war, it is inevitable for war crimes to occur. This is because of the fact that warring nations have only one goal in mind while fighting, and that is to try and stop the enemy the easiest way possible.
- Another reason for inevitable war crimes is that there is no one to stop the winning side, allowing them to do as they please, which includes violating human rights. A good example would be the Rape of Nanking by the Japanese. It was a completely one sided mass murder …
- An unfortunate but inevitable aspect of war is that many unlawful crimes will occur. There is almost no way to prevent them, but that does not make them excusable. War is an extreme time where paranoia, the will to win and belief that what any side is fighting for is right may lead even the most calm and secure leaders to resort to horrible actions. During World War II many Japanese Americans were put in internment camps …

Stacie was especially pleased that, "students not only answered the essential question, but did so in the comparative manner in which the unit was conceived, drawing parallels between No Gun Ri and many other events from Global and American history."

Beyond the question of inevitability, all of the classes focused on responsibility, asking, "Who should be held accountable for war crimes—nations or soldiers—and to what extent?" Josef's students tended to hold governments responsible: "The students, when answering our essential questions, almost universally agreed that not only are war crimes inevitable, but that governments are responsible. For the most part, students did not believe soldiers should be held accountable because, as one student said, 'If soldiers don't do what the government orders them to do then they will be shot.'" Looking specifically at No Gun Ri, one of Josef's students asserted, "The U.S. was responsible for the massacre of Koreans at No Gun Ri. The U.S. Army refused to allow them to continue. Orders issued from the U.S. military allowed for U.S. soldiers to shoot and kill

Koreans." Michael's students considered this issue in depth, with their emphasis on the Clinton apology. He reflected, "They [students] even thought about the major idea that it's impossible to say one whole nation is 'evil' because of an incident, yet we must define what to do and how to hold nations responsible when war crimes do happen." On the related question, "Why is it more acceptable to blame certain groups, like the SS, for war crimes than others, like the *Wehrmacht?*" many of Stacie's students ruminated on the blind eye turned to both "average" people's and victors' actions and the need to believe that goodness exists somewhere in war. Speaking of No Gun Ri, one student observed,

> For many years the horrible killings that were happening were unheard of and undocumented. The U.S. did not want to be seen in any negative lights, and the power they gained by [achieving their war aims] enabled them to hide just that.

Students were inspired to think about the facts they learned, leading them to form articulate responses, orally and in writing, to questions teachers posed in class and in assignments. Their deep engagement shows the power of this material and the comparative approach.

Teachers Reflect on the Unit

Reviewing the impact of the unit in their classes, Josef, Stacie, and Michael all agreed that their students gained from learning rarely taught material in a comparative manner through high quality sources. Although most of their students were not totally shocked that the U.S., or any other nation's soldiers for that matter, could act so brutally, all of the teachers identified opening students' minds and encouraging more critical thinking of the past and present as a major triumph of the unit. While we were concerned that this topic might be too sensitive, our approach and guidance helped students to understand war crimes as a *human* concern and not simply as something that is done by rare "monsters" like Hitler. As Josef explained, "I believe the most successful part of the unit was having students rethink their traditional perspective that the United States is a country free of wrongdoing." Stacie's students "were not shocked by the United States' actions, especially in this day and age." However, Stacie believed that, "understanding the multiple influences that lead one to commit war crimes helped students see the intricacies of this issue, rather than simply accepting that horrible things happen in war." Michael also reported that his students were not shocked, but learning about the events on the Eastern Front and at No Gun Ri helped them gain the necessary perspective to interpret government actions concerning war crimes. He said,

> They had learned throughout the year that bad things happen in the world and here they saw that yes, American does it too. What I found surprising were their reactions to Bill Clinton's apology and their views on America's handling of the events. This they clearly identified as an injustice.

The teachers were overwhelmingly pleased with their students' ability to make meaning of complex information and to confront moral and controversial questions with maturity and respect. Michael began the unit concerned with his students' ability to tackle the information, but these worries subsided as the unit progressed. As he recounted,

> The students' reactions to the lessons on the Nazi invasion of the Soviet Union and the events at No Gun Ri were impressive. The classes I taught the lessons to were

freshmen classes so they had never studied war crimes as its own concept. I was very impressed when I first asked them to define it and they came up with solid examples, though they lacked a proper definition. This did seem to link with how our group felt about society overall.

Josef challenged his students to re-evaluate American exceptionalism, in addition to grappling with the war crimes at the heart of the unit, with positive outcomes: "The students' engagement increased significantly when they were analyzing deep concepts about how a nation that prides itself on freedom and equality could commit this atrocity." Stacie knew her students had learned about war crimes prior to this lesson and therefore emphasized making connections both in the activity she planned—it was crucial that students piece together the story on their own for the task to work effectively—and between the events at No Gun Ri and other war crimes. She spoke of being "amazed at their ability to draw conclusions and discuss, in depth and from many angles, the similarities between No Gun Ri and several other instances of war crimes." Although this topic might be more intriguing at face value than other aspects of history, it is particularly challenging because of its potential to generate discomfort and anger about America's role in wars. However, our experiences confirm Diana Hess's (2009) findings that students are eager to talk about controversial issues, and that doing so in a well-conceptualized and structured manner can be extremely stimulating for young people.

Across the board, the teachers discussed time—or, more precisely, the shortage thereof—as a major difficulty with the unit. Josef relayed that although the human rights violations in the Columbian era and No Gun Ri resonated, he would have preferred to reach a point in his curriculum where he could teach more modern examples of war crimes and use them as a basis for comparison to No Gun Ri. He also stated that he would have liked to have delved deeper into soldiers' accountability and whether or not following orders excuses their brutality. Michael, who struggled with especially tight time constraints as a result of his school's 40-minute periods, asserted that he would modify his lessons to allow for more discussion of the essential questions in addition to covering the information, and that he would add a more human element to the section on the *Wehrmacht* after witnessing his students' reaction to the Korean survivors' testimony. Both classroom teachers look forward to teaching the unit again, with these and other modifications.

Concluding Thoughts: Holding Nations Accountable

A unit on war crimes is especially relevant as scholars continue to explore America's involvement in such atrocities. In *Kill Anything That Moves: The Real American War in Vietnam*, Nick Turse (2013) presents new evidence of U.S. brutality in Vietnam, arguing that U.S. war crimes there were systemic and not aberrational. In his review of the book, Jonathan Schell (2013) wrote,

> It has not been until the publication of Turse's book that the everyday reality of which these atrocities were a part has been brought so fully to light. Almost immediately after the American troops arrived in I Corps, a pattern of savagery was established. My Lai, it turns out, was exceptional only in the numbers killed.

Turse's new study, then, reminds us of the importance of constantly re-examining our past so that we can remain alert to such tragedies in the present.

Reflecting back on our work in planning and teaching this unit, we were excited by the creative teaching methods deployed, stimulating primary sources used, and intensive student learning achieved in what was, for most, new areas and topics of inquiry: war crimes, No Gun Ri, and comparative history. We agreed that greater clarity was needed near the end of the unit on the implications of the history of war crimes that the students studied. While student disagreements about accountability and who should be held responsible for wartime atrocities were a positive sign of student engagement with a weighty moral and historical issue, we feel that the discussion needed to be linked to international law and why it is often violated by nations reluctant to prosecute war crimes. In other words, students need to recognize that when war crimes such as those at No Gun Ri go unpunished, international human rights convention laws are being violated. The discussion of this issue should not end with students thinking the question of punishment of individuals culpable for war crimes—be they by common soldiers or high ranking commanders—is simply a matter of opinion, which seemed to be the case in some of the rushed concluding discussions of the unit. Rather, students must comprehend that prosecution is, in fact, mandated by international law and when nations such as the United States or Germany evade prosecution as war criminals, they are flouting the law, denying justice to the victims of these crimes, and setting precedents of immunity from prosecution that can serve to foster further war crimes in the future. Students, we argue, need to ponder these mandates of international law, how they are flouted by nation states, the political realities that allow such defiance of international law, and what, if any, policies can be adopted to see that justice is done so that war criminals do not continue to go unpunished.

Note

1   Although readers of this chapter might not have this access to Hanley, teachers might offer a similar encounter with him and his work by having students dramatize excerpts from the Hanley interview included at the beginning of this chapter.

Works Cited

Bartov, O., Grossmann, A., & Nolan, M. (Eds.). (2002). *Crimes of war: Guilt and denial in the twentieth century.* New York: The New Press.

Browning, C. (1992). *Ordinary men: Reserve Police Battalion 101 and the final solution in Poland.* New York: HarperCollins Publishers.

Charter of the International Military Tribunal. (1945, August 8). *UN documents: Gathering a body of global agreements.* Retrieved from www.un-documents.net/imtchart.htm

Clinton, B. (2001, January 11). No Gun Ri: Clinton's statement. *PBS Online Newshour.* Retrieved from www.pbs.org/newshour/media/media_watch/jan-june01/clinton_1-11.html

Hamburg Institute. (1999). The battle against the partisans. In Hamburg Institute, *The German Army and genocide: Crimes against war prisoners, Jews, and other civilians in the East, 1939–1944* (pp. 152–161). New York: The New Press.

Hanley, C. J. (2010). No Gun Ri: Official narrative and inconvenient truths. *Critical Asian Studies,* 589–622.

Hanley, C., Choe, S., & Mendoza, M. (2001). *The bridge at No Gun Ri: A hidden nightmare from the Korean war.* New York: Henry Holt and Co. Publishing.

Hersh, S. (2004, May 10). Torture at Abu Ghraib. *The New Yorker.* Retrieved from www.newyorker.com/archive/2004/05/10/040510fa_fact

Hess, D. (2009). *Controversy in the classroom.* New York: Routledge.

Inside Schools. (2012a). International Community High School. *Insideschools.* Retrieved from http://insideschools.org/high/browse/school/1382

Inside Schools. (2012b). Edward R. Murrow High School. *Insideschools.* Retrieved from http://insideschools.org/high/browse/school/899

Kempster, N. (2001 January 12). Clinton "regrets," doesn't apologize for, No Gun Ri. *Los Angeles Times.* Retrieved from http://articles.latimes.com/2001/jan/12/news/mn-11517

Lifton, R. J. (2005). *Home from the war: Learning from Vietnam veterans:* New York: Other Press.

Local School Directory. (2012). Indian Hills High School. *Localschooldirectory.com.* Retrieved from www.localschooldirectory.com/public-school/55461/NJ

Morris, E. (Director). (2003). *The fog of war* [Motion Picture].

Osborne, J. (1950, August 21). Men at war: The ugly war. *Time.* Retrieved from www.time.com/time/magazine/article/0,9171,812987,00.html

Schell, J. (2013). How did the gates of hell open in Vietnam? A new book transforms our understanding of what the Vietnam War actually was. TomDispatch.com. Retrieved from www.tomdispatch.com/blog/175639/tomgram%3A_jonathan_schell,_seeing_the_reality_of_the_vietnam_war,_50_years_late

Stiglitz, J. (2012). *The price of inequality.* New York: W.W. Norton & Company.

Turse, N. (2013). *Kill anything that moves: The real American war in Vietnam.* New York: Metropolitan Books.

Von Brauchitsch. (1941, June 6). Commissar Order. *EUH 3033 History of the Holocaust Professor Geoffrey J. Giles.* Retrieved from www.clas.ufl.edu/users/ggiles/barbaros.html (excerpt only)

Wiggins, G., & McTighe, J. (2005). *Understanding by design.* New York: Prentice Hall.

Williams, J. (Producer), Roberts, T. (Director), (2002). *Kill 'em all: American war crimes in Korea.* [Motion Picture]. UK: BBC Timewatch.

Additional Resources

Hunt, M. (2003). *The world transformed: 1945 to the present.* New York: Bedford/St. Martin's.

Levi, P. (1995). *Survival in Auschwitz.* New York: Touchstone Publishing.

Son My Village Chief. (1998). Summary of Son My chief's letter. In J. Olson & R. Roberts, *My Lai: A brief history with documents* (p. 139). New York: Bedford/St. Martin's.

Thompson, Jr., H. (1998). Hugo Thompson Testimony. In J. Olson & R. Roberts, *My Lai: A brief history with documents* (pp. 90–92). New York: Bedford/St. Martin's.

Weitz, E. D. (2003). *A century of genocide: Utopias of race and nation.* Princeton, NJ: Princeton University Press.

CHAPTER RESOURCES

I. Unit Plan: War Crimes

Common Core Standards

CCSS.ELA-Literacy.RH.9-10.1 Cite specific textual evidence to support analysis of primary and secondary sources, attending to such features as the date and origin of the information.

CCSS.ELA-Literacy.RH.9-10.3 Analyze in detail a series of events described in a text; determine whether earlier events caused later ones or simply preceded them.

CCSS.ELA-Literacy.RH.9-10.8 Assess the extent to which the reasoning and evidence in a text support the author's claims.

CCSS.ELA-Literacy.RH.9-10.9 Compare and contrast treatments of the same topic in several primary and secondary sources.

CCSS.ELA-Literacy.RH.11-12.1 Cite specific textual evidence to support analysis of primary and secondary sources, connecting insights gained from specific details to an understanding of the text as a whole.

CCSS.ELA-Literacy.RH.11-12.3 Evaluate various explanations for actions or events and determine which explanation best accords with textual evidence, acknowledging where the text leaves matters uncertain.

CCSS.ELA-Literacy.RH.11-12.7 Integrate and evaluate multiple sources of information presented in diverse formats and media (e.g., visually, quantitatively, as well as in words) in order to address a question or solve a problem.

CCSS.ELA-Literacy.RH.11-12.8 Evaluate an author's premises, claims, and evidence by corroborating or challenging them with other information.

CCSS.ELA-Literacy.RH.11-12.9 Integrate information from diverse sources, both primary and secondary, into a coherent understanding of an idea or event, noting discrepancies among sources.

Essential Questions

- Are war crimes an inevitable part of war?
- Is there a distinction between war and war crimes?
- Should all war crimes be measured relative to the Holocaust? Why or why not?
- Who should be held accountable for war crimes—nations or soldiers—and to what extent?
- Why is it more acceptable to blame certain groups, like the SS, for war crimes than others, like the *Wehrmacht*?

Enduring Understandings

Students will understand that:

- The definition of war crimes is expansive and it has great moral, political, and historical significance.
- Actions taken on the Eastern Front, in Korea and in Vietnam should be classified as war crimes.
- Perceptions of the war and of the enemy bias the way governments and people perceive war crimes. This often hampers international organizations' ability to hold nations accountable for these crimes against humanity.
- There is an inherent link between war and war crimes, with war providing cover for the crimes that soldiers and nations commit against civilians.
- The myth that only evil nations and governments commit war crimes is just that; in reality, all nations have committed war crimes at some point in their history.

Culminating Assessment

Students in each class will submit written work in the form of an essay or newspaper article in which they evaluate and compare instances of war crimes including No Gun Ri (Korean war), the *Wehrmacht's* actions in the Soviet Union (World War II), the My Lai Massacre (Vietnam), and others.

Selected Learning Activities

- *Stacie*: Students will act as the journalists uncovering the events at No Gun Ri and subsequent cover-up. When their investigation is complete, they will determine if, who, and how the US should be punished for their actions. Students will work in groups, with each group receiving one document that they will read and share with other groups. When all groups have learned about each document they will have time to organize and contextualize the events so that the story makes sense to them; this will culminate in students writing their own investigative journalism pieces in which they compare No Gun Ri to other instances of war crimes.
- *Josef*: Students will use an Activity Guide to learn about Korean geography and key terms related to the Korean War and No Gun Ri massacre, practice reading comprehension skills and document analysis, and synthesize information leading to students drawing conclusions about war crimes in general and a comparison of the events at No Gun Ri and Columbus's slaughter of the Arawaks.
- *Michael*: Students will work cooperatively to analyze the events at No Gun Ri and President Clinton's apology, using that information to create the apologies they would issue if they were president of the United States at the time the Associated Press revealed the massacre.

II. Lesson Plan: Uncovering War Crimes at No Gun Ri

Aim: Are war crimes an inevitable part of war?

Objectives: After this lesson, students will be able to:

- Define: war crimes; crimes against humanity.
- Identify and explain international law discussing treatment of civilians in wartime.
- Describe events at No Gun Ri and evaluate these events in the context of international law.
- Discuss and analyze U.S. attempts to cover up these events at the highest level.
- Analyze whether U.S. military action at No Gun Ri qualifies as war crimes.
- Assess whether the U.S. should be held accountable for these actions and, if so, what the consequences should be.

Do Now: Students will read an excerpt from a *New Yorker* article on Abu Ghraib and answer the following questions: What actions did the U.S. take at Abu Ghraib? Why is this so controversial? Can this type of situation be avoided?

Activity: The class will begin with a discussion of the rules established by the Nuremberg Convention, which will be projected on the Smartboard. Students will answer the following questions:

- What do these documents say about attacking civilians?
- Should military and government leaders be held accountable for civilian deaths, or is this an unfortunate consequence of war?
- Why is the losing party tried for war crimes, but not the victor?

For homework students read *Time* piece on No Gun Ri ("Men at War, the Ugly War"). With that knowledge base, in class they will act as the journalists uncovering the events and subsequent cover-up. When their investigation is complete, they will determine if, who, and how the U.S. should be punished for their actions. Students must remember that journalists don't necessarily learn all the facts in order (or even in a way that makes sense).

Each group will receive one of the No Gun Ri documents (Eighth Cavalry document—detailed timeline of firing on Korean civilians; Kean Order—"Korean police have been ordered to remove all civilians between the blue lines … Civilians are to be considered the enemy and action taken accordingly"; Memo to General Timberlake—"Korean refugees approaching American soldiers, strafed with gun fire. Need to eliminate this activity because it would be an embarrassment if people found out"; Muccio Letter—Refugee "problem"). Each student will receive a chart to organize information on No Gun Ri. They will read and analyze their document, fill it in on their charts, and then select one person from the group to act as the "source," who shares the information with other groups. Groups can ask questions of the "source," then fill in this information on their charts as well. When all groups have learned about each document they will have time to organize and contextualize the events so that the story makes sense to them. They can also use the questions on the back of the handout to assist in this process.

After all of the groups have drawn their own conclusions, as a class students will answer the following questions:

- Were the events at No Gun Ri war crimes?
- Why would you characterize them as such?
- Why do you think the government went to such great lengths to cover up these events?
- Whom, if anyone, would you hold accountable for this atrocity at the time this was exposed? Why?

Closure: Students will consider and discuss the following questions, as well as answering the aim of the lesson:

- Is the U.S. responsible for similar acts today? Explain.
- Why must we deal with this issue now?
- Do we deal with it better, worse, or in the same way we did in the past?
- Are war crimes a natural outgrowth of war? Can they be prevented or legislated against?

Homework: Use the information you discovered through this process to write a one-page newspaper article revealing the Army's actions in Korea in July 1950. At the end of the article, please answer the question: Are war crimes an inevitable part of war? You might want to include information on other war crimes/crimes against humanity in this paragraph (My Lai Massacre, the Holocaust, events in Iraq/Afghanistan, etc.).

III. Student Work from Stacie's Class

On June 25, 1950, Communist backed North Korea invaded and attacked South Korea on the 38tyh parallel in an attempt to spread Communism to the other half of the Korea nation. When this occurred, South Korea did counter-attack, but with little success. At that time, this was known was a civil war since both sides of the nation were fighting each other. However, the status of the war changed when the U.S. became involved in the war effort. When President Truman received a cablegram reporting the North Korean military attack on South Korea, immediate military actions were taken to roll back the Communist controlled North Koreans to where they were before their attack on South Korea. President was able to get the approval of the United Nations Security Council to send out troops under the command of General Douglas MacArthur to try to contain communism and roll back the Communists to the 38th parallel. Much aid had been provided for the success of this military mission such as allocating a certain percentage of the gross national product for military effort. President Truman wanted to convince the Communist nations that the United States is tough when it comes to stopping the spread of a corrupt form government, which is Communism.

Many interviews of U.S. soldiers who fought in the Korean War and official military documents prove that the American was well developed compared to the enemy nation and it also described the horrors of the Korean War. During the war, the American army had the advantage of using powerful military tactics such as firing gun shots by planes and using the refugees, those people who attempted to leave the warring nation, in the war effort. Also, South Korean police and marine units would simply just kill anyone, including innocent civilians of any age, suspected of being the enemy or refugees crossing the blue line. During the Korean War, basic human rights were violated in order to make it easier for the soldiers fight in the war. Unfortunately, during the Korean War, war crimes were inevitable to due to the fact that both the Communist back North Korean and the U.S. wanted to achieve a speedy victory with any means necessary. I think that this fact holds true for all wars, that in times of war, it is inevitable for war crimes to occur. This is because of the fact that warring nations have only one goal in mind while fighting, and that is to try to stop the enemy the easiest way possible. And the easiest way to do that would in some shape or form violate certain human rights of the civilians inhabiting the warring nations.

Figure 6.1   Example #1.

The war in Korea may have seemed like a quick and easy victory for the United States. It was a war that we were considerably well prepared for. However; much is not known about the Korean War. Though many Northern Koreans were portrayed as viscous, it was the United States soldiers that participated in many supposed war crimes. What was worse than the crimes of war themselves was the attempted cover up of the crimes by military officials. Americans tried to make it seem as if the Koreans were savages and claimed they were comparable to Nazis. The reality was that there was a large amount of rape between soldiers and Korean women that was not spoken for. There were huge massacres of Korean people in which Americans did not seem to care if they were the actually the enemy or not. The United States defended these crimes by claiming that they were simply a part of the war tactics that needed to be followed to help prevent the spread of communism. They claimed that they were in a position where they needed to anything possible to stop it. Such a large amount of hysteria was created around the issue of communism between both of the Red Scares that people were willing to stop at nothing. The expense that others would pay was not considered, nor was it seemed to be something that the government cared about taking responsibility in the post Korean time. In July of 1950 hundreds of Korean civilians, mainly women and children were killed without mercy by the U.S. army, this was not the only, but the most known of all the killing sprees that seemed to occur throughout the war, very different from the typical battles that had always occurred in previous wars.

An unfortunate but inevitable aspect of war is that many unlawful crimes will occur. There is almost no way to prevent them, but that does not make them excusable. War is an extreme time where paranoia, the will to win and belief that what any side is fighting for is right may lead even the most calm and secure leaders to resort to horrible actions. During World War II many Japanese Americans were put in internment camps post Pearl Harbor. Although these decisions were extremely rash and an overreaction to the attack, the amount of fear in the American public led to an overwhelming amount of racism that the government needed to deal with. They felt they were protecting American citizens and that after what happened they know longer needed to protect the Japanese, whether they were American or not. Although looking back many people see how unnecessary these internment camps were, at the time, they seemed to be the only option. Another reason that it is almost impossible to stop such severe situations from occurring is the constant focus both economically and politically on winning. No one goes into a war without the mindset that they want and must win, so they do whatever they can to achieve their goal. It is with stubbornness, unawareness and paranoia that horrible things like the Holocaust, Japanese internment camps, and the events during the Korean War were able to occur. It is also the fact that only the winning sides voice is heard, that they go by unnoticed. For many years the horrible killings that were happening were unheard of and undocumented. The U.S. did not want to be seen in any negative lights, and the power they gained by winning the war enabled them to hide just that. What is not realized by many is that war is defined by who wins and who loses. Many things that happen get lost in the shuffle and are brushed off as casualties of war, but they are not just simple casualties, they are people's lives that were lost. Crimes of war are serious offenses that people think they can get away with because of the situation, but war or not, most offenses are inexcusable.

Figure 6.2   Example #2.

IV. Handout on Clinton Apology for No Gun Ri

Information on the Release of No Gun Ri Information in 1999

Very little evidence of the events at No Gun Ri was released in 1950 and many surviving Koreans did not speak of the events. In 1998 after information began to surface in South Korea the AP in America began to investigate, gathering information from Korean survivors, American veterans, and declassified government documents (the ones you examined!). The U.S. Army ran an investigation in 1999 and in 2001 claimed that refugees were killed, but no order was given. This was followed by this statement from then-president Bill Clinton:

STATEMENT BY THE PRESIDENT (January 11, 2001)

On behalf of the United States of America, I deeply regret that Korean civilians lost their lives at No Gun Ri in late July, 1950. The intensive, yearlong investigation into this incident has served as a painful reminder of the tragedies of war and the scars they leave behind on people and on nations …
To those Koreans who lost loved ones at No Gun Ri, I offer my condolences. Many Americans have experienced the anguish of innocent casualties of war. We understand and sympathize with the sense of loss and sorrow that remains even after a half a century has passed. I sincerely hope that the memorial the United States will construct to these and all other innocent Korean civilians killed during the war will bring a measure of solace and closure … As we honor those civilians who fell victim to this conflict, let us not forget that pain is not the only legacy of the Korean War. American and Korean veterans fought shoulder to shoulder in the harshest of conditions for the cause of freedom, and they prevailed. The vibrancy of democracy in the Republic of Korea, the strong alliance between our two countries, and the closeness of our two peoples today is a testament to the sacrifices made by both of our nations fifty years ago.

V. Memo to General Timberlake

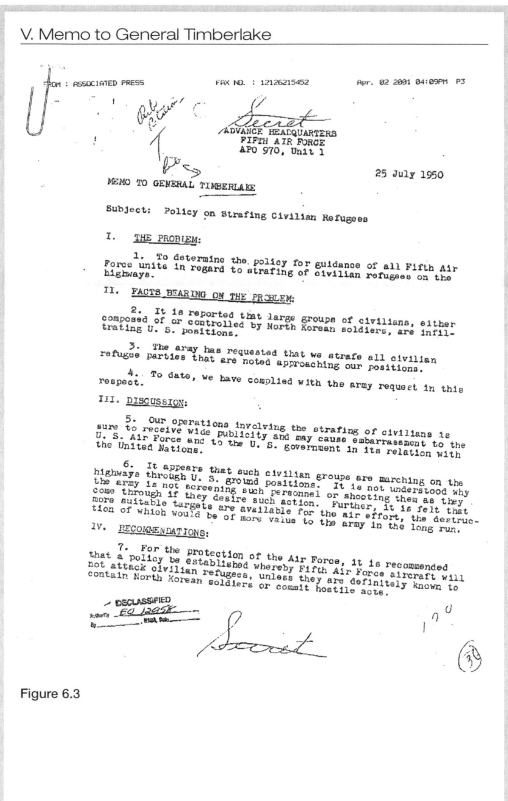

FROM : ASSOCIATED PRESS   FAX NO. : 12126215452   Apr. 02 2001 04:09PM P3

Secret

ADVANCE HEADQUARTERS
FIFTH AIR FORCE
APO 970, Unit 1

25 July 1950

MEMO TO GENERAL TIMBERLAKE

Subject: Policy on Strafing Civilian Refugees

I.   THE PROBLEM:

   1. To determine the policy for guidance of all Fifth Air
Force units in regard to strafing of civilian refugees on the
highways.

II.   FACTS BEARING ON THE PROBLEM:

   2. It is reported that large groups of civilians, either
composed of or controlled by North Korean soldiers, are infiltrating U. S. positions.

   3. The army has requested that we strafe all civilian
refugee parties that are noted approaching our positions.

   4. To date, we have complied with the army request in this
respect.

III. DISCUSSION:

   5. Our operations involving the strafing of civilians is
sure to receive wide publicity and may cause embarrassment to the
U. S. Air Force and to the U. S. government in its relation with
the United Nations.

   6. It appears that such civilian groups are marching on the
highways through U. S. ground positions. It is not understood why
the army is not screening such personnel or shooting them as they
come through if they desire such action. Further, it is felt that
more suitable targets are available for the air effort, the destruction of which would be of more value to the army in the long run.

IV. RECOMMENDATIONS:

   7. For the protection of the Air Force, it is recommended
that a policy be established whereby Fifth Air Force aircraft will
not attack civilian refugees, unless they are definitely known to
contain North Korean soldiers or commit hostile acts.

DECLASSIFIED
Authority EO 12958
By _____

Secret

Figure 6.3

: ASSOCIATED PRESS   FAX NO. : 12126215452   Apr. 02 2001 04:10PM P4

Secret

8. It is further recommended that we so inform 8th Army Headquarters.

TURNER C. ROGERS
Colonel, USAF.
D C/S Operations

2

Secret

Figure 6.3   (Continued)

VI. Letter to Dean Rusk

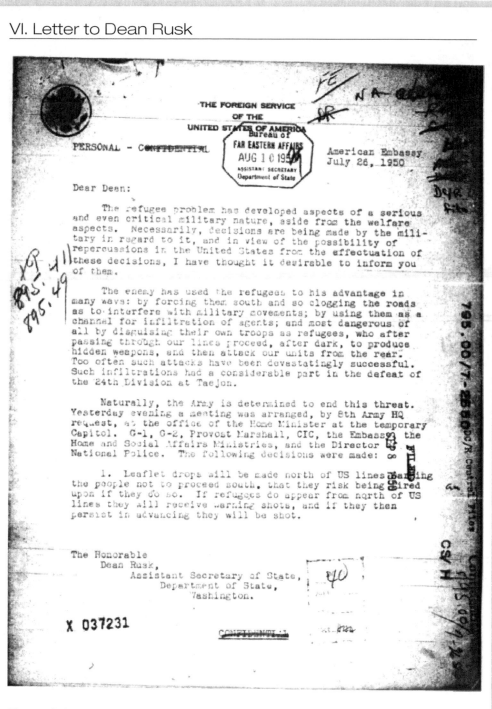

THE FOREIGN SERVICE
OF THE
UNITED STATES OF AMERICA

PERSONAL - CONFIDENTIAL

Bureau of
FAR EASTERN AFFAIRS
AUG 10 195[illegible]
ASSISTANT SECRETARY
Department of State

American Embassy
July 26, 1950

Dear Dean:

  The refugee problem has developed aspects of a serious and even critical military nature, aside from the welfare aspects. Necessarily, decisions are being made by the military in regard to it, and in view of the possibility of repercussions in the United States from the effectuation of these decisions, I have thought it desirable to inform you of them.

  The enemy has used the refugees to his advantage in many ways: by forcing them south and so clogging the roads as to interfere with military movements; by using them as a channel for infiltration of agents; and most dangerous of all by disguising their own troops as refugees, who after passing through our lines proceed, after dark, to produce hidden weapons, and then attack our units from the rear. Too often such attacks have been devastatingly successful. Such infiltrations had a considerable part in the defeat of the 24th Division at Taejon.

  Naturally, the Army is determined to end this threat. Yesterday evening a meeting was arranged, by 8th Army HQ request, at the office of the Home Minister at the temporary Capitol. G-1, G-2, Provost Marshall, CIC, the Embassy, the Home and Social Affairs Ministries, and the Director of National Police. The following decisions were made:

  1. Leaflet drops will be made north of US lines warning the people not to proceed south, that they risk being fired upon if they do so. If refugees do appear from north of US lines they will receive warning shots, and if they then persist in advancing they will be shot.

The Honorable
 Dean Rusk,
  Assistant Secretary of State,
   Department of State,
   Washington.

X 037231

CONFIDENTIAL

Figure 6.4

PERSONAL - CONFIDENTIAL

- 2 -

2. Leaflet drops and oral warning by police within US combat zone will be made to the effect that no one can move south unless ordered, and then only under police control, that all movement of Korean civilians must end at sunset or those moving will risk being shot when dark comes.

3. Should the local tactical commander consider it essential to evacuate a given sector he will notify the police liaison officers attached to his HQ, who through the area Korean National Police will notify the inhabitants, and start them southward under police control on specified minor roads. No one will be permitted to move unless police notify them, and those further south not notified will be required to stay put. —

4. Refugee groups must stop at sunset, and not move again until daylight. Police will establish check points to catch enemy agents; subsequently Social Ministry will be prepared to care for, and direct refugees to camps or other areas.

5. No mass movements unless police controlled will be permitted. Individual movements will be subject to police checks at numerous points.

6. In all cities, towns curfew will be at 9 p.m., with effective enforcement at 10 p.m. Any unauthorized person on streets after 10 p.m. is to be arrested, and carefully examined. This last item is already in effect.

Sincerely,

John J. Muccio

CONFIDENTIAL

Figure 6.4 (Continued)

VII. Kean Memorandum

SECRET

REPRODUCED AT THE NATIONAL ARCHIVES

Headquarters 25th Inf Div
Sangju, Korea
27 July 1950

MEMO TO:

    Commanding Officers, All Regimental Combat Teams
    Staff Sections, This Headquarters

    Korean police have been directed to remove all civilians from the
area between the blue lines shown on the attached overlay and report
the evacuation has been accomplished.

    All civilians seen in this area are to be considered as enemy and
action taken accordingly.

OFFICIAL: KEAN
                                   Maj Gen USA

    HERRMANN
    G-3

SECRET

1365

Figure 6.5

Seven
The U.S. in the World

Globalism and War: U.S. Intervention in the "American Century"

By Diana B. Turk, with Bill Boyce, Vincent Falivene, and Brittany Rawson

Framing the Questions: An Interview with Marilyn Young, conducted by Robert Cohen

Marilyn B. Young is Co-director of the Center for the United States and the Cold War and a professor in the Department of History at New York University. She earned her Ph.D. from Harvard University. Her books include *Rhetoric of Empire: American China Policy, 1895–1901* (1969); *Transforming Russia and China: Revolutionary Struggle in the 20th Century* (with William Rosenberg) (1980); and *The Vietnam Wars, 1945–1990* (1991), for which she received the Berkshire Women's History Prize. She has edited and co-edited several anthologies, including *Women in China: Essays on Social Change and Feminism* (1973); *Promissory Notes: Women and the Transition to Socialism* (with Rayna Rapp and Sonia Kruks) (1989); *Vietnam and America: A Documented History* (with Marvin Gettleman, Jane Franklin, and Bruce Franklin) (1995); *Human Rights and Revolutions* (edited with Jeffrey N. Wasserstrom and Lynn Hunt) (2000); *The Vietnam War: A History in Documents* (with John J. Fitzgerald and A. Tom Grunfeld) (2003); *The New American Empire* (with Lloyd Gardner) (2004); and *Iraq and the Lessons of Vietnam, or How Not to Learn from History* (with Lloyd Gardner) (2008). She has served as an elected member of the American Historical Association (AHA) Council, the Society for Historians of American Foreign Relations (SHAFR), and on the Council and the Board of the Organization of American Historians (OAH). She was awarded a Guggenheim Fellowship in 2000 and an American Council of Learned Society Fellowship in 2000–2001.

Robert Cohen: *What are the most common mistakes that Americans make, the most wrong-headed assumptions they hold when they think about the role that the U.S. has played in the world, on the global stage?*

Marilyn Young: I suppose the biggest mistake is the imagination that the United States was ever absent from the world—a conviction that the United States had once been isolationist and then moved out into the world. And I think that was really never the case. The United States has been in, of, and part of the world from the very start. It was born in empire, in fact; in rebellion against the British for sure, but with its own imperial ambitions as regards this continent. And engaged therefore in imagining and thinking about what the rest of the world was doing. So there has never been a time when the United States was absent from the world—it always been part of it, in the most fundamental ways.

RC: Why do you think there is a tendency for people to think that way—of the U.S. as apart from the rest of the world? The U.S. is taught as separate, as if we are preserving a concept of American exceptionalism.

MY: Precisely. It's part of this notion of America being an exceptional country. And at one level every country is exceptional in the sense of every country is different from any other country. They're all different. They're all unique so to speak. Exceptionalism with respect to the United States is something else. It's the notion that the United States differs morally from the rest of the world, that it is somehow a chosen nation. There is a religious overtone often to the way people are taught to think about the United States, that its values and its history are somehow superior to the values and historical record of any other country.

Part of this has to do with the notion of Founding Fathers. If you have Founding Fathers, then, in a sense, you don't have history because all of it is imminent and contained in the beginning. So you have these Founding Fathers with these wonderful, noble ideals. And then there is American history, which now and then and here and there falls off from those noble ideas but is repaired. There is not a notion of an ongoing history but rather of the repair, the falling off from an ideal, the fixing of it. There was slavery—not very nice—but it was "fixed" in the 19th century. Once it's fixed it somehow disappears from historical consciousness. So that when one teaches about American history it's not as a slave power in the 19th century but rather as a country that was all the time going towards the elimination of slavery and thus the fulfillment of the Declaration of Independence. So this flattening out or a kind of elimination of history means that the United States was always in and of itself conceptualized as this exceptional sphere, protected by two oceans, that would every now and then fare forth into the outer world, rather than being tied up in the world at all points and all the time. America as a debtor nation, which was the case until World War I, was obviously engaged with European bankers, if nobody else. From the very beginning the United States was involved in an extensive effort to challenge European nations in terms of trade with Asia, with Latin America, and so on.

RC: There also seems to be, related to what you are saying, a way of not thinking about American expansionism. And so America's story is reduced to this Whiggish view of everything getting better, moving further and further towards liberty. But then how did we get from having just these 13 colonies expand all the way out west? What happened to the Native Americans? How did the U.S. so expand? There doesn't seem to be any way of thinking about that, according to the kind of exceptionalist narrative that you are describing.

MY: For one thing the very word "expansion" or "expansionism" sort of naturalizes it. Growth is good. Expansion is a kind of growth—not when it's a matter of body fat but when it's a matter of a nation's ambitions. So the United States starts small, these 13 colonies become a nation and then that nation moves out into what is only barely conceptualized as a peopled place; rather, it is this territory. That territory becomes "settled," again as if there is nobody already there. The history of the Spanish Empire in the United States gets wiped out in this way, almost completely. So there is this sense of a natural fulfilling of borders, as if there is anything natural about a border. There is nothing natural at all about a border. Borders are established through all sorts of power politics. Otherwise why does the United States stop where it stops and Canada begin? There is no natural barrier there. So it's all in the history of the becoming of this much larger nation. And what we are really talking about is the building of a powerful nation state that increasingly engages in every direction, west as well as across the Atlantic Ocean as well as across the Pacific Ocean.

RC: *Your point about expansionism is an interesting one. Is there a term that you like better than "expansionism"? Because I think that you are right, it does make it seem like there is a natural quality to expansion.*

MY: I think for myself, there is an earlier expression of this, a book that is rarely used now, but an historian, Richard Van Alsytne [1974] wrote a book called *The Rising American Empire*. Now that book stops in the 1840s so the empire that he is talking about is exactly what's sometimes called westward expansion. I think the words "empire" and "imperial" suit the United States as they have suited other major powers. The United States is not only, in the words of historian Tom Bender, "a nation among nations," but it also an empire among empires. And empires differ among themselves. The British Empire is different from the French Empire, is different from the German, is different from the American. But we're talking about a country that exercises power well beyond its own borders in different forms. It does so territorially; it does so through maximal influence, kinds of protectorates; it does so through the domination of trade and investment. And there are different degrees of all of this. And nothing is fully controlled except of course a full colony … and even a full colony fights back in various ways.

For me, to think of the United States as an empire and American history as the history of American imperialism is useful—keeping in mind always that empires—what goes with empires is war. And at the same time that I would want to incorporate from the very beginning in anybody's sense of American history the notion of empire, I want to incorporate the notion of America's frequent appeal to force, domestically, so to speak in terms of Indian wars, and then in overseas expansion and up to and including the present day. I think also there is a way in which we separate the wartime from peacetime that actually distorts the history. The history of American wars has to be integrated into America's domestic history far more than it is. It isn't [just the] Civil War [and then] World War I. There is a lot more that happens in there, including the interventions in Central America—which are part and parcel of the whole.

RC: *I think your point about war is really important. War is not integrated very well into the teaching of history in the schools. Wars, these big conflicts, just appear. People don't take into consideration all of the different types of force, and the many different ways the U.S. has resorted to force—from coups and military occupations to massive invasions. You don't really get people bringing this all together and thinking about what this all adds up to—all this use of force; all these wars. If you think about it, we have been at war since this century started. War is really central to American history and yet we don't teach it in anything resembling a systematic way—and rarely teach it in a critical way.*

MY: That's no accident. The notion of the society that is always at war feels foreign to almost all Americans. The common conception is that we are a peace loving nation and wars happen. And then there's peace [again]. In fact, peace happens now and then. And it is much more an uninterrupted history of conflict in which military force is a significant element. But that's difficult for people to accept and if it became fully and entirely part of the consciousness of most Americans, I think there would be some protest or difficulty. So it is to the interests of everybody concerned to have a notion of history that is basically pacificist—and where war is wrongly viewed as an aberration.

RC: You'd be changing the theme of American history if the centrality of war and violence was recognized. It's not a minor adjustment.

MY: Oh, yes, that would be very fundamental. And I think from 1945 on, it is hard to escape a narrative that is primarily a narrative of war. What the Cold War was basically about was accustoming the public to a state that was liminal, at neither war nor peace—and far more war-like than peace-like. And in that liminal state, the country could move towards war when necessary. And this has its most profound early expression in the Korean War, but it goes on quite steadily after that.

RC: In the writing of American history, there seems to be a lot of denial about the whole issue of empire. Even that word "empire," if you look at textbooks, empire is something that happens in the late 19th century, an aberration that kind of goes away. I am wondering if you see that issue about the U.S. and empire as one of the central debates in American history? Maybe I shouldn't phrase it quite that way, but how would you define the central debates in the field of U.S. diplomatic history?

MY: That is one of them. I don't think that is the only one. If you describe the United States as an empire, a lot of people right away say, "Well, that is just a curse word, like when you call someone whose politics you don't like a fascist ..." [But] I think *empire* is a functional descriptive word, [though] many American historians don't. They feel that what is going on is flattened out by calling it "empire," and it's not a real analysis, it is just a way of saying the U.S. role in the world is bad.

Those scholars conflate empire with colonialism. If the only kind of empire that you identify is colonial then indeed once the Philippines are declared independent by 1946, with the exception of 900 bases and Puerto Rico, then the United States holds no territory that is not a part of its own polity. I think it is wrong to exclude those, though. I think that it is important that Americans understand that there *are* 900 bases or thereabouts in the world on which American soldiers are stationed in which they have special privileges one could well call colonial. And, then, of course, there is always Puerto Rico and its anomalous state. So, I don't think that you can just limit it to the 1890s. There is another element in which the notion of empire is useful. And that is the sense that America *has* to lead, that it's Number One ... That kind of imperial mentality, which is not called imperial—a lot can be swept under the rug inside that.

But, you asked [earlier] what are the disagreements and conflicts in the field. Empire is one. Even with an empire, do you think it is an empire that has to do more with ideology or more with material interests? In fact, the whole notion of the economic aspects of American diplomacy was very prominent in the 1930s, disappeared in the 1940s, was repressed in the 1950s, and returned very slowly in the 1960s, only to be somehow superseded and forgotten towards the end of the 20th century and the early 21st century. But this notion of what is the nature of America's economic interest globally? How do they function in terms of American domestic policy? What do they predict for in terms of American behavior? What in fact is the nature of American national interests? What does it mean to have a national security state? All of these are subjects of debate.

One way of thinking about divisions is: how do you explain the various wars? What was the Vietnam War about? What was America's entry into World War II about? We could start from there. Or Korea? Or Vietnam? Or the current wars? What were the origins of the Cold War? Can we talk about responsibility? Or was it something mutually constructed by the Soviet Union and the United States? All of these continue to be debated. There are endless books on the Vietnam War—libraries full. And on the Cold War. And lately there are libraries full of books on the 1970s, and the nature of the 1970s. Was this indeed a second Cold War, as Noam Chomsky named it? Or was it the introduction of the U.S. as a definer and defender of a human rights regime internationally? So lots of questions. As history goes on, various decades become historical, historians turn their attention to them.

RC: *There is also a debate about whether the U.S. role is benign, this force for stability and democracy versus the idea of empire; the idea of democracy versus the idea of empire.*

MY: It is a force for stability. The question is, stability for whom? When you say, "We want law and order," it's whose law and whose order? Because it's not neutral. Some people benefit from kinds of order and other people lose.

What is fascinating—and that's the thing about ideology and rhetoric—occasionally you are hoisted by your own words. The United States' … proclaimed dedication to freedom and democracy every now and then comes home to roost in events like the Egyptian Revolution—which the United States could not possibly really oppose, or find itself stripped naked before its own people and the world.

RC: *Do you see the overall trajectory in the 20th century as one of progress or stagnation?*

MY: I think there has been one major advance in human history and that is the flush toilet—that's fundamental. And beyond that, I don't know how you think about progress. There are changes that have made life easier and longer for other millions of people. And then there are changes that make life more difficult. And these changes have often taken place at the same time. So you have an increasing impoverishment of the countryside and the development of industrial capitalism, urbanism, which flourishes as the same time. So progress is for whom? The condition of the overwhelming number of people, depending on the parameter you are talking about, is better than whatever before you wish to choose. But it depends absolutely on the parameter and who[m] you are talking to about it.

All of those people now in the former Soviet Union say, "Oh I long for the days of Stalin." They do? Are they kidding? But what is it that they feel they have lost? Why doesn't it feel like progress to them? Then there are all those who say, "God forbid that we should ever return to anything like that." And then there are the people who wave the Confederate flag. What are they thinking about? What notion of the past do they have that would make all of what we would consider good change appear retrograde? So they have nostalgia for a period in which most of us would have been either enslaved or dead. The notion of progress above all depends on perspective.

RC: *In terms of the United States' role in the world, do you see much in the way of change over the course of the 20th century?*

MY: It gets more prepossessing. The United States becomes a creditor nation. And that lasts a very long time, until suddenly it finds itself massively a debtor nation. But in terms of the reconstruction of Europe, depending upon what historian—you see there again, you ask what are the conflicts in the field [of diplomatic history], depending on the subject there are different views on just about everything. The Marshall Plan is considered by many people to have saved and reconstructed Europe. At the same time, it saved and reconstructed the domestic economy. It did of course save and reconstruct the domestic economy post-World War II. But there are [those] who say, "No, England was going to recover on its own; it didn't really need it," and so on. But there is the general sense that the United States post-World War II played a significant role in perhaps the more speedy recovery of parts of Europe. At the same time it put in place an arms race, a national security state domestically, and an expanding arena of conflict. And, all of that was happening at the same time.

Years ago … John Lewis Gaddis, a very prominent historian in this [Cold War] field, one of his students was in the audience and asked of Gaddis who was on the platform: "Overall has the United States America been a force for good since 1945?" And he answered without hesitation, "Yes, absolutely." Other historians on the platform, Bruce Cumings among them, paused, because it was almost impossible to sort out. "Yes in this arena; emphatically no in that." The flattening of Korea during the Korean War, was that good? Is the flourishing South Korean economy now dependent on it having been flattened and 2 millions Koreans dead between 1950 and 1953? What a strange equation that is. You deserve to die so that we can make cars today? History doesn't really work that way. And the notion of overall force for good? I don't really know what that means. Countries and governments, states, exist, and the history plays out, and it is often unpredictable. Always interesting. And to put a plus or minus sign on that seems odd.

Who is the Greek poet who said, "Not to be born is the best for man." Overall is it better to be alive or dead? Well, it depends on whom you are asking. At any given moment someone might say, "Oh, I wish I were dead." It's not a question that makes any sense to me. One can say that the United States has at various moments demonstrably done unnecessary harm. And this is something one would want to act against. That I think you can say. You might also say that at times the United States has tried to do—*wished* to do—demonstrable good. And occasionally it's worked out, although this also is full of contradictions. As you know, things like the Green Revolution or other such improvements work in multiple ways, some very damaging.

RC: *In thinking about primary source documents, what might be one or two primary sources that are useful for teaching and important in your field?*

MY: I would always start with "National Security Council Report 68" [NSC-68] because it's the moment at which a course is really chosen for post-World War II America that in essence militarizes its policy and creates a powerful military sector, which is defended and justified by casting the Soviet Union in a particular role. I think it's a fundamental document. Parts of it will surprise people, I imagine. Like when the memorandum says that even if the Soviet Union didn't exist we would wish to behave in this way—as sort of the henchmen of the world basically: "And doing this may involve us in behaving in ways that are more like our enemies." Well, what does that mean? In order to defeat someone you become them? What strange paradox is that? So, I think NSC-68 is a really significant document. It lays things out in language that sounds rhetorical, but this was a classified document. So this is the governmental power talking to itself, but it talks to itself in the language of newspaper editorials. And, that is interesting too. There are any number of ways to analyze and look at NSC-68. I think it requires study, and I think it is in many ways determinative because once it is funded, and that happens as soon as the Korean War begins, once it's funded, it is very hard to step back from. The shrinking of defense budgets, as we see, is difficult. Their expansion is easy. And that has happened time and time again.

RC: *Can you say something about the context? Why NSC-68 was written?*

MY: Quite early on, there is the formation of a national security council. It includes the secretary of state and his various deputies who are advisors to the president, and its task is to examine and to think about national security. That's a creation of World War II perhaps, this notion of not being protected by two oceans but having to think globally about the security of the state, the nation state. So here is this council. And they consider all manner of things.

One of the things they consider is the future of relations with the Soviet Union. This was now 1949, there's already tension between the U.S. and the Soviet Union, it's not maximal. And it is a response to the Soviets getting the atomic bomb. Up until the Soviet bomb the U.S. was the sole nuclear power in the world, and its security was defined by its singularity. Now somebody else has it. What does that mean? How do we understand ourselves in a world in which a country organized on different and antagonistic lines is nuclear armed? What do we do about that?

What goes along with NSC-68 is a prior document and that is George Kennan's famous memorandum, which is later published as a memo from "Mr. X." And this lays out, the two go together—Kennan's "Mr. X Memoir" is I believe in 1947—a non-militarized version of containment. Then you have NSC-68, which is a militarized version. This notion of containment, really militarized containment, governs U.S. foreign policy until the fall of the Soviet Union. So I think those are two fundamental post-war documents.

RC: *Why do you think studying history is important? What do you think the study of the U.S. role in global history offers to young people, students, citizens, residents of the U.S.?*

MY: There is that famous dictum of George Orwell's from *1984*: "Who controls the past controls the future. Who controls the present controls the past." What he means by it is that the way that we are taught the past determines how we understand our present, and also what is likely to happen in the future. If you don't want to be, so to speak, a pawn in their game you have got to understand history on your own, and as much as possible independent of the official history that is in a large number but not all of the textbooks that are available both for teachers and for students. The study of history, through its documents, and by reading as many different understandings and interpretations as possible, is a way of giving you control over your own life.

Otherwise you really don't understand what is happening to you or why. You don't understand why all of a sudden you live in a country with a professional army and a mercenary army—both! We imagine that we have X number of troops in Afghanistan. We don't. We have twice that number because there is a contract army there that's not counted. We don't know their numbers. We don't even know who's in it. We do know or should know that they consume an incredible amount of money at the time when everything else is being cut. So, you're a teacher? Compare your salary to that of a contract mercenary solider from Fiji, say, which is among the places from which soldiers are contracted. Now I'm not against Fijians earning money, but not as supposedly defending me. It has nothing to do with me. To have any control of your life, you have to understand your personal history. Who made you what you are? What happened with your parents and grandparents? How did they live in history? How do you live in history? I don't see how anyone can move around without a desire to ask, how did we get here? That's why history is essential.

RC: *I would also add that a few years ago during one of the Bush presidential elections there was a whole village in France writing to some Midwestern town to try to influence them not to vote for Bush. This speaks to the fact that Americans are privileged in that they as citizens in the pre-eminent global power, they are the only ones in the world who through their vote have any hope of restraining that power. So it puts a special obligation on U.S. citizens to be able to think critically, analytically, about the role that the U.S. is playing in the world.*

MY: Why it's important now to understand America's role in the world is because its position may be radically shifting. That is something to try to understand too. This notion that America must lead, at a time when America is weaker than many other countries economically, when its only strength is the size of its military, and that military's fire power in wars in which that sort of fire power has virtually no meaning really does raise the question in what sense America can lead, must less should America lead—that's a separate question. And, the way in which the world as a whole really does reject American leadership when it can.

The fact that the greed of Americans, of a tiny segment of the American ruling group, that greed brought down or nearly brought down the world economy is something that Americans need to think about very carefully. It is nervous making to me that China could sell America at any moment. And then where would we be?

We are inevitably of and with the world and as we change, our position in the world changes— and that is something Americans really need to keep track of. It would be wonderful if America having been an empire among empires could become a nation among nations, full stop. And, understand itself as such. I think it would make a great difference to how we live and what we can do.

Works Cited

Orwell, G. (1983 [1949]). *1984*. New York: Signet Classics.
Van Alstyne, R. W. (1974). *The rising American empire*. New York, NY: W.W. Norton and Company.

Essay: Globalism and War: U.S. Intervention in the "American Century"

By Diana B. Turk, with Bill Boyce, Vincent Falivene, and Brittany Rawson

> You might also say that at times the United States has tried to do—*wished* to do—demonstrable good. And occasionally it's worked out.
>
> Dr. Marilyn Young

In 2006, when historian Thomas Bender challenged the assumption of *nation* as the "natural container and carrier of history" (2006, p. 5) in his groundbreaking book, *A Nation among Nations: America's Place in World History,* few outside the academy had even considered in any meaningful way the implications of bifurcating American history—or any national history—from a study of the history of the rest of the world. After all, the K-12 curriculum in most states throughout the U.S. has, since the 19th century, neatly divided American history from the history of other places (Bender, 2006), a practice reflected in various national exams (Advanced Placement, Achievement, National Assessment of Educational Progress), state tests such as the New York State Regents, and high school course sequences that proscribe one or two years of global history, usually followed by one or two years of U.S. history. Rarely, if ever, are students asked to consider

U.S. and world histories as explicitly intertwined through common themes or common sets of essential questions (Bender, 2006).

Yet this conceptual separation of U.S. history from global history does not make sense in any interpretive framework, given how interconnected the U.S. has been to nations and peoples abroad and how much the events of other nations, particularly with respect to war and peace but also to other political, economic, and social movements, have influenced events and trends in U.S. history. "The history most of us have been taught carries an old, nineteenth century ideology about the nation being the natural, sometimes the only carrier of historical meaning," Bender wrote. "But experience belies that presumption, the persistence of which makes it difficult to understand the world we live in" (2006, p. 297). Further, to consider the U.S. as separate from the rest of the world implies that it is somehow "exceptional," which in Bender's view is a fundamental fallacy:

> The framing of American history that I have offered will give little comfort to proponents [of exceptionalism], for I believe the facts make it clear that there is both a common global history *and* a history that reveals many national differences. On the spectrum of difference the United States is one of many, and there is no single norm from which it deviates—or that it establishes.
>
> (2006, pp. 296–297, emphasis in the original)

As much concerned by intrinsic fallacies that arise from considering the United States as exceptional as by the misguided nature of separating its history from that of the rest of the globe, Bender cautioned,

> [I]f world history is taught separately from that of the United States, then world history leaves out the United States and American history leaves out the world. Is it because of this disconnect that American leaders can so regularly invoke the idea of American exceptionalism even as they propose our country as the model toward which all other nations are or should be tending?
>
> (2006, p. 297)

This chapter seeks to answer the call from Bender raised here and elsewhere (2006; 2002) for a broader analysis of the place of America within the world by considering the impact global events had upon U.S. policies during the middle decades of the 20th century and the impact the U.S. had on other nations around the globe during the same time period. The teaching unit described in this chapter challenges global history teachers to bring an explicit focus on the U.S. to their curricula while also asking U.S. history teachers to reconsider the test-and-curriculum-imposed division between the past of the U.S. and that of the world. At stake is a better understanding of the ways that the U.S. and rest of the globe are, and have always been, interconnected.

According to New York University Professor Marilyn Young, an historian of U.S. foreign relations, a major misunderstanding that has arisen from the way that history has most often been taught in the United States is:

> [T]he imagination that the United States was ever absent from the world—a conviction that the United States had once been isolationist and then moved out into the world. And I think that was really never the case. The United States has been in, of, and part of the world from the very start. It was born in empire, in fact; in rebellion against the

British for sure, but with its own imperial ambitions as regards this continent. And engaged therefore in imagining and thinking about what the rest of the world was doing. So there has never been a time when the United States was absent from the world—it always been part of it, in the most fundamental ways.

Indeed, considering the U.S. as "exceptional," according to Young, is not only a fallacy, as Bender (2002, 2006) argued, but this "difference" can actually lead to a misguided sense of moral superiority. Noted Young,

[A]t one level, every country is exceptional in the sense of every country is different from any other country. They're all different. They're all unique so to speak. [But] [e]xceptionalism with respect to the United States is something else. It's the notion that the United States differs morally from the rest of the world, that it is somehow a chosen nation. There is a religious overtone often to the way people are taught to think about the United States: that its values and its history are somehow superior to the values and historical record of any other country.

In Young's view, some of this sense of innate righteousness stems from conceptions of the nation as having developed in the hands of a set of wise and all-knowing Founding Fathers:

You have these Founding Fathers with these wonderful, noble ideals. And then there is American history, which now and then and here and there falls off from those noble ideas but is repaired. There is not a notion of an ongoing history but rather of the repair, the falling off from an ideal, [and then] the fixing of it. There was slavery—not very nice—but it was "fixed" in the 19th century. Once it's fixed, it somehow disappears from historical consciousness. So that when one teaches about American history it's not as a slave power in the 19th century but rather as a country that was all the time going towards the elimination of slavery and thus the fulfillment of the Declaration of Independence. So this flattening out or a kind of elimination of history means that the United States was always in and of itself conceptualized as this exceptional sphere, protected by two oceans, that would every now and then fare forth into the outer world, rather than being tied up in the world at all points and all the time.

This notion of American exceptionalism—of the U.S. as somehow special and imbued with powers of good that from its infancy were nurtured by the Founding Fathers—led over time to the idea that the U.S. has been empowered, either by a higher power or a sense of moral authority, to colonize and "civilize" those nations and peoples viewed as morally inferior. Whether in the case of Westward Expansion on the North American continent or overseas in places such as the Philippines and Cuba, the United States' expansionist tendencies were read by many to spring from moral rather than economic or political sources. Whereas British and Belgian colonialism got labeled by most as *imperialist* from the start, in the U.S., it is and has been a more complicated—and somewhat more radical—assertion to label the nation's actions as *colonialist* or *imperialist*. "I think the words 'empire' and 'imperial' suit the United States as they have suited other major powers," Young argued.

The United States is not only ... "a nation among nations," but it also an empire among empires ... [W]e're talking about a country that exercises power well beyond its own borders in different forms. It does so territorially; it does so through maximal influence, kinds of protectorates; it does so through the domination of trade and investment.

Young recognized that her words might be controversial, but argued that this kind of re-interpretation was, in fact, necessary:

> If you describe the United States as an empire, a lot of people right away say, "Well, that is just a curse word, like when you call someone whose politics you don't like a fascist" … [But] I think *empire* is a functional descriptive word, [though] many American historians don't. They feel that what is going on is flattened out by calling it "empire," and it's not a real analysis, it is just a way of saying the U.S. role in the world is bad.
>
> Those scholars conflate empire with colonialism. If the only kind of empire that you identify is colonial then indeed once the Philippines are declared independent by 1946, with the exception of 900 bases and Puerto Rico, then the United States holds no territory that is not a part of its own polity. I think it is wrong to exclude those, though. I think that it is important that Americans understand that there *are* 900 bases or thereabouts in the world on which American soldiers are stationed in which they have special privileges one could well call colonial. And, then, of course, there is always Puerto Rico and its anomalous state. So, I don't think that you can just limit it to the 1890s. There is another element in which the notion of empire is useful. And that is the sense that America *has* to lead, that it's Number One … That kind of imperial mentality, which is not called imperial—a lot can be swept under the rug inside that (emphases in the original).

Therefore, according to Young, reading the U.S. as a fundamentally imperialist nation is a more useful and accurate framework for viewing American interactions with the rest of the world than the more politically palatable narrative of the U.S. as a fundamentally beneficent nation that sometimes goes astray. The imperialist framework also enables us to acknowledge that the U.S. has for most of its history been at war, with some pockets of peace, rather than a peaceful nation that occasionally—and only when deeply provoked—goes to war:

> For me, to think of the United States as an empire and American history as the history of American imperialism is useful—keeping in mind always that what goes with empires is war. And at the same time that I would want to incorporate from the very beginning in anybody's sense of American history the notion of empire, I want to incorporate the notion of America's frequent appeal to force, domestically, so to speak, in terms of Indian wars, and then in overseas expansion and up to and including the present day. I think also there is a way in which we separate the wartime from peacetime that actually distorts the history. The history of American wars has to be integrated into America's domestic history far more than it is. It isn't [just the] Civil War [and then] World War I. There is a lot more that happens in there, including the interventions in Central America—which are part and parcel of the whole.

From 1945 on, Young argued, it is hard to read U.S. history except as a narrative of war: "What the Cold War was basically about," she noted, "was accustoming the public to a state that was liminal, at neither war nor peace—and far more war-like than peace-like." Still, in her view, the notion that war is so central to American history feels anathema to most Americans because this is not the narrative popularly shared in textbooks or that espoused by most social commentators. "The notion of the society that is always at war feels foreign to almost all Americans," Young argued.

> The common conception is that we are a peace loving nation and wars happen. And then there's peace [again]. In fact, peace happens now and then. And it is much more an uninterrupted history of conflict in which military force is a significant element.

In Young's mind, this imagination of the U.S. as fundamentally peace-loving is a central part of the consciousness of most Americans, so re-conceptualizing a nation built on the principles of "all men are created equal" and guided by the Bill of Rights as a forceful, warlike nation would be a difficult step for many to take. And, as she also noted,

> [I]f it became fully and entirely part of the consciousness of most Americans, I think there would be some protest or difficulty. So it is to the interests of everybody concerned to have a notion of history that is basically pacificist—and where war is wrongly viewed as an aberration.

A New Framework for Teaching and Learning About the Cold War in U.S. and Global History Classrooms

For the group of educators who came together to design and teach a unit focused on the role of the United States within the world, re-thinking the U.S. as a fundamentally imperialist, warlike nation as opposed to the more standard narrative of a fundamentally good, peaceful nation proved particularly eye-opening. This narrative countered the one learned—and taught—by most of our group. What would happen, we wondered, if we presented this argument to students to "test" against an analysis of Cold War events related to U.S. and global history during the middle decades of the 20th century? How would students react and what would be the implications for our students' conceptions of America's role within the world?

Taking seriously Bender's (2006) argument against the bifurcation of U.S. history from global history, we explicitly designed our unit (Chapter Resources I) to be taught in both traditional U.S. history classes and in regular global history classes, as well as in a semester-long international relations course that spanned U.S. and global content. Aware that each course would require different sets of materials for student to access, while addressing themes and events found in both U.S. and global history, our group decided to adopt the same enduring understandings, essential questions, and culminating project, but to allow each teacher to select readings and materials appropriate for his or her classroom. Adopting the backwards planning model called for in Wiggins and McTigue's (2005) *Understanding by Design,* our group crafted the following enduring understandings for students to take away from the lessons:

- Nationalism can be both constructive and destructive—notions of American "exceptionalism" (and others' notions of exceptionalism) come with costs and far-reaching implications.
- *Change* does not always represent *progress* for all players in geopolitical enterprises.
- Intervention on the part of the United States in other countries has had major intended and unintended consequences—both for the U.S. and for the countries in which it has intervened.
- How we conceptualize the United States, whether as an essentially "good" country that goes astray sometimes, or as an essentially "bad" country that sometimes does right,

fundamentally alters how we consider and evaluate past actions of the country with respect to other (often weaker) nations.

- Other nations around the globe do not view the U.S. in the same light as those within the U.S. view themselves.
- The U.S. has acted in imperialistic ways, and there have been economic, political, and social implications of those actions.
- Social Darwinism and racism have played important roles in American intervention and rule abroad.

We also sought to underscore the following two historical thinking concepts in our unit: first, that historical events are not monolithic, but instead involve multiple perspectives and influences; and secondly and related to the first point, that historical narratives are shaped by their authors' social, cultural, economic, and political worldviews, and the narratives that become "accepted" are often created by the winners.

In order to help students arrive at the enduring understandings we laid out above, our group crafted the following essential questions for the teachers to choose from and use to frame their units of study:

- In what ways was the United States an "empire" during the 20th century? What have been the implications of its imperialist tendencies?
- How do narratives of equality play into nation-building? In what ways does nationalism serve as both a constructive and destructive force?
- How did other countries in the world view the United States during the mid-20th century, and how have these views changed over time?
- What happens when *change* does not represent *progress* for all players?
- To what extent has the United States bullied other countries in its pursuit of social, political, and economic ends? How might we evaluate this "bullying" in light of the outcomes of those quests? What have been the implications—for the U.S. and other countries—of the U.S. pursuit of natural resources?
- How much has the United States been a "good" country? Is the status quo "good," with a few "pitfalls"? Or is the status quo immoral and bullying, with a few episodes of "right" during the 20th century?
- Whom has the U.S. helped in the world? Whom has it hurt and what have been the unintended consequences of U.S. actions?
- In what ways did Social Darwinism and racism support American intervention and rule abroad during the 20th century?

A Common Unit for U.S. History and Global History: U.S. Interventions Abroad during the Cold War Era

Three teachers and a social studies education professor came together to design the unit for this chapter. The first teacher, Vincent Falivene, has been teaching in well-regarded public schools for ten years, the first five at Williamsburg Prep High School in Brooklyn and the most recent five at the highly ranked South Side High School in Rockville Center, NY. Vincent teaches international relations to twelfth graders enrolled in the acclaimed school's International Baccalaureate (IB) program. A large school of 1,100 students, nearly 75% of them white, offering relatively small classes and a large number of advanced and IB courses (US News and World Report, 2013), South Side is known as a competitive place to work: the students are extremely motivated and well prepared, and they demand excellent teachers. A casually dressed white man in his late thirties,

Vincent's commitment to enlightened, participatory democracy manifests in his efforts to develop students' critical, inquiry-based historical thinking skills while cultivating decision-making, open discourse, and imagination in his students.

Bill Boyce teaches eleventh grade U.S. history at Talent Unlimited High School on the Upper East Side of Manhattan. Located in one of the wealthier sections of New York City, Talent Unlimited High School enrolls a highly diverse student body, 36% of which is black, 39% Hispanic, 20% white, and 5% Asian. Forty-six percent of the students qualify for free and reduced lunch (Inside Schools, 2013a). Bill has been at Talent Unlimited for three years; prior to coming here, he taught for three years at Urban Peace Academy in East Harlem and one year at Fordham Leadership for Business and Technology in the Bronx. A tall white man in his early thirties who dresses in a shirt and tie at work, Bill brings to his classes a concern with issues surrounding inequality, over-enrollment, and what he sees as a troubling increase in focus on high-stakes testing.

The third teacher in the group, Brittany Rawson, is a white/Native American teacher who works at the Dr. Susan S. McKinney Secondary School for the Arts in Brooklyn, where she is in her first year of teaching tenth and twelfth grades. McKinney is an under-resourced urban school with 71% of its student body—three-quarters of whom are black and one-quarter Latino—qualifying for free or reduced lunch (Inside Schools, 2013b). Prior to McKinney, Brittany taught for a year at a transfer school in Brownsville, Brooklyn. A tall and thin native Minnesotan in her mid-twenties, Brittany cares deeply about developing in her students an understanding that they should question standard narratives, such as those in their textbooks. Through her curriculum writing and classroom instruction, she aims to inspire students to "push back at things that don't sit right with them, especially when it comes to issues of rights and freedoms." She wants her students to develop the skills and understandings needed to create powerful, well-supported arguments against traditional narratives and injustices.

The final member of the group, social studies education professor Diana Turk, served as the convener and leader of the group. An American studies scholar and teacher educator with a central concern for using history as a way of fostering students' sense of civic engagement in the communities and polities surrounding them, Turk encouraged the teachers to craft a unit that would be historically rich and innovative: different from anything they had taught before in terms of content, and centrally connected to the arguments raised in the interview with Marilyn Young. At the same time, she pushed the group to incorporate a strong creative component into the unit project as a way to propel students to *want* to learn, wrestle with, and ultimately demonstrate their responses to the historical arguments at hand.

To support these goals, the group chose to follow a project-based learning (PBL) approach to the Cold War unit. Project-based learning, sometimes referred to as "problem-based learning," is an approach to teaching and learning that forefronts projects or problems, and invites students to bring multiple sources and often different disciplinary approaches to bear in a way that privileges creative engagement with material to answer and respond to the project or problem assignment. Rather than serving as passive recipients of a teacher-directed unit, Frank and Barzilai (2004) explained, citing Thomas,

> The PBL approach engages learners in exploring important and meaningful questions through a process of investigation and collaboration ... Students build their own knowledge by active learning, ... working independently or collaborating in teams, while the teacher directs and guides, and they make a real product.
>
> (2000, p. 42)

As Turk, Fraser, and Berman (2012) have shown, classroom projects completed following a PBL approach can demonstrate not only students' subject matter competence but also their historical and analytical thinking skills and their abilities to connect their learning to real-world applications. Indeed, when well designed and well executed, a PBL approach can allow for a more authentic mode of assessment than traditional testing allows (Turk et al., 2012).

Project-based learning units, according to Turk and colleagues, contain the following properties: they last several class periods to a week or more; they are rigorous and meaningful, both "internally authentic" in that they ask for the demonstration of real disciplinary skills and also "externally authentic," in that they have real-world application and meaning for the students; they are teacher shaped but student driven, where the teacher acts as "coach"; the guidelines and grading criteria are known to students in advance and are well scaffolded and clear; and finally, the projects matter deeply in terms of student learning and assessment—they are not "add-ons" to the curriculum after the "real" work has been done (Turk et al., 2012).

In initial planning meetings, during which we combed through the historian's interview to identify compelling arguments and ideas for our unit, our group was drawn to the question of U.S. culpability with respect to inflicting harm in its interactions with other countries during the Cold War era. As we considered U.S. interventions in Cuba, Guatemala, Iran, Korea, Panama, and Vietnam, we began to shape the unit's project around a trial in which the international community, represented by all or many of the countries listed above, would weigh the U.S. culpability regarding violations of the United Nations Charter, Article 1, which calls for member nations to resist aggression, support the right to self-determination for nations, and also protect human rights and dignity. With all the teachers equally excited about the trial project, we set to work to gather materials and craft a unit that would have as its central focus the researching, planning, and carrying out of a trial for the U.S. The judges, we decided, would be students serving as representatives of the United Nations Security Council.

Putting the U.S. on Trial: How did U.S. Policies and Actions during the Cold War Era Affect Cuba, Guatemala, Iran, Korea, Panama, and Vietnam?

To introduce students to the historical context of a trial for the U.S., our group seized on the recommendation of historian Marilyn Young to begin our explorations of U.S. actions abroad during this time with the classic Cold War document, "National Security Council Report 68" (NSC-68), dated April 12, 1950:

> I would always start with NSC-68 because it's the moment at which a course is really chosen for post-World War II America that in essence militarizes its policy and creates a powerful military sector, which is defended and justified by casting the Soviet Union in a particular role … Parts of [the document] will surprise people, I imagine. Like when the memorandum says that even if the Soviet Union didn't exist we would wish to behave in this way—as sort of the henchmen of the world basically: "And doing this may involve us in behaving in ways that are more like our enemies." Well, what does that mean? In order to defeat someone you become them? What strange paradox is that?

Alongside NSC-68, we also chose to introduce Deputy Chief of the U.S. mission in Moscow George Kennan's 1946 Long Telegram, also recommended by Professor Young as important for conceptualizing the U.S. as a country fundamentally at war. In explaining the formation of the

National Security Council in the late 1940s and its concern with the Soviet Union as a new atomic power, Young noted, "Up until the Soviet bomb, the U.S. was the sole nuclear power in the world, and its security was defined by its singularity. Now somebody else has it. What does that mean? How do we understand ourselves in a world in which a country organized on different and antagonistic lines is nuclear armed? What do we do about that?" These questions served as the underpinnings for both NSC-68 and Kennan's Long Telegram, with the militarized approach of the former document combining with the containment principles of the latter to largely guide U.S. foreign policy throughout the Cold War. In addition to these crucial documents, all three teachers also included an examination of Article 1 of the United Nations Charter, taking the goals of the Charter as the standard against which their classes would evaluate U.S. actions abroad. From there, however, Brittany decided to focus on U.S. Cold War actions and interventions only in Iran and Southeast Asia, while Vincent and Bill introduced their classes to events in Latin America as well.

Introducing the Trial Project – Brittany's Tenth Grade Global History Class

Your team will be assigned a country to represent. We will have two teams representing each country.

1. South Korea
2. Vietnam
3. Iran
4. The United States

Each team will be either defending (the United States, South Korea) or prosecuting (Vietnam, Iran) the United States based on their actions in your country and the United Nations Charter.

Each team must create an opening and closing statement, as well as a list of questions to ask their country, and a list of questions for the opposing country. All three of these should work together to prove that the United States either worked within the limits of the United Nations Charter, or against it.

Documents to use:

- Article 1, United Nations Charter;
- NSC-68;
- Vietnamese Declaration of Independence;
- class reading on American involvement in Korea;
- Shirin Ebadi's "A Tehran Girlhood" from *Iran Awakening*.

Additionally, you and your group should use your class notes, paying particular attention to notes on mutually assured destruction and U.S.–Soviet relations.

With this opening outline, Brittany introduced the Cold War Trial Project to the 15 students— 8 girls and 7 boys, all of them African American or Latino (or both)—who were present in her tenth grade global history class one windy and cold afternoon in late March. Brittany walked briskly around the room, which was decorated with bright posters and samples of student work, eagerly engaging her students in conversation as they slowly filtered into the classroom. The windows were closed to keep the chill out, but this made the room rather stuffy. One girl began complaining under her breath immediately upon coming into class, her discontent quickly escalating to yelling. She was hot and wanted the window opened, but other girls in the class didn't agree. Brittany seemed unfazed, however, and calmly asked the upset girl if she needed to step outside to take a deep breath. The girl jumped out of her seat but instead of going to the door, ran to the window and flung it open—but then quickly adjusted it back so it was open just a crack. A solution reached, and breathing easier in the classroom, Brittany smiled at the girl, who calmed down immediately.

Each student in the class collected upon entry a packet of materials to use for the trial preparation, including a series of prompts for how to write the statements they would use, as lawyers and as witnesses, at their trial. Brittany kept the reading materials somewhat simple: Article 1 of the United Nations Charter; an excerpt from NCS-68; an excerpt from the 1945 Vietnamese Declaration of Independence; a summary of events related to the Korean War; and Shirin Ebadi's "A Tehran Girlhood" from *Iran Awakening,* on the U.S.-orchestrated overthrow of Prime Minister Mohammed Mossadegh in 1953 that resulted in the installation of the Shah. To facilitate her students' comprehension of the materials—some of whom, she felt, would simply give up if confronted with such difficult reading—Brittany condensed and heavily excerpted the complicated documents and materials. The piece on Korea she borrowed from Bill, another teacher in our group, but she edited it significantly for both length and vocabulary. In addition, for each source, Brittany provided guided reading questions for the students to answer as they moved, paragraph by paragraph, through the material during a class session. In pairs or groups of three, the students worked through each of the sources, spending one day on NSC-68, one day on materials related to Southeast Asia, one day on Iran, and several days on trial preparations and the trial itself. Overall, the class spent more than a week on the unit, including taking time after the trial to debrief the experience and the project.

While Brittany had 87 sophomores enrolled in three sections of her global history class, attendance in any given class hovered only around 60%. When it comes time to take the New York State Regents in global history, an exam the students must pass to graduate, Brittany estimates that only about 30 to 35 of them will pass the first time they take it, largely due to poor attendance. Still, as she explained the trial to the students and charged them to build their cases either for or against the U.S. in evaluating whether it violated the United Nations Charter, the students' energy and excitement were clear. Diligently, they worked through the complicated readings and assignments, even asking a visitor to explain things to them when they did not understand. While the essential question on which their unit was based, "To what extent has the U.S. bullied other countries in its pursuit of social, political, and economic ends?," clearly stemmed from the Young interview, Brittany chose not to address the full interview specifically in class, instead offering small excerpts as "do-nows" for her students to respond to at the beginning of class. Even with just a short introduction to Young's arguments, the students in Brittany's class seemed to share Young's view of the U.S. as a largely imperialist, bullying country. Working through "A Tehran Girlhood," many of them paused to roll their eyes and exclaim in disgust at the increase in oil exports to the U.S. and Britain that occurred once Mossadegh was forced out so that the CIA-backed Shah could be put in power. In the students' view, this was just "one more example" of U.S. over-reach in Middle East affairs, something they stated they still saw today with the U.S. wars in Iraq and Afghanistan. In the arguments they made—voiced from their perspectives as relatively disadvantaged young men and women of color living in the urban inner city—the U.S. was usually at fault for exploiting weaker countries and peoples, especially those with valuable natural and capital resources. To Brittany's students, the essential question she posed to them, designed to inspire debate and provoke disagreement, appeared somewhat obvious. *Of course* the U.S. has bullied other countries. The only debatable point was whether this in fact violated Article 1 of the United Nations Charter, and that would be the subject of the trial for which they next needed to prepare.

Working through the Trial Materials: Vincent's Twelfth Grade International Relations: History of the Americas Class

Vincent's students—whiter, wealthier, and in general far better prepared for their high school studies than Brittany's students—embarked upon the Cold War unit with more favorable views of U.S. actions than Brittany's students did. While South Side's inclusive approach to the IB program does not require students to "test in" to take Vincent's IB history of the Americas class, this bubbling group of 10 boys and 13 girls—the vast majority of them Caucasian—still seemed more like participants in a college seminar than like a class of high school students in the spring of their senior year. Vincent—called "Mr. Falivene" by his students—exuded a relaxed and informal manner as he moved through the room on a sunny March day. He exchanged warm comments and playful jokes with the students, particularly a group of gregarious boys and girls clustered in the back of the room, as he handed back the previous day's homework. At one point, when the volume of conversation rose beyond what he deemed acceptable, Vincent calmly called out, "Hey guys, stay with me," and the students immediately re-focused on the materials before them. Overall, a calm and focused feel suffused the bright and spacious classroom, and the students appeared to feel safe taking intellectual risks, answering Vincent's questions even when not thoroughly sure of the answers and engaging and disagreeing with each other in respectful tones.

The volume of reading Vincent's students did in their Cold War unit was vast in comparison to the materials assigned by either Brittany or Bill. The students received thick packets of readings that Vincent had collected over his years of teaching, many of them scholarly articles, which they had to read, digest, and be prepared to debate. Vincent's PowerPoint presentations were challenging and complicated too, and the students knew he would not accept easy, pat explanations in response to his open-ended, analytical questions. Viewing history through multiple lenses and putting disagreeing historians into "conversation" with each other were both hallmarks of Vincent's teaching. In their "The Cold War: The Early Years" reading packet, for example, the students encountered the writings of academic historians such as Arthur Schlessinger, Thomas Bailey, Bruce Cumings, Tony Judt, and John Lewis Gaddis, as well as charts that prompted them to group the historians into "traditional/orthodox," "revisionist," and "post-revisionist" historiographical camps. As they moved through the unit, the students read and parsed through much of the interview conducted with Professor Young, using its historical constructs to frame their explorations and also subjecting her claims to analysis and evaluation. At one point, Vincent prompted the students to put Young's arguments into dialogue with those of conservative historian Niall Ferguson (2004), whose controversial embrace and celebration of U.S. empire provided a complicated foil to Young's more critical evaluation of U.S. imperialistic tendencies.

By the time Vincent's students encountered the trial project, then, they had already amassed a sophisticated understanding of U.S. Cold War involvement in other nations around the globe. In addition, Vincent pushed the students to develop at least rudimentary political perspectives on the topic, and he took these into consideration when he assigned each student's role—sometimes in opposition to their actual political beliefs—to play in the trial itself.

Vincent assigned students to the following roles, a list that Bill also adopted:

> *In the aftermath of the failed Bay of Pigs Invasion, several non-aligned nations have accused the United States government of violating Article 1 of the United Nations Charter for Cold War interventions in the 1950s and early 1960s:*

Lawyers for the Prosecution

Lawyer 1: Opening Statement
Lawyer 2: Concluding Statement

Lawyers for the Defense

Lawyer 1: Opening Statement
Lawyer 2: Concluding Statement

Witnesses for the Prosecution

1. Mohammed Mossadegh
2. Jacobo Arbenz
3. Fidel Castro
4. Patrice Lumumba
5. Nikita Khrushchev
6. Howard Zinn

Witnesses for the Defense

1. Dwight D. Eisenhower
2. John Foster Dulles
3. John F. Kennedy
4. Robert S. McNamara
5. Shah Mohammed Reza Pahlavi
6. Colonel Carlos Castillo Armas
7. Fulgencio Batista

UN Security Council

1. China
2. France
3. Soviet Union
4. United Kingdom
5. United States
6. Philippines

For their IB-prescribed "in-papers," and to help students prepare for the trial, Vincent assigned his students to write the following tasks that required them to draw from the readings he provided them, their class discussions, and his extensive PowerPoint presentations:

In-Papers
Lawyer 1 Tasks

A   Write an opening statement that summarizes the charges and explains your case.
B   Develop a series of questions for each of your witnesses. These should center on:
    1   The relationship between the witness and the US.
    2   The social, political, and economic policies created, supported, or enacted by the witness.
    3   The reasons for these policies and actions.
    4   The consequences of these policies and actions.

Lawyer 2 Tasks

A   Write a concluding statement that summarizes your argument for or against the defendant.

B Develop a series of cross-examination questions for the opposition witnesses. These should center on:

1 The relationship between the witness and the U.S.
2 The social, political, and economic policies created, supported, or enacted by the witness.
3 The reasons for these policies and actions.
4 The consequences of these policies and actions.

Witnesses Bio Sketches

- Who are you?
- What is your background? (What led you to be in your current position?)
- What are your chief accomplishments?
- What would you most be criticized for?
- What social, political, and economic policies did you create, support, or enact?
- What were the reasons and consequences of these policies?
- What are the direct or indirect connections to Kennedy's Cuban policy?

UN Security Council

- What country do you represent?
- Describe your relationship with the U.S.
- Provide a brief history of your nation.
- Highlight key national achievements and set-backs.

Vincent later expressed some disappointment with the "in-papers" and vowed to help future classes "take their preparations for the trial more seriously," thereby saving them from having to do additional work overnight between the first and second day of the trial when the students realized they were not as prepared as they wanted to be. However, to Diana, the teacher educator who observed the class and read the materials the students produced, the in-papers seemed largely well researched and carefully planned biographical summaries that gave the students a clear sense of how their characters would have testified at a trial for the U.S. (see Chapter Resources IV). Certainly, the depth of the "in-papers" helps explain why the trial in Vincent's classroom ended up taking three and a half days. The students not only had much to say for their own roles, but when it came to questioning and cross-examining the witnesses, the lawyers—selected from among the top performers in the class—built their cases meticulously, selectively showcasing their own witnesses and seeking to discredit those of their opponents. And when it came time to evaluate the U.S.'s culpability with respect to violations of Article 1 of the United Nations Charter, the UN Security Council members proved equally thoughtful, their statements and positions historically compelling—and, as we will see, at times surprising.

Putting the United States on Trial: Bill's Eleventh Grade U.S. History Class

At 8:50 am on the day of the trial in Bill's eleventh grade U.S. history class at Talent Unlimited High School, the hallway buzzed with an air of expectancy. A school for students who are interested in the performing arts, Talent Unlimited occupies the third floor of a large building shared by several other schools. The sounds of singing filled the hallways that morning, both during and in between class times—ahhhhhh went the voices rising up the scale, ohhhhhh they came back down in song. Somehow, the other students appeared to take the loud background music in their stride as they went about their business in school.

A popular teacher who sports khakis, brightly-colored button-downs, and catchy prep-school ties, Bill, known as "Mr. Boyce" to his students, loped down the hallway toward his assigned room, where he stopped to greet his students outside and welcome them personally, and with affection, into his classroom. The 20 students—18 of them female—quickly filed in, glancing anxiously at note-cards clutched in their hands. Most smiled nervously at Diana, who was there to observe the class. Mistaking the visit for an evaluation of their teacher, a few came over to volunteer how much they liked Mr. Boyce.

The students took seats that had nametags such as "U.S. Lead Attorney" and "First Witness for the Global Community" attached to them. At 8:54, Bill sent the students representing the UN Security Council out of the room to set the stage for the trial. When they came back in, he announced "All rise," and "Please be seated," in somber tones, and then declared the court in session. The lead attorney for the Global Community walked to the center of the room, tossed her long dark hair to the side, and confidently began her opening statement in a voice that rose as it unfolded:

> The U.S. is corrupt; simple as that. From the time of killing innocent Native Americans to even going to other countries and starting wars, the U.S. is a killing machine. The U.S. figures just because it's stronger, has better weapons, and "pities" other countries and wants to "help," but only in the most unconventional ways. "Helping" means sticking the U.S.'s nose where it doesn't belong … Always the same excuse, "promote democracy," "we need to help," "we need natural resources." The U.S. shouldn't put people like the Shah and Carlos Armas in power in Iran and Guatemala because we don't like the way they handle things. It isn't the U.S.'s country so they shouldn't feel obligated to help … Again, we ask, why does the U.S. feel the need to "help"? If a country's government is corrupt let that country figure it out for themselves!

By the time she was done, the lead attorney for the Global Community was almost shouting. With her words still echoing in the room, she nodded toward the UN Security Council, and strode back to her seat. A stunned silence filled the room, and one could see on the students' faces the thought sinking in: *this trial is for real.* Slowly, the lead attorney for the United States stood and came to the front of the room:

> Good morning ladies and gentlemen. I would first like to bring your attention to the fact that the United States has made a huge impact on the world. These impacts have resulted in both negative and positive effects; however, in the end the decisions made have proven to be justified. In the mid-1960s the U.S. became involved with Vietnam. Before their involvement, Vietnam was in a terrible place … With Vietnam in such terrible shape the United States had to offer their assistance … Communism is evil, they limit freedom of speech and imprison their people for no reason. For those reasons our actions are justified. In the end the United States should not be punished for their involvement in other countries because of the help they provided.

What happened during the next hour can only be described as astounding for anyone who has experienced what is often a lack of enthusiasm and engagement in many high school classrooms: one by one, the additional lawyers came forward to present their arguments and call their witnesses to testify. First, the Global Community lawyers called the student playing

Mariana Rodriguez of Guatemala, who testified emotionally to the horrors of the CIA-backed military coup that toppled President Jacob Arbenz—suspected by the U.S. of communist leanings—and installed the military dictator Colonel Carlos Castillo Armas. The coup left her country in tatters, the student playing Rodriguez testified, her voice cracking. The military-backed and U.S.-supported Civil Defense Patrols, authorized by the new dictatorship, tortured and "disappeared" thousands of Guatemalans, including her sister, Carmen. The U.S. must be held culpable, she argued forcefully, not only for supporting a ruthless military dictatorship but also for stripping away, with Arbenz's defeat, the last curbs against the mercenary power of the United Fruit Company. She and other witnesses gave accounts of the oppression Guatemalans suffered in their jobs with United Fruit (later re-named the Chiquita Company), which paid poorly and exploited the labor of the peasants, who had few options except to work for the huge fruit conglomerate.

When the student playing Mariana Rodriguez finished her testimony, another student playing the role of the historian and veteran Howard Zinn came forward to turn the discussion to Vietnam and add additional testimony to the horrors wrought by the U.S. Speaking, the girl playing Zinn said, as a representative of veterans of U.S. wars, the atrocities U.S. soldiers were accused of perpetrating on the Vietnamese went far beyond the "normal ravage of war." She spelled out in great detail many of the crimes—rape, beheadings, electrocutions, random shootings, poisoning of food stocks, etc.—that the U.S. soldiers allegedly committed. As she offered her extensive testimony, the attorneys for the U.S. began to shift uncomfortably in their seats: how would they defend their nation against such powerful accusations?

But then it came time for the defense to call its witnesses, and as they began to offer their testimony, the picture became far more complicated: a student representing Harry S. Truman argued that countries all over the world were being "threatened by communist take-over," and that it was the U.S. who came to the rescue, investing hard-earned U.S. profits into foreign nations to protect them from the "great communist threat." Another student stood as Robert S. McNamara, former Secretary of Defense, testifying,

> The ultimate goal of the United States in Southeast Asia, and the rest of the world, is to help maintain free and independent nations who can develop politically, economically, and socially, so they can be responsible members of the world community … As the admired super power of the world, we cannot abandon the people of Vietnam.

Ultimately, the student representing McNamara asserted, the U.S. did what it did for the sake of the Vietnamese who needed their help so desperately. Thus, she argued, it cannot be held liable for violation of Article 1 of the United Nations Charter because, throughout, its *intentions* were good.

The trial proceeded at a fast clip, the lawyers standing to call their witnesses and the witnesses going forward to testify in well rehearsed order. At one point, when a student hesitated, seemingly paralyzed by the public speaking required of her, Bill attempted to reassure her by saying, "Don't worry, it's not a real trial." But this statement defied the feel of the trial setting, and the students would later say that it struck many as wrong and out of place, because the sense of *realness* in the trial was palpable throughout. The students took their roles very seriously. As they showed during the trial and as they would claim later in their reflections on the activity, much felt at stake in whether the U.S. would be found guilty or not by those representing the UN Security Council.

The Trial Verdict: Was the United States Guilty of Violating Article 1 of the United Nations Charter?

Article 1 of the United Nations Charter calls for member nations to pledge to uphold the following UN goals:

1. To maintain international peace and security, and to that end: to take effective collective measures for the prevention and removal of threats to the peace, and for the suppression of acts of aggression or other breaches of the peace, and to bring about by peaceful means, and in conformity with the principles of justice and international law, adjustment or settlement of international disputes or situations which might lead to a breach of the peace;
2. To develop friendly relations among nations based on respect for the principle of equal rights and self-determination of peoples, and to take other appropriate measures to strengthen universal peace;
3. To achieve international co-operation in solving international problems of an economic, social, cultural, or humanitarian character, and in promoting and encouraging respect for human rights and for fundamental freedoms for all without distinction as to race, sex, language, or religion; and
4. To be a centre for harmonizing the actions of nations in the attainment of these common ends.

In both Brittany's global history class and Bill's U.S. history class, the UN Security Council's verdict on U.S. culpability in violating the above charter proved easy to decide: all sections found the U.S. guilty. In doing so, the students did not take on the roles of the different countries that made up the members of the Security Council at the time; instead, they simply evaluated the evidence and arguments as they saw them, and in their view, the case was clearly stacked against the defense. The students playing the roles of the Security Council in Bill's class would later admit in a debriefing session with Diana that during the trial, they had a difficult time giving equal weight to the arguments put forth by the U.S. attorneys and their witnesses because the evidence they had analyzed in class made it harder to argue for U.S. innocence. As a "bullying" nation, they explained, it was difficult to consider the United States as anything but guilty for violating several statutes outlined in Article 1, including allowing other nations the right to self-determination, refraining from aggressive actions, and respecting human rights and fundamental freedoms. In Brittany's class, too, the students took a similar approach, arguing in reflective pieces written in the wake of their trial that their findings rested on what they saw as clear U.S. violations of other countries' right to self-determination, especially with respect to Iran and Vietnam (most students in Brittany's class wrote that they considered the U.S. not guilty in Korea).

In Vincent's class, where the students representing the UN Security Council had to vote not as judges who simply evaluated the cases presented, but rather as they thought the nations they were assigned to represent on the Council would have voted during that time period, the verdict proved much more complicated, and in fact ended with a U.S. acquittal. In some cases, the position the Security Council member nation took fell in line with expectations: Communist China declared the United States guilty, whereas the United Kingdom sided with its ally and voted not guilty. But in other cases, the position proved unexpected and showed careful analysis on the part of the students representing certain countries: the student representing France, for example, found the U.S. guilty, despite France's alliance with the United States, whereas the student representing the Soviet Union voted, surprisingly, to acquit. These decisions prompted fascinating discussion in Vincent's class, the unfolding of which showed the extent to which the students had both understood the complicated historical arguments raised during the trial, as well as their own recognition of *realpolitik*.

The student representing France defended his decision to find the U.S. guilty by arguing that since the United States had not backed France during the crisis in the Suez in 1956, France, in his view, would not have backed the United States in this case: "France was concerned with America's domination of the Atlantic alliance" in the wake of Suez, the student noted.

> I voted the U.S. guilty due to the acts of aggression they took against some nations. This made me question their intentions for getting involved in foreign affairs. I believe their intentions were slightly imperialistic and mainly aided countries because they wanted something in return.
>
> (Student in Vincent's class, out-paper)

France may have been an ally of the United States, in other words, but at this point in history, according to the student, that alliance was tenuous and fraught with bitterness over Suez so may well have resulted in a guilty verdict.

The student representing the Soviet member of the UN Security Council also took an interesting and unexpected tack in voting: fearing that finding the U.S. guilty would open the Soviet Union up to similar charges, he chose to vote the Soviet arch-enemy not guilty and thus potentially spare his own country from facing similar charges at a future trial. As another student argued,

> The UN Security Council ultimately decided that the U.S. was not guilty of violating the UN Charter. While this may not be entirely justified, it was perhaps necessary because holding the United States accountable could have set a precedent that would require the UN to hold several other nations, such as the Soviet Union, accountable for their imperialistic actions [as well]. [Chapter Resources V.]

Despite the overall vote of not guilty by the UN Security Council in the class, most of the students wrote in their IB "out-papers," which asked them to analyze the verdict and assess their own level of agreement with the outcome, that they personally considered the United States guilty of violating the United Nations Charter. One student wrote,

> I do agree that we need countries to set up and enforce rules and laws, but this doesn't exempt them from following [those laws] either. The evidence against the United States is appalling. Self interest was the major reason [the] United States intervened in smaller nations and they use the threat and fear of communism to justify their actions.
>
> (Student, out-paper)

Another student agreed, citing events in Guatemala in 1954:

> [There,] the CIA replaced the democratically elected leader of Guatemala, Arbenz, with US-backed Armos. Arbenz had taken land from the American-run United Fruit Company (U.F.C.), much of which was uncultivated, and distributed it to poor peasants. The U.F.C. was compensated for the land, and the Guatemalan people started towards a better life. The prosecution explained how then the people were hurt, not

helped, when the U.S. intervened and returned the land to the U.F.C. Although redistribution of land appears communist, the prosecution showed again how the U.S.S.R. had no influence over Arbenz. The prosecution also revealed the conflict of interest in the U.S. government. Many government officials, such as Secretary of State John Foster Dulles, were on the U.F.C. board or held shares in the company. They violated the self-determination of Guatemala to protect their economic interests.

(Student in Vincent's class, out-paper)

In these cases, the students clearly shaped their views based on their interpretations of the readings they did in preparation for the trial. The same held for the students playing the UN Security Council in Bill's class, who found themselves so swayed by the readings that they had a hard time really hearing the U.S. defense. At the same time, though, it is important to note that political beliefs certainly played a role in some students' assessment of U.S. culpability in violating the United Nations Charter. In another section of Vincent's class, for example, the student he assigned to represent the Philippines did not wish to vote the United States guilty for its Cold War actions due to his conservative political leanings. He thus researched the history of U.S. involvement in the Philippines and decided that since the United States had granted the Philippines independence in 1946, in the wake of World War II, it was possible that the Philippine representative to the UN Security Council would have been more grateful for the recent actions toward independence than angry about the initial U.S. annexation of his nation, so he voted to acquit the United States of wrong-doing. In other words, he found a creative way to find the U.S. innocent of violating the UN principles, a position in keeping with his own pro-America political leanings.

Latent political beliefs also played a role in Brittany's class, in which the students were quick to find fault with the U.S. policies in Iran, Vietnam, and Korea as a result of their own sense of disenfranchisement as young men and women of color living in a socioeconomically disadvantaged area. "They love anytime that we can talk about history from the point of view of the underdog," Brittany stated of her students, because they see themselves in the role of underdog as well.

Lots of them live in a world where the government does shortchange them. So on one hand, they hear how great America is and all these awesome things we do, and how we're such a wealthy country, and we're such a privileged country, and I think it's sort of chafing to hear how wealthy and awesome and privileged America is and to so often not experience that.

As young people who themselves feel disenfranchised from the larger narratives of American success and benevolence, it turned out to be a somewhat cathartic experience in Brittany's class for the students to cry false to U.S. claims of "benevolent involvement" and "greater good" as they weighed the outcomes of U.S. interventions in Iran and Southeast Asia during the 1950s and 1960s.

Evaluating the Trial Project: An Assessment of Teaching and Learning

The proceedings against the United States for alleged violations of Article 1 of the United Nations Charter proved an engaging and powerful project for the students in all three history classes. Framed around a series of rich essential questions, the unit introduced students to complicated historical arguments and pushed them to weigh competing and often contradictory evidence.

Offered in three very different settings and courses—Brittany's lower-performing tenth grade global history class, Vincent's higher-performing twelfth grade IB history of the Americas class, and Bill's mid-level eleventh grade U.S. history class—the unit served as a vision of what history can look like: an examination of the complex relationships and history of the modern world, a history that transcends borders, yet remains rooted in and related to notions of the nation (Bender, 2006). While the three teachers made some modifications to the unit readings and the countries covered, as a result of their students' differing reading levels and degrees of academic preparation, what really stood out was the way the unit engrossed and excited students across a vast range of socioeconomic and ethnic/racial backgrounds.

As a model of a PBL approach, the trial proved successful in all classes as an "internally authentic" and an "externally authentic" learning activity. With respect to internal authenticity, students engaged deeply with the project assignment, evaluating a rich and important set of historical materials in the same rigorous manner as historians do and arriving at their own conclusions about the meaning of the events they studied. With respect to external authenticity, the students in the three classes certainly recognized the "real world value" of what they were doing in the trial and wrestled with the ramifications of their actions in ways that are rarely done in history classrooms. The proceedings *felt* real in all three settings, and the students had a definite sense that there was much at stake in the final outcome. The students' negative reaction to Bill's assurances to the nervous presenter that the trial wasn't "for real" underscored this sense of realness. As one girl in Bill's class wrote in an assessment of the activity,

> Overall I think the trial went very smoothly, and everyone showed a lot of effort. Considering the content, I think I understand the content better than I [otherwise would have] … I'm proud of how much each student put into this trial, knowing how important it was for this class.

In Vincent's class, the students became so worried about their level of preparation after the first day of the trial that they conducted still more research at home in preparation for the second day. And in Brittany's class, where only about 40% of students turn in their work on any given project, the trial so engaged the class that they turned in their work at a rate exceeding 85%. For these students, as for those in Bill and Vincent's classes, the historical research and analysis they did enabled them to understand and ultimately speak with some degree of authority on matters of deep and important significance to them as students and citizens.

As our group reflected on the work the students did in all three classes and the level of historical understanding they demonstrated through the trial preparations completed in Brittany and Bill's classes and through the IB "in-papers" and "out-papers" in Vincent's class, it became clear to us that the students had indeed mastered the knowledge we had outlined for them in the enduring understandings. Namely, they clearly demonstrated understanding of the following:

1. Intervention on the part of the United States in other countries has had major intended and unintended consequences—both for the U.S. and for the countries in which it has intervened.
2. How we conceptualize the United States, whether as an essentially "good" country that goes astray sometimes, or as an essentially "bad" country that sometimes does right, fundamentally alters how we consider and evaluate past actions of the country with respect to other (often weaker) nations.
3. The U.S. has acted in imperialistic ways, and there have been economic, political, and social implications of those actions.

The narrative of U.S. benevolence and essential peacefulness in its interactions with other nations is one that has been inscribed in the received story most students learn (and teachers teach) due to American dominance and ultimate success in the Cold War. The portrait offered by Marilyn Young in the interview that framed this chapter sought explicitly to *interrupt* that received narrative of U.S. peacefulness and goodness by offering a counter-analysis that reframed the U.S. in what Young considered a more accurate, if less flattering, light. This served as a central focus for the unit, and as we examined the students' oral and written products created during and after the unit, it became clear that in all three classes, they understood Young's argument and were able to test its value as an historical lens through their classroom trial projects.

Young's perspective in the interview proved particularly important for all three teachers as a lens that pushed them to rethink U.S. actions during the Cold War era. Reflecting back on the unit, Vincent stated, "One of the major contributions and validations provided by the Young interview was in the primacy of the notion of American empire, U.S. exceptionalism, and the role each played in the Cold War." For him, these arguments proved essential in revisiting topics he had taught dozens of times before. He noted about Young's interview,

> In one sense it was very validating because in the past [my colleague teaching the same class and I] have done these comparisons between George Kennan and NCS-68, but I don't think we were able to do it in a very effective way. In the past it seemed to be—it tended to be very dry and not as well contextualized—we tended to contextualize it in the Korean War, but connecting it to notions of American exceptionalism, to notions of imperialism and different types of imperialism [was hard]. So being able to draw on the interview to help us define those words and provide a lens, I think, is really one of the great things about the interview, aside from obviously the very insightful lens through which it looks.

Bill agreed: "It was really powerful showing the United States in a different light," through the use of the Young interview, and in fact, it helped him reframe his entire approach to teaching U.S. history, not just the unit on the Cold War. With his students, Bill spent much more time this year than he had in the past examining the Indian Removal Act and other policies by Andrew Jackson, America's role in getting the Panama Canal built, and other U.S. interventions that showed a "bullying" nation expropriating natural resources and land, regardless of the human cost to those displaced through its actions. Young's arguments helped him "really show the students how the United States treats other people, especially in North America. And from there we transitioned to thinking about how the United States treats people abroad, in Central America, Southeast Asia, and so on." As he noted,

> The kids had a good idea that something's not right here in U.S. history. The U.S. has really bullied people. We [the U.S.] find things we want and we go in to other countries and just take it … So we focused on Guatemala and how they treated the Guatemalans, and how, you know, there was a fruit business, and there was a monopoly to be made, and you look at how they were able to put people into power to continue monopolies around the world. We saw that in Southeast Asia and Iran and you know, throughout the 20th century. It's where we [the U.S.] leave one place, we kind of go searching for another location.

Brittany, too, found the Young interview vital in shaping and structuring the unit she taught. As one of only two social studies teachers in her school, Brittany noted that she often feels alone in curriculum planning, so having the guidance of Young and the collaboration of the other teachers really made a difference for her teaching in this unit. Although she considered the language of the interview too complicated to share in its entirety with her students, Brittany noted that she benefited from working with it and especially appreciated Young's suggestion to start with NSC-68:

> [The interview] helped me frame what I did a lot. It got me thinking about how I can structure how we were going to get through a certain idea. We used NSC-68 a lot, which I don't think I would have thought to use in a global history class at all, so that was really helpful ... I think the coolest thing is that [for] my students, something like NSC-68 easily could have been a throw away for them. But they're still talking about it, which they don't do [about other sources]. I can't overstate how interesting this is because they are still referring to that stuff, they are still going back. We're in a unit on Revolution now, we're back in the 1700s now with the French Revolution, and they are still talking about it.

When asked why she thought NSC-68 had resonated so meaningfully with her students, Brittany offered this poignant and provocative reply, which spoke to both the sense of dislocation her largely poor, minority students feel with respect to the nation they live in and also their eagerness for the historical knowledge and awareness to be able to frame their dislocation in a broader social context:

> So here's a document [NSC-68] that is like, "America's awesome, we're the good guy, we defend the little guy, we are always out for the best," and then they got to really shine a light on that and be like, "Is America really out for the little guy, are we really supporting [them]?" and have real examples of where that hasn't happened. I think it justified their own feelings in a way that made them feel very educated and intelligent. You know, not to say, "My own personal experience is that this sucks," but to say, "I know that in Iran [in the 1950s], the people got screwed. I know there are people in other places, in other times that were seeing what I'm seeing."

As these reflections show, involvement in this project helped all three teachers—thoughtful, deeply committed educators with experience that varied from two to ten years—to re-imagine the history of U.S. involvement with other nations. And this *act* of rethinking on the part of teachers—of considering *how* to frame the historical events they teach—has enormous implications, Young argued, for *what kind of history* students learn:

> [T]he way that we are taught the past determines how we understand our present, and also what is likely to happen in the future. If you don't want to be, so to speak, a pawn in their game you have got to understand history on your own, and as much as possible independent of the official history that is in a large number but not all of the textbooks that are available both for teachers and for students. The study of history, through its documents, and by reading as many different understandings and interpretations as possible, is a way of giving you control over your own life. Otherwise you really don't understand what is happening to you or why.

Explaining the importance of why we should learn history, Young noted,

> To have any control of your life, you have to understand your personal history. Who made you what you are? What happened with your parents and grandparents? How

did they live in history? How do you live in history? I don't see how anyone can move around without a desire to ask, how did we get here? That's why history is essential.

In order for students to understand the history of the Cold War, both from a U.S. and from a global framework, and in order to see U.S. policies and actions as many throughout the world saw (and continue to see) them, it is important for them to really grapple with what happened and from whose perspectives the stories are being told. Young concluded,

> We are inevitably of and with the world, and as we change, our position in the world changes … It would be wonderful if America, having been an empire among empires, could become a nation among nations, full stop. And understand itself as such. I think it would make a great difference to how we live and what we can do.

Students who are taught a history in which the U.S. is both a nation among nations, *and* a nation that has engaged in imperialistic actions with all the problems and responsibilities that that entails, may find it easier as they come of age to recognize both their rights and their responsibilities as citizens and residents of the U.S. *and* of the world, to speak out when they see their own and other nations transgressing against the fundamental human rights that the United Nations Charter calls on its member nations to protect. By asking students to evaluate and judge historical events, to weigh intention and determine culpability, we call on them to help their own and other nations chart a course for the future where peace, not war, can become the status quo.

Works Cited

Bender, T. (Ed.). (2002). *Rethinking American history in a global age.* Berkeley, CA: University of California Press.

Bender, T. (2006). *A nation among nations: America's place in world history.* New York: Farrar, Straus, Giroux.

Ebadi, S. (2006). *Iran awakening: A memoir of revolution and hope.* New York: Random House.

Ferguson, Niall. (2004). *Colossus: The rise and fall of the American Empire.* New York: Penguin Books.

Frank, M., & Barzilai, A. (2004). Integrating alternative assessment in a project-based learning course for preservice science and technology teachers. *Assessment & Evaluation in Higher Education, 29*(1), 41–61.

Inside Schools. (2013a). Talented Unlimited High School. *Insideschools.* Retrieved from http://insideschools. org/high/browse/school/100

Inside Schools. (2013b). Dr. Susan S. McKinney Secondary School of the Arts. *Insideschools.* Retrieved from http://insideschools.org/high/browse/school/599

U.S. News and World Report. (2013). South Side High School. *U.S. News and World Report.* Retrieved from www. usnews.com/education/best-high-schools/new-york/districts/rockville-centre-union-free-school-district/ south-side-high-school-14024

Thomas, J. W. (2000). A review of research on project-based learning. Prepared for Autodesk Foundation. Retrieved from www.bie.org/research/study/review_of_project_based_learning_2000

Turk, D., Fraser, J., & Berman, S. B. (2012). "Project-Based Advanced Placement U.S. History: A Collaborative." Paper presented at College and University Faculty Association, National Council for the Social Studies, Seattle, WA.

Wiggins, G., & McTighe, J. (2005). *Understanding by design.* Alexandria, VA: Association for Supervision and Curriculum Development (ASCD).

CHAPTER RESOURCES

I. Unit Plan: U.S. in the World

Common Core Standards

CCSS.ELA-Literacy.RH.11-12.1 Cite specific textual evidence to support analysis of primary and secondary sources, connecting insights gained from specific details to an understanding of the text as a whole.

CCSS.ELA-Literacy.RH.11-12.3 Evaluate various explanations for actions or events and determine which explanation best accords with textual evidence, acknowledging where the text leaves matters uncertain.

CCSS.ELA-Literacy.RH.11-12.9 Integrate information from diverse sources, both primary and secondary, into a coherent understanding of an idea or event, noting discrepancies among sources.

Essential Questions

- In what ways was the United States an "empire" during the 20th century? What have been the implications of its imperialist tendencies?
- How do narratives of equality play into nation-building? In what ways does nationalism serve as both a constructive and destructive force?
- How did other countries in the world view the United States during the mid-20th century, and how have these views changed over time?
- What happens when "change" does not represent "progress" for all players?
- To what extent has the United States bullied other countries in its pursuit of social, political, and economic ends? How might we evaluate this "bullying" in light of the outcomes of those quests? What have been the implications—to the U.S. and other countries—of the U.S. pursuit of natural resources?
- How much has the United States been a "good" country? Is the status quo "good," with a few "pitfalls"?" Or is the status quo immoral and bullying, with a few episodes of "right" during the 20th century?
- Whom has the U.S. helped in the world? Whom has it hurt and what have been the unintended consequences of U.S. actions?

Enduring Understandings

Students will understand that:

- Nationalism can be both constructive and destructive—notions of American "exceptionalism" (and others' notions of exceptionalism) come with costs and far-reaching implications.
- *Change* does not always represent *progress* for all players in geopolitical enterprises.
- Intervention on the part of the United States in other countries has had major intended and unintended consequences—both for the U.S. and for the countries in which it has intervened.
- How we conceptualize the United States, whether as an essentially "good" country that goes astray sometimes, or as an essentially "bad" country that sometimes does right, fundamentally alters how we consider and evaluate past actions of the country with respect to other (often weaker) nations.
- Other nations around the globe do not view the U.S. in the same light as those within the U.S. view themselves.
- The U.S. has acted in imperialistic ways, and there have been economic, political, and social implications of those actions.

- In what ways did Social Darwinism and racism support American intervention and rule abroad during the 20th century?

- Social Darwinism and racism have played important roles in American intervention and rule abroad
- Historical narratives are shaped by their authors' social, cultural, economic, and political worldviews; the narratives that become "accepted" are often created by the winners
- Historical events are not monolithic and involve multiple perspectives and influences.

Culminating Assessment

Students will create a mock trial in which the United States is charged by members of the international community—namely Iran, Guatemala, Panama, and Vietnam—of violating Article 1 of the United Nations' Charter. Students will research the positions of various individuals and leaders in the different countries and will also research the defense that the United States and its allies, the South Koreans, may have mounted. Students will present oral testimony at trial and will write reflective assessments on how different countries may have voted should such a trial have taken place during the Cold War era.

II. The Cold War Trial Project

Brittany Rawson's Tenth Grade Global Class
Cold War Unit Project

Directions: Your team will be assigned a country to represent. We will have two teams representing each country.

1. South Korea
2. Vietnam
3. Iran
4. The United States

Each team will be either defending (the United States, South Korea) or prosecuting (Vietnam, Iran) the United States based on their actions in your country, and the United Nations Charter.

Each team must create an opening and closing statement, as well as a list of questions to ask their country, and a list of questions for the opposing country. All three of these should work together to prove that the United States either worked within the limits of the United Nations Charter, or against it.

Documents to use:

- Article I, United Nations Charter
- NSC-68
- Vietnamese Declaration of Independence
- Class reading on American involvement in Korea
- Shirin Ebadi's "A Tehran Girlhood" from *Iran Awakening*.

Additionally, you and your group should use your class notes, paying particular attention to notes on mutually assured destruction and U.S.–Soviet relations.

In this packet, you will find all of the pieces you need to build your case. As a group, you will turn in one complete version of this packet, but don't expect one member to do all of the work. You will evaluate each other and your contributions to the group as a part of your final grade. This packet will be due on the day of your presentation. In order for your group to present, it must be completed fully. (No winging it!)

- Project Roles
- Argument Outline
- Opening Statement
- Direct Examination Questions
- Cross-Examination Questions
- Closing Statement

Project Roles

Assign each member of your team a role. Write your name next to your role.

Three lawyers

Opening Statement Lawyer _____

Lawyer for Questioning _____

Closing Statement Lawyer _____

Two "witness" representatives of your country

Witness One _____

Witness Two _____

Outline of Team Argument

The country we represent is _____.

We believe America acted (in line with/against) the United Nations Charter during (explain the situation)

What did the United States do?

How did your country view the actions of the United States?

Three things that support our position on whether or not the United States violated the United Nations Charter are:

1.
2.
3.

The documents we will use to prove this are (use at least two):

1.
2.
3.

Opening Statement Outline

Directions: Paint a picture for the audience. What has happened, and what should be done? Give a summary of your argument in a persuasive way. Tell the audience what you are going to argue, describe why the other side is wrong, and then request a specific decision from the judge (i.e., you should/should not find the United States in violation of the United Nations Charter).

Your Honor, Ladies and Gentleman:

We represent _____. Today, we are here to seek justice for our people. We believe the way the United States acted in _____ was _____ ...

We will prove this to you today by showing (explain what you will argue)

The other side will argue (describe what you think the other side is going to say)

But we will show (describe your counter argument)

Therefore, we ask you to find the United States (state the outcome you are seeking)

Questions and Answers for Direct Examination (for you to ask your country)

For your direct examination, you want to let your country representatives tell their story. Avoid yes or no questions and use open ended questions. (*Example:* Instead of "Did the Americans attack in 1953?" Ask "What happened in the capital city in 1953"?) Start at the beginning and guide your representative through questions that help them tell the story of your country. Stick to the facts. Do not make things up.
   Include at least 10 questions.

Questions for Cross-Examination (for you to ask the other side)

In your cross-examination, you want the lawyer to control the story, not the other country's representative. Ask yes or no questions. Don't ask questions you don't know the answer to. Confront the representative with specific evidence. (Question starters: "Isn't it true ...?" "Is it correct ...?" "Do you deny ...?" etc.)
   Include at least 10 cross-examination questions.

Outline for Closing Statement

Your Honor, Ladies and Gentlemen:

Today you have heard testimony from _____.
We have proved _____

Our representatives have shown (summarize the argument of your representatives)

The other side said (describe the counter-argument)

We proved that wrong by

Therefore, we find the United States (repeat the outcome you are asking for)

III. Rubric for Evaluating Trial

Vincent's Twelfth Grade IB International Relations: History of the Americas Class

Lawyer Rubric

Performance	Excellent 25	Above Average 23	Average 20	Poor 18
	Student spoke clearly, loud enough for all to hear; was confident and persuasive in their opening/closing statements; asked relevant questions in direct and cross-examination effectively; rarely or did not use notes. Demonstrated extensive historical knowledge and understanding of context.	Student spoke clearly most of the time; was loud enough most of the time; was confident and persuasive in their opening/closing statements most of the time; asked relevant questions most of the time effectively; used notes at times. Demonstrated strong and specific historical knowledge and understanding of context.	Student mumbled at times; spoke quietly some of the time; at times lacked confidence and persuasiveness in opening/closing statements; did not ask relevant questions or was ineffective in asking questions; used notes often. Demonstrated general historical knowledge and understanding of context.	Student was difficult to hear; student was not confident or persuasive in opening/closing statements; student did not ask relevant questions; used notes most of the time. Demonstrated little historical knowledge and understanding of context.

Witness Rubric

Performance	Excellent 25	Above Average 23	Average 20	Poor 18
	Student spoke clearly, loud enough for all to hear; was confident in their responses; answered all questions effectively; rarely or did not use notes. Demonstrated extensive historical knowledge and understanding of context.	Student spoke clearly most of the time; was loud enough most of the time; was confident in their responses most of the time; answered most of the questions effectively; used notes at times. Demonstrated strong and specific historical knowledge and understanding of context.	Student mumbled at times; spoke quietly some of the time; at times lacked confidence; did not answer all of the questions or was ineffective in answering a question; used notes often. Demonstrated general historical knowledge and understanding of context.	Student was difficult to hear; student was not confident; student did not answer questions; used notes most of the time. Demonstrated little historical knowledge and understanding of context.

Security Council Rubric

Performance	Excellent 25	Above Average 23	Average 20	Poor 18
	Student responded while taking their oath; was attentive during the trial and took notes; student participated in deliberation; student completed the verdict form.

Demonstrated extensive historical knowledge and understanding of context. | Student responded while taking their oath; was attentive most of the time during the trial; took notes most of the time; student participated in deliberation; student completed the verdict form.

Demonstrated strong and specific historical knowledge and understanding of context. | Student mumbled while taking their oath; was attentive some of the time during the trial; took notes some of the time; little participation during the deliberation; student completed the verdict form.

Demonstrated general historical knowledge and understanding of context. | Student did not respond while taking their oath; student was not attentive during the trial; student took few, if any notes; little or no participation during deliberation; student did not complete the verdict form.

Demonstrated little historical knowledge and understanding of context. |

IV. Student Work: Sample In-Paper

Vincent's Twelfth Grade IB International Relations:
History of the Americas Class

3/10/13
Assignment: Witness Bio Sketch
Witness for the Defense: John Foster Dulles

Background

- Served as legal counsel to the U.S. delegation to the Versailles Peace Conference after World War I.
- Oversaw and did business with Nazi Germany companies.
- Helped draft the preamble to the United Nations Charter in 1945.
- Strongly opposed and criticized U.S. nuclear attacks on Japan.
- Briefly served as New York Republican Senator in 1949.
- Secretary of State to Eisenhower.

Accomplishments

- Contributed to containment efforts in neutralizing the Taiwan Strait during the Korean War.
- Supervised construction of the Japanese Peace Treaty, which allowed Japan to regain full independence under United States' terms.
- Worked to reduce French influence in Vietnam.
- Drafted Operation Ajax plan, which overthrew Prime Minister Mossadegh in a coup d'état and put the American-supported Shah Pahlavi into power.

- Organized the Southeast Asia Treaty Organization (SEATO).
- Contributed to the Guatemalan coup d'état in 1954, which overthrew leader Arbenz.

Criticisms

- Benefited directly from business with the Nazi regime in the 1930s.
- Viewed as a war hawk and adamant nuclear weapons supporter.
- Coup d'états in Iran and Guatemala worsened long-term relations with the nations, and encouraged the unsuccessful Bay of Pigs Invasion.
- Supported massive retaliation and nuclear brinkmanship.
- Supported Guatemalan coup because of family ties to the United Fruit Company.
- Did not respond to Hungarian Revolution.

Policies

- Containment as "liberation."
- Japanese Peace Treaty.
- Built up NATO.
- Use of massive retaliation against Soviet Union.
- The Australia, New Zealand, United States Security (ANZUS) Treaty for mutual protection with Australia and New Zealand.
- Coup d'états of governments that did not benefit American interests.

Consequences

- Coup d'états and "containment as liberation" resulted in positive short-term success in American economic benefit, but negative long-term effects. Actions led to detrimental relations between the U.S. and many nations.
- Previous "successes" set a precedent for overthrowing governments the U.S. did not benefit from. As a result, the CIA believed overthrowing Castro would work as it had in Iran and Guatemala.
- Caused Kennedy to alter his views on Latin America, which were moderately accepting of leftist governments in the beginning of his presidency.

V. Student Work: Sample Out-Paper

Vincent's Twelfth Grade IB International Relations:
History of the Americas Class

3/19/13

The UN Security Council ultimately decided that the U.S. was not guilty of violating the UN Charter. While this may not be entirely justified, it was perhaps necessary because holding the United States accountable could have set a precedent that would require the UN to hold several other nations, such as the Soviet Union, accountable for their imperialistic actions. While the United States did violate the UN Charter by intentionally undermining the principles of self-determination, they did not actually use their military to do so and thus would be able to say that they were supporting self-determination by giving the people the ability to fight an oppressive communist leader. Despite the potential justifications for their actions, the United States was guilty of undermining self-determination during the Bay of Pigs invasion and the argument that they were protecting the peace and human rights of people in weaker nations is undermined by the fact that they installed totalitarian leaders who were just as harsh as communist leaders. It is not the place of the United States to condemn all of communist ideology. If the people support communism, then it is in line with the UN Charter's emphasis on self-determination. On the other hand the UN and the U.S. are within their rights to bring about peace and stop human rights violations. However, this can lead to a slippery slope because the human rights violations of non-communist leaders are no less atrocious than the human rights violations of communist leaders.

The strength of the defense's argument lay mostly in the evidence that the U.S. did not use its military to invade Cuba, but rather used Cuban exiles, trained them, and provided them with supplies for the invasion. Consequently, the U.S. could argue that they were not undermining the will of a suppressed people. Their strength also lies in the argument that communist leaders have a history of acting aggressively. The evidence provided included the Soviet Union's invasions to suppress uprising in Berlin in 1953, the invasion of Hungary in 1956 after Imre Nagy attempted to withdraw from the Warsaw Pact and Hungarians protested for more independence from the Soviet Union, and the Soviet aid in building the Berlin Wall in 1960 to prevent East Berlin's people from fleeing to the non-communist, more economically prosperous West Berlin. In all of these cases, the Soviet Union not only demonstrated a tendency of communist governments to suppress the self-determination of the people and act aggressively towards other nations, but also established a paradigm where the United States stayed out of their sphere of influence. Why, then, should the U.S. be held accountable for dominating Cuba, which is in its sphere of influence, especially since they did not use military force like the Soviets did? China's actions in the Taiwan Crisis, of bombing Jinmen and Matsu, also provide evidence that communist nations are often aggressive and threaten peace.

The defense's weakest argument lay in their assessment of Castro's human rights violations as a reason to intervene. This argument falls to the evidence that Armas, Batista, and Shah Reza Pahlavi were equally brutal and oppressive to the people of their nations.

The strength of the prosecution's argument was that the U.S. did not have a right to condemn all communist governments and that human rights violations were just an excuse to secure their own economic interests. The prosecution accurately brought up the evidence that several U.S. leaders had personal claims to the United Fruit Company and thus were motivated by self-interest. The argument that the U.S. was supporting self-determination was effectively countered by the fact that Castro had widespread support of the Cuban people. The CIA used propaganda and deception to convince some people to oppose Castro, but did not have popular support. The prosecution used evidence of U.S. actions in Guatemala and Iran to effectively demonstrate how the U.S. acted against the self-determination of the people. Mossadegh and Arbenz were elected and largely supported.

The weakness of the prosecution's argument lies mostly in the fact that there is a slippery slope if the U.S. is held accountable for the Bay of Pigs invasion. Would the UN then need to assess the actions of the Soviet Union? This is likely why the Soviet Union voted that the U.S. was not guilty.

Conversely France likely voted that the U.S. was guilty although the two were historically allies because of the events of Suez Crisis. In this crisis there was a parallel situation in which Nassar, president of Egypt nationalized the Suez Canal. Coaxing Israel to invade, just like the U.S. did with the Cuban exiles, France and Britain created excuses to invade Egypt. This again demonstrates the slippery slope weakness of the prosecution's argument. Not every dominant or imperialistic action can be punished.

Despite this weakness, the United States was guilty for violating the UN Charter.

Contributor Biographies

Bradley Abel is a ninth grade social studies teacher at John Hersey High School in Arlington Heights, Illinois. He currently teaches human geography with an emphasis on implementing college readiness standards into the content-based classroom. He is a 2011 recipient of the Milken National Educator of the Year award.

Stacie Brensilver Berman is a doctoral student in Teaching and Learning at New York University's Steinhardt School of Culture, Education, and Human Development. She holds a B.A. in Diplomatic History from the University of Pennsylvania, an M.A. in History from Hunter College and an M.A. in Social Studies Education from New York University. She previously taught high school social studies for 10 years at Edward R. Murrow High School in Brooklyn, New York and has worked with teachers across the country on implementing and evaluating Project Based Learning units in U.S. history.

Bill Boyce is a history teacher at Talent Unlimited High School in the Upper East Side neighborhood of Manhattan, New York. He teaches American history and global studies. Boyce earned his B.A. in Journalism at the University of Massachusetts-Amherst. He also received his M.Ed. in Secondary Education at Boston College and is currently pursuing a second master's degree in Administration and Supervision at Fordham University.

Allyson Candia is a tenth grade social studies teacher at the High School for Environmental Studies. She teaches global studies and Advanced Placement world history. She is a graduate of Boston University and is currently earning her master's degree in History at Hunter College.

Michael Catelli is a high school social studies teacher at Indian Hills High School in Oakland, New Jersey. He holds a B.A. from Seton Hall University and an M.A. from Teachers College, Columbia University. He currently teaches world history, American history, and sociology with a focus on citizenship at both the local and global level.

Robert Cohen is a professor of history and social studies in New York University's (NYU) Steinhardt School of Culture, Education, and Human Development. He is an affiliated member of NYU's History Department. Cohen's recent books include: *Rebellion in Black and White:*

Southern Student Activism in the 1960s (2013), co-edited with David J. Snyder; *Freedoms' Orator: Mario Savio and the Radical Legacy of the 1960s* (2009); and *Teaching U.S. History: Dialogues Among Social Studies Teachers and Historians* (2010), co-edited with Diana Turk, Rachel Mattson, and Terrie Epstein. Cohen's other books include *Dear Mrs. Roosevelt: Letters from Children of the Great Depression* (2002); *The Free Speech Movement: Reflections on Berkeley in the 1960s* (2002), co-edited with Reginald Zelnik; *When the Old Left Was Young: Student Radicals and America's First Mass Student Movement, 1929–1941* (1993). He is also consulting editor for *Emma Goldman: A Documentary History of the American Years,* whose most recent volume (3) covers 1910–1916 (2013).

Bernadette Condesso is an eleventh and twelfth grade history teacher at Poughkeepsie Day School in Poughkeepsie, New York. She currently teaches American history, European history, world religions, and modern China studies. She is the recipient of three NEH Summer Scholars grants and a Gilder Lehrman Teacher Seminar Participant.

Josef Donnelly is a ninth and tenth grade social studies teacher at International Community High School in the South Bronx, New York. His school has a 100% English Language Learner student population. He is a graduate student at Teachers College, Columbia University, where he is earning his M.A. in teaching social studies. Prior to becoming a teacher in New York, he was a Peace Corps Volunteer on a tiny atoll in the Federated States of Micronesia.

Laura J. Dull is an associate professor and the Coordinator of the Graduate Secondary Social Studies Program at the State University of New York at New Paltz. She earned a B.A. from Hiram College, M.A. from Teachers College, and Ph.D. in Comparative and International Education from New York University. She taught social studies for seven years in New York City public schools. She wrote a book about educational reform in Ghana (*Disciplined Development: Teachers and Reform in Ghana,* 2006) and has written articles on textbooks in Ghana, service learning and neo-liberalism in Serbia, and discussion in American classrooms. She received a Fulbright Scholar Award to Serbia in 2007 and a Korea Society Fellowship in 2013.

Vincent Falivene is a twelfth grade IB and global history as well as theory of knowledge teacher at South Side High School in Rockville Centre, New York and adjunct instructor at New York University's Steinhardt School of Culture, Education, and Human Development. Previously, he was a founding teacher at Williamsburg Prep High School in Brooklyn and worked in Education and Educational Media at the Metropolitan Museum of Art. Additionally, Vincent aided in the development of the Urban Memory Project, an oral and photographic history of several neighborhoods in New York City. Vincent received his M.A. from Teachers College, Columbia University and has been recognized as a distinguished educator by the Nobel Committee and the University of Chicago.

Paul Kelly is the Principal of Elk Grove High School in Elk Grove Village, Illinois. He completed a B.S. and M.Ed. at the University of Illinois at Urbana-Champaign and an M.Ed. at Benedictine University. Kelly received the Milken National Educator Award in 2005 as a social studies teacher and served for six years as the Division Head for Social Science and World Languages at John Hersey High School in Arlington Heights, Illinois. As an educational consultant, he has delivered professional development workshops to urban, suburban, and rural school districts in Illinois, Wisconsin, and Ohio.

Michelle Lewis-Mondesir is an instructional specialist for social studies at New Visions for Public Schools. Michelle has an M.S.Ed. in Educational Leadership from Brooklyn College, an M.A. from New York University and a B.A. from Hunter College. As an instructional specialist, she creates challenge-based curricula for all social studies courses and coaches teachers at the New Visions Charter High Schools. She previously held the position of history educator and department leader at the Academy for Environmental Leadership. During her time as a history educator, she taught global studies and Regents review courses.

Melissa Mabry has taught world history and human geography to ninth graders at John Hersey High School in Arlington Heights, Illinois for the past 14 years. She earned her B.S. in Secondary Education from the University of Illinois at Urbana-Champaign and her M.A. in Liberal Studies at Northwestern University.

Brittany Rawson teaches global history and economics at the Susan S. McKinney High School in Brooklyn. She earned her B.S. in Social Studies Education from New York University. Brittany brings to her curriculum writing and classroom instruction a commitment to helping her students develop the skills and understandings to fight injustice and social exclusion.

Abby Rennert teaches at KAPPA MS215, a public middle school in the Bronx, NY. She currently teaches sixth grade English and social studies. Abby received her B.A. from Vassar College, her M.S. in English Education from Lehman College, and recently completed an Advanced Certificate in STEM from New York Institute of Technology. She is always seeking ways to improve her teaching practice and has participated in different programs, including Teaching American History grants, the Common Core Fellows, and the New York City Writing Project.

Alejandro Sosa is an eleventh grade global history and AP world history teacher. He received his B.A. from Hunter College, his M.A. in Social Studies Education from New York University and holds a graduate degree in Leadership and Technology from the New York Institute of Technology. He has worked with many organizations in helping to promote college and career readiness, including the College Board, National Association for Secondary School Principals, the National Writing Project, and Educators for Excellence.

Michael R. Stoll is an instructor of education at William Jewell College in Liberty, Missouri. He holds a B.A. from Haverford College, an M.A. and M.S.Ed. from Northwestern University, and is currently completing his doctoral degree in Teaching and Learning at New York University's Steinhardt School of Culture, Education, and Human Development. A former high school social studies teacher and educational consultant, he has worked with teachers in Illinois, New York, New Jersey, and Missouri to develop and implement innovative social studies curricula.

Diana B. Turk is an associate professor and the Director of the Social Studies Education Program in the Department of Teaching and Learning at New York University's Steinhardt School of Culture, Education, and Human Development, and as of fall 2013 is serving as the Director of Teacher Education at Brandeis University. She holds a B.A. in American Studies from Hamilton College and an M.A. and Ph.D. in American Studies from the University of Maryland, College Park. Her books include *Bound by a Mighty Vow: Sisterhood and Women's Fraternities, 1870–1920* (2004) and *Teaching U.S. History: Dialogues among Social Studies Teachers and Historians* (2010), co-edited with Rachel Mattson, Robert Cohen, and Terrie Epstein. Her scholarship centers on helping teachers to teach history in ways that are innovative, student centered, and rigorous, and will inspire students to use their voices toward democratic ends.

Dawn Vandervloed is a social studies teacher at Washingtonville High School in Orange County, NY. She teaches global history and geography and economics and government. Previously, she has taught as an adjunct instructor in history at Orange County Community College and Mount Saint Mary College, NY. She received her master's degree from New York University in Public History. She is currently Vice President of Membership for the Mid Hudson Social Studies Council and a Teacher Consultant for the Hudson Valley Writing Project.

Rebecca Vercillo currently teaches ninth grade human geography and tenth grade world history and AP world history at John Hersey High School in Arlington Heights, Illinois. She has a B.A. in History and Political Science from the University of Illinois at Urbana-Champaign and is currently working on an M.A. in Liberal Studies at Northwestern University. Vercillo has also been a professional development team leader and has helped in the development of a common core curriculum in world history.

Index

|| ||| | || | ||| || ||| | ||| || | || | |||| | ||||| || || ||